AA

Too a Alan Holmes
1999.

Explorer
California

Mick Sinclair

KT-434-544

AA Publishing

Front cover a: surfing is a popular pastime; front cover b: in-line skating at Joshua Tree National Monument; front cover c: Mission La Purisma Concepcion; front cover d: view across the Merced River in Yosemite National Park; spine: negotiating a desert track; back cover: the impressive Hearst Castle at San Simeon; page 2: Mission San Diego de Alcala; page 4: making music on Venice Beach; page 5 a: a colourful display; page 5 b: stretch limos are a common sight; pages 6–7: downtown LA at night; page 8: Muir Beach at sunset; page 9: Calico is a re-creation of a gold-rush town.

Written by Mick Sinclair
Revision verified by Mick Sinclair

Revised fourth edition 1999

First published 1993
Edited, designed, produced and distributed by AA Publishing.
Maps © The Automobile Association 1993, 1995, 1996, 1999

The contents of this publication are believed correct at the time of printing. Nevertheless, the publishers cannot be held responsible for errors or omissions, or for changes in details given in this guide, or for the consequences of any reliance on the information provided by the same. Assessments of attractions, hotels, restaurants and so forth are based upon the author's own personal experience and, therefore, descriptions given in this guide necessarily contain an element of subjective opinion which may not reflect the publisher's opinion or dictate a reader's own experiences on another occasion. We have tried to ensure accuracy in this guide, but things do change and we would be grateful if readers would advise us of any inaccuracies they may encounter.

A CIP catalogue record for this book is available from the British Library.

ISBN 0 7495 1884 7

Published by AA Publishing (a trading name of Automobile Association Developments Ltd, whose registered office is Norfolk House, Priestley Road, Basingstoke, Hampshire RG24 9NY. Registered number 1878835).

Colour origination by Fotographics Ltd
Printed and bound in Italy by Printer Trento srl

Titles in the Explorer series:
Australia • Boston & New England • Britain • Brittany Caribbean • China • Costa Rica • Crete • Cuba • Cyprus Egypt • Florence & Tuscany • Florida • France • Germany Greek Islands • Hawaii • India • Indonesia • Ireland • Israel Italy • Japan • London • Mallorca • Mexico • Moscow & St Petersburg • New York • New Zealand • Paris • Portugal Prague • Provence • Rome • San Francisco • Scotland Singapore & Malaysia • South Africa • Spain • Thailand Tunisia • Turkey • Turkish Coast • Venice • Vietnam

AA World Travel Guides publish nearly 300 guidebooks to a full range of cities, countries and regions across the world. Find out more about AA Publishing and the wide range of services the AA provides by visiting our Web site at www.theaa.co.uk.

How to use this book

ORGANISATION

California Is, California Was
Discusses aspects of life and culture in contemporary California and explores significant periods in its history.

A–Z
A listing of places to visit. The book begins with San Francisco, and is subsequently divided into other major cities and regions. Places of interest are listed alphabetically within each section. Suggested walks, drives and Focus On articles, which provide an insight into aspects of life in California, are included in each section.

Travel Facts
Contains the strictly practical information that is vital for a successful trip.

Hotels & Restaurants
An alphabetical listing of places to stay and places to eat. Entries are graded budget, moderate or expensive.

ABOUT THE RATINGS
Most places described in this book have been given a separate rating. These are as follows:

▶▶▶ **Do not miss**

▶▶ **Highly recommended**

▶ **Worth seeing**

MAP REFERENCES
To make the location of a particular place easier to find, every main entry in this book is given a map reference, such as 176B3. The first number (176) indicates the page on which the map can be found, the letter (B) and the second number (3) pinpoint the square in which the main entry is located. The maps on the inside front cover and inside back cover are referred to as IFC and IBC respectively.

Contents

My California by Mick Sinclair

Simply put, California has everything. You can surf and ski on the same day, climb mountains, explore deserts, dine in chic restaurants among famous faces, or sample life in a rural community little changed in appearance since the Gold Rush. The California landscape that encompasses volatile features such as geysers and sulphur vents, and is regularly stirred by earthquakes (usually too small to cause damage), also includes the serene beauty of Yosemite Valley and no fewer than 264 state parks giving protection to 1.4 million acres of pristine land. The coastline, too, has the power to thrill, with the beach-and-surfer dominated southernmost third and the scenic drama of the bluffs and cliffs that lie further north.

The discovery of gold made California independently wealthy and stimulated an independence of mind that lasted into the present. Today's Californians include individuals pushing back the boundaries of everything from new technology to adventure sports, and a multitude of cultures and creeds that continually reshape the demography of the US's most populous state.

California has been the apple in the eye of travellers for 500 years. Seventeenth-century Spanish explorers, the 'forty-niners' of the gold rush, Hollywood hopefuls of the 1920s, and the Asian immigrants of the 1980s are just a few of those for whom the state has held the promise of a new life and a brighter future.

While the social mixture can be stimulating – not least for the opportunity to spread New Year celebrations over several months (Asian celebrations follow the lunar cycle) and sample the cuisines of the world without leaving the neighbourhood – it also contributes to the stresses and strains of the state's infrastructure, at times threatening to erode California's tradition of support for the underdog as immigration issues move increasingly to the centre of state politics.

Yet lessons learned from the inner-city riots and the widespread financial downturn of the early 1990s have caused California to perform a remarkable self-transformation. The state has reinvented itself, creating a diversified economy and regaining enough social cohesion to once again be a vibrant and welcoming place: the California dream seems very much alive.

On innumerable trips, Mick Sinclair has explored California from its mountaintops to its desert floors. He is the author of several guidebooks to the state and has also written guides to other US regions and cities, including Florida, New York, Chicago, and Miami, and to other countries. His magazine and newspaper features on travel, culture and the arts have appeared all over the world.

California Is
California Was

California Was

CALIFORNIA
OREGON
IDAHO
NEVADA
UTAH
ARIZONA
PACIFIC OCEAN
MEX
Crescent City
Yreka
Mt Shasta 4317m
Cascade Range
Pit
Alturas
Eureka
Cape Mendocino
Trinity
Shasta Lake
Redding
Lassen Volcanic National Park
Susanville
Red Bluff
Coast Range
Quincy
Fort Bragg
Chico
Yuba City
Ukiah
Clear Lake
Sacramento
Lake Tahoe
Point Arena
Auburn
Sierra Nevada
Santa Rosa
Napa
SACRAMENTO
Point Reyes
Stockton
Sonora
Mono Lake
Oakland
Yosemite National Park
San Francisco
Modesto
San Jose
Merced
Bishop
Santa Cruz
San Joaquin
Kings Canyon National Park
Fresno
Independence
Salinas
Monterey
Sequoia National Park
Mt Whitney 4418m
Death Valley
Santa Lucia Range
Coast Ranges
Big Sur
Visalia
3368m
Salinas
Delamo
San Simeon
Ridgecrest
Bakersfield
Mojave Desert
San Luis Obispo
Santa Maria
Barstow
Lancaster
Needle
Colorado
Santa Barbara
Lompoc
Point Conception
Sonora Desert
Ventura
Pasadena
Oxnard
San Bernardino
Los Angeles
Anaheim
Palm Springs
Blythe
Channel Islands
Long Beach
Salton Sea
Oceanside
Escondido
Brawley
San Diego
0 100 200 km
0 50 100 miles

10

The golden state

Rarely has a region captured the imagination for as long or as strongly as California. Spanish explorers, the forty-niners, would-be film stars, and millions of tourists have all arrived in anticipation of finding America's promised land. Few of them have been disappointed, although California is never quite what people expect it to be.

California is a land of golden beaches only along the most southerly quarter of its 1,000-mile coastline; the rest is typified by bracing, pristine bluffs lashed by crashing ocean waves.

Inland California embraces parched deserts and snow-capped mountains, but also finds room for the lush valleys of the wine country and the lava landscapes of the far north.

The state's two major cities are poles apart. San Francisco is small and visually attractive, and it exudes a warm, cultured atmosphere. By contrast, brash Los Angeles, while never dull, struggles to justify its glamorous

Part of California's golden coast: a beach to the north of Malibu

image and gives new meaning to the word 'sprawl.'

California is far too diverse and complex – socially, geographically, and politically – to be defined by a single, simple image. Of 32 million Californians, surprisingly few were born in the state and barely half fit the traditional Anglo-American stereotype.

A flourishing New Age movement strengthens California's anything-goes reputation, while increased environmental protection is a product of many years of legislation. Yet California has plenty of conservatives, and Ronald Reagan's eight-year reign as state governor was far from unrepresentative of the state's political mind.

State Motto	*eureka* (I have found it)
State Song	'I love you, California'
State Mineral	gold
State Flower	golden poppy
State Animal	grizzly bear
State Bird	valley quail
State Fish	golden trout
State Reptile	desert tortoise
State Insect	dog-face butterfly
State Mammal	gray whale
State Fossil	sabre-toothed tiger

Even before its European settlement, California was thought to harbour treasures beyond man's wildest dreams. The discovery of gold compounded this belief and set the state on the road to becoming a financial super-power, with a multitude of diverse industries underpinning an economy that would make today's California – if it were a country – one of the richest in the world.

END OF TRADITION California's long reliance on several key industries, particularly automobile production and aerospace research, was ended in the late 1980s by declining federal expenditure, national recession and demographic changes. Simultaneously, Silicon Valley's computer industry hit a sharp decline, as did Hollywood's TV and film companies, locked into a downward spiral only compounded by the late 1992 LA riots that destroyed the city's tourist industry.

DIVERSE REVENUE By the late 1990s, however, California had made a remarkable recovery, deviating from traditional sources of income to create the most diversified economy in the state's history. Established areas such as film and computers boomed, but so did newer industries as varied as clothing and biotechnology. Tourism also rose, nowhere more so than in LA where visitors – up by more than 25 per cent since 1990 – spent over $10 billion annually. Overall, the state is creating around half a million jobs each year, and a total output valued at a trillion dollars.

❑ Discovered in the 1860s, California's oil reserves continue to be lucrative. There are major wells in Los Angeles and in the Central Valley, although exploitation of offshore deposits was curtailed after a huge spill off Santa Barbara in 1969 caused widespread environmental damage. ❑

SILICON VALLEY From the 1970s, the development of the silicon chip turned computer whiz-kids into millionaire corporate executives overnight and made so-called Silicon Valley – a region south of San Francisco, long at the forefront of electronics research – the state's fastest-growing area.

The early 1990s stabilisation of the computer industry led to recession in Silicon Valley. Now, though, the Valley is again drawing massive amounts of venture capital, around $850 million annually, and opportunities created by multimedia and the Internet have created a new army of highly skilled software designers.

AGRICULTURE California's most reliable commodity is not film stars but farm produce. The Imperial and Central valleys produce half the fruit, nuts and vegetables grown in the United States, a crop that is worth around $16 billion annually. Yet there is controversy surrounding the over-use of chemicals and the long-term ecological upsets caused by the conversion of desert to farmland.

Agriculture: a boon or a threat?

Jogging, rollerblading, and skateboarding are wildly popular throughout the state, often in specially designated areas. So are cycling (including mountain biking), hiking and river rafting; toning one's physique in a health club or fitness centre is a state ritual. The ocean and winter's snow-covered mountain slopes are other playing fields for this health and fitness orientated culture.

OCEAN SPORTS Although it may seem the most Californian of all the state's participant sports, surfing arrived from Hawaii in 1907 and did not capture the Californian imagination until the invention of lightweight surfboards in the 1950s.

Subsequently mythologised by the songs of the Beach Boys and the beach-blanket films of the early 1960s, surfing became a lasting symbol of the sun-kissed Californian beach life.

From the masses gathered at San Diego's Mission Beach to the hardy loners spotted off the rocky Central Coast, surfing has evolved into a subculture with its own barely penetrable language and customs. In some areas, local surfers actively deter outsiders from encroaching on the breakers they consider their own.

❏ Few of California's professional sports teams have roots in the state: the Rams moved west from Cleveland in 1946; the Dodgers arrived from Brooklyn in 1958; the L.A. Lakers were based in Minneapolis until 1960; the Oakland A's played in Kansas City until 1968. ❏

Scuba diving and snorkelling are pursued in numerous locations, especially along the central coast where the beaches are not crowded.

BEACH SPORTS Back on the sand, volleyball nets line many southern California beaches and

anyone-can-join 'pickup' games are common. If you play, don't expect mild exertion – sand is brutal on the leg muscles. You will soon appreciate the stamina of Californians who play beach volleyball professionally – they are the big-earning stars of televised tournaments held each summer.

WINTER SPORTS During the winter, many coast-dwelling Californians head inland. The 1960 Winter Olympics at Squaw Valley (near Lake Tahoe) gave many residents a sense of the magnificence of their own state's skiing. The winter resorts of Lake Tahoe and Mammoth Lakes are now major destinations for skiers and snowboarders, who are present in rapidly swelling numbers and who dazzle two-footed snow lovers with swooping downhill descents on their four-foot-long boards.

Although born in Hawaii, surfing has become inextricably linked with California

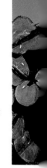

The price of more than a century of unrestrained growth has been the wreckage of California's ecosystems by the diverting of rivers and the decimation of forests, factors that have wrought havoc on the state's wildlife and created the worst air pollution in the country. From the founding of the Sierra Club in 1892 to the antipollution initiatives of the 1970s, California has led the country in encouraging environmental protection, but the greening of the Golden State is a far from settled issue: state bureaucrats, conservationists and commercial interests regularly do battle in the courts.

14

AIR POLLUTION Twenty-five million vehicles and a cruel combination of geography and climate make smog a major Californian headache. Infamously bad in Los Angeles, smog also affects many southern areas and Silicon Valley in the north.

Catalytic converters and the use of unleaded petrol have had some effect, but attempts to encourage car pooling (employees sharing vehicles) have been less successful. A multi-million dollar public transportation programme in Los Angeles hopes to have weaned 8 million drivers off their cars by the year 2000.

IN THE HOME Antismog measures also apply in the home. California's Air Resources Board has created a list of 3,400 household items, among them carpet cleaners, hair sprays, and disinfectants, that must comply with new safety standards by 2005. Detergents and face creams are among products currently being evaluated. The board claims that the targeted products daily release hydrocarbons equivalent to 500,000 car exhaust emissions.

NO SMOKING To improve air quality for staff and non-smoking customers in California's licensed premises, it became illegal to smoke in bars, restaurants and nightclubs from the first day of 1998. Although only 18 per cent of Californians smoke, the new law was widely condemned by bar owners, fearing lost business; many kept polishing their ashtrays and turned a blind eye to customers who continued to smoke. In general, the ban has been more widely adhered to in upscale establishments. In 1996, San Francisco became the first local government to sue the tobacco industry to recover money spent treating smoking-related illnesses.

> ❏ California has more endangered, rare or threatened species than any other state: 283 at the last count. ❏

Golden Gate Bridge

DANGER TO HABITATS Half a million people settle annually in California, and the demand for new homes causes fragile coastal and desert regions to disappear beneath tract housing and shopping malls. In some areas, residents have voted for higher taxes to ensure undeveloped land stays that way, and to maintain protected wildlife areas.

A stimulus to southern California's growth and the productivity of the Central Valley farmlands was the diverting of water from the state's northern rivers. Consequently, the Sacramento delta, the confluence of rivers from the Sierra Nevada mountains, and the San Francisco Bay underwent profound changes, adversely affecting migratory birds and fish stocks, and leaving inhabited land prone to flooding. Legal arguments rage over water rights, and droughts have led to rationing.

LA WATER Los Angeles finally got some comeuppance for the devious practices that brought the city its first fresh water supply via a 250-mile aqueduct, which stimulated its growth, when, in 1997, it was ordered to spend $300 million annually to improve the source area around Owens Lake in the Sierra Nevada. Although the city is contesting the ruling, it is now required to reduce the amount of water taken and partially flood the

California's surge of economic growth has an environmental price tag…

lake to reduce the dust, laden with arsenic toxic metals, that makes the Owens Valley one of the most polluted places in the United States. In an unrelated incident the same year, a toxic chemical used in the production of rocket fuel was found in the drinking water of three California counties, including Los Angeles.

FORESTS Ninety per cent of California's redwood and Douglas fir trees have been chopped down since the gold rush. Even the federal protection of some strands of coastal redwoods and giant sequoias does not guarantee their survival – the felling of the forest leaves them exposed to erosion.

❑ After years of overcrowding and smog in one of the US's most beautiful natural areas, it was decided to end private vehicular access to Yosemite Valley. In 1998, work began on removing the 2,300 parking places and developing a new system of bicycle routes around the valley floor, with visitor access by shuttle bus. ❑

There is precious little evidence of it as yet on the state's governing bodies, but currently only 57 per cent of Californians are white Anglo-Americans. In the future, there is expected to be no ethnic majority at all in the state, just several large ethnic minorities.

Military conflicts and eased entry restrictions brought substantial increases in Asian immigration into California from the 1950s, and the state's already established Hispanic population grew by more than 70 per cent in the 10 years to 1992. Of 7 million new arrivals and births in California during the 1980s, 85 per cent were Asian or Hispanic.

Meanwhile, migration from California to other US states reached record levels with 250,000, mostly non-Hispanic whites departing for economic reasons in 1994. In the same year, international migration into California, increasing by 60 per cent through the early 1990s, reached a record with 200,000 documented new arrivals, mostly from Asia or

Variety is the spice of California: Melrose Avenue, LA

Latin America. Additionally, an estimated 125,000 settle illegally in California annually.

NATIVE AMERICANS Enduring removal from their ancestral lands since the time of the Spanish missions and with few recognised rights until the 1960s, California's Native Americans increased in number during the 1970s and 1980s and there are now around 250,000 living in the state. Despite being indigenous residents, Native Americans are the least conspicuous of all California's ethnic communities, not least the (approximately) 20 per cent of them living on reservations.

> ❑ More people live in California than in Canada. ❑

BLACK AMERICANS Blacks of African descent were a significant element in some of California's earliest Spanish settlements, though the state's black population underwent its biggest expansion during the 1940s, when wartime heavy industry attracted labour from the rural and economically ailing Deep South.

Subsequently, sheer weight of numbers provided the electoral clout to put blacks into important positions in California political life, but not the economic power to regenerate the cheaply built housing projects that evolved into inner-city ghettos. In some instances, the arrival of Asians into black neighbourhoods has caused resentment and violence among already established communities.

Simultaneously, California's uncertain job market is tempting some Californian blacks back to the Deep South.

16

Pictures of a diverse and lively culture from the Mission District in San Francisco

HISPANICS California's Spanish history is echoed in its place-names and street names, while its Spanish-speaking present is evident in the TV and radio stations catering to a Hispanic population now accounting for one in four of the state's inhabitants.

As early as 1945, Los Angeles had the biggest Mexican community outside Mexico; many more Mexicans crossed the border between 1951 and 1964, when the US government encouraged the import of agricultural labour. Since then, the depressed Mexican economy, and trouble and strife throughout Central and (to a lesser extent) South America, have contributed, along with a compara-tively high birthrate, to the growth of California's Hispanic numbers.

ASIANS Thirty-five per cent of the Asian population of the United States lives in California, where Asians make up one in ten of the state's inhabitants. This grew by 127 per cent during the 1980s.

California's earliest Asians were Chinese who arrived at the time of the Gold Rush. Many of these immigrants became labourers, some became merchants, and all experienced the racism that caused them to band together in Chinatown districts. The Chinese population did not significantly change until the repeal of anti-Asian immigration laws in 1965. After that year many new arrivals left their traditional homes in Chinatown as soon as they could afford to in favour of homes in the suburbs. Those left behind tended to be the poor and elderly, those least able to integrate into US society.

Following the first Chinese, Japanese labourers and farmers settled in California and laid the foundations of the state's prosperous agricultural industry between 1890 and 1910. After the Japanese attack on Pearl Harbor in 1941, their internment devastated an entire generation of Japanese Americans; among their children, who are increasingly adept at balancing two cultures, are success stories spanning most walks of Californian life.

> ❏ Approximately 30 per cent of US immigrants settle in California. If California were a country, it would be the 30th most populous. ❏

Koreans became a strong presence in parts of Los Angeles beginning in the 1950s; in the 1970s, following the fall of Saigon, 100,000 Vietnamese, Cambodians, and Laotians arrived in California.

In San Francisco, the Laotians and Vietnamese have been evident opening businesses in the Tenderloin district. Less happily, teenage Cambodians in Long Beach's 'Little Phnom Penh' are integrating into American society by joining black and Hispanic street gangs.

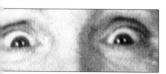

From Marxist logging colonies to the ragbag of beliefs of the New Age movement, cults have been a mainstay of California life for decades and show few signs of abating.

18

Idealistic cooperative communities appeared as early as the 1880s, the largest being the 400-strong Kaweah Colony, who followed a Marxist plan for self-sufficiency that included a potentially devastating project to scythe down all the state's giant sequoia trees.

Oriental mysticism and arcane magic had stolen the cult spotlight from utopian politics by the 1920s, when the Krishnamurti Foundation was founded in Ojai, and the Rosicrucian Order built a home in San Jose, both of which still exist. In Los Angeles, inspired by a visit by English occultist Aleister Crowley, the Builders of the Adytum formed; their tarot-decorated temple continues to explore the mysteries of the Kabbala. Mount Shasta is thought by some to be inhabited by Lemurians, a race of highly advanced beings from a lost city of the Pacific.

In 1930, one G. W. Ballard claimed he had quenched his thirst while hiking on the mountain with what turned out be the Elixir of Life, handed to him by a youth who proceeded to reveal the secrets of the universe. Ballard responded by forming the I AM Foundation of Youth that, by the 1950s, was attracting 3,000 brightly robed believers to its ceremonies.

While Ballard was being enlightened on Shasta's slopes, mining engineer W Warren Shufelt was producing a map of tunnels beneath Downtown Los Angeles that, he thought, were the home of an ancient race of 'Lizard People,' mentioned in Hopi Indian legends.

❑ Tales of 'glowing humanoids' and three-fingered aliens buying supplies in local grocery stores have convinced some Californians that the Joshua Tree National Monument is a UFO landing site. ❑

In 1969, the Charles Manson 'family' (see page 33) committed gruesome murders; in the 1970s, Jim Jones's California-based People's Temple moved to Guyana where Jones and 900 followers committed mass suicide in 1978. Another mass suicide took place in 1997, when 39 members of the Heaven's Gate UFO cult committed suicide in Rancho Sante Fe, near San Diego, believing that it was time to 'shed their containers' and join a spacecraft behind the Hale-Bopp comet.

Have aliens gathered at Joshua Tree National Monument?

Cults might flourish in California but they are, by definition, of limited appeal. Of more lasting consequence is the state's unique ability to allow alternative approaches to life and living to be tried and tested before, in many instances, being adopted throughout the world.

ON THE NET Long at the front line of computer technology, California was among the first places in the world to begin exploring the possibilities of the Internet. In unwitting anticipation of the worldwide information superhighway, many San Francisco cafés were linked by SF Net by the early 1990s, a method of communication through cyberspace with customers in other on-line cafés throughout the city.

Such is the popularity and wide-spread use of the Internet through-out California that users elsewhere have become familiar with access to the Net becoming blocked once the state wakes up and goes on-line.

MEDICINAL MARIJUANA As the effectiveness of marijuana to ease the pain of those suffering serious illness is increasingly recognised by the medical profession, California had led the way in enabling the illegal drug to become available to those who have medical reasons for using it. From the early 1990s, a buyer's club in San Francisco sold marijuana to its 11,000 members with the tacit approval of the city authorities, and a statewide referendum in November 1996 led to the legalisation of medicinal marijuana use within the state, even though its cultivation and possession remains illegal under US law.

NEW AGE In the early 1960s, the Esalen Institute near Big Sur became the home of the human potential movement. Twenty years later, many of its tenets of self-discovery were echoed in the New Age movement, in full swing during the 1980s and an umbrella term that encompassed long-standing pursuits such as dream interpretation, astrology and tarot reading, with newer areas such as channeling, rebirthing, and belief in the powers of crystals. In August 1987, thousands of Californians participated in a 'Harmonic Convergence' gathering on the slopes of Mt Shasta, intended to welcome the Age of Aquarius, but while many of these topics continue to be popular in California and beyond, by the 1990s many were regarding the New Age as old hat.

19

❏ A 1991 survey revealed 25,000 people claiming to be pagans or wiccans (practitioners of witchcraft) in San Francisco and the Bay Area. ❏

Californians were among the first to benefit from the convenience of cyber cafés

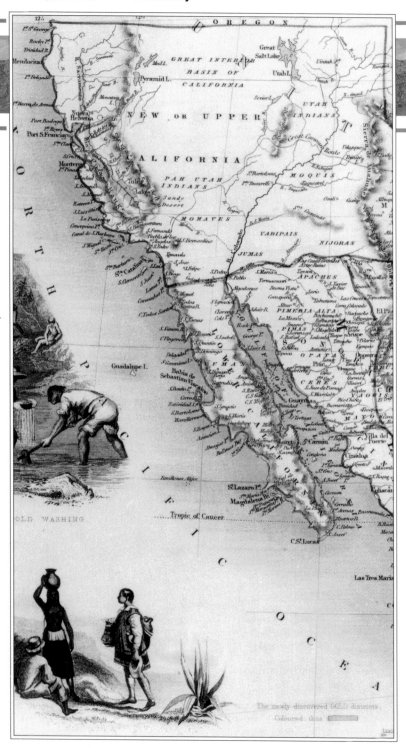

Some 200 million years ago the area that is now California was consumed by the Pacific Ocean, with the western edge of the North American continent being defined by the mountains of what is now Nevada.

GEOLOGY Around this time, two of the 20 tectonic plates that form the earth's crust – the Pacific plate and the North American plate – began moving. The heavier ocean plate slid beneath the continental plate and caused buckling, which eventually created undersea mountain ranges.

MOUNTAINS One mountain group would become California's coastal ranges; another group, farther east, would become the Sierra Nevada mountains. The latter formed along an east–west geological fault line that caused the northern section to move slowly 60 miles west, becoming what are now the Klamath Mountains.

Pressure within the earth forced the mountains continually up, and they broke surface 25 million years ago.

PLAINS Because of the movement of the Klamaths, the Pacific Ocean continued to cover north-eastern California until its sediments created a plain. As high temperatures in the earth's mantle forced the plain to fracture, lava flowed to the surface through fissures and solidified to become the Modoc Plateau.

The Coastal Ranges and the Sierra Nevada mountains had also trapped a section of the Pacific between them. This too filled with sediment and became the Central Valley.

DESERT Sixteen million years ago, the Sierra Nevada mountains became tall enough (though well short of their present height) to influence the weather. Blocking the passage of rain from the ocean, the mountains caused the land on their eastern side to become arid and evolve into deserts.

Over several ice ages, the most recent ending 30,000 years ago, glaciers smoothed the Sierra's granite peaks and carved great U-shaped valleys, such as the great valley in Yosemite.

❏ The first Europeans to experience a California earthquake were the members of the Portolá expedition of 1769. At the time, they were encamped by the Santa Ana River in what was to become Orange County. ❏

THE SAN ANDREAS FAULT
California's immensely varied landscapes lie on one of the world's most geologically active zones, part of the 'Ring of Fire' that girdles the Pacific Ocean. Of hundreds of fault lines running across the state, the longest, and most famous, is the San Andreas fault, which runs for 600 miles and marks the meeting point of the Pacific and the North American plates.

The solid granite slopes of Yosemite National Park, carved and shaped by the passing of glaciers

Recent discoveries indicate that human habitation in the Americas may date much farther back than previously believed, but it is still widely accepted in scientific circles that the earliest North Americans arrived by crossing by a land link over the Bering Strait, between Alaska and Siberia, around 12,000 years ago.

Estimates suggest that at the time of European discovery 300,000 Native Americans lived in California (their forebears having settled around 6,000 years before), split into just over 100 groupings, each of which comprised several hundred people – communities too small to fit the usual definition of a tribe.

CULTURE AND BELIEFS Across the land, a host of different skills and belief systems developed. In central California, for example, the Maidus, Pomos, and Wintuns observed the Kukso cult, creating elaborate feathered costumes for use in dances and ceremonies, with the Pomos becoming renowned for their feathered basketry.

Farther south, the Chumash demonstrated advanced artistic skills with the most intricate of rock art, and the Gabrieleño followed a one-god

Preaching to Native Americans

religion and meted out severe punishment on any member who deviated from a strict moral code.

Despite these differences, and with food abundant for all (except for those in the desert regions), there were none of the tribal wars that occurred elsewhere in North America, and trading between different groups was common.

❏ Believed to be the last surviving Yahi, 'Ishi' (as he was named) was discovered in California's far north in 1911, and spent the next five years living in the anthropology museum of the University of California in San Francisco, passing on details of his people's culture before dying of tuberculosis as a result of his first cold. ❏

ARRIVAL OF THE EUROPEANS The talent that the Native Americans displayed for living in harmony with each other, and with nature, were not traits shared by California's European settlers, who considered the 'Indians' barbarians, fit only for labouring tasks.

Although many of the first European settlers were guilty of mistreating the Native Americans, greater damage to the native population was caused by European-borne diseases, such as measles and smallpox, to which the indigenous people had no immunity, and by the enormous influx of land-hungry whites at the time of the gold rush, which resulted in most Native Americans being forcibly resettled on reservations.

An expedition in 1533 under the Spaniard Hernando Cortés is credited with making the first sighting of Baja (or Lower) California, a long peninsula that was mistakenly believed to be an island. This geographical error also applied to Alta (or Upper) California – what is now the state of California – for many years.

In 1542, the crew of Juan Rodríguez Cabrillo, a Portugese navigator in the employ of Spain, became the first to drop anchor off Alta California, pausing at what is now San Diego Bay and at the Channel Islands off Santa Barbara.

Not for another 25 years did a European set foot in California, and it was not a Spaniard but a Briton, Francis Drake, who landed at a site near Point Reyes (the actual location is disputed) in 1579, claiming California – which he named Nova Albion – for Queen Elizabeth I.

Without fixed settlements it was impossible for any territorial claims to be made firm, however. After Sebástian Vizcaíno landed at what he called Monterey in 1602, he toured the coast bestowing many of the bays and headlands with their enduring Spanish names. Vizcaíno's claims for the area's topography were less successful, though, and his cartographer was hanged for producing a wildly inaccurate map of Monterey Bay.

With a Jesuit mission established in Baja California in 1690 and Alta California discovered to be part of the North American mainland in 1742, the Spanish king ordered the construction of a north–south string of Franciscan missions across California, with Monterey becoming the province's administrative centre.

Ostensibly, this was a religious crusade to convert the Native Americans to Catholicism, but the building of the missions (fully described on pages 110 and 111), and four attendant presidios, each housing several hundred troops, was also intended to bring a social infrastructure to the region that, it was (rather optimistically) hoped, would deter any rival colonial power from intruding on California.

❏ The first European sighting of California's greatest natural harbour, San Francisco Bay, was made from land in 1769 by a Spanish expedition heading north from San Diego hoping to find an overland route to Monterey. ❏

Symbol of a religious crusade: San Diego Mission

Despite 21 missions and the base at Monterey, California remained sparsely inhabited, and it had barely been explored inland from El Camino Real, the route linking the missions from San Diego to Sonoma. Many of the missions – most of which were not completed until the early 1800s – became extremely prosperous, mainly by exploiting Native American labor on vast tracts of farmland grazed by imported cattle.

THE RUSSIANS During the mission period, a colony of Russian fur trappers had advanced into California from Alaska (part of the then-expanding Russian empire), seeking beaver and sea otter pelts. The Russians established Fort Ross, 60 miles north of San Francisco, in 1812. Through mutual necessity as much as anything else, the Russians and Spanish enjoyed friendly relations, neither side having the facilities to mount a serious challenge to the other.

THE BRITISH They had been plotting routes across Canada from the late 1700s, in the hope of locating the Northwest Passage to speed trade between Europe and Asia. They failed to find the Northwest Passage but did succeed in developing British influence in the area through the Vancouver-based Hudson Bay Company, and were ever-mindful of Drake's claim of California for the British crown as they mounted fur-trapping expeditions throughout the West Coast.

THE FRENCH Their interest in North America was growing, and they made several expeditions to California during the 1820s. A few citizens of the United States (whose ships were forbidden to land in California) also arrived.

THE CALIFORNIOS As conflicts between the European powers became focused on issues closer to home (namely the rise of Napoleon), a change of control in California

eventually came from those most directly affected by such a move: the Californios, the mostly California-born Mexicans, who took advantage of Mexico's independence from Spain to declare themselves under Mexican rule in 1822.

> ❏ Total livestock holdings of the California missions in 1828: 252,000 cattle, 268,000 sheep, 3,500 mules, 34,000 horses, 8,300 goats, 3,400 pigs. ❏

Russian stronghold: Fort Ross

In Mexico City, California was generally considered to be an unimportant outpost and the governing of the province was left to the Californios themselves. Through the distribution of enormous land grants, a handful of Californio families became prominent and organised life on the ranchos with themselves at the top of a feudal-type system.

Native Americans. In fact, the Californios simply seized the land for themselves.

Through the early decades of the 1800s, many US citizens – some making the perilous overland journey, many more arriving after a three-month sea voyage around Cape Horn – arrived in California and acquired great influence by marrying into the leading families

The Pala Mission, San Diego

Like their Spanish predecessors, the Californios exploited Native American labour but, unlike the Spanish, they lacked agricultural skills. Rather than developing the land, the Californios were content to slaughter cattle and sell the hides to US traders – who turned the hides into leather goods and sold them back to the Californios.

> ❏ 'I am afraid we shall see a great deal of trouble in California this year. There are 7,000 or 8,000 emigrants from the USA expected.' ❏
> – WDM Howard, San Francisco merchant and landowner, 1846.

The missions' influence declined after Spanish rule, and their secularisation was ordered by the Mexican government in 1834. This act provided for mission land to be split equally between Californios and

and displaying the entrepreneurial zeal that some Californios lacked.

As the expansionist doctrine of Manifest Destiny came to hold sway over US foreign policy, California (and much of the present south-western United States) was increasingly seen as a desirable acquisition.

The United States had made various illegal incursions into California, and even attempted to buy the province from Mexico by the time the Mexican War broke out in 1846, after US actions in Texas. In June of that year, a group of US soldiers took over a barely defended presidio in Sonoma and declared California an independent republic – the short-lived Bear Flag Republic. In July, there were unopposed US landings at Monterey and San Francisco, and very soon every major settlement in California had the stars and stripes flying over its Spanish plaza.

The conclusion of the Mexican War allowed the United States to acquire California – also Nevada, Utah, New Mexico, and parts of Wyoming and Colorado – for $15 million, in a deal ratified in February 1848.

On January 24, 1848, just nine days before California was formally handed over to the United States, gold was discovered on the land of John Sutter, a European immigrant of the Mexican era, 50 miles east of his Sutter's Fort headquarters (the future site of Sacramento). Washed down from the Sierra Nevada, flakes of gold had accumulated in California's rivers over countless centuries and, to all intents and purposes, were there for the taking.

The news of the gold strike was delayed, however, as Sam Brannan, owner of the *California Star* newspaper, waited until May 12 (and until he had equipped his supply store at Sutter's Fort) before running down a San Francisco street waving aloft a vial of gold dust.

LINGERING DOUBTS Outside California, people continued to have doubts over the truth of the discovery of gold until December, when President James K Polk not only

A 1905 prospector hits the trail

verified the existence of California gold but exhibited 230 ounces of it.

GOLD FEVER Destined to be one of the greatest population movements in world history, the Gold Rush began in 1849, increasing the size of California from 7,000 non-native inhabitants in 1848 to 100,000 four years later.

These figures would certainly have been higher were it not for the fact that reaching California still required a marathon sea trip or a high-risk overland trek across mountains or deserts.

POPULATION BOOM A vast seaborne influx of men and mining machinery swelled San Francisco's population from 500 to 25,000 within two years (at one point, San Francisco Bay became blocked by abandoned ships whose crews headed for the gold-laden rivers), and inland river ports such as Sacramento and Stockton became major population centres.

Other new towns were established on the bays and inlets of the north and central coasts, while scores of mining communities grew in the centre of the gold-producing area (what eventually became known as the Gold Country), on the western slopes of the Sierra Nevada mountains.

> ❏ The biggest gold nugget found in California weighed 195 pounds. ❏

The Wells Fargo Museum, LA

Finding gold was the stuff of dreams, but more solid profits stemmed from feeding and housing the booming population: farming and lumber quickly became lucrative industries (this was the start of the decimation of the state's forests).

WILD TIMES Socially, the California of this time was the epitome of the fabled Wild West. The vast majority of its inhabitants were single males, and catering to their baser desires provided plenty of scope for unscrupulous entrepreneurs. San Francisco's Barbary Coast area (demolished in the 1940s) became infamous the world over for its prostitution, gambling, and drinking, yet it was only the largest and most notorious example of what was to be found in virtually every California community of the mid-1800s. What law there was tended to be upheld by vigilante groups, and in many towns the gallows saw frequent use.

END OF AN ERA Within three years, the Gold Rush was over. The river gold had quickly been picked clean, and company-owned mines provided the only access to the gold-bearing quartz still embedded in the Sierra Nevada hillsides. Those who had arrived seeking their fortunes either returned to the East or settled in the new towns along the coast.

Though no longer promising instant riches, gold mining continued to generate tremendous revenue – $81 million in the peak year of 1852 – and was to have a lasting effect on California's development.

> ❏ The great migration into California included many European vintners aware of the grape-producing potential of the Napa and Sonoma valleys north of San Francisco, where the state's first winery was established in 1857. ❏

Because of the mines' wealth, California bypassed the usual transition period as a frontier territory and attained full statehood in 1850. Geographically distanced from the core of the conflict and too busy getting rich to worry about it, California was barely affected by the Civil War, which raged through the rest of the United States from 1864 to 1869. Attention focused instead on the construction of the State Capitol Building in Sacramento, which was completed in 1874 and which became a symbol of California's emergence as a self-reliant, economically powerful entity.

The gold rush had made rich men of California's shop owners and merchants, but one group of Sacramento storekeepers – Charles Crocker, Mark Hopkins, Collis P. Huntington and Leland Stanford, later dubbed the Big Four – were set to become the wealthiest and most powerful men in the state by investing in what was to be the next key component in California's rapid development: the railroads.

Armed with the plans of an established railway engineer, Theodore D. Judah (who was later elbowed aside), the Big Four set about transforming the long-cherished dream of a coast-to-coast railroad link into reality and formed the Central Pacific Railroad Company in 1861.

BIG MONEY Playing on the US government's fear of losing California to the Confederate States as the Civil War loomed, the Big Four extracted enormous subsidies for their transcontinental railroad project. For each mile of construction they received 12,800 acres of land and $18,000 in cash, more for building over difficult terrain.

POWER AND WEALTH Employing a host of scandalous schemes, the Big Four got the US government to meet the entire cost of the railroad and bought themselves luxurious mansions in San Francisco's exclusive Nob Hill district.

After the transcontinental railroad was completed in 1869, the Big Four absorbed the rival Union Pacific Railroad to create the Southern Pacific Railroad and they then held a monopoly on trade routes across the state.

RESENTMENT AND RACISM Able to control the fate of entire communities, and with immense personal wealth, the Big Four wielded a level of political power unparalleled in California's history. There was much resentment of the rail barons, however, not least from the growing numbers of poor, who were feeling the effects of the post-Gold Rush depression by the late 1860s.

❏ Of the Big Four, it was Charles Crocker who oversaw the actual construction of the transcontinental railroad. Crocker, who weighed 250 pounds, allegedly stood on the freshly completed tracks 'bellowing like a bull' at the labourers. ❏

SUPPORT The spread of poverty in northern California also spawned racism, directed in particular at the Chinese, who had provided the bulk

Knotts Berry Farm, Buena Park

of the labour force and who were obliged to seek support from one another in the Chinatown areas taking root in San Francisco and in numerous other communities around the state.

THE BOOM SPREADS SOUTH As northern California had been enjoying the prosperity unleashed by the Gold Rush, southern California had remained isolated and arid, inhabited by only a few thousand people, mostly divided between Los Angeles and San Diego, cities the Big Four considered too remote to be worth joining to their rail network.

When a rival company, the Santa Fe Railroad (later to be taken over by the Big Four), began pushing west through Arizona in search of an outlet on the Pacific, the people of southern California saw their chance.

THE RAIL RACE Tremendous competition developed between San Diego and Los Angeles to be first with a rail link. With its natural harbour, San Diego was the logical choice, but a subsidy (in effect a bribe) of $602,000 underwritten by the 5,000 citizens of Los Angeles swayed the balance, and the Angelenos were duly connected to the rest of the nation in 1886. San Diego acquired a spur line a year later.

There followed a vigorous advertising campaign promoting southern California as a Mediterranean paradise. This, together with absurdly cheap train fares (round-trip tickets from Kansas City for just $1), brought tens of thousands of people to the newly accessible region. In the property-selling frenzy that ensued, plots of southern California land increased tenfold in value within the space of a year.

❏ In 1899, the Los Angeles Police Department sought to improve their response time by forming their first bicycle squad. ❏

The railroad also boosted the trade of southern California's harbours, making San Pedro (in Los Angeles), San Diego, and Santa Barbara outlets for the agricultural products of the Central Valley and for the sweet, seedless oranges that had recently been introduced to southern California. New communities took shape – Pasadena, Venice and Hollywood (which was originally founded by two Methodists as a temperance colony); oil was discovered beneath Los Angeles in 1892, and, through the early years of the 20th century, what were to evolve into gigantic aeronautical and automobile industries got started.

LOOKING SOUTH While all of California had its share of earthquakes, the San Francisco Earthquake of 1906, which razed the city and caused fires to rage for three days, encouraged many in the depressed north to seek their share of the wealth that was now being generated in the state's booming southland.

THE EARTH—"I HOPE I SHALL NEVER HAVE ONE OF THOSE SPLITTING HEADACHES AGAIN."

After the 1906 earthquake

The prosperity of the mid- and late 1800s did much to foster the myth of California as the American promised land, but it was Hollywood – a placid farming community on the outskirts of Los Angeles that transformed itself into the centre of the fledgling film industry – that was to present California as a latter-day Garden of Eden to the world at large.

30

EARLY DAYS In the early days of film, a monopolistic patent company, the Film Trust, had sewn up film-making on the East Coast, forcing aspiring directors to turn their attentions elsewhere. In 1907, William Selig's *The Count of Monte Cristo* became the first feature film to use a Los Angeles location, and news of the area's suitability for film production quickly spread.

Besides being too distant for patent laws to be enforced, southern California promised daily sunshine at a time when technical limitations made it necessary to shoot even indoor scenes outdoors. It also boasted a great stock of readily available natural backdrops that, with a few strategically placed props, could replicate almost any landscape in the world.

Nonetheless, once they had reached the West Coast, film-makers and their entourages were not welcomed with opened arms. In the small California towns where hardworking settlers were carving out new lives for themselves, filmshoots disrupted

Cecil B De Mille and Jesse Lasky, two greats from Paramount

business and the riotous behaviour of the crews outraged the God-fearing locals.

Several LA communities banned film-making altogether and, with rents in downtown Los Angeles too high for impecunious movie makers, many camera-wielding arrivals travelled eight miles west to the farming town of Hollywood, quickly turning disused barns into production offices and filling the streets with standing sets.

❏ One early Hollywood arrival was Cecil B De Mille, who in 1913 completed the first western feature to be shot in the district, *The Squaw Man*. In the make-do spirit of the times, De Mille shared his office with a horse. ❏

Most early films were cheap one-reel Westerns, but by 1916 D W Griffith was employing 15,000 extras on the set of *Intolerance* and had re-created the Hanging Gardens of Babylon on Hollywood and Sunset boulevards.

THE BIG TIME Five years later, 100,000 Los Angeles residents were making a living from the movies, which were now grossing a billion dollars annually, and the best-known faces in the country were the screen stars, such as Douglas Fairbanks and Mary Pickford, ensconced in the new mansions of Beverly Hills.

As the fame of Hollywood spread, so did its notoriety. Sensation-seeking scandal sheets fed an eager public, and found plenty to fill their pages in the bars, clubs and bedrooms of Tinseltown.

As one sordid revelation followed another, an initiative by top studio bosses to 'clean up' Hollywood resulted in the Hays Code of 1930. It was a form of self-censorship limiting what could be shown on the screen (in force until the 1960s, when it was replaced by the ratings system).

THE STUDIO SYSTEM Formed as Hollywood's earliest producers banded together to create large companies such as Paramount, RKO, and Warner Brothers, this also exerted a tight grip on what made it onto celluloid by signing staff – including actors and actresses – to exclusive, long-term contracts.

The creative inertia inherent in this system was apparent by the 1950s, when a loosening of control enabled independent productions to thrive – particularly so during the 1960s and 1970s. Despite this, the major studios still carried considerable clout in deciding exactly what reached the screen, and by the 1980s there was a swing back toward carefully marketed big-budget blockbusters.

Through diversification into TV and record production, the film companies have retained a large slice of the world entertainment market and continue to be major southern California employers. This enables Los Angeles to justify its reputation as a stomping ground for budding actors, screen-writers and directors – and the home of the stars – despite the fact that Hollywood has become a slum and most of the studios have moved to the suburbs.

> ❑ 'It's not true I was born a monster. Hollywood made me one.'
> – Boris Karloff. ❑

Mann's Chinese Theater

Often to the amusement, and sometimes to the horror, of Americans living elsewhere, there has been an undertow of radicalism in California life since the Gold Rush. While it was lampooned for many years as the place to which all of America's nuts eventually rolled, radical California really got into gear during the 1950s and the 1960s with the beatniks, hippies and political protesters.

BIRTH OF THE BEATNIK Intent on breaking free from the conventions of American society, and variously inspired by bebop jazz, cheap wine and Zen Buddhism, a small band of unconventional writers and painters began colonising the Italian coffee shops and cheap rooming houses of San Francisco's North Beach during the mid-1950s. They called themselves 'Beats' but were derisively dubbed 'beatniks' by a local newspaper columnist mindful of the recent Soviet satellite, sputnik.

The fame of the Beats was confirmed when Allen Ginsberg's epic poem *Howl* was banned for obscenity in 1956, and when Jack Kerouac's breathless novel, *On the Road*, became the literary sensation of 1957. Devoted to constant travel, the Beats were actually much less of a California phenomenon than the subculture that succeeded them, the hippies.

The genesis of hippiedom was a mind-altering drug called LSD (lysergic acid diethylamide), being tested on volunteers at Stanford University through the mid-1960s. While teaching a writing course at the university, Ken Kesey (author of *One Flew Over the Cuckoo's Nest*) brought a supply of the still-legal drug to San Francisco, where it was enthusiastically consumed at multimedia events.

LSD was soon outlawed, but not before its ability to send the user on a quasimystical, psychedelic 'trip' had been widely recognised, and it was soon under production in illicit laboratories.

FLOWER POWER The Victorian homes of San Francisco's Haight-Ashbury made ideal communal hippie pads, and by 1967 it seemed every disaffected youth in the United States had arrived there. Free concerts in Golden Gate Park were attended by tens of thousands of long-haired, painted-faced people, drawn to hear the bands of the era, such as the Grateful Dead,

❑ 'Women and men alike carried flowers and wore ribbons in their hair. There were more clean, long-haired males assembled in one place than at any time since the Crusades.' ❑
– Journalist Ralph Gleason describing 1967's Human Be-In in Golden Gate Park.

Flower children announce the 'death of the hippie', 1967

Jefferson Airplane, and Country Joe and the Fish.

As more addictive substances replaced LSD in popularity and Haight-Ashbury became squalid and overcrowded, hippiedom's slide from peace and love to horror was compounded by the activities of Charles Manson. Recruiting his infamous 29-member 'family' in Haight-Ashbury, Manson moved with them to a desert base to launch a series of grisly killings in Los Angeles, including that of film director Roman Polanski's pregnant wife, Sharon Tate. Manson was subsequently convicted of seven murders and is currently making regular appeals for parole.

In their own ways, the Beats and the hippies both rejected the entire social order, but 1960s California also found the political establishment being challenged in (comparatively) more orthodox ways.

POLITICAL PROTEST Formed on the campus at Berkeley in 1964, the Free Speech Movement (see pages 84 and 85) was the stimulus for a decade of nationwide campus revolts and anti-Vietnam War protests. Meanwhile, the increasingly diverse ethnic make-up of what was fast becoming the nation's most populous state was not reflected in the white-dominated corridors of power, and discontent simmered in various quarters.

Anger erupted most dramatically in Watts (a depressed section of Los Angeles) in 1965, when the National Guard was called upon to quell a six-day battle that left 34 dead and caused $40 million of damage.

During the following year the militant Black Panthers formed, pledging themselves to armed struggle against the ruling classes.

STATE POLITICS The turbulent 1960s had mellowed by the following decade, when there was (at least some) assimilation of ethnic minorities into policy-making bodies. Simultaneously, state governor Ronald Reagan – nicknamed 'Ray-guns' for his willingness to use force in response to protest – lost the election to Jerry Brown, a fourth-generation Californian who was viewed by many as the embodiment of Golden State wackiness.

❑ The formation of the National Farm Workers' Union by Cesar Chavez in 1962 brought about improved conditions for California's vast army of undervalued agricultural workers through a series of strikes and public-supported boycotts. ❑

Eschewing the governor's luxury mansion built by Reagan in favour of a simple apartment, and conducting a much-publicised romance with fashionable rock singer Linda Ronstadt, Brown imposed strict controls to reduce smog, decriminalised possession of marijuana, and set California on course to being the country's most environmentally aware region by the time he left office with an eye on the White House in 1983.

SAN FRANCISCO

| 0 | 1 | 2 km |
| 0 | | 1 mile |

● Bay Area Rapid Transit (BART) Stations

— 49 Mile Scenic Drive

South Bay

A BEAUTIFUL CITY Set on a small, hilly peninsula, San Francisco is an easy place to fall in love with. Since Gold Rush times, settlers from the far corners of the globe have arrived here. Their sheer diversity fosters the live-and-let-live attitude for which the city is renowned.

The city splits into a mosaic of tightly grouped neighbourhoods. The Financial District and the Civic Center mark either end of Downtown, linked by the city's main artery, Market Street. North of Downtown, Nob Hill, Russian Hill, and Telegraph Hill are prime residential areas, yet they nestle close to the bustling streets and alleyways of Chinatown and the Italian-flavoured North Beach. Fisherman's Wharf, to the north,

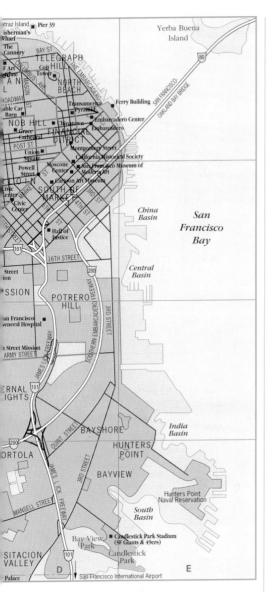

is the one place in San Francisco where tourists outnumber locals.

South of Market Street, up-and-coming SoMa borders the mostly Spanish-speaking Mission District, just west of which the Castro is a predominantly gay and lesbian area.

West of Downtown, Haight-Ashbury saw the rise and fall of flower power, and adjacent, the bucolic Golden Gate Park stretches almost to the ocean. North of Haight-Ashbury lies tiny Japantown and the broad streets of Pacific Heights, which lead on to the woodlands of the Presidio area, covering the city's north-west tip.

36

FESTIVALS
Hardly a week passes without some kind of festival happening in San Francisco. The highlights are the Chinese New Year, usually in February, celebrated with firecrackers and a three-hour dragon-led parade through Chinatown; the St Patrick's Day parade in March; the Cherry Blossom parade in Japantown during April; the Bay-to-Breakers fun run across the peninsula in May; the Mission District Carnaval, also in May; and the Halloween parade along Castro Street in October.

Districts

▶ The Castro   34C3

The largest and most famous of San Francisco's gay areas, the Castro is much changed from 15 years ago when its streets were a wild celebration of gay lifestyles. The city's raunchiest Halloween parades continue to happen here, but the success of the Castro's many gay-run businesses – and the threat of AIDS – has instilled a sense of quieter respectability.

Regardless of their sexual persuasion, few people could be left unmoved after visiting the **Names Project**▶▶ (2362 Market Street), where each grave-sized patch of a gigantic quilt represents one local victim of the AIDS virus – at present, the quilt has 6,000 patches.

▶▶▶ Chinatown   35D4

Squeezed into a few chaotic blocks between the Financial District and North Beach, Chinatown is a riot of exotic sights and smells, and the base for the banks, newspapers and schools that serve what is claimed to be the largest Chinese community outside Asia.

Dragon-tail-entwined streetlights and pagoda-style buildings overlook a ceaseless procession around the food stalls on Stockton Street and the herbalist shops, tearooms, bakeries, and gaily painted, century-old temples that fill numerous alleyways.

▶ Civic Center   35D3

Rightly regarded as the best beaux-arts grouping in the United States, the public buildings of the compact Civic Center are dominated by the dome of the elegant **City Hall**▶▶▶ – raised in 1915 (see page 52) – and by hundreds of homeless people occupying their neat plazas.

▶ Downtown/Union Square   35D4

Downtown San Francisco encompasses the Civic Center, Tenderloin, and the Financial District, and holds the bulk of the city's hotels, big-name stores, and the well-known – though uninteresting – Union Square.

▶ Embarcadero Center   35D4

The best views of San Francisco are from the **Skydeck**▶▶ on the 41st floor of One Embarcadero Center, one of a group of four soulless high-rises housing offices, shops and hotels between the Financial District and Chinatown.

▶ Financial District   35D4

Stride among the power-dressed power brokers of the Financial District to find out why San Franciscans dread the 'Manhattanisation' of their city, a condition exemplified by the sterile glass and steel corporate towers built here during the 1970s and early 1980s.

▶ Fisherman's Wharf   35D4

The base of a large fishing fleet until the 1940s, today's Wharf is almost entirely devoted to the tourist. T-shirts and trinkets are sold in every store, street stands do a brisk trade in overpriced sourdough bread and seafood, and the best among a glut of attractions are **Underwater World**▶ (Pier 39), and **Hyde Street Pier Historic Ships** (see page 41).

▶▶ Haight-Ashbury

34C3

Haight-Ashbury found itself at the forefront of the flower-power revolution of the late 1960s, when thousands of long-haired youths poured into what had been a declining middle-class neighbourhood.

Haight Street, the area's main thoroughfare, still bears a distinct counter-culture bias, even though the offbeat bookstores and wacky clothes shops are steadily being replaced by pricey restaurants and fashion boutiques as the neighbourhood becomes increasingly gentrified, its many well-tended Victorian homes becoming sought-after properties.

▶▶ Japantown

34C4

Concealed behind Japantown's usually unexciting exteriors are the shops, temples and social centres serving the city's Japanese community, only a small percentage of whom actually live here. Between Post Street and the Geary Expressway, the large **Japan Center▶** contains numerous outlets for quality Japanese arts and crafts, and several temptingly priced restaurants. Within the centre, Kabuki Hot Springs offers a traditional Japanese steambath and shiatsu massage.

▶▶ Mission District

35D3

A Spanish-speaking enclave whose population is chiefly drawn from Central and South America, the Mission District also attracted some of the city's writers and artists. A number of left-wing political activists are based on Valencia Street.

Other than Mission Dolores (see page 54), the draws are well-preserved Victorian houses and vivid street murals. To find the former, walk south from Mission Dolores and turn left along Liberty Street; for the latter, walk south from the corner of Mission and 24th streets.

SAFETY
The closest San Francisco gets to being seriously seedy is the 10-block strip between Union Square and the Civic Center, where most of the city's homeless congregate and where prostitutes ply their trade from street corners. The Western Addition, a rough neighbourhood between Haight-Ashbury and Japantown, is also best avoided after dark.

Looking north across San Francisco, with Alcatraz Island and Telegraph Hill's Coit Tower clearly visible

DASHIELL HAMMETT
The master of hard-boiled detective fiction, Dashiell Hammett, moved to San Francisco in 1920 to work for the Pinkerton Detective Agency. The booming but corrupt city made the ideal setting for his cynical investigator Sam Spade, and Hammett's writing reached a peak with *The Maltese Falcon* in 1930. Hammett's most productive years were spent at 1155 Leavenworth Street in Nob Hill. He departed to write film scripts in Hollywood, only to be imprisoned for refusing to testify during the anti-Communist witch hunts of the 1950s.

Two of the Mission District's many murals, reflecting the artistic traditions of the area's predominantly Hispanic population

▶▶ **Nob Hill**   35D4

In the late 1800s, California's first tycoons erected lavish homes on Nob Hill, overlooking the Financial District. Only one of the mansions survived the 1906 earthquake – it is now the ultraexclusive ivy-covered **Pacific Union Club**▶ (1000 California Street) – though Nob Hill remains among the city's priciest and most prestigious addresses, and holds exclusive hotels and restaurants patronized by famous faces.

One place meriting a stop is the reposeful **Grace Cathedral**▶▶▶ (1051 Taylor Street), modelled on Paris's Notre-Dame. While ministering to the spiritual needs of its ultra rich congregation, the cathedral has – controversially – also sheltered the city's homeless in its basement.

▶▶▶ **North Beach**   35D4

Italians were the first to give North Beach a lasting style, arriving in force from the late 1800s and opening the first of the restaurants and cafés that make this the city's best place for pasta and pizzas, and for lingering over a cappuccino beside the seething Columbus Avenue.

During the mid-1950s, North Beach's (then) cheap rents, wine and food made it the home of the first beatniks – so dubbed by San Francisco newspaper columnist Herb Caen – the most illustrious of whom are remembered by street names in their honour and by their still-standing haunts, such as the City Lights Bookstore and Vesuvio, a café and bar. See the walk on page 50.

▶ **Pacific Heights**   34C4

A yuppie stronghold, Pacific Heights' Union Street – once the location of several dairy farms, and known as Cow Hollow – is packed with chic clothes shops and arts-and-crafts galleries. Close by are several landmark Victorian homes. These include the 8-sided **Octagon House**▶ (2645 Gough Street) and the **Haas-Lilienthal House**▶▶ (2007 Franklin Street), the only fully period-furnished house in San Francisco open to the public.

► Russian Hill   35D4

Most people stay in Russian Hill only long enough to photograph a section of **Lombard Street**►►, hailed as the crookedest street in San Francisco; its descent between Hyde and Leavenworth streets landscaped into a series of curves decorated by plants and bushes.

While in Russian Hill, find time for the **San Francisco Art Institute**► (800 Chestnut Street), the oldest art school on the West Coast, with displays of student work, an outstanding mural by Diego Rivera, and an inexpensive café with excellent views.

► SoMa   35D3

Until recently an uninteresting sector of warehouses, rail-freight yards, and factories, SoMa ('South of Market Street') has changed faster than any other part of the city. Fashionable nightclubs and restaurants have made Folsom Street the playground of the city's hipsters, while new buildings, such as the Moscone Convention Center, the Museum of Modern Art, and the Yerba Buena Gardens complex (see panel) are appearing all over SoMa.

Many factory outlet stores here offer designer products at discount prices (see pages 60 and 61).

► Telegraph Hill   35D4

Telegraph Hill is a coveted address with some splendid modern residential architecture lining the steep streets that wind up to **Coit Tower**►►►, a memorial to the city's volunteer firemen, erected in 1933.

The tower is notable less for the views from its summit than for the outstanding Depression-era murals decorating its inner walls. Depicting scenes of Californian life of the time, the murals' militant symbols upset the authorities and delayed their unveiling for several years. After visiting the tower, get down from Telegraph Hill by way of the **Filbert Steps**►►, a steep and partially wooden walkway fringed by effusive vegetation.

CROOKED STREETS
Anyone will tell you that Russian Hill's Lombard Street is the crookedest street in San Francisco. But nearly as crooked, and much less crowded, is Vermont Street in the Potrero Hill area, just east of the Mission District. Vermont Street also has the distinction of being the only city thoroughfare that fire-engine drivers refuse to navigate because of its tortuous twists.

YERBA BUENA GARDENS
Filling a 12-block section of SoMa bordered by Market, Harrison, Second, and Fifth streets, Yerba Buena Gardens is an ambitious complex of new buildings and landscaped gardens to which some of San Francisco's smaller museums, such as the Mexican Museum, are – on the heels of the eye-catching new Museum of Modern Art – hoping to relocate in the near future. Check with the Visitor Information Center (see page 71) for the latest details.

A bird's-eye view across North Beach and Telegraph Hill to Fisherman's Wharf

San Francisco

CABLE CARS

Invented by Andrew Hallidie, the first cable car ran along Clay Street on August 1, 1873. A safer way of negotiating steep streets than horse-drawn wagons, the cable car also made possible the development of hitherto inaccessible high areas such as Nob Hill. By 1906, there were 600 cable cars in operation but that year's earthquake, and the subsequent rise of motorised transportation, conspired to render them obsolete. Preserved as a National Historic Landmark, the system in use today – mostly for the enjoyment of tourists – was improved by a $60 million facelift in 1982.

The US's only moving National Historic Landmark, cable cars provide public transportation in San Francisco along three routes

Museums and galleries

▶ African American Historical and Cultural Society 35C4

Building C, Fort Mason Center

African-American history and achievements in the San Francisco area and beyond are chronicled through archival material and paintings. An annex at 762 Fulton Street in the Western Addition holds more material.

▶▶ Cable Car Museum 35D4

1201 Mason Street

Giving a rather dull, pictorial record of the 120-year history of San Francisco's famous cable cars, and showing off some early examples, the museum also reveals the simple but clever engineering principle that keeps the cable cars working: each car is pulled along the streets by an underground cable that never stops moving. The heavy whirring sounds, audible as you enter, are the steel cable being pulled over 14-foot-wide winding wheels, visible in the museum's lower level.

▶▶▶ California Academy of Sciences 34B3

Golden Gate Park

Pitched at children and intended to stimulate an interest in the natural world, the California Academy of Sciences gets a D for its static exhibits on California ecology and the native cultures of the world, but an A-plus for the wide-ranging selection of marine life in the **Steinhart Aquarium▶▶▶** – from bloated Amazon Basin predators to the mysterious splitfin flashlight fish.

Elsewhere, the safe-quake exhibit, inside in the **Hall of Eart and Space Sciences▶▶**, vibrates the floor with the same magnitude with which the earthquakes of 1865 and 1906 shook San Francisco's streets. Regain your balance by visiting the **Far Side of Science Gallery▶▶▶**, lined with the hilarious cartoons of Gary Larson.

An additional fee brings admission to the adjoining Morrison Planetarium, humorously billed as 'California's largest indoor universe'.

▶ Cartoon Art Museum 35D3

814 Mission Street

Changing exhibitions taken from a vast permanent collection trace the development of a cartoon or comic strip from the hand of the artist to the finished product.

▶▶ Chinese Historical Society of America 48C3

650 Commercial Street

An engrossing accompaniment to a walk through Chinatown, outlining the Chinese arrival in California, their labour on the region's first railroads, and their banding together for mutual support in the face of 'Yellow Peril' racial hostility. Look, too, around the shows of the **Chinese Cultural Center▶**, on the third floor of the Holiday Inn, 750 Kearny Street.

▶ Exploratorium

3601 Lyon Street

The best place in San Francisco to amuse young minds with low boredom thresholds, the Exploratorium is a

single vast hall filled with 650 interactive exhibits designed to illustrate and explain the fundamentals of natural science and human perception. The exhibits, such as crackling tesla coils or coupled resonant pendulums, stand alongside the results of an innovative artist-in-residence programme that produced *Tornado*, a reservoir of fog continually pulled upward in an inverted vortex, and *Alien Voices*, allowing two people in separate wooden telephone booths to speak to each other in a choice of 16 computer-altered voices.

The Exploratorium's most popular area (reservations necessary) is the Tactile Dome, a dark space that you can only leave by feeling your way out on hands and knees.

▶ Fort Point 34B4

Beneath Golden Gate Bridge
Finished in 1861 to protect the entrance to San Francisco Bay, Fort Point was never attacked despite becoming obsolete a year after its completion by advances in weaponry design. Some rooms within the three-storey granite fortress store historical artefacts, and enthusiasts in Civil War uniforms give tours.

▶ Hyde Street Pier Historic Ships 35D3

Hyde Street Pier, close to Fisherman's Wharf
Back when Fisherman's Wharf was full of fishermen rather than tourists, ferries to Berkeley and Sausalito sailed from Hyde Street Pier, which now permanently moors several historic vessels. Among them are the 1890 ferry *Eureka*, once the world's largest passenger ferry,

The Balclutha, *built to move grain between California and Europe, forms part of the Hyde Street Pier Historic Ships collection*

A GHOST SHIP
On chilly nights when the Golden Gate Bridge is eerily shrouded in fog, look for a phantom clipper, the *Tennessee*, gliding through the waves. The two-masted vessel sank here 100 years ago but is regularly sighted – most famously in 1942 by several of the crew of a naval destroyer.

and the *Balclutha*, a square-rigged sailing ship that was launched in Scotland in 1886, which rounded Cape Horn several times before ending its days transporting Alaskan salmon. The National Maritime Museum, nearby at Aquatic Park, is rather staid, displaying mostly models of seagoing vessels.

▶▶ Mexican Museum   34C4
Building D, Fort Mason Center
Besides giving new Mexican-American artists a chance to break into the museum exhibition circuit, the Mexican Museum mounts outstanding shows on many aspects of Mexican arts and culture.

▶▶ M H de Young Memorial Museum   34B3
Golden Gate Park
There are few better places to observe how American art gradually turned away from European tastes and acquired a distinctive national identity. Works by many of the country's most influential artists are here, such as John Smibert, noted for his 18th-century society portraits, and Albert Bierstadt, whose 19th-century landscapes chronicled the settlement of the American West. Few pieces, however, are as entertaining as the room of trompe-l'oeil paintings, notably William Michael Harnett's *After the Hunt*.

In contrast to the strong theme of the de Young collection, the breadth and diversity of the **Asian Art Museum**▶▶▶, now in an adjoining building (but planning to move to Civic Center), is almost too vast to comprehend. It is the small pieces that stick in the mind: the 15th-century votive stele from China, Japanese Netsuke – wooden toggles for boxes and pouches, fashionable during the 18th and 19th centuries – and a human thigh-bone trumpet from Tibet.

FREE ENTRY
Museums that normally have an entry fee are free on the following days of the month: Asian Art Museum, first Wednesday (10–12); California Academy of Sciences, first Wednesday; California Palace of the Legion of Honor, second Wednesday; M H de Young Museum, first Wednesday (10–12); Exploratorium, first Wednesday; Museum of Modern Art, first Tuesday; Mexican Museum, first Wednesday.

42

The Egyptian-style main building of the M H de Young Memorial Museum

▶▶▶ Museum of Modern Art   35D3
151 Third Street
The centrepiece of the Yerba Buena Arts Center development that has totally changed the face of SoMa over the last few years, San Francisco's new Museum of Modern Art opened in 1995 in an architecturally striking six-storey building.

The second-floor galleries highlight painting and sculpture from 1900 to 1970, and include significant contributions from Europeans – among them Picasso's *Head in Three-quarter View* and *The Coffee Pot*, Braque's *Violin and Candlestick*, and Matisse's seminal *Woman with the Hat*. Amid many notable abstract expressionist canvases are works by Pollock and de Kooning, and the last completed work by Barnett Newman. A separate gallery houses works bequeathed by California abstract expressionist Clyfford Still. Over 100 works by Paul Klee are included in the collection of German Expressionists, and surrealism is represented by offerings from primary figures such as Dali and Ernst.

Complementing the painting are architecture and design exhibitions, while the third floor houses photography from the likes of Man Ray and Moholy-Nagy, and from much admired local practitioners such as Ansel Adams and Edward Weston.

▶ Museum of Money of the
   American West   49D3
400 California Street, Bank of California basement
Stable currency was not a feature of pioneer-era California, and here you will see a variety of bills issued by different states, and even by the Mormon religion, before standardised laws were adopted.

▶ North Beach Museum   48B4
1435 Stockton Street, in the Eureka Savings Bank
Temporary shows, often made up of the possessions of local people, illuminate the rise of one of San Francisco's most fascinating districts.

▶ Pacific Heritage Museum   49D3
608 Commercial Street
The exhibitions displayed here on the history of the countries of the Pacific Rim are varied and rarely uninteresting. On the lower level, the permanent displays recall the building's time as the city's original mint, established on the heels of the Gold Rush in 1854.

▶▶▶ Palace of the Legion of Honor   34A4
Lincoln Park
Modelled on its namesake in Paris and erected in memory to California's dead of World War I, the Palace of the Legion of Honor, on a bluff overlooking the ocean, makes an architecturally imposing showcase for San Francisco's major collection of fine art.

Amid a rich endowment of paintings and decorative arts spanning several centuries, and the Achenbach Foundation's excellent collection of graphic art, it is the superb collection of Rodin sculptures, ranging from early experiments such as *Man with a Broken Nose* to the accomplished *Victor Hugo*, which steals the show.

FREE MEDIA
Each week the *San Francisco Bay Guardian* and *SF Weekly* provide excellent city-wide news, views, and events listings. You will find the papers distributed on street corners and in many shops and restaurants. Also free, the monthly *North Beach Now* covers goings-on in the North Beach area, and the biweekly *Bay Times* serves the city's gay and lesbian community, as does the weekly *Bay Area Reporter*.

43

A Thinker, *from the original cast, is among the selection of Rodin sculptures at the Palace of the Legion of Honor*

HILL TALK
'When you get tired of walking around San Francisco you can always lean against it.' – *Transworld Getaway Guide*, 1975–6.

Though the sign outside claims it to be the oldest building in San Francisco, the 1776 Commandante's Quarters at the Presidio contains few original sections

▶ Performing Arts Library and Museum   *34C3/35C4*
399 Grove Street
As a prelude to an evening at the ballet or opera, take a peek at these changing exhibitions relating to San Francisco's performing arts heritage. The displays include vintage costumes, photos, posters and programmes galore.

▶ Presidio Army Museum   *34C4*
Corner of Lincoln Boulevard and Funston Avenue
Housed in a one-time military hospital in an 1863 building with verandas, the Presidio Army Museum charts the growth of San Francisco's military garrison, from its Spanish beginnings through its role in two world wars to the present. Alongside the massed uniforms and insignia lies an excellent display on the city's 1906 earthquake, and outside are two of the 'refugee cottages', which were rented to homeless survivors of the catastrophe for $2 a month.

The museum is just one building of the 1,500-acre **Presidio**, founded by the Spanish as a military base in 1776 and owned by the Sixth Army until being de-commissioned and given to the National Park Service in 1994. Many early buildings remain (within an easy walk from the museum); the **military cemetery▶** holds graves dating back to the Civil War and is the subject of a park ranger-led tour on Saturdays.

▶ San Francisco Craft and Folk Art Museum   *34C4*
Building A, Fort Mason Center
Always worthwhile shows of curious arts and crafts: from California decoys to mythical African figures.

▶ Wells Fargo History Museum   *49D3*
420 Montgomery Street
In the 1840s, Wells Fargo ran the first stagecoaches between the eastern and western United States, transporting people, gold and mail thousands of inhospitable miles. An 1860s stagecoach suggests the discomfort of public transportation, and much more in the museum represents the banking wing of the company, now one of the nation's biggest financial institutions.

Over the last decades, San Francisco's fabled tolerance of unconventional lifestyles has helped to make it the home of the largest and most assertive gay and lesbian communities in the world.

Many gay men landed in San Francisco toward the end of World War II after being discharged from the US military in disgrace for their homosexuality – or suspected homosexuality. Unable to face the stigma awaiting them at home, most stayed in the city, socialising in a network of discreet bars and clubs.

Gay rights The radicalism of the 1960s, and anger fuelled by continued police raids on gay-patronised establishments, brought many gays to the streets to proclaim their sexuality and to demand their civil rights. Simultaneously the Castro district began changing from a working-class Catholic area to an almost exclusively gay neighbourhood.

As the Castro's fame spread far and wide, gays from all over the country moved into the district, their sheer force of numbers making the gay vote of crucial concern for aspiring city politicians. Many liberals running for public office adopted the gay rights agenda, and in 1977, Harvey Milk, who ran a camera store on Castro Street, became the country's first out-of-the-closet public official.

Slow integration Homophobia was by no means eradicated, however. A year after his election, Harvey Milk and the city's gay-supportive mayor, George Moscone, were assassinated. The light sentence of five years' imprisonment passed on Dan White, the right-wing politician who committed the double murder, so incensed the gay population and large numbers of heterosexuals as well that 50,000 people took part in the protest that culminated in police cars being overturned and

City Hall being attacked in 1978's 'White Night Riot'.

Several decades of standing up and being counted have left San Francisco's gays – and, to a lesser extent, lesbians – with a unique level of integration into mainstream city life.

AIDS Tragically, the impact of AIDS has perhaps been felt more powerfully here than anywhere else in the western world. Yet the crisis has revealed hitherto unknown reserves of community solidarity and has provided a new focus for political activity.

45

Gay culture is an established part of the San Francisco community

Walk

Looking around Chinatown

See map on pages 48–9.

Begin at the Chinatown Gates at the corner of Bush Street and Grant Avenue.
Since 1970, the **Chinatown Gate** has made a less than imposing entrance to Chinatown's main street.

Walk north along Grant Avenue, pausing at the corner of California Street.
At 600 California Street, the **Old St Mary's Church** was the first Catholic cathedral on the West Coast, blessed in 1854.

Turn east off Grant Avenue onto Commercial Street for the Chinese Historical Society of America.
At 650 Commercial Street is the **Chinese Historical Society of America** (see page 40).

Turn left onto Kearny Street, turning left again after one block onto Clay Street and cross onto Waverly Place.

Chinatown's distinct style

Here are many Chinatown buildings such as the 1852 **Tien Hou Temple**, on the top floor of Nos. 123–129.

Exit Waverly Place turning left onto Washington Street and then left onto Stockton Street.
Crowded **Stockton Street** is where the city's Chinese community buys its fresh meat, fish and vegetables.

From Stockton Street, take any street to Grant Avenue, a block east, and return to the Chinatown Gate.

● **Stroll** *Entering Golden Gate Park (see page 56) on John Kennedy Drive takes you past the ivy-covered McLaren Lodge, now the park headquarters and formerly the home of John McLaren, a Scot who spent 50 years cultivating the park, and on to the colourful blooms and luscious palms which surround the Conservatory. Just ahead, Hagiwara Teagarden Drive branches left, running between the California Academy of Sciences and the M H de Young Museum (see pages 40 and 42 respectively), and the wistful Japanese Tea Garden with its statue of Buddha, cast in 1790. A short walk farther on, two bridges cross Stow Lake to the foot of Strawberry Hill, the highest point in the park.*

Walk

The Financial District

See map on pages 48–9.

Begin at the Federal Reserve Bank at 101 Market Street.
Using computer simulations in the **Federal Reserve Bank** lobby, you can rearrange the country's finances.

Cross Market Street and walk west along Pine Street to the corner of Montgomery Street for the Bank of America building.
At the foot of the Bank of America building, a severe black granite sculpture has earned the nickname 'Banker's Heart'.

Continue north along Montgomery Street for the Wells Fargo History Museum.
At 420 Montgomery Street, this museum documents the rise of the Wells Fargo company (see page 44).

Continue three blocks north along Montgomery Street for the Transamerica Pyramid.
The city's tallest structure, the 853-foot-high Transamerica Pyramid, at 600 Montgomery Street, displays mildly diverting works of art on its lobby-level walls.

Continue north along Montgomery Street, turning right onto Jackson Street for Jackson Square.
Around Jackson Square, many buildings that predate the Financial District's high-rises by a century or more have been restored.

From Jackson Square, walk west along Washington Street and return to Montgomery Street.
Throughout the year, the City Guides conduct hour-long walking tours around particular places of interest, including City Hall, Coit Tower, Nob Hill, Japantown and the Mission District murals. For more details, call 415/557–4266.

47

● **Stroll** *From Mission Dolores walk south along Dolores Street to Liberty Street, turning left for the heart of the Liberty Hill Historic District, filled by late 19th-century buildings.*
   From the end of Liberty Street, walk north along Valencia Street and turn right onto Twentieth Street. At the corner of South Van Ness Avenue, Tribute to Carlos Santana is among the biggest and boldest of the Mission District's many murals.

Begin at Aquatic Park, just west of Fisherman's Wharf.
Nearly four miles of breezy waterside walking, the Golden Gate Promenade covers a tiny section of the Golden Gate National Recreation Area, leading

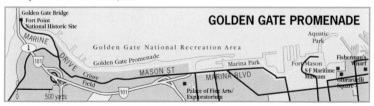

GOLDEN GATE PROMENADE

Golden Gate Promenade

over the hills of Fort Mason (see page 53) and past the flashy yachts that are tethered alongside the marina, by the old Presidio military base (see page 44), finally concluding close to Fort Point (see page 41) at the foot of Golden Gate Bridge (see page 54).

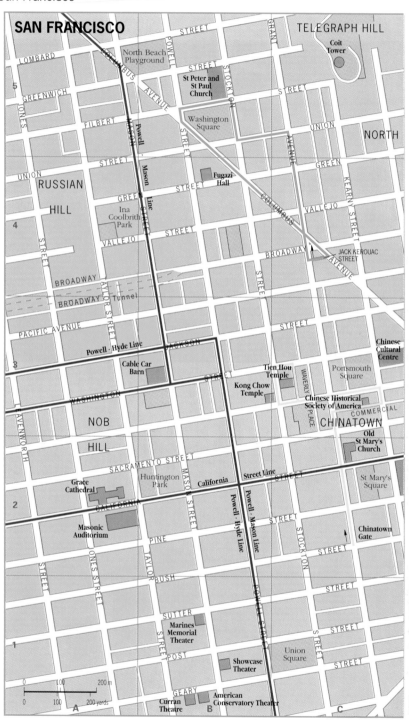

SAN FRANCISCO

TELEGRAPH HILL

Coit Tower

LOMBARD STREET

North Beach Playground

GREENWICH

St Peter and St Paul Church

STREET

Washington Square

UNION

NORTH

FILBERT STREET

GREEN

UNION

RUSSIAN HILL

Powell

Mason Line

GREEN STREET

Fugazi Hall

STREET

VALLEJO

Ina Coolbrith Park

VALLEJO STREET

STREET

COLUMBUS AVENUE

KEARNY STREET

BROADWAY

JACK KEROUAC STREET

BROADWAY

BROADWAY Tunnel

AVENUE

PACIFIC AVENUE

Powell - Hyde Line

JACKSON

Chinese Cultural Centre

Cable Car Barn

STREET

Tien Hou Temple

Portsmouth Square

WASHINGTON

Kong Chow Temple

WAVERLY

Chinese Historical Society of America

PLACE

COMMERCIAL

NOB

CHINATOWN

HILL

Old St Mary's Church

SACRAMENTO STREET

Huntington Park

MASON STREET

California

Street Line

St Mary's Square

LEAVENWORTH

Grace Cathedral

Powell - Hyde Line

Powell - Mason Line

STOCKTON STREET

CALIFORNIA

Masonic Auditorium

Chinatown Gate

PINE

TAYLOR

JONES STREET

BUSH

STREET

POWELL STREET

SUTTER

Marines Memorial Theater

Union Square

POST

Showcase Theater

STREET

1

GEARY

0   100   200 m

0   100   200 yards

Curran Theatre

American Conservatory Theater

A   B   C

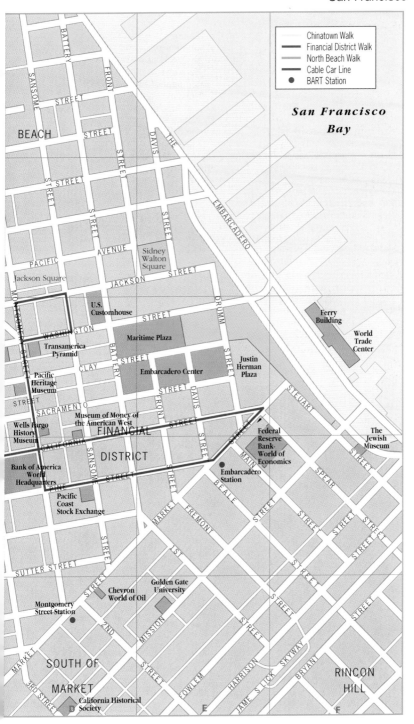

Legend
- Chinatown Walk
- Financial District Walk
- North Beach Walk
- Cable Car Line
- ● BART Station

San Francisco Bay

BEACH

BATTERY STREET

SANSOME STREET

FRONT STREET

DAVIS STREET

THE EMBARCADERO

STREET

STREET

STREET

STREET

PACIFIC AVENUE

Sidney Walton Square

Jackson Square

JACKSON STREET

MONTGOMERY STREET

WASHINGTON STREET

U.S. Customhouse

STREET

DRUMM STREET

Ferry Building

World Trade Center

Maritime Plaza

Transamerica Pyramid

BATTERY STREET

CLAY STREET

Embarcadero Center

Justin Herman Plaza

Pacific Heritage Museum

STREET

FRONT STREET

DAVIS STREET

STEUART

SACRAMENTO STREET

Museum of Money of the American West

STREET

STREET

Wells Fargo History Museum

FINANCIAL

Federal Reserve Bank-World of Economics

The Jewish Museum

CALIFORNIA STREET

SANSOME STREET

DISTRICT

MAIN STREET

SPEAR STREET

STREET

Bank of America World Headquarters

PINE STREET

Embarcadero Station

Pacific Coast Stock Exchange

BEALE STREET

STREET

STREET

STREET

SUTTER STREET

MARKET STREET

FREMONT STREET

STREET

1ST STREET

Chevron World of Oil

Golden Gate University

Montgomery Street Station

2ND STREET

MISSION STREET

STREET

STREET

STREET

SOUTH OF MARKET

California Historical Society

3RD STREET

MARKET STREET

FOLSOM STREET

HARRISON STREET

JAMES LICK SKYWAY

BRYANT STREET

RINCON HILL

E

F

Walk

A journey through North Beach

See map on pages 48–9.

Begin at Jack Kerouac Street, on the 1000 block of Grant Avenue.
Named after one of the Beat Generation's brightest lights, **Jack Kerouac Street** marks the transition from Chinatown to North Beach.

Take a few strides north to the corner of Columbus Avenue and Broadway.
With strip joints nestling alongside jazz and other music clubs, the area around the **corner of Broadway** and **Columbus Avenue** is the scene of some of the city's lewdest and loudest nightlife – as it has been for decades.

Walk north along Columbus Avenue for the City Lights Bookstore.
At 261 Columbus Avenue, the **City Lights Bookstore** became the first

paperback bookshop in the country when it opened in 1953; its owner, poet and painter Lawrence Ferlinghetti, published many works of the best of the Beat writers, beginning with Allen Ginsberg's controversial poem, *Howl*, in 1956. Facing City Lights across Adler Place, **Vesuvio** is another beatnik-era survivor.

Continue north along Columbus Avenue for Washington Square.
Overlooked by the twin spires of the Romanesque Church of St Peter and St Paul, **Washington Square** has amateur art exhibitions each weekend, and elderly Chinese practice the slow, artful exercises of Tai Chi every morning.

Cross Washington Square and walk south along Grant Avenue.
From here to Broadway, **Grant Avenue** has some of the area's best-priced restaurants, many funky shops, and some venerable R&B clubs.

Continue south along Grant Avenue and return to the starting point, Jack Kerouac Street.

The Octagon House, in the Union Street area of Pacific Heights

Given a week or a weekend in San Francisco, there are endless permutations of places to go and things to see. The following itineraries will give you a balanced look at the city.

Week's itinerary

Day one Explore the Financial District and Chinatown on foot (see pages 46 and 47). Lunch in North Beach. Take a cable car north to explore both Fisherman's Wharf and Fort Mason, or take a journey by bus to Golden Gate Bridge.

Day two Take a cable car to Nob Hill, explore the area and adjoining Russian Hill on foot. Lunch on Union Street. Walk south through Pacific Heights to Japantown.

Day three Travel by BART to Berkeley and explore the town and university campus. Lunch on Telegraph Avenue. Take BART to Lake Merritt for the Oakland Museum. Return by BART to the city.

Day four Visit Alamo Square, and continue to the Haight-Ashbury area. Lunch on Haight Street and spend the rest of the day exploring Golden Gate Park.

Day five Tour Alcatraz in the morning (see page 80). Have lunch in North Beach. During the afternoon, explore Telegraph Hill and walk along the Embarcadero to Embarcadero Center.

Day six Sail across the bay and spend the day at Sausalito or Tiburon.

Day seven Tour the Civic Center and walk south into SoMa for lunch on Folsom Street. Visit the small museums and factory outlet shops in SoMa, or take a journey by bus into the Mission District.

Weekend's itinerary

Day one Spend a day following the blue and white seagull signs marking the 49-mile Scenic Drive. The route is designed to take in all the major areas and points of interest in San Francisco. A map of the drive is available free from most hotels and tourist information offices.

Day two On the second day, walk around Chinatown (see page 46), and take a bus to Golden Gate Park for a picnic lunch by Stow Lake. Visit the Academy of Sciences (ideal for children) or the M H de Young Memorial Museum and Asian Art Museum. Or simply walk around the park.

NOT 'FRISCO'
You will know you are talking to a Bay Area resident if they refer to San Francisco as 'the city'. You will know you are talking to a tourist if they call the city 'Frisco'.

TAI CHI
Visit Washington Square or Huntington Park on any morning and you will see dozens of people engaged in slow-motion movements. Tai Chi is based on coordinated, carefully balanced rhythmic movements that use all the body's joints, ligaments, and muscles, and help to regulate blood flow.

With Alcatraz Island in the background, one of the city's pleasure cruises leaves Fisherman's Wharf for a tour of San Francisco Bay and the Golden Gate

ADOLPH SUTRO
Prussian-born Adolph Sutro devised a tunnel that improved ventilation and drainage in Nevada's silver mines. The idea earned him a fortune. Mayor of the city from 1894 to 1896, Sutro also founded the Sutro Library.

THE BUDDHIST CHURCH
The plain exterior of the Buddhist Church of San Francisco, at 1881 Pine Street, conceals a richly furbished interior, complete with screens of painted peacocks flanking the altar and carvings from Kyoto gracing the ceiling's beams.

San Francisco City Hall, its green dome visible across much of the city. Behind the three large central windows is the mayor's office

Buildings

▶ Buddha's Universal Church
48C3

720 Washington Street
Built by donations from its congregation, Buddha's Universal Church welcomes the public every Sunday to its free lectures and tours of the church, whose symbolic design culminates in a rooftop lotus pool.

▶ The Cliff House
34A1

1066–90 Point Lobos Avenue
The seven-storey 'French-château-on-a-rock', erected by wealthy one-time Populist city mayor Adolph Sutro in 1896, remains the most famous of several Cliff Houses that have occupied the headland site since 1853. A limp collection of souvenirs and a touristy restaurant fill the present Cliff House. You can also pick up information here on the Golden Gate National Recreation Area and enjoy a clear view of sea lions and marine birds.

Just to the north, ruins are all that remain of the 1896 Sutro Baths, where up to 24,000 people at a time could swim in a lavish three-acre complex of saltwater tanks beneath a massive glass dome – for just 10¢ a day.

▶▶▶ City Hall
35D3

Civic Center, Van Ness Avenue
Easily the city's most opulent building and the centrepiece of the Civic Center's grouping of often exquisite public buildings, San Francisco's 1915 City Hall was conceived by the young architectural firm of Brown and Bakewell, headed by former students of the influential École des Beaux-Arts in Paris, who decided they had nothing to lose by submitting the boldest, grandest scheme they could think of, which was budgeted at a then-astronomical $3.5 million. Marble, granite, gold inlays and sumptuous arches are the building's characteristics.

Time-lapse photography reveals the volume of night-time traffic along Columbus Avenue running between North Beach, Chinatown and the Transamerica Pyramid. To the left, Café Tosca is thought to be one of the city's oldest bars; to the right are Chinese restaurants

53

► Columbus Tower   48C4

Corner of Kearny Street and Pacific Avenue

Bought and restored by locally based film director Francis Ford Coppola in the 1970s, the flat-iron Columbus Tower dates from 1905. With the towering Transamerica Pyramid nearby, Columbus Tower adds considerable character to the view from North Beach toward Chinatown.

►► Ferry Building   49F3

Eastern end of Market Street

Until the construction of the city's bridges, the turn-of-the-century Ferry Building was the emblem of San Francisco – also its tallest structure – and the landing point for tens of thousands of commuters who made the daily voyage across the bay. A greatly reduced number of sailings still depart from the rear terminal, but the building itself is filled with uninteresting offices.

►► Fort Mason   34C4

West of Fisherman's Wharf, across Van Ness Avenue

In 1796, the Spanish garrison based at the Presidio (see page 55) built a battery on this bluff overlooking the bay. It became a US Army command post from the 1860s, and 80 years later was the embarkation point for over a million soldiers headed for war in the Pacific. The fort remained under military ownership until becoming part of the Golden Gate National Recreation Area in 1972.

Some Victorian buildings on the hilltop are still used by the military, while the former hospital serves as the headquarters of the Golden Gate National Recreation Area (of which Fort Mason is a part; see page 56).

At the foot of the bluff, several converted warehouses house the **Fort Mason Center►►**, which includes the African-American Historical and Cultural Society (see page 40), the Mexican Museum (see page 42), and the San Francisco Craft and Folk Art Museum (see page 44).

MAJOR EARTHQUAKES

On April 18, 1906, an earthquake measuring 8.3 on the Richter scale, and a three-day fire that followed it, destroyed much of the city, leaving 3,000 dead and 300,000 homeless. Increased earthquake awareness and strict building codes helped prevent a similar catastrophe when a 7.1 earthquake struck the city on October 17, 1989. Eleven were killed and 1,800 lost their homes.

The Golden Gate Bridge seen from the west side, overlooking the inlets holding Baker Beach and China Beach

BRIDGE SUICIDES
The Golden Gate Bridge found instant popularity as a suicide stop, the first fatal jump into the cold waters and fast currents of the bay taking place just three months after its opening. Over 900 people are known to have leapt to their death from the bridge and the true figure is probably over a thousand. In 1993, phones linked directly to suicide counsellors were installed on the bridge for would-be jumpers.

►►► Golden Gate Bridge 34B4

Taking its name from the bay it crosses rather than its colour (a reddish orange, the color most visible in fog), the Golden Gate Bridge is a remarkable artistic as well as engineering feat. Its construction defies the currents and depth of the bay, and the simplistic designs look entirely at home in a stunning natural landscape.

Designed by Joseph B Strauss (although controversy still ensues as to whether Strauss was genuinely responsible for the bridge's form), the bridge was completed in 1937 at a cost of $35 million (a sum paid off in tolls by 1971). Almost two miles long, with towers as high as a 48-storey building, it is still among the world's largest suspension bridges. The bridge can be crossed by car or on foot, though the steady rumble of traffic tends to upset contemplation of the views – as do the often ferocious winds.

►►► Mission Dolores 34C3

320 Dolores Street

Originally titled Mission San Francisco de Asís to honour the patron of the Franciscan order, Mission Dolores was completed in 1791. It was the sixth of the 21 Spanish missions that spread the length of California.

Thick adobe walls have enabled the mission to withstand earthquakes and years of neglect, and to become the oldest building in San Francisco – even the original bells and various other artefacts that arrived from Mexico by mule remain – an evocative reminder of the California of two centuries ago.

Behind the atmospheric chapel, with frescoes on its walls, a museum houses a small collection of early mission items, and a courtyard leads to the cemetery, where over 5,000 Castonoan Indians – many of them victims of European diseases – are buried in unmarked communal graves. Several Spanish and Anglo-American bigwigs lie in marked tombs.

▶▶▶ Palace of Fine Arts   *34C4*

Baker and Beach streets

A collection of dreamy beaux-arts structures grouped around an immense rotunda, Bernard Maybeck's Palace of Fine Arts was intended as a temporary contribution to the city's Panama-Pacific Exposition of 1915. At the Expo's conclusion, public feeling staved off the planned demolition and a well-heeled local resident funded a total restoration during the 1960s.

▶ Presidio   *34B4*

Main Gate on Lombard Street, junction with Lyon Street

Across the 1,500 acres of hills and woodlands that cover the north-west corner of the city, a Spanish Presidio (or garrison) was founded in 1776. Until being decommissioned in the 1990s, the area served as the base for the US Sixth Army, but has long been freely accessible to the public and a couple of its buildings are noteworthy. The **Officers' Club▶** (on Moraga Avenue) is still partly walled by Spanish-era adobe; across Pershing Square, the 1857 Old Station Hospital, which holds the Presidio Army Museum (see page 44), is the oldest complete building on the base. In the nearby **National Military Cemetery▶**, some tombs date back to the Civil War.

▶▶ Rincon Center   *49F2*

101 Spear Street

Enter the spacious indoor plaza of the Rincon Center at lunchtime and you will find snack-munching office-workers and the gentle music of a fountain and a pianist in a dinner jacket. This modern building has enclosed the delectable art-deco form of the 1940 Rincon Annexe Post Office Building. A series of controversial **murals▶▶** by Anton Refregier, grittily portraying several murky moments in San Franciscan history, make for stimulating viewing on the post office walls.

▶ St Mary's Cathedral   *34C3*

Corner of Geary and Gough streets

In a city better known for its Victorian architecture, St Mary's Cathedral is a forceful piece of modern design by Pietro Belluschi, completed in 1971 at a cost of $7 million. The open-plan cathedral can seat 2,500 people and was built to replace the previous St Mary's, which served as the city's Catholic Cathedral from 1891 until being destroyed by fire in 1962.

STEEPEST STREET

You will often find yourself thinking that San Francisco's steepest street must be the one you are on. You will be correct if you are climbing the section of Filbert Street between Hyde and Leavenworth streets, which rises at an angle of 31.5 degrees.

Forming the shape of a Greek Cross, towering paraboloids give St Mary's Cathedral a 190-foot-high ceiling, and help the interior eliminate the traditional divisions between apse, nave, transept, baptistry and narthex

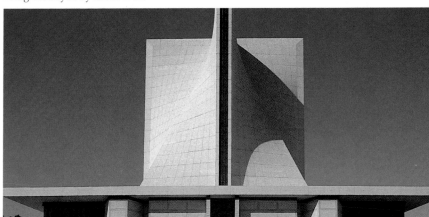

With the Financial District to the rear, Alamo Square's 'Painted Ladies', built in the 1890s, contribute to one of San Francisco's most reproduced photographic juxtapositions

SAN FRANCISCO'S TWINS
San Francisco is twinned with 13 cities: Abidjan, Assisi, Caracas, Cork, Esteli, Haifa, Manila, Osaka, Seoul, Shanghai, Sydney, Taipei, and Thessaloniki.

GGNRA
Created in 1972 to limit commercial development, the Golden Gate National Recreation Area safeguards nearly 70 square miles of mostly coastal terrain, embracing much of the city's northern and western edges and extending across the bay to the rugged Marin County Headlands. There are several museums, as well as the blustery Coastal Trail between Lincoln Park and the Golden Gate Park.

Parks and gardens

►► Alamo Square   34C3
A pretty, rolling park on the crest of a hill between the Western Addition and Pacific Heights, Alamo Square's eastern side is faced by six 'Painted Ladies', well-maintained Victorian homes with the modern city skyline for a backdrop – a regular stop for photo-hungry visitors.

►► Aquatic Park   34C5–35D4
A grassy area with a concrete bandstand close to Fisherman's Wharf and the historic ships of Hyde Street Pier, Aquatic Park is mostly used by walkers and joggers following the Golden Gate Promenade (see page 47).

► Baker Beach   34B4
Access from Lincoln Boulevard
Breezy mile-long Baker Beach is a pleasant place to pass half a day; enthusiastic anglers spend considerably longer.

► Buena Vista Park   34C3
Blocks 1100 and 1200 of Haight Street
The name means 'good view', and that is precisely the reward for scrambling through the twisted mass of Monterey pine and California redwoods filling this very steep park, encircled by graceful Victorian mansions and a short walk from the heart of Haight-Ashbury.

► China Beach   34B4
Near Seacliff Avenue
A small and marvellously secluded beach hemmed in by bluffs. Its name comes from the Chinese fishermen who once camped here. Though often cold, the calm waters make China Beach one of the few places in San Francisco where swimming is safe. The lifeguard post is occupied during the summer months.

►►► Golden Gate Park   34A3–C3
City parks rarely come any better or bigger than Golden Gate Park, which extends for more than three miles between Haight-Ashbury and the ocean. Large enough

to hold a polo field, soccer fields, a golf course, 10 separate lakes, and a couple of major museums, the park also has several busy roads; pedestrian crosswalks make life safe for walkers.

A **Dutch windmill▶**, a **Japanese tea garden▶ ▶ ▶**, and a large assortment of enigmatic statuary are unexpected features.

▶ Mission Dolores Park   *34C3*
Blocks 500 and 600 of Dolores Street
Often bathed in sunshine when the rest of the city is shrouded in fog, Mission Dolores Park is a few blocks from the Dolores Mission and makes a fine place for a picnic when exploring the Mission District.

▶ ▶ San Francisco Zoo   *34A2*
Sloat Boulevard
Founded in 1889, San Francisco Zoo has benefited from a major renovation, swapping its cages for detailed re-creations of its inmates' natural habitats. Another welcome addition is the excellent **Primate Discovery Center▶ ▶**, which explains more than you will ever need to know about such creatures – many of whom swing merrily from the branches of the zoo's artificial rain forest. Koalas, penguins, pygmy hippos, and leopards are among the zoo's other residents, while the tarantulas, black widows and scorpions of the insect zoo are creepy in every sense.

▶ Sutro Heights Park   *34A3*
Scattered with ruined statuary, this covers the former estate of Adolph Sutro, one of the leading figures of his time (see page 52). On a bluff above the Cliff House, the park is great for sunset watching.

WHAT'S IN A NAME?
There is no beach in the North Beach, no statue of George Washington in Washington Square, and no square in Jackson Square

TWIN PEAKS
The nearly 1,000-foot-high dual summits of Twin Peaks give unmatched views of San Francisco and beyond. The first Spanish arrivals named these humps of high ground *Los Pechos de la Chola* – Breasts of the Indian Girl – and they're easy to locate by looking for the Sutro TV Tower, which is nearby on Mount Sutro.

Golden Gate Park's Japanese tea garden

Excursions

From hikes in untamed hills to wine-tasting amid the state-renowned vineyards, you have many day-tripping options out of San Francisco. Most can be undertaken on public transportation or by car; you can also use one of the tour operators listed opposite.

Suggested Routes

Coast Seaside towns seldom come more picturesque than **Sausalito**, an eight-mile ferry ride north of San Francisco, where scores of expensive hillside homes rise steeply above a waterfront lined by enjoyable cafés, galleries and shops.

Many high points in San Francisco give views of the strikingly barren headlands of **Marin County**, directly north across the bay and forming part of the **Golden Gate National Recreation Area (GGNRA)**. A network of hiking trails winds over them, passing through sheltered valleys to isolated beaches, and there are other routes leading to the shady redwood groves of **Muir Woods**.

Travelling by BART east from the city brings you to **Berkeley**, its famous university, and the more industrialised **Oakland**, noted for the restaurants of its Chinatown area and the outstanding Oakland Museum of California. Both make a pleasurable day's break. Further descriptions are on pages 76, 77 and 83.

Scenery Ninety-four miles to the south of San Francisco, California's one-time capital, **Monterey** (see page 99), and the mission town of **Carmel** (see page 92) stand on either side of the scenic Monterey Peninsula, and within easy reach of Big Sur (see page 92), rightly

A typically wild and rugged section of Golden Gate National Recreation Area, which fills 74,000 acres of San Francisco's coastline and was created in 1972 by an amalgamation of city parks, private land, and formerly military-owned areas

acclaimed as the most photogenic portion of the entire central coast.

Wineries are found all over California, but the major centre of production is the so-called Wine Country (see pages 244–55), occupying the verdant valleys of **Sonoma** and **Napa**, beginning 50 miles north of San Francisco. Many wineries are open for tastings, and balloon rides above the valleys are widely available. A more unabashed tourist attraction is **Marine World/Africa USA**, 25 miles north-east of the city close to Vallejo, where exotic animal species fill a 160-acre park, and where tigers, lions, sea lions and dolphins are expertly trained to entertain.

Tour Operators and Special Tours

Blue and Gold Fleet (tel: 415/705–5444). Daily crossings to Oakland from Pier 39 in Fisherman's Wharf and from the Ferry Building, and in summer (less frequently in winter) to Angel Island. Daily crossings from Pier 41 to Sausalito and Tiburon, and to Vallejo from Pier 39.

59

California Wine Tours (tel: 415/434–8687). Offers several tour options to the wine-producing Napa Valley, including one that begins with a cruise across the bay to Vallejo and continues in a chauffeur-driven stretch limo.

A Day in Nature (tel: 415/673–0548). Half-day naturalist-led tours of the Marin Headlands and Muir Woods, and full-day tours to the Napa Valley; price includes a gourmet picnic.

Golden Gate Ferries (tel: 415/923–2000). Frequent crossings daily to Sausalito and Larkspur from the Ferry Building.

Golden Gate National Recreation Area Any GGNRA visitor centre will supply maps and general information. GGNRA's headquarters is at Building 201, Fort Mason (tel: 415/556–0560).

Gray Line (tel: 415/958–9400). Excursions by bus to Monterey and Carmel, Muir Woods and Sausalito, and the Wine Country.

Great Pacific Tour Co. (tel: 415/626–4499). Excursions by bus to Monterey and Carmel, Muir Woods and Sausalito, and the Wine Country.

Haight-Ashbury Flower Power Walking Tours (tel: 415/863–1621). Visit the landmarks of 1960s Haight-Ashbury on a two-hour stroll.

Red & White Fleet (tel: 415/447–0597). Ferries to Sausalito and catamaran trips to Africa USA/Marine World, from Pier 41 in Fisherman's Wharf.

San Francisco Helicopter Tours (tel: 800/400–2404). A bird's-eye view of the city and points beyond.

Tom's Scenic Trailwalks (tel: 510/845–0856). Guided, easy-paced walks around the Bay Area's most scenic stretches of shoreline.

Ghirardelli Square (below) is housed in a former chocolate factory

Shopping

Vast shopping malls, a common sight in other cities, are not much in evidence here. However, San Franciscans can be enthusiastic shoppers and every neighbourhood has a street worth browsing along.

Predictably, it is mostly tacky tourist fare that fills **Fisherman's Wharf**, although the shops and galleries filling two converted factories – the **Cannery** (2801 Leavenworth Street) and **Ghirardelli Square** (9800 N. Point Street) – are entertaining places to wander around and can turn up unexpected finds, such as the fine crafts sold by Folk Art International.

If you are shopping for more interesting souvenirs, fruitful territory might be the Chinatown section of Grant Street, where dozens of places display unusual items, from carved jade figures to cheap toys. While in Chinatown, drop in at the Ten Ren Tea Company (949 Grant Avenue), where many fine imported brews can be sampled at the counter. Investigate the neighbourhood's herbalists, such as Chung Chou City (898 Stockton Street) or Fung Yun Wah (868 Jackson Street).

For more mainstream buying Classy stores of Macy's, Neiman-Marcus and Saks Fifth Avenue stand within a credit card's throw of one another beside Union Square. If you have time to visit only one such emporium, though, make it **Nordstrom's** (865 Market Street), where spiral escalators whisk you between fashionably stocked floors.

For those with eyes bigger than their bank accounts, the windows to watch are along Maiden Lane. Among this street's stylish boutiques, **Chanel** (No. 155) has three floors laden with the French company's finest products, and **Candelier** (No. 60) displays candles and candleholders in countless unusual shapes.

Take a peek also at the nearby **Gump's** (135 Post Street), an institution among the city's swells for its fine crystal and world-class jade and pearls – all at world-class prices.

60

The toughest antiques hunt This could well end amid the historic brick buildings of Jackson Square, a number of which have ground-level shops stuffed with European 18th- and 19th-century furnishings, Turkish rugs, and fine Asian tapestries and decorative pieces. The price tags can be steep, but well-heeled, knowledgeable collectors should find the selection tempting.

There is more that is old among the stores of Haight-Ashbury. Much of the clothing here is salvaged from decades past, or imported: Aardvark's (1501 Haight Street) carries some great gear of yesteryear; more of the same fills Held Over (1537 Haight Street); Spellbound (1670 Haight Street) has finer clothing from the 1890s to the 1920s. For mindblowing day-glo T-shirts, try Positively Haight Street (1159 Masonic Avenue).

In the same neighbourhood, Revival of the Fittest (1701 Haight Street) recycles and re-creates American household knick-knacks of the 1940s and 1950s, Curios & Candles (289 Divisadero Street) turns crystals and semiprecious stones into pricey talismans, and Pipe Dreams (1376 Haight Street) has giant rolling papers and waterpipes. Haight Street is also the place to find used CDs and records: try Reckless Records (number 1401) and Recycled Records (number 1377).

In a city of bookworms, you will discover plenty of bookshops in which to browse and buy. Nationally known chain stores such as Barnes & Noble and Borders are well stocked with the latest titles, often at reduced prices.

Specialty bookstores include Forever After (1475 Haight Street), with a tremendous stock of used volumes on all subjects; City Lights (261 Columbus Avenue), carrying the definitive range of writings by and about the Beat Generation, plus political and general titles; The Sierra Club Bookstore (730 Polk Street) has a tremendous stash on natural California and is a recommended stop for hikers and walkers; William Stout Architectural Books (804 Montgomery Street) has an unmatched inventory of what its name suggests.

Defined by chic boutiques, antique shops and fashionable restaurants, the section of Union Street between Gough and Fillmore streets is the main shopping strip of Pacific Heights, one of the city's wealthiest areas

DISCOUNT SHOPPING
Well within the range of the average pocket are the numerous factory outlets occupying former warehouses in the SoMa area. Cruise the multistore complexes of the Six Sixty Center (660 Third Street) and Yerba Buena Square (899 Howard Street). Many top companies discount their damaged or discontinued lines here, and the bargains can be tempting. Elsewhere, Esprit (499 Illinois Street) is one of the major names for California casualwear.

**FISHERMAN'S WHARF
EATING**
While visiting Fisherman's
Wharf it is wise to limit
your eating to snacks
from the seafood stalls
on the street and preserve
your appetite for a meal
in more inspiring
surroundings.

Food and drink

Food and drink are major preoccupations in this city, and
its restaurants offer everything from downhome American
fare to cuisines culled from every corner of the globe. For
Californians with cultured palates – or just big appetites –
San Francisco is much less about bay views, cable cars, and
the Golden Gate Bridge than it is about eating.

Prices Fierce competition helps keep prices low, and all
but the most exclusive restaurants are well within the
range of the majority of travellers. Even the tourist-
packed eateries of Fisherman's Wharf are not the
gastronomic wastelands that they could be. Despite
claims to the contrary, though, comparatively little of
what is offered in the area's seafood restaurants comes
from local waters.

Although San Francisco is serious about its food and
restaurants, the atmosphere of most eateries is casual.
Men almost never require a tie and they can usually get
away without even a jacket.

Italian The streets of North Beach, just south of
Fisherman's Wharf, are jammed with Italian restaurants
offering authentic regional cuisine from every inch of
this Mediterranean country and providing excellent
value. A simple fresh pasta dish is unlikely to cost more
than $10, and even three-course dinners for less than $25
are not unknown.

North Beach dining is no secret, however, and for
evening you should plan to dine early (before 7) to avoid
crowds. Earlier in the day, you will have no problem
finding a cosy niche inside one of the neighbourhood's
many atmospheric cafés, where you can linger over a
cappuccino and a light Italian lunch and dessert, to your
heart's content.

Crab During its mid-November to June season, look for
Dungeness crab, which many Italian restaurants serve as

*One of the oldest and
most popular of North
Beach's many Italian
restaurants, Fior d'Italia
has occupied the same
site since 1886*

the centrepiece of a seafood dish called *cioppino*. The same creature turns up in Chinese restaurants, deliciously flavoured with ginger and garlic.

The Empress of China— a San Francisco favourite

Chinese This type of food has long been a feature of San Francisco, and Chinatown is its culinary hotspot, despite the fact that many of the top Chinese chefs have departed for other areas – notably the Richmond district, just west of Pacific Heights, where Clement Street in particular holds many Asian restaurants of merit.

Within Chinatown, cooking styles reflect the diverse ethnic backgrounds of recent immigrants: besides Cantonese (and variations on it such as Hakka and Choazhou), Hunan and Szechuan fare, unusual Vietnamese-Chinese and Peruvian-Chinese dishes enliven many menus.

The best way to sample Chinatown's food is inside one of the large and lively dim sum restaurants, which cater mostly to a local Chinese clientele and usually open between 11 and 3. Only in Hong Kong are you likely to encounter a bigger variety of dim sum – pastries and dumplings filled with seafood, meat and rice and noodles.

Pointing is the surest way to get what you want, as the dishes are wheeled on trolleys in front of diners. If, as is likely, you are not sure what you are looking at, ask the waiter or waitress for advice or simply select whatever looks interesting. When you have finished, the bill is determined by the number of empty dishes on your table. Many dim sum restaurants serve regular Chinese dinners in the evening.

Other Asian and Far Eastern For Japanese food aim for Japantown's Japan Center and you will come across several dozen reasonably priced Japanese restaurants and sushi bars.

Many Thai and a lesser number of Indian restaurants are well established in San Francisco. Particularly hot and spicy dishes are usually marked as such on the menu.

Among the gritty fast-food joints of the Tenderloin (be careful, as it is not the safest area in the city, see page 36), dozens of small Vietnamese, Laotian and Cambodian cafés have appeared, providing exotic, spicy food at giveaway prices.

63

DIM SUM DISHES
Popular dim sum dishes in Chinese restaurants include *Jow Ha Gok*, shrimp turnovers; *Siu Mai*, steamed meat dumplings; *Cha Siu Bow*, barbecued pork inside buns; and Gee Cheung Fun, rolls of rice and noodles.

San Francisco is well-stocked with bakeries selling delicious fresh snacks

Contemporary fare Elsewhere around town, particularly on Union and Fillmore streets in Pacific Heights, some of the city's more innovative restaurants are blazing a trail with contemporary American cuisine – modernised variations on regional American dishes that bear the nutritional and aesthetic imprint of California cuisine (see page 78), which itself has largely faded from fashion.

French The city's more traditionally inclined and the longer-established power brokers don suits and head for the upper-crust restaurants of Nob Hill, noted for their classic French food.

Latin American Much more down to earth than the city's expensive restaurants – and usually with much more filling food – are the innumerable low-priced Mexican and other Latin American food outlets crammed into the Mission District. These range from dirt-cheap hole-in-the-wall takeout stands to fully fledged restaurants where the food is tasty and well priced and the service is swift and cheerful – they're Brazilian, Guatemalan, El Salvadorean, Chilean, Peruvian and beyond.

Bohemian For a meal in the company of the city's artists, writers, lesser media celebrities and full-time nightclubbers, try any of the restaurants and cafés along Haight-Ashbury's Haight Street or SoMa's Folsom Street. Many of these serve no more than basic, filling American food – such as massive omelets and huge sandwiches – but do so in bizarre settings with a carefully cultivated bohemian atmosphere.

Tea and coffee A growing band of hotels in San Francisco has taken up the practice of serving afternoon tea, which usually features a good range of real teas and snacks such as scones and pastries.

In North Beach, the rich aroma of roasting coffee beans regularly drifts across the streets. Certainly, there is no better place than a North Beach café to down an invigorating espresso. Many of the city's hundreds of cafés are patronised by serious coffee drinkers, alert to bean type and nuances of flavour.

NEECHA
THAI CUISINE

(415) 922-9419
2100 SUTTER STREET
(Near Steiner)
SAN FRANCISCO, CA 94117
LUNCH 11 a.m. - 3 p.m.
DINNER 5 p.m. - 10 p.m.

17

Alcohol California's wines are world-renowned, but the best of them rarely make it outside the state. Dining in San Francisco, the biggest city in close proximity to California's wine country, affords you the best opportunity to sample the widest range of California wines at very reasonable prices.

The most popular derive from the Cabernet Sauvignon (red) and Chardonnay (white) grapes. You will also find fine examples of other varietals and blends, including reds from Zinfandel, Shiraz, Merlot, Pinot Noir, Sangiovese and Nebbiolo, and whites from Sauvignon Blanc, Riesling, Gewürztraminer and Viognier.

Many but not all restaurants serve alcohol; in those that do, a glass or two of **California wine** makes a nice accompaniment for a meal. To mix your alcohol with a view, try sampling one of San Francisco's rooftop hotel cocktail lounges (see page 66).

It is more in keeping with the mellow mood of the city, though, to drink the night away in a street-level bar – of which there are many, and most of these are much safer than their somewhat scruffy appearance might at first suggest.

American brew Beer-lovers are in for a treat in San Francisco. Alongside the usual wines and spirits, most bars stock the products of the area's many micro-breweries: beers whose body and flavour – and strength – are well worth sampling.

Anchor Steam Beer is among the most widely found of the local brews in San Francisco, but there are many more, their names often chalked up on a board above the counter.

Smoking A new state law decrees that smoking is now barred in all enclosed public spaces, so that means most restaurants. If they have an outdoor terrace, you may be permitted to smoke there, but check first.

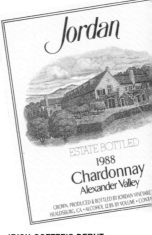

IRISH COFFEE'S DEBUT
Irish coffee (allegedly) made its first US appear-ance in 1952 in San Francisco, at the Buena Vista Café, Fisherman's Wharf (2765 Hyde Street).

65

A damp morning brings plenty of customers to Fisherman's Wharf's Buena Vista Café

Nightlife

For a major city, San Francisco's nightlife is surprisingly small-scale and friendly, with little evidence of the social snobbery and price-hiking that goes on down the coast in Los Angeles.

What's on The free weekly papers, the *San Francisco Bay Guardian* and *SF Weekly* (see page 43), are the best sources of nightlife listings.

The main ticket agency is BASS (for bookings, or recorded information tel: 510/762–2277), which has outlets all over the city. TIX, on the Stockton Street side of Union Square (open Tuesday to Thursday 11–6; Friday and Saturday 11–7; tel: 415/433–7827), offers half-price, day-of-performance tickets for selected performing arts shows.

Watering holes Affable and socially very diverse, cafés and bars are found all over the city, with the greatest concentration in North Beach, The Mission, and SoMa districts. You should also plan to spend a few daylight hours at one of the rooftop cocktail lounges, which provide views along with the (usually expensive) drinks. Top of the tops is the Carnelian Room, on the 52nd floor of the Bank of America Building at 55 California Street.

Classical music, opera, and ballet San Francisco enjoys a deservedly strong reputation for its classical music, opera and ballet. Major performances by the **San Francisco Symphony**, based at the Louise M Davies Symphony Hall, 201 Van Ness Avenue (tel: 415/864–6000), take place from September to May, with many special shows in summer.

The **San Francisco Opera** has a star-studded September to December season at the War Memorial Opera House (tel: 415/864–3330). In summer, the **Pocket Opera** (tel: 415/575–1100) mounts lesser-known operas in smaller venues (which change from year to year).

Rated among the world's best, the San Francisco Ballet performs from February to May at the Opera House, 301 Van Ness Avenue (tel: 415/865–2000), returning for special Christmas performances.

Theatre Between October and May, there is drama at the Geary Theater, 415 Geary Street (tel: 415/749–2228), from the respected **American Conservatory Theater**, and throughout the year at the tiny Magic Theater, Building D, Fort Mason Center (tel: 415/441–8822). More in the mainstream, Broadway hits are performed at the Curran Theater, 445 Geary Street (tel: 415/ 776–1999).

The witty and raucous *Beach Blanket Babylon* is the longest running theatrical show in San Francisco, a revue popular since the early 1970s; see it at Club Fugazi, 678 Green Street (tel: 415/421–4222).

Comedy Cutting-edge comic Lenny Bruce got arrested in San Francisco in the early 1960s. The gags of today are unlikely to bring police raids, but the city still has a fair number of lively comedy clubs. The pick are the

Evening rush hour: the Ferry Building in the middle distance, once the tallest structure in the city, is dwarfed by Financial District towers; the lights of Oakland are visible across the bay

Punch Line, 444 Battery Street (tel: 415/397–7573). At Josie's Cabaret and Juice, 3583 16th Street (tel: 415/861–7933), predominantly gay and lesbian comedians appear throughout the week and on the entertaining 'open mike' night each Monday.

Completed in 1923, the Castro Theater is a popular venue for cult movies

Cinema Each spring, the popularity of the San Francisco Film Festival confirms the city's love of good movies. Besides many first-run complexes, such as the eight-screen Kabuki Center, corner of Post and Geary streets (tel: 415/931–9800), there are a number of cinemas that screen rarely seen cult and arthouse films: the Castro Theater, 429 Castro Street (tel: 415/621–6120), the Roxie, 317 16th Street (tel: 415/863–1087), and the Red Vic, 1727 Haight Street (tel: 415/668–3994).

Jazz, rock, and R&B Many of the top US and international bands include the city on their tours. Major venues for contemporary sounds are the Paradise Lounge, 11th and Folsom streets (tel: 415/861–6906), and the DNA Lounge, 375 11th Street (tel: 415/626–1409).

On the local live music circuit, it is R&B that predominates and sounds best at rough-and-ready venues like The Saloon, 1232 Grant Street (tel: 415/989–7666). For the novelty value alone, show up at one of the early evening shows at Brain Wash, 1122 Folsom Street (tel: 415/861–3663) – a combined bar and laundromat.

The best of the mainstream jazz clubs are Slim's, 333 11th Street (tel: 415/522–0333), and Up & Down Club, 1151 Folsom Street (tel: 415/626–2388).

Dance Clubs San Francisco's club scene is varied and changeable. Most venues have a different theme each night, and are in SoMa. Two geographical exceptions are the dependable Club 181, 181 Eddy Street (tel: 415/673–2181) and Bahai Cabana (1600 Market Street; tel: 415/626–3306), with captivating salsa and world beat nights.

JOKES, JAZZ, BREAST IMPLANTS
These days, North Beach is best known for its restaurants, but from the 1950s its comedy clubs showcased cutting edge comics such as Lenny Bruce and Mort Sahl, while jazz clubs in local cellars hosted wild nights of bebop that inspired the Beat movement. Another pioneer was Carol Doda, whose silicon-implanted breasts starred in the nation's first topless show, at the Condor Club in 1964. The event is remembered by a wall plaque at 300 Columbus Avenue.

There's no shortage of accommodation in the city; some hotels, like the Marriott, are hard to miss

BEYOND THE CITY
Spending a night across the bay provides an enjoyable change of pace and scenery. Several hotels perch on the Sausalito hillsides. None are cheap and most are full at weekends, but they offer a chance to stroll through the quaint village after the day-trippers have departed. A stopover in Berkeley encourages a leisurely gourmet meal in one of the town's award-winning restaurants without the need to dash back to the city.

HIDDEN EXTRAS
Be warned that quoted prices for accommodation rarely include the city's 14 per cent 'transient occupancy' tax, which guests have to pay.

Accommodation

From fax-equipped suites in marble towers to four-poster beds in wood-framed Victorian mansions, places to stay in San Francisco are as abundant as the hills and as varied as the views. In fact, this is one of the best places in California to find affordable and atmospheric alternatives to chain hotels and motels.

Making an advance booking is always a good idea, but is only essential during the busiest period – summer and early autumn, when prices are around $10–$20 higher than during the rest of the year.

The **San Francisco Visitors and Convention Bureau** (see page 71) publishes a free guide to lodgings, with copious listings and room rates, and its office stocks many leaflets detailing individual properties.

Hotels In a city that is small and easy to get around, precisely where you stay is of minor consequence. Most large hotels are close to Union Square, and there is a group of newer chain hotels close to Fisherman's Wharf. But it is a smart move to avoid these congested areas in favour of the more characterful residential areas.

The luxurious 'grand hotels' of Nob Hill pride themselves on pampering their guests, often with complimentary newspapers and magazines, and drinks and snacks laid out for guests to help themselves, though the price (starting at around $200 and rising swiftly) will deter all but the most wealthy visitor.

A better bet are the so-called 'boutique hotels' ($80–$140), several of which are situated between Nob Hill and Downtown. These are small hotels with attentive staff and a limited number of rooms in what used to be an affluent family home. The fittings and fixtures are carefully chosen to add period charm, breakfast is included, and often complimentary wine or sherry is served in the afternoon. Reservations are advised.

Broadly similar to the boutique hotels, many rambling Victorian homes throughout the city have been refurbished and converted into bed-and-breakfasts. Widely fluctuating prices ($60–$190) reflect the fact that both the individual properties and the rooms within them vary greatly: some rooms may be small with a shared bathroom; others might be large and equipped with a whirlpool and CD player.

It is the very lack of hotel-like standardisation that is part of the appeal of B&Bs, however, and describing one's room is a favourite topic at breakfast, usually a hearty affair served around a communal table.

The enormous popularity of B&Bs means that you should make a reservation early, especially if arriving in summer or staying over a weekend. Use one of the special agencies such as Bed & Breakfast International, PO Box 282910, San Francisco, CA 94128–2910, reservations (tel: 1-800-372–4500); information (tel: 415/696–1690).

Budget accommodation While prices are generally above what you will pay elsewhere in the state, and campsites are non-existent, San Francisco is good news for travellers on tight budgets, with dozens of privately run hostels and guesthouses, plus two Hosteling International properties, offering dormitory beds, single rooms and double rooms.

The hostels include the 170-room San Francisco International Hostel at Fort Mason, one of the largest youth hostels in the United States; others are across the city. Many impose a three-night maximum stay during the busy summer season, and some may impose a curfew. In summer, the Residence Hall of San Francisco State University, 800 Font Boulevard (tel: 415/338–6219), offers a small number of twin-bedded rooms and one- and two-bedroom apartments at rates of around $80 for a double.

GAY AND LESBIAN ACCOMMODATION
Wherever they stay in this tolerant city, gay and lesbian travellers are unlikely to encounter discrimination. Indeed, a number of hotels and bed-and-breakfasts, particularly in the Castro area, are staffed by and cater specifically to gays and lesbians.

69

One of seven luxury hotels on Nob Hill, the Mark Hopkins Hotel opened in 1926 and occupies the site of the mansion of early California railroad mogul Mark Hopkins

Practical points

Listings of recommended San Francisco accommodation begin on page 266.

Arriving by air San Francisco's airport (tel: 415/761–0800) is 14 miles south of the city. Links into the city are generally quick and reliable.

A number of companies, such as Super Shuttle (tel: 415/558–8500), and Lorrie's Airport Service (tel: 415/334–9000) run minivans from the traffic island directly outside the terminal's upper (departures) level. The information desk on the airport's lower (arrivals) level can supply a full list of operators and prices, usually around $15 to any city address.

Alternatively, the SFO Airporter (tel: 415/495–8404) bus runs every 20 minutes (5am–11pm) between the airport – departing from the blue column outside the lower level – and the main hotels around Union Square.

Routes 7F and 7B of the local SamTrans bus service (tel: 800/660–4BUS) are cheaper but slower, and baggage (on the 7F) is limited to one small item. The buses depart from marked stops outside the airport's upper level.

Airline phone numbers American (tel: 800/433–7300); British Airways (tel: 800/247–9297); Delta (tel: 800/221–1212); Northwest (tel: 800/225–2525); United (tel: 800/241–6522); USAir (tel: 800/428–4322); Virgin (tel: 800/862–8621).

Arriving by train Arriving by train (tel: 800/872–7245 for information) in San Francisco means disembarking at the gleaming terminal at Emeryville, across the bay, and continuing into the city aboard one of the free shuttle buses that meet arriving passengers.

Arriving by bus Greyhound buses (tel: 800/231–2222) to San Francisco stop at the Transbay Terminal, 425 Mission Street.

Car hire In a city that is so easy to walk around and served by an excellent public transportation system, you

TAXI FARES
Only for three or four people sharing the cost are taxis from the airport to the city financially worthwhile. Fares are likely to range from $28 to about $35.

The wavy lines on the side of this San Francisco bus spell 'MUNI', the name of the city's transportation authority, derived from 'San Francisco Municipal Railway'

will not need a car. If you are travelling further afield, however, you may want to hire one (see pages 257–8); all the main firms have desks at the airport and offices around the city.

Alamo (tel: 800/354–2322)
Avis (tel: 800/331–1212)
Budget (tel: 800/527–0700)
Hertz (tel: 800/654–3131)
Thrifty (tel: 800/367–2277)

Parking Local law requires a car's front wheels to be turned toward the curb when parked, to prevent the vehicle from rolling down the street.

Climate San Francisco enjoys mild weather year-round, with temperatures seldom above 70°F (21°C) or below 40°F (4°C). Stiff breezes often whip in off the bay, however, and fogs are a regular feature, liable to make the city feel cooler than it actually is. Play it safe by bringing a warm sweater or jacket even in summer, and in winter, be prepared for chilly evenings, when a coat is essential.

Consulates Most foreign embassies are based in Washington DC. For passport emergencies and other needs, you should contact the relevant consular office in San Francisco:
UK, 1 Sansome Street (tel: 415/981–3030); Ireland, 44 Montgomery Street (tel: 415/392–4214); Germany, 1960 Jackson Street (tel: 415/775–1061); Netherlands, 1 Maritime Place (tel: 415/981–6454); Norway, 20 California Street (tel: 415/986–0766); Sweden, 120 Montgomery Street (tel: 415/788–2631).

Travellers with disabilities All public buildings are wheelchair accessible and have adapted toilets for people who use wheelchairs; most buses can 'kneel' to the curb, and all BART stations have elevators between street and platform levels. Information on other facilities can be obtained from the Disability Co-ordinator, Mayor's Office of Community Development, 10 United Nations Plaza, Suite 600, San Francisco, CA 94102 (tel: 415/252–3100).

Foreign exchange Foreign currency and foreign currency travellers' cheques can be changed at the airport and at the following locations:
AFEX, Associated Foreign Exchange, 201 Sansome Street (tel: 415/781–7683).
Bank of America, 345 Montgomery Street (tel: 415/622–2451).
Thomas Cook, 75 Geary Street (tel: 800/CURRENCY). These offices all open during regular business hours, and all except Thomas Cook also open on Saturday morning.

Information For free maps, brochures and general information, call into the Visitor Information Center, on the lower level of Hallidie Plaza near the corner of Market and Powell streets.
Open: Monday to Friday, 9–5:30; Saturday 9–3; Sunday 10–2 (tel: 415/391–2000).

EMERGENCY NUMBERS
Dial 911 for fire, police, or ambulance. Other emergency numbers include the Rape Crisis Hotline: 415/647–7273 or 206–3222.

FREE MUSEUMS
To save money, avoid the rain, or simply to enjoy something for nothing, San Francisco has several major museums offering free admission on certain days (see page 42). The following are always free:
Cable Car Museum (page 40)
Chinese Cultural Center (page 40)
Chinese Historical Society (page 40)
Fort Point (page 41)
Museum of Money of the American West (page 43)
North Beach Museum (page 43)
Presidio Army Museum (page 44)
Wells Fargo History Museum (page 44)

71

SAN FRANCISCO'S FOG
Visitors underestimate San Francisco's infamous fog at their peril. Particularly during the summer, fog rolls in from the ocean and engulfs much of the city in a blanket of white. The fog usually burns off by mid-day but in the morning expect cool temperatures and restricted views.

One of the city's most popular sports: jogging

Pharmacies Several **Walgreen** drug stores have 24-hour pharmacies, including those at 500 Geary Street near Union Square (tel: 415/673–8413) and 3201 Divisadero Street at Lombard Street (tel: 415/931–6417). Also try the Walgreen on Powell Street near Market Street (135 Powell Street, tel: 415/391–7222). Open: Monday to Saturday, 8am–midnight, Sunday 9–8. AE, MC, V.

Newspapers Both the city's daily newspapers, the morning *San Francisco Chronicle* and the evening *San Francisco Examiner* (combined on Sundays), are the obvious places to find local and state news, although they tend to be thin on national and foreign coverage.

The widely found *LA Times* and *New York Times* are better for hard news from further afield and make a better read, and for city features and events listings, the free papers detailed on page 43 are the prime source.

Also worth flipping through are the free tourist magazines such as *San Francisco Key* and the *Bay City Guide*, found in most hotels.

TV and radio Affiliated to national networks, the main San Francisco TV channels are 2 KTVU (FOX); 4 KRON (NBC); 5 KPIX (CBS); 7 KGO (ABC); and 9 KQED (PBS). Many hotels also offer selected cable TV channels. A multitude of radio stations cover the AM and FM frequencies.

Participant sports Like most Californians, San Franciscans are enthusiastic participants in outdoor activities, and visitors will find a whole range of physical pursuits.

Cycling The city has two excellent signposted bike routes, one through Golden Gate Park, the other crossing the city to the Golden Gate Bridge. Bike rental costs start at $20 a day, and outlets are plentiful along Stanyan Street.

Golf There are public 18-hole courses at Lincoln Park (tel: 415/221–9911) and Harding Park (tel: 415/664– 4690), and a pitch-and-putt nine-hole course in Golden Gate Park (tel: 415/751–8987). Rates range from $23 to $28 at Lincoln Park to $10 to $13 at Golden Gate Park, all per person.

Hang-gliding Constant breezes make San Francisco a popular place for hang-gliding; the 200-foot-high cliff at Fort Funstan, near Lake Merced, is the main venue.

Sailing and parasailing Numerous companies operate yachts and other small craft from Pier 39 in Fisherman's Wharf. If you want a rush of adrenalin along with the views, contact Capt. Case Powerboat and Waterbike Rental (tel: 415/331–0444), from whom you can rent a 'high-tech' jetski to plough through the waves on the bay, or a powerboat to skim across it.

Spectator sports Tickets for most major sport events are available through BASS Ticketmaster (tel: 510/762–2277) and the outlets mentioned below.

Baseball During the April to September season, the San Francisco Giants draw crowds to 3-Com Park, eight miles south of the city. Tickets are from the stadium box office (tel: 415/467–8000). On the day of a game, the 'Ballpark Express' bus runs between Downtown and 3-Com Park.

Football The city's football team, the San Francisco 49ers (tel: 415/468–4949), also play at 3-Com Park.

HEALTH
For a doctor or dentist, look under 'Physicians and Surgeons' or 'Dentists' in the Yellow Pages. Alternatively, call Visitors' Medical Services (tel: 415/353–6000) for referral to a doctor, or the San Francisco Dental Office (tel: 415/777–5115) for a dentist. Hospitals with 24-hour emergency rooms are San Francisco General, 1001 Potrero Avenue (tel: 415/ 206–8000) and Davies Medical Center, Castro and Dubuce Streets (tel: 415/565–6060).

Baseball and basketball Further professional sporting action takes place across the bay, with the Oakland A's baseball team and the Golden State Warriors basketball team, who appear at the Oakland Coliseum and Oakland Coliseum Arena, respectively (tel: 510/762–BASS).

Public transport San Francisco's famous **cable cars** are tourist attractions rather than a practical way of getting around. They operate on two routes between Downtown and Fisherman's Wharf, and another between Nob Hill and the Financial District. Tickets can be bought from self-service machines.

More useful are the **buses** and **streetcars** run by MUNI (tel: 415/673–MUNI). Exact change ($1) is necessary on buses, and a single-journey ticket with free transfers is valid for two changes of route within 2 hours. A MUNI Passport saves money when using public transport a lot (valid on all MUNI services for one, three or seven days). MUNI routes are shown in the phone book, and at bus stops.

The state-of-the-art **Bay Area Rapid Transit (BART)** system is chiefly of use for crossing the bay to Berkeley and Oakland. Fares range from $1 to over $4 according to distance travelled; tickets can be bought from machines at BART stations.

Taxis can be ordered by telephone but are usually easy to hail in the street. Average charges are approximately $1.70 for stopping to pick you up and $1.80 for each mile of the journey. Scores of cab companies are listed in the phone book.

Read the fine print: the cable car 'fun tours' advertised here are aboard a 'motorised' cable car which, by definition, is not a cable car at all but a small bus designed to resemble a cable car

73

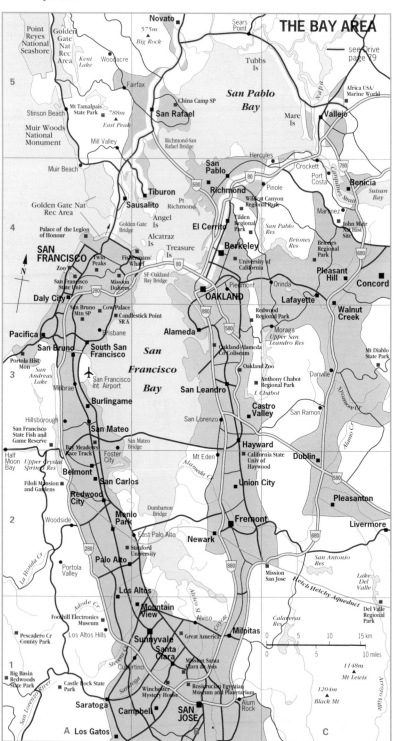

THE BAY AREA

74

CONTRASTS From the wild hills of Marin to the high-tech suburbia of Silicon Valley, the Bay Area encompasses a host of contrasting communities with only their proximity to San Francisco Bay in common. The area is by no means dull, but there is no single spot justifying a long-term stay and it is ideally examined on day-trips from San Francisco.

In the East Bay, backed by steep hills holding rustic homes and covered by a great number of parks, life in Berkeley (for all but devoted gastronomes, who know it as the birthplace of California cuisine) revolves around a world-famous university campus, noted as much for its student politics as for its breakthroughs in nuclear physics. Neighbouring Oakland is enjoying a revival of its fortunes, and tempts passers-by with one of the state's best museums and an immense tidal lake.

MAIN ROUTES Along the 55-mile-long peninsula stretching south from San Francisco, Highway 1 charts the coast (see pages 90–101) while Highway 101 keeps to the bayside of the peninsula's central mountains, passing tree-shrouded foothill communities before hitting the dense suburbia filling Santa Clara Valley, now better known as Silicon Valley, home of high-tech industries and San Jose – the fastest growing US city.

Stanford University is the outstanding sight here, although Silicon Valley's towns are at pains to polish up whatever historical remnants and natural areas they possess to make themselves attractive to visitors whose interests extend beyond micro-circuitry.

North from San Francisco, the green spaces of Marin County were partly colonised two decades ago by San Francisco's original hippies, whose inner-self explorations developed into the New Age pursuits of Marin's more recent, much better bankrolled, arrivals.

Marin is best tasted as part of a loop around San Pablo Bay, on the inland side of which lie several small towns of historical interest on the scenically appealing Carquinez Straights. The wild and scenically spectacular Point Reyes area is covered in the North Coast chapter (see pages 240–1).

The Bay Area

76

*Previous page:
Fireworks over the San
Francisco-Oakland Bay
Bridge*

*Berkeley students stroll
around Sproul Plaza,
overlooked by the
Campanile and by the
distant hills that hold the
university's science
laboratories*

▶ Angel Island   74B4

Native Americans hunted seal and otter from the banks
of Angel Island long before its discovery by the Spanish
in 1775. The island – the largest in San Francisco Bay –
was used in various ways by the US government,
including as an arrival point for Asian immigrants, as a
quarantine centre, and as a prisoner-of-war camp, before
becoming a state park. Walking trails cross the tree- and
scrub-covered island, and the wind-sheltered beaches at
Ayala Cove (landing point for Fisherman's Wharf
ferries) and Quarry Point are perfect for picnics.

▶ Benicia   74C4

In the frenzy of the gold rush years, a deepwater
harbour enabled the town of Benicia to keep pace with
San Francisco in the race to become California's number
one port. It even enjoyed 13 months as state capital from
1853, and the **Benicia State Capitol Park▶** preserves the
handsome Greek Revival building in which state
business was carried out. The **Fischer-Hanlon House▶**, a
renovated gold rush hotel beside the park, is also open
for tours, and in the nearby **Benicia Arsenal▶** building
local artisans have studios and shops.

▶▶ Berkeley   74B4

Beginning with the Free Speech Movement of the early
1960s, student activity on the campus of the **University of
California at Berkeley▶▶▶** has brought one of the
country's top educational establishments a reputation
for radicalism and caused the town of Berkeley to be
nicknamed 'Berserkely.' Paradoxically, the university
began as a Christian college in the 1850s; it was taken
over by the state of California in 1873.

Stalls dispensing literature and views on any number
of controversial topics are common on campus, and

Berkeley has one of the most left-leaning local governments in the country. But these days revolt against authority seems the last thing on the minds of the 30,000 students, most of whom earnestly pursue their studies with an eye on the ever-shrinking job market.

Berkeley is easy to reach by BART from San Francisco, and the campus is within easy walking distance, directly east of the station. Devote most of your time to the campus, as only the well-stocked bookstores and lively restaurants along **Telegraph Avenue▶▶** are of interest elsewhere. For more on Berkeley's militant past, see pages 84–5.

Once the scene of anti–Vietnam War protests, **Sproul Plaza▶▶**, close to Berkeley's Bancroft Way, is jammed by milling students and makeshift stalls manned by ecological and political activists. The 200-foot-high **Campanile▶▶** (to the right), modelled on the bell tower of St Mark's in Venice, has been a landmark since 1914. Immediately north, safeguarding the university's rare books, the **Bancroft Library▶** also has a small museum of Californian history. The adjoining **Le Conte Hall** is where physicist Robert Oppenheimer laboured over plans for the first atomic bomb.

Farther north, across University Drive, is the 1907 **Hearst Mining Building▶**. Beneath its impressive rotunda the building displays mineral collections and exhibits on mining in California. The **Phoebe A. Hearst Museum of Anthropology▶**, on Bancroft Way (to the south), holds an intriguing stash, including much from Native American cultures; and across Bancroft Way is an architectural tour de force – the imposingly modern **University Art Museum▶▶**, which has an impressive permanent collection and regularly stages important temporary exhibitions.

▶ Fremont   74B2

If you are passing through Fremont, you might be tempted by the 1797 **Mission San José de Guadalupe▶** (43300 Mission Boulevard), although a $5 million rebuilding has left the mission looking far grander than it ought to.

A better stop is the **Ardenwood Historic Farm▶** (on State Road 84), whose animals, gardens and shops re-create local rural life around the turn of the century. Between August and April, thousands of migratory birds also pass through Fremont, some of them using the **San Francisco Bay National Wildlife Refuge▶▶** (on Marsh Land Road) as a food stop.

▶ Hayward   74B3

Eight miles south of Oakland, Hayward's **Historical Society Museum▶** (22701 Main Street) charts the growth of this sizable residential community from its origins as a supply stop on the gold mine route. A peek into the spacious rooms of the **McConaghy House▶** (18701 Hesperian Boulevard) shows how the town's wealthy enjoyed life during the late 1800s, and a leisurely hour can be passed strolling among the native Californian vegetation artfully arranged in the **Japanese Garden▶** (22372 N Third Street).

77

In no part of California is eating taken more seriously than it is in and around San Francisco, and it was in the upmarket restaurants on Berkeley's Shattuck Avenue – an area known as the 'gourmet ghetto' – that California cuisine was first served to the Bay Area's salivating foodies.

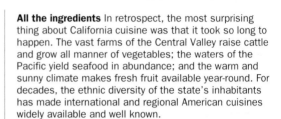

PIZZA: CALIFORNIA STYLE

Outlets of California Pizza Kitchen, now a nationwide chain, bake pizzas in brick ovens and serve them with exotic toppings such as goat's cheese, duck or lobster.

CALIFORNIA AGRICULTURE

California's fertility helps make fresh produce a regular feature of the meal table. During the 1920s, the diverting of northern river to irrigate the 400-mile-long San Joaquin Valley, which runs through the centre of the state, enabled it to become one of the world's most agriculturally productive regions. Together with the more southerly Imperial Valley, the San Joaquin Valley enables California to grow more food than 90 per cent of the world's nations.

Date cultivation near Palm Desert in the Coachella Valley near Palm Springs, one of the world's major date-producing regions

All the ingredients In retrospect, the most surprising thing about California cuisine was that it took so long to happen. The vast farms of the Central Valley raise cattle and grow all manner of vegetables; the waters of the Pacific yield seafood in abundance; and the warm and sunny climate makes fresh fruit available year-round. For decades, the ethnic diversity of the state's inhabitants has made international and regional American cuisines widely available and well known.

A unique blend In the late 1970s, Berkeley's top chefs began crossing the borders of international cuisine, juxtaposing methods of preparation, flavouring and styling, using whatever local produce was in season. In some cases, animals were reared and a range of vegetables grown to the exact specifications of a particular restaurant, and chefs bought seafood directly from individual fishermen.

A matter of taste Coming to the fore just as healthy eating was becoming a national preoccupation, California chefs selected ingredients for their nutritional balance, appealing to the digestive tract as much as the taste buds. And the artful presentation of food on the plate was also important.

Although the fame of California cuisine spread far and wide, the highly valued individuality of each chef prevented any single dish – which might be anything from grilled pigeon breasts to red snapper in peanut sauce – from becoming uniquely associated with California cuisine.

The rise of California cuisine was matched by the rise of the celebrity chef, none more illustrious than Wolfgang Puck, credited with inventing the 'designer pizza' and owner of several renowned restaurants in California, including Postrio in San Francisco and Spago in Los Angeles.

Drive

Marin County, the North Bay, and the East Bay

See map on page 74.

Leave San Francisco on the Golden Gate Bridge, entering Marin County on Highway 101 and shortly exiting for Sausalito.
A picturesque and very upmarket 'artist's colony,' **Sausalito▶▶** is a pleasant bayside town of steep, narrow streets and a strollable – though very commercialised – waterfront area.

Return to Highway 101 and drive north for two miles, exiting for Tiburon.
Another affluent bayside community, placid **Tiburon▶** boasts the **Richardson Bay Audubon Center and Sanctuary▶**, which offers bird-watching from an effortless and rewarding nature trail.

Return to Highway 101 and drive north for six miles to San Rafael.
The seat of Marin County, **San Rafael** holds a 1949 replica of an 1817 mission chapel and the architecturally significant **Marin County Civic Center▶▶**.

Continue north on Highway 101, after nine miles reaching Novato.
In **Novato**, a dairy-farming town named after a Hookooeko Indian chief, the **Marin Museum of the American Indian▶** details local Native American prehistory and culture.

Leave Highway 101 and drive 20 miles east on State Road 37 to Vallejo.
The large shipbuilding town of **Vallejo** is mostly visited for the Marine World/Africa USA theme park located on its outskirts (see page 87), although the **Naval and Historical Museum▶** merits a quick look.

Drive south from Vallejo, crossing the Carquinez Strait on Highway 80 and landing at Crockett. Turn left to follow the Carquinez Strait Scenic Drive as far as Port Costa.
In the pretty riverside hamlet of **Port Costa**, a look inside **Muriel's Old Doll House Museum** reveals an astonishing doll collection.

Return to Crockett and head south along Highway 80 for Berkeley.
The university town of **Berkeley▶▶** is described on pages 76 and 77.

Take any road south from Berkeley for Oakland.
A major East Bay community with an outstanding museum, **Oakland▶▶** is described on page 83.

Return to San Francisco on Interstate 80, crossing the Bay Bridge.

79

Sausalito's waterfront district

Angel Island (see page 76) might be the largest of San Francisco Bay's islands, Treasure Island (see page 88) may have the best views, but the lump of granite known as Alcatraz is by far the most famous – or most infamous.

80

High security A mile and a half north of Fisherman's Wharf, Alcatraz (whose Spanish name means 'Pelican') became the most feared place of incarceration in the United States from 1934, when 'incorrigible' criminals – those deemed beyond salvation and considered too dangerous to be held in conventional jails – were moved to this top-security, strict-discipline penitentiary. Its most notorious residents were Al Capone, Machine Gun Kelly and Robert Stroud – the so-called 'Birdman of Alcatraz' – see panel on page 77.

At Alcatraz, even work was regarded as a privilege and had to be earned by a prisoner through good behaviour. There was one guard for every three inmates, and any prisoners who did escape from their cells were faced with the prospect of crossing the freezing, swiftly moving waters of the bay to freedom.

Although stays at Alcatraz averaged nearly 10 years, inmates were denied access to newspapers, radios and TVs, and 80 per cent of them never received a visitor. Only 36 of the 1,576 convicts imprisoned here ever attempted escape: all but five were recaptured within an hour; of those five, nothing was ever heard again.

Change of use The costs and difficulties of running an island prison, and the severity of the regime, led to Alcatraz's closure in 1963. After a period of Native American occupation, Alcatraz became part of the Golden Gate National Recreation Area, in 1972 throwing open its once tightly guarded doors to the curious public.

Most of the semi-ruined prison buildings – the cellblock, the mess hall with its tear-gas cylinders fixed to the ceiling, and the prison hospital –

can be toured, and there is a small museum and a short documentary film. It is also worthwhile taking the audio-cassette tour, which carries a terse commentary by former Alcatraz guards and inmates.

Frequent crossings between Pier 41 on Fisherman's Wharf and Alcatraz are operated by the Blue & Gold Fleet (tel: 415/705–5555), though you should book a few days in advance during the summer.

An Alcatraz prison cell

► **Los Altos Hills** 74A1

When Silicon Valley techies get bored with their microchips, they head for Los Altos Hills and wallow in nostalgia at the **Foothill Electronics Museum►**, where dozens of valve-driven radios, TVs, and other vintage electrical devices are lovingly maintained.

The John Muir National Historic Site, Martinez

► **Los Gatos** 74A1

Sumptuous homes fill the hillsides and lanes of Los Gatos, 16 miles west of San Jose, whose owners sometimes emerge to scour the pricey shops and boutiques of the **Old Town►** (on University Avenue) for antiques. Other pastimes include visiting the art and nature displays of **Tate Avenue Art and Natural History Museum►** (4 Tait Avenue), and riding the **Billy Jones Wildcat Railroad►** in Oak Meadow Park.

► **Martinez** 74C4

When he wasn't blazing a hiking trail through California's backcountry, Scottish-born naturalist John Muir lived in comfort in Martinez, in a 17-room house built by his father-in-law in 1882. Known as the **John Muir National Historic Site►►** (4202 Alhambra Avenue) and kept as it was at Muir's death in 1914, it is well worth a visit. Be sure to catch the free film show, which reveals Muir's crucial role in the presentation of the country's wilderness areas – particularly Yosemite and other sections of the Sierra Nevada – and in the creation of national parks and forests.

The Martinez Adobe, built in 1849, and occupied for a time by Muir's daughter, shares the site and has displays on Mexican life in early California.

LIVERMORE VALLEY
Top-secret weapon research is one of the main sources of employment in the Livermore Valley, 48 miles east of San Francisco, site of the Lawrence Livermore National Laboratory, though since the end of the Cold War the research emphasis has tilted in favour of peaceful applications. More noticeable on the approach to Livermore are the hundreds of windmills spread across the hillsides, using the almost constant wind to produce low-cost energy.

► **Menlo Park** 74A2

Many Californians bury their noses once a month in the pages of *Sunset*, a magazine devoted to the stylish upkeep of gardens, homes and lifestyles in the western United States, and whose own experimental gardens, kitchens, and offices can be visited in Menlo Park, north of Palo Alto. Also in town, a group of elegant Spanish-style buildings set across a 3-acre garden holds the **Allied Arts Guild**, where several crafts studios are open to the public.

It may lack the majestic peaks of Yosemite or the mysterious landscapes of Death Valley but, as natural regions go, San Francisco Bay is one of the most ecologically important places in California – and one of the most threatened.

BAY STATISTICS
At low tide, the surface of San Francisco Bay covers approximately 450 square miles. The greatest depth of water is 216 feet, although slightly more than 70 per cent of the bay is less than 12 feet deep. Since the arrival of the first American settlers, the bay's shallowness has encouraged 'landfill', the filling in of its edges to create new land for building.

82

Delicate balance The bay forms a huge estuary, with much of its 100-mile shoreline lined by cordgrass, an important oxygen- and nutrient-producing plant. In the bay's marshes, microscopic marine creatures thrive and provide food both for migratory birds – beneath whose flight path the bay stands – and, once the tiny organisms are swept out to sea, for large sea dwellers, including the celebrated (and enthusiastically watched) California gray whales, who pass by the bay on their annual journey between the frozen Arctic Ocean and the warmer waters off Baja California.

Damage There are two main causes for the damage to the bay's subtle ecology: increased urbanisation, which has led to 75 per cent of the marshland disappearing beneath new housing districts and industrial sites; and the diverting of the Sacramento and San Joaquin rivers to the farms of the Central Valley, which has severely reduced the amount of fresh water tempering the salty environment of the bay.

Conservation measures In the mid-1960s, continued lobbying by concerned citizens forced the state government to create the San Francisco Bay Conservation and Development Corporation, which first stopped the pumping of raw sewage into the bay, and then introduced new laws in order to restrict landfill practices.
   Nonetheless, the decline of the bay has been slowed rather than halted, despite marshland reclamation projects and the requirement for any new landfill project to be matched by an area of equal size being returned to the water.
   Currently, groups such as Save The Bay and the Bay Institute are focusing attention on the toxic substances that are building up in the bay, destroying its vital wetlands.
   Another ongoing problem is the thirst of expanding Southern California – a region without its own water supply – which places ever-greater demands on the bay's freshwater rivers.

A nature refuge and ornithological research centre, Marin County's Audubon Canyon Ranch

Further information More about the bay and its ecology can be gleaned at San Mateo's Coyote Point Museum (see page 88), Palo Alto's Baylands Nature Interpretive Center (2775 Embarcadero Road), the Environmental Education Center of the San Francisco Bay National Wildlife Refuge (at Alviso, on the northern edge of San Jose), and at Hayward Regional Shoreline (eastern end of San Mateo Bridge, close to Hayward), a major marshland reclamation project.

▶ Mount Diablo   74C3

The highest point in the Bay Area, moody Mount Diablo is well named as Devil's Mountain. Spanish soldiers reported seeing a mysterious figure taking the side of the Indians during battles around its slopes, and another group believed they had encountered Satan himself when a Native American shaman appeared. From the 3,849-foot summit you will see (fogs permitting) the Pacific and the Sierra Nevada mountains 200 miles east.

A bust of Jack London commemorates the opening of Oakland's Jack London Square, though the area holds little of substance to remember the San Francisco-born writer

▶▶ Oakland   74B4

Most tourists see no more of Oakland than the waterfront shops of **Jack London Square▶**, which can be reached by free shuttle bus from the 12th Street BART stop, but this is far less interesting than Oakland's **Chinatown**, or the **Oakland Museum of California▶▶▶** (corner of 10th and Oak streets; tel: 510/834–2414), with its accounts of Californian history, art and ecology.

▶▶ Palo Alto   74A2

Affluent Palo Alto is the site of **Stanford University**, founded by railroad magnate Leland Stanford in 1885. Long viewed as the conservative counterpart to radical Berkeley, Stanford reputedly earns $5 million a year in royalties on its inventions. Romanesque sandstone buildings sit at the heart of the campus, the nicest being the mural-decorated **Memorial Church▶** on the Main Quad. The quad is also a pick-up point for free shuttle buses across the 9,000-acre campus, best appreciated from the observation level of the **Hoover Tower▶**.

'Must sees' include the Asian and Egyptian collections of the **Stanford Museum of Art▶** the **Cantor Sculpture Garden▶**, where an eight-ton *Gates of Hell* is the most imposing of several pieces by Rodin, and the **Stanford Linear Accelerator Center▶▶**, located in the hills two miles from the main campus, tours of which (appointment only; tel: 415/926–2204) are conducted by students.

FESTIVALS
A pale shadow of the goings-on in San Francisco, the Bay Area's festivals tend to be very small, local affairs. Among them, the enjoyable Marin and San Mateo county fairs (based in San Rafael and San Mateo, respectively) are held each July; the Sand Sculpture and Sandcastle competition takes place on Alameda Island, off Oakland, in June; and September is enlivened by Redwood City's Great Milk Carton Boat Race, when local crazies race boats made from milk cartons.

California is much less a hotbed of revolution than the world at large often seems to think it is. The only time complete social upheaval was seriously on the Californian political agenda was during the nationally turbulent years of the 1960s, and it was the Bay Area that saw the bulk of the action, with student unrest and violent agitation by the Black Panthers and the Symbionese Liberation Army.

REPUBLIC OF BERKELEY
The Berkeley campus may have a history of radical politics, but the administration of Berkeley itself is acknowledged as the most left-wing in the US, often nicknamed the Peoples' Republic of Berkeley. Over recent years, community legislators have passed laws aimed at improving the lot of disabled, gay and homeless citizens, and changed Columbus Day to Indigenous Peoples Day, drawing attention to the negative impact of the arrival of European settlements on the Americas.

Organized student revolt This began in Berkeley during the autumn of 1964, when the university authorities attempted to halt fund-raising activities and the distribution of political leaflets on the edge of campus by citing a clause in the state constitution requiring the university to be free of religious or sectarian influence.

Fronted by Mario Savio, the resultant Free Speech Movement (FSM) arranged student sit-ins and protest rallies and an occupation of Sproul Hall, which led to the largest mass arrest in California's history as police dragged 750 students from the building.

Eventually the university powers softened their attitudes, forced to heed student demands for participation in the running of the university.

The success of the FSM in encouraging student activism across the country laid the foundations for the massive anti-Vietnam War demonstrations of later years, when Berkeley was again the state's focal point of dissent. The civility of the FSM actions had become a very distant memory by 1968, though, when several days of rioting took place after the police blocked a student march along Telegraph Avenue.

More violence Berkeley saw more violence in 1969 when a pocket of university ground earmarked for development was turned – by the spades of a disparate bunch of radicals – into People's Park, an open space intended for community use. To take possession of the park (which for many years provided a refuge for the area's homeless), the county sheriff and the National Guard fired tear gas and buckshot, causing the death of one bystander and blinding another.

The Black Panthers While Berkeley was a centre for student activity, Oakland was the birthplace in 1966 of the Black Panthers, who advocated self-determination for America's blacks by any means necessary. Although founded by Bobby Seale and Huey Newton, the Black Panthers' best-known figure was their minister for information, Eldridge Cleaver.

Influenced to varying degrees by Malcolm X, Karl Marx, Che Guevara, and Mao Tse-tung (one way the Panthers raised money was through buying 20¢ copies of Mao's Little Red Book in San Francisco's Chinatown and then reselling them to Berkeley's students for $1 each), the Black Panthers dressed in a uniform of black jackets, black berets and dark glasses.

Described by the FBI as the gravest threat to domestic peace as their message spread across the country, the Black Panthers were far smaller in number than their publicity suggested. Following shoot-outs with police and the imprisonment of many of its members (including Cleaver who, while on parole, stood as a US presidential candidate for the Peace and Freedom Party), the Oakland Panthers grew increasingly less militant, devoting their time to local community projects and canvasing black support for the Democratic Party. Cleaver, incidentally, who went underground in 1968 and moved to Cuba, Algeria, and then France, reappeared in the US in 1975, declaring himself a born-again Christian.

The SLA The demise of the Black Panthers did not mean the end of armed insurrection in the Bay Area, however. By killing an Oakland schools superintendent with arsenic-coated bullets for his plans to instigate surveillance of high-school students, the Symbionese Liberation Army (SLA), an underground revolutionary group, announced their presence in 1973.

The following year, the SLA kidnapped the heir to the Hearst publishing fortunes, Patti Hearst. The ransom for her return involved a programme of food distribution to California's poor, following which Hearst announced that she had decided to join the organisation.

After a bank raid, six SLA members were killed in Los Angeles and in 1975 Hearst herself was arrested in San Francisco and sentenced to seven years' imprisonment. Now she is a Connecticut housewife.

Since then, the emphasis of Bay Area politics has largely switched toward community and ecological issues. The Berkeley campus has been quiet – perhaps a mark of the lasting achievements of the FSM – while, as in San Francisco, the clearest gains have been made by the Bay Area's gay and lesbian communities.

WOMEN EMPOWERED
In 1992, the unprecedented election of two women – former San Francisco mayor Dianne Fienstein, and Barbara Boxer – to represent California in the Senate reflected the ascent of women to positions of power within the state. In the Bay Area, achievements of the women's movement have been many, and it came as no surprise in the early 1990s when the San Francisco-ruling Board of Supervisors had a female majority, including two out-of-the-closet lesbians.

85

Bobby Seale, co-founder of the Black Panthers, speaks to students in 1968 during the height of the movement's fame

JAMES LICK'S OBSERVATORY

Atop Mount Hamilton, 19 miles east of San Jose and reached by a twisting road, the 36-inch telescope of the Lick Observatory has been scanning the heavens since 1888 – less efficiently since urbanisation filled the sky with smog. The observatory was created with the money of James Lick, whose body lies here, an eccentric gold rush-era millionaire who believed there was life on the moon. Open daily, the observatory conducts an informative interpretive programme each Friday evening (tel: 408/274–5061 for details).

The architectural anomaly that is Winchester Mystery house – said to be haunted

▶ Redwood City

Everything from cement to chrysanthemums passes through the port at Redwood City, a few miles north of Palo Alto, but the sole attraction for visitors is the Gothic Revival **Lathrop House▶** (627 Hamilton Drive).

▶▶ San Jose

San Jose is loaded with unlikely sights. Within the sphinx- and hieroglyph-decorated Rosicrucian Park (1342 Naglee Avenue), run by the mystical order, a re-creation of an avenue from ancient Thebes leads to the **Egyptian Museum**, whose collection includes everyday objects from ancient Egypt and a striking collection of mummified cats, crocodiles and people, plus an explorable replica of a 2000 BC pyramid. Close to Interstate 280, the **Winchester Mystery House** (525 Winchester Boulevard) is extraordinary – 160 rooms, with stairways leading to ceilings, corridors leading nowhere and doors opening on to walls. Its construction was financed by Sarah Winchester, heir to the weaponry fortunes, to appease the spirits of those killed by Winchester rifles. Sarah believed she would die if the house was completed, so work continued for 38 years until her death in 1921.

Other local discoveries include the **Chinese Cultural Gardens**, inside Overfelt Gardens (Educational Park Drive); the Japanese Friendship Garden and **San Jose Historical Museum** in South Kelley Park (635 Phelan Avenue); and the **Tech Museum of Innovation** (145 W San Carlos Avenue) with interactive displays echoing the area's scientific achievements.

▶ San Leandro   74B3

Just south of Oakland, San Leandro once had a large Portuguese farming community but is now a residential and manufacturing base, of note for **Casa Peralta▶**, a 1897 home that can be toured.

The pick of California's theme parks are in the south of the state, close to Los Angeles (see pages 160–1), although there are a couple of major parks in the Bay Area, not to mention several places to put on a bathing suit and splash around when the temperature soars. The parks have a range of dramatic rides based on TV shows and movies, marine and African wildlife and some spectacular water slides.

Paramount's Great America►►
Close to Santa Clara between highways 101 and 237, Paramount's Great America fills 100 acres with daredevil roller-coaster rides and all-action simulations, some based on Paramount's most popular film and TV shows, and some simply designed to terrify.

Most spectacular are Invertigo, a suspended coaster that rises 138 feet before a spine-tingling plummet; Drop Zone, with a 224-feet freefall descent, and A License To Thrill, with participants cast in the role of super-spy James Bond. Alongside are calmer items such as Martian jokes and songs of Jetson's Space Blast as well as gentle rides intended for small children.

A day is ample time to see and do everything.

Marine World/Africa USA►► Near Vallejo (on Marine Parkway, off Interstate 80), this one is more about watching than participating. In the Marine World section, killer whales, dolphins, and sea lions demonstrate their tricks, while in Africa USA, it is lions, tigers, orang-utans and elephants who put on the shows. Not to be outdone in the intelligence stakes, a group of specially trained humans entertains audiences with a waterskiing performance.

Lesser attractions include a tropical aviary, a walk-through greenhouse filled with dazzling butterflies, and a children's playground equipped with nets, ropes, and tunnels.

Raging Waters If you are in San Jose when the sun beats down, cool off at **Raging Waters►** (in Lake Cunningham Regional Park, off the Capitol Expressway), a 14-acre park where everything involves getting people wet.

Much the same applies if you are in the Livermore Valley, where four twisting flumes make up the Rapids Waterslide, part of the **Shadow Cliffs Regional Recreation Center►** (two miles east of Pleasanton on Stanley Boulevard), or at Milpitas, which holds the **Splashdown Waterslide►** (1200 S Dempsey Road).

A dolphin show at Marine World

FILOLI

Of several rambling mansions secreted in the foothills and forests of the Bay Area, only the Filoli Estate, a 43-room dwelling with exquisitely landscaped gardens, is likely to be familiar – it was the Carrington estate in the top TV soap, *Dynasty*. You will find it on Canada Road in Woodside (tel: 415/364–2880 for a guided tour).

TREASURE ISLAND

A manmade island in San Francisco Bay, created for the 1939 Golden Gate Exposition, Treasure Island was taken over by the US Navy. The Treasure Island Museum details the history of the navy, although a stronger reason for making the ferry crossing from Fisherman's Wharf might be the fantastic views of the Golden Gate and Bay bridges and of San Francisco itself.

The Bay Bridge, seen from Treasure Island

▶ San Mateo   74A3

With computers, diaramas and films, San Mateo's four-storey **Coyote Point Museum▶▶** (Coyote Point Drive) presents an exceptionally informative account of the intricacies of – and the threats faced by – the natural life of San Francisco Bay. The museum, designed to blend in with its wooded surroundings, also exhibits a functioning beehive and an industrious colony of termites, while the tranquillity of the bayside setting – interrupted only by the jets flying in and out of nearby San Francisco airport – makes it a good place for a picnic.

San Mateo is the seat of San Mateo County, whose past can be traced at the **San Mateo County Historical Museum▶** (1700 W Hillsdale Boulevard).

▶ Santa Clara   74B1

A fast-growing but largely uninteresting community just north of San Jose, Santa Clara evolved around Mission Santa Clara de Asís, founded in 1777 but survived only by a replica of its third (1825) church within the grounds of Santa Clara University.

The university's **de Saisset Museum▶** has objects from the original mission, and an illuminating collection devoted to California's indigenous cultures and the impact of European settlements. Most visitors pass right through the town, however, headed for the Great America theme park (see page 87).

▶ Saratoga   74A1

One of many to live comfortably in Saratoga, nestling in the lower slopes of the Santa Cruz foothills west of San Jose, was James D Phelan, one-time US senator and three-time mayor of San Francisco. Since 1930, Phelan's 19-room **Villa Montalvo▶▶** (15400 Montalvo Road), complete with terraced gardens, arboretum and bird sanctuary, has been a retreat for writers and painters, and numerous cultural events take place in the theater occupying the villa's converted carriage house.

If Saratoga's wealth becomes overwhelming, focus on higher things at the reposeful 15-acre **Hakone Gardens▶** (21000 Big Basin Way), landscaped along formal Japanese lines.

Though large parts of the Bay Area may be densely residential, an impressive area is wide-open countryside, where hiking trails, sedate lakes, and threatened wildlife all exist within an hour's drive of suburbia.

Bubble-juggling, Golden Gate Park

Big is beautiful On the hills above Berkeley and Oakland, the second-largest park system in the United States comprises 63,000 acres and divides into 43 separate parks. The largest and most popular section of the network is **Tilden Regional Park▶▶** (off Grizzly Peak Boulevard), where weekend crowds enjoy swimming in and sunbathing around Lake Anza, honing their competitive edge on the golf course and tennis courts, and strolling in the botanical garden as their children amuse themselves riding a miniature steam train and getting dizzy on a vintage merry-go-round.

Peacefully pastoral Nice though it is, the recreational development of Tilden is at odds with the purely pastoral landscapes of the East Bay's other parks. **Wildcat Canyon Regional Park▶**, borders Tilden but its appeal is thoroughly rustic, with quiet hiking trails winding around a creek and across wooded hillsides.

From Wildcat Canyon, ambitious hikers can pick up the **Skyline National Trail▶▶** and thread their way south over 30 view-laden miles to the Anthony Chabot Regional Park, well known to local anglers for the bass and trout in its Lake Chabot and to wildlife watchers for the deer, raccoons, and bobcats resident in the neighbouring **Redwood Regional Park▶**.

Landscapes are generally less dramatic directly south of San Francisco, although part-time lepidopterists should make a stop at **San Bruno Mountain Regional Park▶** (take the Brisbane exit off Highway 101), the last remaining habitat of the mission blue and a couple of other waning butterfly species. The Friends of Endangered Species lead free guided walks to see the butterflies, and to the sites of Native American significance within the park.

Elsewhere, earthquake enthusiasts might enjoy a close inspection of the San Andreas fault, the geological hiccup behind many of California's earthquakes, a section of which runs through the **Los Trancos Open Space Preserve▶** (seven miles south-west of Palo Alto, on Page Mill Road) and which is flanked by a walking trail.

❏ Oakland's Lake Merritt is the world's largest saltwater tidal lagoon. Canoes and a variety of boats can be hired for $4 to $10 per hour from the Sailboat House (tel: 510/444–3807). ❏

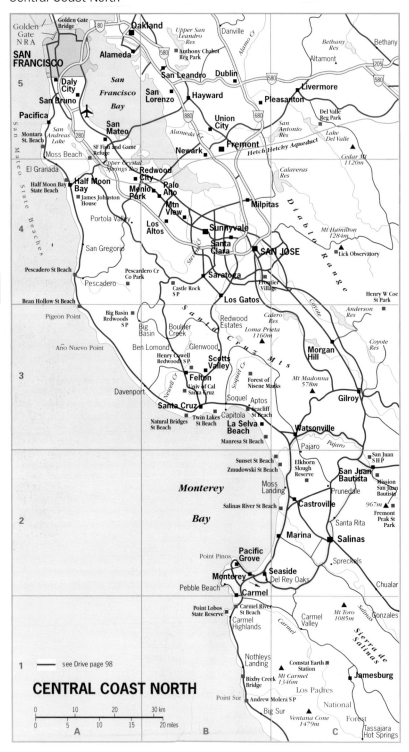

CENTRAL COAST NORTH

see Drive page 98

LARGELY UNCHANGED Much of California's Central Coast, covering almost 400 miles between San Francisco and Los Angeles, has not changed a great deal since it was first sighted by seafaring Spaniards in the 16th century.

Pacific breakers continue to smash against the granite headlands, groves of towering redwood trees still smother many of the coastal valleys, and the colonies of honking sea lions and seals underscore the fact that, even today, it is nature that holds the upper hand.

Completing the sense of remoteness from the state's developed regions, the sole coastal road (Highway 1, also called the Coastal Highway) makes hair-raising crossings of deep canyons as it charts a winding two-lane course linking the area's scattered towns.

The first settlement of appreciable size is Santa Cruz, an affable university community noted for its eccentrics, left-wing politics and the surfers who mass off its attractive beaches.

Fifty miles south, Monterey was California's capital for a period beginning in 1770 and documents the fact by keeping many of its historic buildings intact. The town also marks the edge of the Monterey Peninsula, a fist of forested granite jutting into the ocean, on whose southern edge sits the pretty – if heavily visited – village of Carmel.

A few miles inland from the coast, state parks cover many of the hikable hillsides, and out-of-the-way farming towns form the heart of what is sometimes called Steinbeck country, after the Salinas-born writer, John Steinbeck, one of many literary figures associated with the Central Coast.

BEYOND THE MONTEREY PENINSULA Big Sur comprises more than 70 miles of dramatic, wide-open country populated by barely a thousand souls, and brings the northern section of the Central Coast to an end on the outskirts of San Simeon.

Half Moon Bay pumpkins, harvested for Halloween

The pine-cloaked hillsides of Big Basin Redwoods State Park

GENDER-BENDING, FRONTIER STYLE
Born in New Hampshire in 1812, one-eyed Charley Parkhurst chewed tobacco with the best of them and piloted stagecoaches over a rough route through the Santa Cruz Mountains. Only on Parkhurst's death in 1879 was 'he' discovered to be a 'she.'

▶▶▶ Big Basin   90A3

The first of California's state parks, Big Basin Redwoods State Park was created in 1902 to protect groves of 2,000-year-old redwood trees covering the ocean-facing slopes of the Santa Cruz Mountains, 25 miles south of Half Moon Bay. A simple self-guided walking trail leads around the biggest and best of the park's majestic redwoods, and 100 miles of hiking trails descend from the inland hills, passing waterfalls, fern glades, and meadows, on the way to secluded sandy beaches. There is hiking and horseback riding amid the 4,000 pristine acres of the Henry Cowell Redwoods State Park, close to Big Basin, and also an excellent self-guided walking trail through the Redwood Grove, home to some of the Central Coast's most handsome trees.

▶▶▶ Big Sur   90B1

Coastal California reaches its scenic climax with Big Sur, a barely populated stretch between Carmel and San Simeon, where the scrub-covered slopes and forested river canyons of the Santa Lucia Mountains meet the ocean in a captivating spectacle of granite and sandstone bluffs being pounded by crashing surf.

Obscure tracks lead to hidden beaches, but even from the winding and dipping Highway 1, Big Sur cannot fail to impress. The **Henry Miller Memorial Library▶** recalls just one of numerous writers and artists who have found inspiration here, and the Esalen Institute (see panel) further attests to Big Sur's mood-enhancing qualities.

▶ Bixby Creek Bridge   90B1

The largest of a series of tall, narrow bridges carrying Highway 1 across the canyons of Big Sur is the Bixby Creek Bridge, some 10 miles south of Point Lobos State Reserve, completed in 1932 and claimed to be the world's largest single-arch bridge.

▶▶ Carmel   90B2

Founded by the Spanish and turned into an unconventional leafy retreat by turn-of-the-century San Franciscan bohemians, Carmel is a self-consciously quaint seaside town with about 5,000 wealthy residents (including ex-mayor Clint Eastwood) fiercely protective of their cottage homes and narrow streets, who have banned neon signs, traffic lights and hot dog stands.

Carmel's lanes and courtyards merit a brief browse, although most hold only souvenir shops, pricey restaurants and art galleries touting depictions of coastal landscapes. More deserving of time are the town's beach, the granite **Tor House▶▶** (on Ocean View Avenue), built by poet Robinson Jeffers, and the **Carmel Mission▶▶▶** (3080 Rio Road), where Junípero Serra, founder of California's earliest missions, died in 1784.

▶▶ Castle Rock   90B4

Rising high above coastal fogs and city smogs, the 3,600 acres of Castle Rock State Park offer rich pickings for backcountry fans. The mountain ridges, waterfalls, giant boulders, and fantastic views cannot be fully appreciated without the requisite equipment and stamina for at least a day's heavy-duty hiking.

▶ Felton
90B3

A handy accommodation base when exploring the parks that lie around it, Felton, a mountain town five miles north of Santa Cruz, also boasts the century-old **Covered Bridge▶** spanning the San Lorenzo River valley, and two scenic railways: the Roaring Camp Big Trees Narrow Gauge Railroad, which navigates redwood groves on the way to Bear Mountain, and the Santa Cruz Big Trees & Pacific Railroad, which descends to Santa Cruz (both run daily in summer; less often at other times).

▶ Forest of Nisene Marks
90B3

By 1923, 40 years of commercial logging had decimated 10,000 acres of forest inland from Santa Cruz. When logging finished, the land was purchased by a Danish immigrant family, who later put it under state protection. Hiking trails reveal young redwoods – proof of the forest's regenerative powers – and take you past many remnants of the lumber industry.

▶ Half Moon Bay
90A4

Increasingly populated by rich refugees from Silicon

ESALEN INSTITUTE
A flag bearer of the human-potential movement, the Esalen Institute took its name from the local Native Americans, and grew up around the natural hot springs at Big Sur in 1962. With yoga, meditation, holistic medicine, Gestalt therapy, and much more, Esalen's workshops and seminars attract the wealthiest of California's New Agers. Expect little change from $300 for an introductory weekend, though if your head is already screwed on right, you might treat the rest of your body to a massage (for details, tel: 408/667–3000).

93

Valley suburbia, the small oceanside town of Half Moon Bay maintains a picturesque main street, where Victorian buildings house various cosy restaurants and bakeries.

Several miles of quiet, scenic beaches add to the town's appeal, and if you are passing through in October, you may find the local Art and Pumpkin Festival in full swing.

Just south of Half Moon Bay, the **Higgins Purisima Road▶** branches from Highway 1 to wind for eight miles through tiny, time-locked farming settlements, before rejoining the main highway.

Well-tended grounds, carefully preserved adobe buildings, and a handsome Moorish-towered church help make Carmel Mission one of the prettiest of California's missions

From turn-of-the-century bohemians to 1950s beatniks, writers and poets have long been a feature of the Central Coast. Inspired by fleeting visits or besotted enough to take up permanent residence, they have put the area's powerful landscapes to use as potent backdrops, or simply waxed lyrical about the region's natural splendour.

Steinbeck House in Salinas, now a lunch restaurant, where writer John Steinbeck was born in 1902

Steinbeck No writer has had stronger links to the area than Salinas-born John Steinbeck, whose early jobs were as a ranch hand and fruit picker. Much of his work focused on California's forgotten people, such as the migrant farming communities around his hometown and the fish-cannery workers of nearby Monterey.

Of a prolific output during his peak years of the 1930s and early 1940s, one of Steinbeck's best-known books, *The Grapes of Wrath*, dealt with the plight of a Depression-era family arriving in California from the Dust Bowl of Oklahoma in search of the promised land but finding only an exploitative system of agricultural labour. It won the Pulitzer Prize but enraged the state's land barons, who branded Steinbeck a communist. In Salinas he was widely condemned as a traitor to his native town, and for many years, some local libraries refused to stock his titles. By contrast, Salinas now acknowledges the author with an annual festival and the displays of the National Steinbeck Center (see page 96).

Other famous names Long before Steinbeck was born, Robert Louis Stevenson arrived flat broke in Monterey in pursuit of Fanny Osbourne, a married woman from Oakland whom he had met in France; he married her the following year. Although he was in the town for only a few months during 1879, Stevenson was employed by the local newspaper and wrote two perceptive essays, *The Old Pacific Capitol* and *The New Pacific Capitol*, respectively contrasting Monterey's decline with San

FESTIVALS
Anti-Steinbeck feeling in Salinas has subsided sufficiently for the town to mount a Steinbeck Festival in early August, with tours, films, lectures and discussions relating to the author. Among the region's many other festivals, none is stranger than Half Moon Bay's Art and Pumpkin Festival throughout October, or the Brussels Sprout Festival held during the same month in Santa Cruz, celebrating the town's major farm crop with dozens of sprout-themed events.

Francisco's rise – and tramped the local coastline gaining inspiration for the landscapes which were later to appear in his famed *Treasure Island*.

From 1906, Carmel was home to an infamous, if comparatively short-lived, bohemian community led by romantic poet George Sterling. Many influential writers of the day – including Upton Sinclair, Mary Austin and Jack London – joined him in what was then an idyllic, unheard-of coastal town. In 1926, Sterling published a biography of a longer-lasting Carmel resident, Robinson Jeffers. Born in Pittsburgh, Jeffers was a graduate in forestry and medicine who published his first volume of poetry in 1912 and moved to Carmel two years later.

Carmel's natural beauty and what Jeffers saw as the earthy purity of the local people kept him there. These things convinced Jeffers to abandon conventional poetry and devote himself to lengthy verses, likened to Greek epics, that used a wild, coastal setting in their explorations of human dilemmas.

Not content with constructing epic poems, Jeffers also constructed an epic dwelling, Tor House, using granite stones hauled up from Carmel Beach.

Henry Miller Given the salacious content of his 1930s novels, *Tropic of Cancer* and *Tropic of Capricorn* (denied publication in the United States until the 1960s), Henry Miller's 17-year presence in Big Sur, beginning in 1944, caused local speculation as to what debauched scenes were taking place in his secluded house.

In fact, other than an awful lot of writing, not much was taking place, although Miller's intensely personal narrative style had attracted fledgling Beat generation authors to him, who in turn became obsessed with Big Sur's landscapes. Miller wrote about the area in 1958's *Big Sur and the Oranges of Hieronymus Bosch*, while Beat author Jack Kerouac who liked its fiction potential but hated Big Sur's isolation loosely used Miller as the inspiration for his 1962 novel, *Big Sur*, a tale of a retired Beat idol seeking peace and seclusion.

ARTICHOKE QUEEN
Just north of Monterey, in Castroville, the self-styled 'artichoke capital of the world', Marilyn Monroe was crowned California Artichoke Queen in 1947 at the Artichoke Festival. It is still held each September to celebrate the vegetable that provides the community with its main source of income.

95

Tor House, the Carmel home of Robinson Jeffers, completed in 1919 and occupied by the influential poet until his death in 1962

Seen from the aptly named Ocean View Boulevard, waves crash against the rocky shoreline of Pacific Grove

OLDENBURG'S HATS
The California Rodeo is amusingly commemorated by *Hat in Three Stages of Landing*, a Claes Oldenburg sculpture in the gardens of Pacific Grove's Community Center (940 N Main Street).

THOMAS DOAK
A sailor from Boston who jumped ship in then Mexican-owned California in 1816, Thomas Doak became the first US citizen to settle in the region. Before marrying into the wealthy Castro family, Doak painted the reredos of Mission San Juan Bautista in return for room and board.

►► Pacific Grove — 90B2

A band of tent-carrying Methodists moved to the northern tip of the Monterey Peninsula 1875, and the town that became Pacific Grove evolved into a fenced-in enclave of religious devotion and high moral virtue; its laws restricting the sale of alcohol were not repealed until 1969.

An abundance of shingle cottages gives this quiet seaside town a homey appeal. Monarch butterflies certainly find Pacific Grove to their liking – tens of thousands of them migrate here from March to November to hang from the pine trees (especially plentiful on Ridge Road), forming vast rippling flags of orange and black.

The **Museum of Natural History►** (165 Forest Avenue) has a good display on the butterflies. If visiting on a weekend, round off your tour with a stop at the 1855 **Point Pinos Lighthouse►►** (Lighthouse Avenue).

► Salinas — 90C2

Author John Steinbeck was born in 1902 in Salinas, a down-to-earth town dominated by the agricultural industry and off the beaten tourist track despite being just 18 miles from Monterey. Steinbeck's birthplace and boyhood home at **132 Central Avenue** is now a restaurant but retains much of the appearance of the writer's time; very informal free tours are given during limited periods on weekdays; for details tel: 408/424–2735. A room of the **John Steinbeck Public Library►** (110 W. San Luis Street) displays photographs and manuscripts relating to the prize-winning writer, who featured the town and its problems in many of his books. Much more about Steinbeck, and his uncomfortable relationship with Salinas, can be found amid the interactive exhibits and temporary displays of the **National Steinbeck Center** (371 Main Street), which is also the hub of the Steinbeck Festival, staged each August.

For many locals, however, Salinas is much less about John Steinbeck than the **California Rodeo►►**, four days of ropin' and ridin' staged each July at the Rodeo Stadium on the northern edge of town.

Tear yourself away from the scintillating coastal scenery for even half a day and you will discover natural sights of no less beauty just a few miles inland, in the foothills of the Santa Cruz Mountains and in the untamed territory above Big Sur.

It is here, too, that you will encounter the southernmost strands of the coastal redwood trees; though slightly smaller than their counterparts farther north, they are still wide enough and tall enough to be the highlight of any backcountry ramble.

Wilderness The region's major parks are described elsewhere, but many smaller state- and locally run tracts make the wilderness accessible. There is a particularly strong grouping close to the hamlet of La Honda, on State Road 84, between Half Moon Bay and Santa Cruz. The best of the bunch here is **Portola State Park▶**, a deep, rugged canyon lined by redwoods and firs, with trails leading up to the chaparral-covered higher slopes, and others winding through the thicker vegetation carpeting the forest floor.

Camping and hiking Thirty miles south of Monterey, Highway 1 passes through part of the redwood forest making up a large section of **Pfeiffer Big Sur State Park▶▶**. There is an excellent programme of ranger-led walks and hikes here, and views of the surf-pounded coast that are better than those from the coastal highway.

The main base for camping in the Big Sur area, the park – named after a family who settled the area from the 1860s, a time when Monterey was a four-day horse-ride away – is rarely short of customers, but the crowds can be left far behind as you follow one of the hiking trails, some of which cross into the Ventana Wilderness, a region of oak-cloaked gorges, scrublands, and even a few bristle-coned pines, which in turn feeds into the immense Los Padres National Forest.

Before setting out on foot, however, give due respect to the region's notoriously variable weather and remember that chilly fogs are a regular occurrence. It rains a lot, too, and if you get caught in a downpour, some solace might be found in the knowledge that the redwoods cannot grow without at least 40 inches of rainfall a year.

PICK-YOUR-OWN PRODUCE
The pick-your-own produce of the rich farmlands around Santa Cruz will improve the quality of the best-stocked picnic basket. Depending on season, large and juicy apples, strawberries or raspberries will be among the crops that can be stuffed into your bag for a very modest sum. Look for the roadside signs, or drop into the Santa Cruz Visitor Council (701 Front Street) for the free Country Crossroads brochure.

A park ranger introduces the intricacies of coastal ecology to youngsters at Monterey State Beach, just north of the peninsula

Drive

The Monterey area

See map on page 90.

From Monterey, drive 18 miles east on State Road 68 to Salinas.
Birthplace of the writer John Steinbeck and the home of the California Rodeo, **Salinas** is described on page 96.

Drive 15 miles north from Salinas on State Road 68 to San Juan Bautista.
With an impressive collection of 19th-century adobe buildings, **San Juan Bautista ▶▶** gives a distinct taste of a bygone California (see page 100).

Drive west from San Juan Bautista on State Road 156, turn north on to Highway 101, and after three miles turn west on State Road 129 for Watsonville.
Famed for its apples, strawberries and mushrooms, the small town of **Watsonville ▶** has several streets of well-preserved Victorian homes.

Drive south from Watsonville, joining Highway 1 to reach Moss Landing.
A weather-beaten fishing village dwarfed by a gigantic power station, **Moss Landing** provides access to the **Elkhorn Slough Reserve ▶**, where a four-mile boardwalk crosses wildlife-rich mud flats and salt marshes.

From Moss Landing, continue south on Highway 1 for 10 miles to Marina.
The sand dunes of **Marina ▶** hold hardy shrubs and wildflowers, and hang-gliders soar overhead.

From Marina, continue south on Highway 1, turning west at Monterey for Pacific Grove to join the 17-Mile Scenic Drive toll road.
The **17-Mile Scenic Drive ▶▶** loops through the **Monterey Peninsula**, passing the hilly peninsula's most photogenic sections.

Leave the 17-Mile Scenic Drive following signs for Carmel.
The pretty and affluent town of **Carmel** is described on page 92.

From Carmel, drive three miles north on Highway 1 to return to Monterey.

View along the 17-Mile Scenic Drive

In his 1945 novel **Cannery Row,** *John Steinbeck described the mean streets of Monterey at a time when the town – set on an impressive bay – was the world's busiest sardine processing centre, annually canning 250,000 tons of the greasy creatures until stocks were fished to exhaustion.*

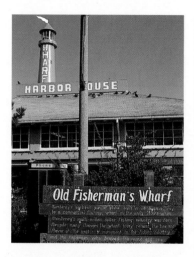

Fisherman's Wharf, Monterey

The former fish factories of Cannery Row are now occupied by trinket shops aimed at the town's 3 million annual visitors. Close by, Fisherman's Wharf, where ocean-going schooners once berthed, is now full of seafood restaurants and snack bars, and is chiefly of appeal for the noisy sea lions basking around it.

History Make a short walk inland from these tourist traps, however, and you will discover well-preserved evidence of Monterey's crucial role in California's past. Settled by the Spanish in 1770, Monterey became capital of Mexican California in 1822, and gave birth to California's first state government in 1849.

New England seafarers who settled in Monterey adapted much of the town's Spanish Colonial architecture to what became the 'Monterey style',

typified by the 1835 **Larkin House►** (corner of Jefferson Street and Calle Principal), a redwood-framed, porched adobe with an added second storey supporting a balcony.

This antique-stuffed structure, and many other landmark buildings nearby, comprise **Monterey State Historic Park►►►**, a seven-acre area spreading out from Custom House Plaza, near Fisherman's Wharf.

If the magnitude of Monterey's 19th-century glories as a seaport still hasn't sunk in, tour the excellent **Maritime Museum and History Center►►►**, opposite Custom House Plaza.

❏ The three-day Monterey Pop Festival in 1967 was the first large outdoor rock festival. It starred Jimi Hendrix, Janis Joplin and local psychedelic stalwarts The Grateful Dead and Jefferson Airplane. ❏

Monterey's literary associations continue at the memento-filled **Robert Louis Stevenson House►►** (530 Houston Street), where the Scottish writer lived in the autumn of 1879.

One place of absolutely no historical significance that should not be missed is the $40 million **Monterey Bay Aquarium►►►** (886 Cannery Row), a state-of-the-art facility cogently displaying and describing the ecology and the creatures of the ocean. Within a hundred galleries that replicate local underwater habitats lurk everything from octopuses to anchovies and seahorses to sharks.

A MYSTERY MAMMAL

The creature washed up on a Santa Cruz beach in 1925 was nearly 50 feet long, with its body tapering to a finlike appendage and with what looked like an elephant's foot sticking from its neck. One expert claimed the foul-smelling beast to be a plesiosaurus – a marine species believed to have become extinct 65 million years ago – and suggested it had been preserved by glacial ice. However, an official explanation held that the creature was a rare type of North Pacific whale, but this is still disputed.

▶▶ San Juan Bautista   90C2

Being an important stagecoach stop promised a rosy future for San Juan Bautista in the mid-1800s, but missing out on the railroad a few years later condemned the town to stagnation – and enabled many of its earliest buildings to survive intact into the present.

The town, three miles east of Highway 101, began in 1797 with one of the largest of California's missions, **Mission San Juan Bautista▶▶**, in use ever since. San **Juan Bautista State Historic Park▶▶** holds several 19th-century adobe structures, including the 1840 Castro House, the two-storey Plaza Hotel (opened as a one-storey bar in 1858 with an extra deck for travellers), and the Plaza Stables' stagecoach memorabilia.

▶▶▶ Santa Cruz   90B3

Scores of congenial bars and restaurants, 30 miles of beaches, and a population spanning all income levels,

A sign points the way to Henry Cowell Redwoods State Park, where the tallest redwood tree reaches 285 feet. The park was once part of the ranch of Henry Cowell, who developed local limestone deposits and died in 1903.

age groups and political persuasions make Santa Cruz one of California's most instantly likable towns.

When conservation got the upper hand over logging, Santa Cruz switched from being a timber-shifting centre to being a resort, and since 1904 its major landmark has been the **Boardwalk▶▶**, a beachside amusement strip with a vintage carousel, a 1924 roller coaster and tacky charm in abundance. Other interesting points of call are the **Surfing Museum▶▶** (in the lighthouse on W. Cliff Drive), with surfers practising in the ocean below, and the **City Museum of Natural History▶** (1305 E Cliff Drive).

Do not expect to tour the **Santa Cruz Mission▶**: founded in 1791, it succumbed to disuse and earthquakes, and only a dull half-size model of it can be seen (at 126 High Street). And do not expect to find real mystery at the **Mystery Spot▶**, a patch of redwood forest where clever distortions of perspective are entertainingly disguised as mystical phenomena.

Anyone drawn to the Central Coast by the stereotypical picture-postcard view of sun-drenched Californian beach life is in for a surprise. You will find more sea lions than surfers, an ocean that is usually too cold and too treacherous to swim in, and a shoreline that has more coves and tidal pools than tanning torsos.

Natural beauty Few of the protected parks and beaches along Highway 1 will disappoint; those mentioned below reveal the Central Coast – whether with wildlife, geology or classic coastal views – at its natural best.

Eighteen miles north of Santa Cruz, **Año Nuevo State Reserve▶▶▶** was set up in 1958 to protect the elephant seal, a sea mammal weighing up to three tons that had been hunted almost to extinction for its oil-rich blubber. Between December and March, thousands of the creatures waddle ashore here, and the males indulge in macho shows of strength prior to mating with 50 or so females. To join the large crowds of humans observing the noisy rituals, reserve a place on the three-hour ranger-led tour (tel: 800/444–7275).

Just south of Carmel, surf crashes against six miles of oddly shaped granite bluffs protruding from **Point Lobos State Reserve▶▶**. Sharp eyesight might reveal sea otters feeding from the offshore kelp forest, while sea lions honk from Sea Lion Rocks. Spare a thought for the Monterey cypress tree, a species unique to the area that sprouts on granite peaks only to spend its life tormented by ocean winds.

In Big Sur, turn off Highway 1 about two miles south of Julia Pfeiffer Burns State Park (not to be confused with the inland Pfeiffer Big Sur State Park) for **Pfeiffer Beach▶**, whose sands are sheltered by an extraordinary multicoloured rock formation situated just a short distance offshore.

Follow Pfeiffer Beach south and you cross into **Andrew Molera State Park▶▶**, set around the lagoon marking the mouth of the Big Sur River. Sixteen miles of hiking trails run through the sycamores and maples.

ELEPHANT SEAL BIRTH
Once fertilised by a successful male, the egg of a female elephant seal does not move to the mother's uterus for between 10 and 14 weeks. This delay, part of an 8-month pregnancy, enables pups to be born on land rather than at sea, where their chances of survival would be far worse.

A section of Point Lobos State Reserve, bestowing protection to 1,250 acres of untamed coast just south of Carmel

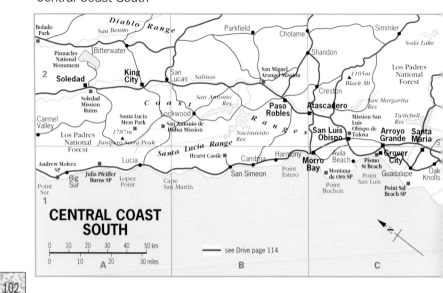

Oil platform off the California coast

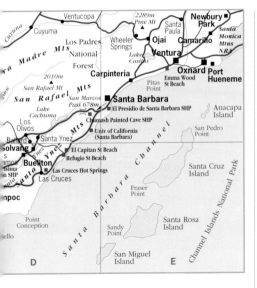

ENDLESS BEAUTY Passing from the northern into the southern section of the Central Coast does not bring any immediate changes: crashing waves and jagged bluffs, and occasional quiet, secluded beaches, continue to dominate the view from Highway 1.

As a manmade introduction to the region, however, it is hard to beat Hearst Castle, a monument to incredible wealth – and incredible architectural aspirations – that sits dreamily on a mountain slope above the village of San Simeon, just beyond Big Sur.

San Luis Obispo grew up around one of the area's several Spanish missions and now draws most of its energy from a student population.

For picturesque settings, though, it is smaller towns like Cambria that rule the day, even if the numerous artists and artisans who have populated them are locked in permanent battle with the souvenir shops that are steadily encroaching into their serene, wooded valleys.

One of the richest and also one of the nicest looking towns in California is Santa Barbara, whose mission-style architecture enhances what is already an enviable setting beside a palm-fringed beach where hedonistic southern California beach life announce themselves for the first time on the Central Coast.

Thirty miles from Santa Barbara is Ventura, the region's southernmost town, which is only just spared the sprawl of Los Angeles. It is notable for another fine set of sands and an historic quarter and provides an embarkation point for the Channel Islands National Park, volcanic islands free of human settlement that share this section of the ocean with oil rigs: a symbol of the Central Coast's struggle between commercial and ecological interests.

In Sedate Cambria, shops offer a mix of Hearst Castle souvenirs and handicrafts produced by local artisans

JAMES DEAN'S LAST RIDE
Forty-seven miles east of San Luis Obispo, at the junction of State Roads 41 and 46, 24-year-old teen idol James Dean was killed when his Porsche careered off the road on September 30, 1955. The actual site of the junction has changed since Dean's last journey, but a memorial to the actor stands outside the Cholame post office.

A MISSION GHOST
On more than one occasion, guards at the Fort Hunter-Liggett military base have drawn their weapons only to see the suspected intruder vanish before their eyes. The apparition is thought to be the ghost of a headless Native American woman who roams the grounds of Mission San Antonio de Padua in search of her head, which her furious husband tore from her body as a punishment for her infidelity.

▶ Cambria   102B1

Great fun to explore despite its contrived Olde Worlde atmosphere and preponderance of half-timbered gift shops, Cambria lies about nine miles south of Hearst Castle and splits its time between pandering to tourists and providing the rural serenity that has inspired a community of artists, whose work can be seen in a dozen browse-worthy galleries.

Friendly and affordable restaurants are also a feature of the pine-shrouded town, and culinary overindulgence can be remedied by a lengthy stroll along the town's magnificent beaches: a scene of picturesque coves, broad sands, a large sea otter refuge and seals sharing waves with surfers.

Just outside Cambria, **Nit Wit Ridge▶** (on Hillcrest Drive) provides an anarchic counterpoint to Hearst Castle. Beginning life in 1928 as a one-room shack, it became a wild and unwieldly mansion after generous applications of cement, seashells, glass, old car parts, and other bits and pieces and ultimately provided an unusual (not to mention eccentric) home for its enigmatic, unique creator into the 1990s.

▶ Carpinteria   103E2

Named by Spanish arrivals impressed with the woodworking skills of the local Chumash Indians, Carpinteria is a quiet coastal town between Ventura and Santa Barbara worth a pause for **Carpinteria State Beach▶**, beckoning sands and – thanks to an offshore reef – some of the safest swimming waters along the entire coast.

▶ Harmony   102B1

Blink and you will miss Harmony, a minuscule privately owned town just inland from Cambria. Nearly all of its 20-strong population are either glassblowers, potters or jewellery-makers, who sell their wares from roadside shops. In the fields around Harmony, Arabian horses are bred and trained on ranches still owned by the Hearst family.

▶ King City 102A2

There is a very worthwhile detour to be made from Highway 1 along the Nacimiento-Fergusson Road, which cuts dramatically across Plaskett Ridge in the Santa Lucia Mountains toward King City, a speck-on-the-map community on Highway 101.

Twenty miles south-west of King City stands **Mission San Antonio de Padua▶▶**, one of the most isolated and most evocative of the Californian missions. Authentic restoration of the buildings makes it easy to appreciate the mission lifestyle, but it is the secluded setting, in a quiet river valley, that really makes the place special. Oddly, although the mission sits miles from any urbanised area, it is inside the Fort Hunter-Liggett military base and you must go through a security check at the gates. If you have the chance, visit on June 2, when the mission celebrates the feast day of San Antonio.

▶ Morro Bay 103C1

Some agreeable seafood restaurants cook up the daily catch of the fishing fleet in Morro Bay, a moderately interesting coastal town whose best feature is the volcanic hunk of Morro Rock, a near-vertical slab rising to 576 feet little more than a pebble's throw offshore, the last visible link in a chain of nine volcanic rocks between here and San Luis Obispo, nine miles south.

Morro Rock is a protected nesting ground for peregrine falcons, and climbing it – once a popular local pastime – is prohibited. You can visit the **Bay Aquarium▶** (595 Embarcadero), which holds minor marine displays and nurses injured otters and seals back to health.

Just south of the town, Morro Bay State Park stretches over the inland hills and around the flat coastal marshlands, which are one of the country's foremost bird-watching spots, home to an abundance of great blue herons. The ecological significance of the area is described in detail at the **Museum of Natural History▶▶**, opposite the park's entrance.

▶▶▶ REGION HIGHLIGHTS

Hearst Castle *page 109*

Santa Barbara County Courthouse *page 113*

Mission La Purisima Concepcion *pages 110, 114*

Mission San Antonio de Padua *pages 105, 110*

Mission Santa Barbara *page 113*

Farmer's Market, San Luis Obispo *page 108*

Nipomo Dunes Preserve *page 107*

Santa Barbara beaches *pages 106–7*

Morro Bay *page 105*

Sailing craft in Morro Bay are dwarfed by the huge volcanic extrusion known as Morro Rock

Whether you are looking for palm-fringed beaches covered with bronzing flesh or you want to seek out secluded coves and spend hours discovering the secret life of the tidal pool, the southern section of the Central Coast has something to please.

CENTRAL COAST FISHING
Albacore, salmon and rock cod are among the species that make the Central Coast a happy hunting ground for anglers. Fishing piers are plentiful, and rare is the coastal town that does not also offer guided fishing trips or run specialist sportfishing excursions to do battle with marlin. Prices for guided trips start at around $30 per day.

One of several quiet beaches close to Morro Bay

North–south split The coast has two distinct faces north and south of Point Conception (although the name has been anglicised, the local post office still uses the original Spanish form 'Concepcion'). To the north, between San Luis Obispo and Santa Barbara, the predominantly rocky coast faces west, and fogs are prone to roll in off the ocean and fill the inland valleys. South of Point Conception, the coast faces south, and the beaches are generally better suited to sunbathing and surfing.

After you sample the opulence of the multi-millionaire's castle (see page 109), the **William Randolph Hearst Memorial State Beach**►►, close to San Simeon, is the ideal spot to rediscover life's simpler pleasures: a rustic fishing pier juts out from the quiet sands, which are fringed by eucalyptus trees and shaded picnic tables.

To the north The 1874 Piedras Blancas Lighthouse marks the edge of Big Sur (see page 92) and the start of the northern section of the Central Coast. A few miles in the other direction, the sands of **San Simeon State Beach**► are broad but busy, especially in summer when the campground is usually full.

Heading south Six miles beyond Morro Bay (see page 105), the Estero Bay area has a trio of rewarding stops. You can swim at peaceful **Morro Strand State Beach**►

(though there are no lifeguards), and the **Los Osas Oaks State Reserve▶** protects one of the longest surviving strands of handsome coastal oaks.

The biggest natural draw around Estero Bay, however, is **Montano de Oro State Park▶▶**, whose Spanish name means 'Mountain of Gold', and derives from a springtime bloom of wildflowers that turn the park's hillsides into a bright carpet of yellows and oranges.

The park's 8,000 acres encompass sandy beaches, tidal pools and surf-pounded cliffs – around which seals, sea lions and sea otters are commonly sighted – and reach inland to raccoon-infested river canyons, through which deer descend to spend the evening grazing on the coastal plain. Several trails snake through the most scenic sections of the park, and a four-mile loop trail climbs Valencia Point, a trek repaid by a stirring view of the coast – fogs permitting.

With a livelier time in mind Head for **Avila Beach▶**, 10 miles west of San Luis Obispo, whose beachside boardwalk is lined with bars and snack stands and where scores of surfers challenge the waves.

The surfers' presence helps make Avila Beach relatively lively at night – a striking contrast to sedate **Pismo Beach▶**, a coastal town a few miles south along Highway 101. Pismo State Beach is worth a look, though – it is well known to Californians for its Pismo clams, a succulent crustacean that has been hunted almost out of existence.

Magnificent sand dunes These are another feature of Pismo State Beach and they reach south, almost obliterating the diminutive community of Oceano, into the 10-mile-long **Nipomo Dunes Preserve▶▶**. Propelled by wind and wave action, the dunes are ever moving and belie their forlorn appearance by performing an important ecological service, allowing numerous species of coarse vegetation to thrive, and providing a habitat for brown pelicans and California least terns, among other creatures.

The tallest dune reaches almost 500 feet high, but the most famous dune is the one where moviemaker Cecil B de Mille buried the set of his 1923 film, *The Ten Commandments*, four-ton plaster sphinxes and all. Since 1990, excavation has been underway in an attempt to salvage the evidence of one of Hollywood's greatest cinematic excesses. The southern edge of the preserve is marked by Point Sal, an imposing headland best admired by scrambling down the cliff wall of the usually empty **Point Sal State Beach▶**.

SANTA BARBARA BEACHES
A set of state beaches occupies the approaches to Santa Barbara. Thirty miles north of the town, Gaviota State Beach spreads across either side of Highway 101 and is enticing less for its sands than its trail inland, winding to Gaviota Hot Springs. Palm-lined Refugio State Beach, 12 miles ahead, is a nicer place to catch some rays and is linked by foot and bike paths to El Capitan State Beach, where seals and sea lions bask offshore alongside surfers.

107

CHANNEL ISLANDS NATIONAL PARK
Five islands off the coast between Ventura and Santa Barbara comprise the Channel Islands National Park, whose unique plant and bird life are staging a comeback after being devastated by California's first white settlers, who trampled over the islands hunting sea lions and seals. The islands have no tourist facilities and can be explored only on marked hiking trails. Trips are run by the Nature Conservancy, based in Santa Barbara (tel: 805/888–7792), and from Spinnaker Drive in Ventura (see page 115).

THE FIRST MOTEL
In 1925, a San Luis Obispo hotel owner renamed his property, at 2223 Monterey Street, the 'Milestone Motel', thereby creating the world's first motel. As the affordable, mass-produced automobile changed the travel habits of millions, motels sprang up beside every busy highway and along the main approach routes to towns, becoming the most popular form of budget accommodation for travellers on the move.

The elegant shops of Ojai suggest the town's popularity with the well-heeled Californian weary of big-city life

▶ Ojai 103E2

With its tennis courts, golf courses, luxury hillside homes, and a summer festival, Ojai (pronounced 'O-hi') has all the trappings of a rich country retreat but enjoys a more enduring reputation as a place where the mystically minded seek enlightenment.

The idyllic crescent-shaped valley that the town occupies has long promised a spiritual Shangri-La (and did indeed provide the setting for Shangri-La in the 1937 film, *Lost Horizon*). The well-stocked library of the **Krishnamurti Foundation▶** (1130 MacAndrew Road)

commemorates an Indian mystic who lectured here in the 1920s, while the similarly Eastern-influenced **Krotona Institute of Theosophy▶** (on Krotona Hill) also has a library packed with esoteric tomes, and landscaped grounds affording exquisite views of the valley's orange and avocado groves, and the mountains that encircle the town.

Less ethereal matters are dealt with by the **Ojai Valley Historical Museum▶** (109 S Montgomery Street). Housed in a former fire house, the museum is filled with entertaining paraphernalia.

▶▶ San Luis Obispo 102C2

The 1772 **Mission San Luis Obispo de Tolosa▶▶** sits at the heart of likable San Luis Obispo, 12 miles from the coast but within easy striking distance of Hearst Castle. If you are only passing through, try to do so on a Thursday evening, when the **Farmer's Market▶▶** brings the whole town to Higuera Street to feast on barbecue.

The mission is not the most striking in California, but the historic plaza on which it stands – split by a creek and filled with lunchtime picnickers – is also the site of the **County Historical Museum▶** (969 Monterey Street), where the community's past is put on show, and the **Art Center▶** (1020 Broad Street), determined to raise the profile of local artists.

Dominated today by the agricultural students of nearby Cal Poly, who often gather around the art-deco Fremont Theater (on Santa Rosa Street), San Luis Obispo in the late 1800s housed a large community of Chinese who were employed in railroad construction: the **Ah Louis Store▶** (800 Palm Street), now a gift shop, is a rare reminder of their presence.

THE MADONNA INN
Impossible to miss, beside Highway 101, San Luis Obispo's shocking pink Madonna Inn offers food and lodging to anyone who wants to put their tolerance of kitsch excesses to the test: the waterfall flushing the coffee shop's men's urinal is just the appetizer for 100 individually themed rooms.

In California, only Disneyland attracts more visitors than Hearst Castle, the former part-time home of publishing mogul William Randolph Hearst. Set on a hilltop above the village of San Simeon, Hearst Castle was built (but never officially completed) at an estimated cost, at today's prices, of $400 million.

Given the *San Francisco Examiner* by his father in 1887, Hearst went on to head a media empire that spanned newspapers, magazines, radio stations and film studios. Aside from becoming phenomenally wealthy, Hearst also had incredible power to influence: most notoriously, he fanned the nationalistic fervour that led to the Spanish-American War in 1898.

After work began on Hearst Castle in 1919, architect Julia Morgan spent the next 28 years struggling with Hearst's constantly changing ideas and the five-ton wagonloads of Flemish tapestries, French fireplaces, Italian ceilings, Persian carpets, candelabras and coats-of-arms Hearst collected from the great homes of Europe. Visiting the castle, it is impossible not to be struck by the incongruity of a would-be medieval palace sprouting on the rugged slopes of a California coastal mountain, or be less than awed by the sheer scale and extravagance of the place.

It is also easy to imagine the likes of Charlie Chaplin, Greta Garbo and Clark Gable (friends of Hearst's long-time companion, actress Marion Davies) lurking amid the million-dollar classical statuary or admiring the lions and cheetahs that once roamed the grounds, enclosed in the world's largest privately owned zoo.

An informative visitor centre lies at the foot of the hill on which the castle stands, and is also the starting point for tours.

HEARST'S LOSS; CALIFORNIA'S GAIN
Plagued in his later years by debts and astronomic tax bills, Hearst died in 1951 (10 years after his life had been the subject of Orson Welles's film *Citizen Kane*), and six years later the Hearst family donated the castle to the state in return for a $50 million tax write-off.

109

GUIDED TOURS
Three separate 90-minute guided tours visit different sections of the castle, while a fourth tour concentrates on the lavish gardens. All tours begin from the visitor centre next to Highway 1. Reservations are essential, especially in summer (tel: 800/401–4775).

The Neptune Pool, the memorable first sight of opulent Hearst Castle for visitors arriving on guided tours

Some are beautiful and some are just ruins, but although they don't have many religions or historical treasures, all of California's 21 Spanish missions (plus five smaller branch missions, or asistencia), established between 1769 and 1823, offer a glimpse into the region's past.

JUNIPERO SERRA

Junípero Serra, the leader of Spain's Sacred Expedition into California, was born in 1713 on the Spanish island of Majorca and arrived in Mexico as a Franciscan missionary in 1749. Serra founded nine of California's 21 missions, and died at Carmel Mission in 1791. In the 1980s, the Vatican's decision to canonise Serra became a controversial issue within California, where many regard him as a major contributor to the destruction of native cultures.

San Diego Mission, founded in 1769, was the first Spanish mission in California, though poor irrigation led to its relocation

Historical significance Beginning at San Diego in the south and finishing with Sonoma in the north, the missions (each one a day's horse-ride from the next) played a crucial role in the development of the state – but you should be selective about which ones you visit if you want to discover more than a few dusty ruins beside the highway.

The southern portion of the Central Coast has some of the better examples: Mission Santa Barbara maintains a majestic presence in the town that grew around it; Mission San Antonio de Padua, near King City, survives in moody isolation; and Mission La Purisima Concepcion, near Lompoc, is so comprehensively re-created that you cannot fail to leave it without gaining some insight into the trials and tribulations of the mission times.

Origins The missions began when Spanish possession of what was then undeveloped Alta (or Upper) California was perceived as being under threat from Russia, active to the north, and the European settlers becoming established on North America's east coast.

The Spanish king dispatched a missionary party – the Sacred Expedition, led by Father Junípero Serra – to establish a series of missions across the territory. Their intention was to convert the indigenous population to Christianity while gaining their loyalty in any future colonial conflict; several missions were constructed side by side with a presidio – or fort – in which Spanish troops were barracked.

Effects on the native people Besides learning the rudiments of Spanish, the indigenous people were supposedly taught skills such as farming, building, blacksmithery, weaving and winemaking. In reality their labour was exploited to further the wealth and self-sufficiency of the missions, many of which had vast landholdings and many heads of cattle.

Few solid facts of mission life have been recorded, although reports of torture and other abuses of the neophytes (as the mission Native Americans were known) have greatly tarnished the benevolent façade that the Spanish sought to maintain.

It is certainly true that many Native Americans resisted the lure of beads and brightly coloured clothes, used to tempt them into the missions, and in some cases they attacked the mission buildings.

Eventually, the mission system all but destroyed California's native cultures and caused the death of

many thousands (thought to be half the indigenous population) through contact with European diseases, such as measles, to which Native Americans lacked immunity.

Some 88,000 Native Americans had been baptised and around 24,000 married in Catholic ceremonies by the time ownership of California switched to Mexico and the missions underwent secularisation at the behest of the Californios (California-born people of Spanish or Mexican descent).

In theory, the neophytes were then allowed to live free, independent lives, but in fact many became the servants of the Californios, who grew rich by cultivating the former mission land which they usurped in its entirety, ignoring the Mexican ruling that half should go to natives.

Although the mission churches were usually maintained to serve as parish churches, other mission buildings – such as the workshops, priests' living quarters and the outbuildings where the neophytes slept – were put to general public use, and during the early years of US rule in California, some were functioning as saloons and hotels.

The mission buildings Always simple structures of tiled roofs and stuccoed adobe lightly decorated with Moorish designs, the missions endured earthquakes as well as decades of neglect, and not until 1903 was there any concerted effort to protect and restore their buildings.

All the missions are open to the public and each has a museum displaying at least a few original objects; some missions are still used by the Franciscan order of monks. Comparatively few original features remain, but the small mission chapels, often bathed in candlelight and decorated by frescoes painted by the neophytes, are charged with atmosphere.

Strolling the grounds can be rewarding, too, both for the well-kept gardens and for the sombre feelings evoked by the cemeteries, where thousands of neophytes lie in unmarked graves beside ostentatious markers to their Spanish masters.

Mission Santa Barbara is one of the most impressive of California's missions

SERRA'S SUCCESSOR
Following the death of Junípero Serra, Fermín Francisco de Lasuén was chosen as his successor. Serra had envisaged the missions declining as the Catholicised native became self-supporting, but Fermín oversaw an expansion and strengthening of the mission system and replaced the simple churches with stronger, grander structures – many of which still stand today.

Walk

A tour around Santa Barbara

Begin at the County Courthouse, 1100 Anacapa Street.
The architecturally magnificent **County Courthouse** is described on page 113.

Walk south-east from the County Courthouse along Santa Barbara Street, turning right on to Cañon Perdido for El Presidio State Historic Park.
Several buildings form the **El Presidio State Historic Park**: on the north side of Cañon Perdido, the **El Presidio Chapel** is a detailed re-creation of a mission-era Spanish chapel; and across the street, the 1788 **El Cuartel adobe** is the second-oldest surviving building in California.

Return to Santa Barbara Street, walking one block south-east to De La Guerra Street for the Historical Museum.
The displays of the **Historical Museum** fill the gap between Santa Barbara's Spanish origins and its emergence as an affluent US town.

Walk south-west along De La Guerra Street, turning right on to State Street and continuing to the Museum of Art.
On the corner of Anapamu Street, the

Santa Barbara County Courthouse

112

Museum of Art spreads over three floors and features many major American and European names.

From the Art Museum, walk two blocks north-east on Anapamu Street to return to the County Courthouse.

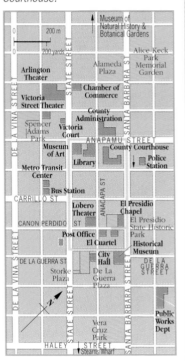

❑ Heritage celebrations make the largest and most enjoyable festivals along the southern section of the Central Coast. The biggest bash is Santa Barbara's weeklong Old Spanish Days held in August; the following month, Solvang remembers its Scandinavian founders with the traditional events of Danish Days; while the strangest annual spectacle takes place 16 miles north of San Luis Obispo in the otherwise unexciting Atascadero, where September Mud Olympics honour the town's Spanish name – which means 'muddy place'. ❑

▶▶▶ Santa Barbara   *103E2*

In a wealthy and conservative but appealingly sybaritic community, Santa Barbara's low-lying red roofs poke through thickly wooded green hillsides, the town having rebuilt itself in the image of California's missions after being flattened by an earthquake in 1925.

Ironically, **Mission Santa Barbara▶▶▶** (2201 Laguna Street), overlooking the town, is architecturally far grander than the average mission, with classically influenced twin towers and columns that were added in 1820. Restored rooms and a museum record the mission's heyday, and an atmospheric cemetery holds the unmarked remains of 4,000 Chumash.

Nearby, displays at the **Museum of Natural History▶** (2599 Puesta del Sol Road) provide a thorough background on the Chumash tribe, and five miles of walking trails weave around diverse native Californian vegetation at the **Botanical Gardens▶▶** (1212 Mission Canyon Road).

Except for the mission, Santa Barbara's historical sights are concentrated downtown. The jewel is the 1929 **County Courthouse▶▶▶** (1100 Anacapa Street), whose architecture embodies the exaggerated mission style Santa Barbara's architects adopted after the 1925 earthquake.

Fine Tunisian tilework and outstanding murals are among the courthouse's decorative features; take the lift

SOLVANG

Founded by Danes in 1911, Solvang's thatched roofs, wooden storks, and pseudo-windmills are intended to convince tourists that a piece of Denmark has been transported to California. Any Dane visiting today would struggle to hold back the laughter, but the village does make an enjoyable interlude between Santa Barbara and San Luis Obispo, if only to discover that Danish pastries prepared to traditional recipes are much nicer than the sugar-saturated imitations sold elsewhere.

Stearns Wharf, built as the base for Santa Barbara's commercial fishing fleet in 1872

113

to the top of the **El Mirador bell tower▶▶** for a view over the town. Within a few strides stand a couple of 18th-century adobe buildings and the State Historic Park (123 E Cañon Perdido Street), where several Spanish military buildings are being renovated; the **Historical Museum▶** (136 E De La Guerra) is, at present, a more rewarding call.

A mile west of downtown, joggers and skaters are a constant sight beside the broad and inviting Santa Barbara beaches, which centre on 19th-century Stearns Wharf. Here gift shops and seafood eateries are joined by the Nature Conservancy, which can provide you with informative literature on the Channel Islands National Park.

SANTA PAULA'S OIL

Twelve miles east of Ventura, Santa Paula's California Oil Museum explains oil production with computer simulations and a working model of an oil rig. There is little, though, to explain why offshore drilling is among the state's most sensitive topics, not least in Santa Barbara, where an offshore spill in 1969 devastated local wildlife.

Drive

The reconstructed version of Mission La Purisima Concepcion

114

The Santa Ynez Valley

See map on pages 102–3

From Santa Barbara, drive 10 miles north on State Road 154, turning right along the twisting Painted Cave Road for the Chumash Painted Cave. Brilliantly coloured abstract designs, which date from AD 1000 and are used in rituals by the Chumash people, can be glimpsed through a screen at the **Chumash Painted Cave▶▶**.

Return to State Road 154 and continue north, crossing the San Marcos Pass and descending into the Santa Ynez Valley; after 26 miles turn left onto State Road 256 for Santa Ynez.
In Santa Ynez, the **Valley Historical Society Museum▶** records the 19th-century settlement of the valley. On the town's periphery, at the **Gainey Vineyard▶** and the **Santa Ynez Winery▶**, you can sample the wines that have made the valley famous among California's discerning wine drinkers.

From Santa Ynez, continue for three miles on State Road 256 to Solvang.
The Danish features of **Solvang** are described on page 113.

From Solvang, drive 10 miles north on Ballard Canyon Road, passing the hamlet of Ballard, for Los Olivos.

In 1975, the **Firestone Vineyard▶** in Los Olivos was the first to use local grapes in the wine-making process; sitting amid 275 acres of vines, the winery is open for tours.

From Los Olivos, drive three miles north on State Road 154 and turn south on to Highway 101, continuing for six miles to Buellton.
Buellton is the site of **Pea Soup Andersen's**, a California legend for the pea soup first offered to travellers in the 1920s.

Leave Buellton on State Road 256, driving west for 17 miles to Mission La Purisima Concepcion.
Founded in 1787, **Mission La Purisima Concepcion's▶▶** original buildings have long been destroyed, but detailed reconstructions make this the most authentic-looking mission site in the state.

*From the mission, join Highway 1 and drive 26 miles east to the junction with Highway 101, then take the side road to **Las Cruces Hot Springs**.*
Two geothermal springs at the end of a short foot trail, Las Cruces Hot Springs▶ (see page 115).

Continue east on Highway 101, passing Refugio and El Capitan state beaches (see page 107) on the 35-mile drive back to Santa Barbara.

▶▶▶ Ventura 103E2

Mainly concerned with farming and industry, and blighted by a large oil refinery, Ventura looks immeasurably better once you locate the town's two-mile-long beach.

There is more to enjoy on foot in the historic area of Old San Buenaventura, which surrounds the Spanish mission from which the town adapted its name. Founded in 1782 and completed in 1809, the small church of **Mission San Buenaventura▶▶** (211 E Main Street) is all that survives of the mission's buildings, described in a small museum, while the once famous 17-acre gardens now stand buried beneath gift shops.

Close to the mission, a productive archaeological dig has yielded valuable finds from the time of Spanish settlement, and also unearthed native American relics dated to 1600 BC, some of which are in the **Albinger Archeological Museum▶** (113 E Main Street). Within a few strides is the **Ortega Adobe▶**, dating from 1857 and looking its age – but nonetheless a good example of the adobe building style.

Across the street, the **Ventura County Museum of History and Art▶** (100 E Main Street) documents the diverse nationalities who settled the region in the late 19th century, and charts the discovery of oil deposits.

Elsewhere in Ventura, **Olivas Adobe Historical Park▶** (4200 Olivas Park Drive) is the site of a two-storey adobe house. A prime example of the Monterey style prevalent in California during the mid-1800s, it is packed with furnishings typical of the period, while the grandiose columns of the **Ventura County Courthouse▶** (501 Poli Street) highlight a later period's obsession with neo-classical architecture.

HOT SPRINGS
Mineral-rich hot springs, some of which have been adopted by commercial spa resorts, crop up fairly often throughout the Central Coast. One place to see springs as nature intended them is at Las Cruces Hot Springs, near the junction of Highway 101 and Highway 1, four miles north of Gaviota. From the parking lot, a trail leads to two pools of water fresh from the bowels of the earth: the first is fairly cool, while the second is warm and ideal for a dip.

Ventura's Mission San Buenaventura, from which the town took its name, was the last to be founded by Junípero Serra

CHANNEL ISLANDS TOURING
A good reason to be in Ventura is to visit the Channel Islands National Park, 15 miles offshore. The Visitor's Center (1901 Spinnaker Drive) provides background on the islands, and Island Packers (1867 Spinnaker Drive; tel: 805/642–1393) runs boat trips to them.

LOS ANGELES CITY

Angeles National Forest

Veterans Memorial Park

SAN FERNANDO

FOOTHILL FREEWAY

GOLDEN STATE FREEWAY

SAN FERNANDO ROAD

San Fernando Mission

Big Tujunga Res

Tujunga

ANGELES CREST HIGHWAY

Switzer Camp

Hansen Lake

MISSION HILLS

SEPULVEDA BOULEVARD

Verdugo Mountains

LA CRESCENTA

LA CANADA FLINTRIDGE

MONTROSE

Descanso Gardens

Devil's Gate Res

Woodbury University

Stough Park

Wildwood Canyon Park

BURBANK

Brand Park

GLENDALE

San Rafael Hills

Arroyo Seco Highway

Rose Bowl

VAN NUYS

Los Angeles

Tujunga Wash

VENTURA FREEWAY

ALAMEDA AVE

VENTURA BOULEVARD

NBC Studios

Autry Museum of Western Heritage

Norton Simon Museum of Art

Universal Studios

Griffith Park

Forest Lawn Memorial Park

Zoo

Santa Monica Mountains National Recreation Area

Planetarium

GLENDALE FREEWAY

PASADENA FREEWAY

Stone Canyon Res

Hollywood Bowl

SUNSET BOULEVARD

WEST HOLLYWOOD

Chinese Theatre

SANTA MONICA BOULEVARD

Silver Lake Res

Southwest Museum

Arroyo Seco Park

HUNTINGTON DRIVE

BEVERLY HILLS

Getty Center

UCLA

LA County Museum of Art

Farmers Market

La Brea Tar Pits

WILSHIRE BOULEVARD

Page Museum

Elysian Park

Lawry's California Center

Dodger Stadium

California State Univ LA

SAN DIEGO FREEWAY

WEST WOOD

HOLLYWOOD FREEWAY

Chinatown

El Pueblo

SAN BERNARDINO FREEWAY

Century City

Museum of Tolerance

Ballona Creek

Music Center

Civic Center

Little Tokyo

WHITTIER BLVD

POMONA FWY

SANTA MONICA FREEWAY

SANTA

MONICA

VENICE BOULEVARD

University of S California

SANTA ANA FREEWAY

Santa Monica Heritage Museum

LINCOLN BLVD

CULVER CITY

Exposition Park

Memorial Coliseum

Maywood

HUNTINGTON PARK

Venice

Marina del Rey

Fisherman's Village

MANCHESTER AVENUE

The Forum

INGLEWOOD

Hollywood Park Race Track

FLORENCE

Cudahy

SOUTH GATE

Watts Towers

Los Angeles International Airport

SERPULVEDA BOULEVARD

Santa

Monica

Bay

EL SEGUNDO

CENTURY FREEWAY

HARBOR FREEWAY

LYNWOOD

WILLOW BROOK

MANHATTAN BEACH

HAWTHORNE

GARDENA

Alondra Park

California State University Dominguez Hills

COMPTON

ARTESIA FRWY

HERMOSA BEACH

ARTESIA BOULEVARD

GARDENA FREEWAY

LONG BEACH FREEWAY

LAKEWOOD BOULEVARD

REDONDO BEACH

HAWTHORNE BOULEVARD

TORRANCE

WESTERN AVE

SAN DIEGO FREEWAY

Dominguez Channel

CARSON

LOS ANGELES BOULEVARD

0   2   4   6   8 km

0   2   4 miles

A   B   C

EXTREMES The second-largest city in the US, Los Angeles has an identity all its own. Here, the finest of fine art collections are surrounded by garish billboards; image-conscious trendies strike a pose in clubs a short distance away from the homeless; and celebrity-filled movie premières vie with gang wars and interethnic feuding for attention on national TV.

The entertainment industry has brought parts of LA more wealth than it knows what to do with and a population packed with household names, but for every fat cat living it up in the Hollywood Hills, there are thousands enduring grinding poverty in LA's less salubrious areas, and discontent among the city's dispossessed has been known to erupt into violence.

PLEASURES At the same time, 99 per cent of visitors to LA can enjoy the fabulous beaches, the madcap architecture and the excellent museums, and generally soak up the LA lifestyle without ever exposing themselves to anything more dangerous than exceeding their credit limit in one of the world's greatest consumer paradises.

NEIGHBOURHOODS Around the skyscrapers of Downtown the historic El Pueblo de Los Angeles, Chinatown and Little Tokyo sit at the core of this enormous city. To the east of Downtown, East LA occupies miles of urban sprawl and houses the bulk of LA's vast Latino population.

LA, as most visitors envisage it, stretches 16 miles west from Downtown, taking in Hollywood, Beverly Hills and Westwood, reaching the coast at Santa Monica.

South of Santa Monica, Venice Beach, Manhattan Beach, Hermosa Beach and Redondo Beach occupy the low-lying land that soon rises into the tall bluffs of the Palos Verdes peninsula, LA's south-western extremity.

East of Palos Verdes, San Pedro and Long Beach sit on the LA harbour, south of Downtown and separated from it by the run-down and dangerous South Central LA. Everything is linked by a network of freeways, clogged during rush hours but essentially the only way to get around this sun-kissed megalopolis.

Blazing sunsets are a feature of balmy LA evenings

▶▶ Beverly Hills 116A3

When you see rows of open-topped Rolls Royces waiting at traffic lights and immaculately groomed poodles being exercised along thoroughly scrubbed pavements, then you know you are in Beverly Hills.

From the 1920s, LA's movie idols followed the lead of Douglas Fairbanks and Mary Pickford and colonised the hills and canyons above Hollywood. Soon Beverly Hills had become a byword for glamour and mind-boggling wealth.

The stately and secluded hillside homes of the rich and famous still fill Beverly Hills. But it is around the designer-label stores on Rodeo Drive that you are most likely to spot the 'big names', even though today's Beverly Hills residents (whose $100,000 average yearly income is four times the national average) are as likely to be plastic surgeons as film stars.

▶ Century City 116A3

On the one-time backlot of 20th Century Fox studios, the metal and glass high-rise towers of Century City form LA's most anodyne district. The sterile mood is eased only by the theatres of the ABC Entertainment Center and the Century City Shopping Center – and the chance to peek at the New York street set that starred in the 1960s film *Hello Dolly!*

▶▶ Chinatown 116C3

Pagoda-shaped buildings and dozens of ornamental fire-breathing dragons were among the things LA's sizable Chinese community acquired when it relocated to present-day Chinatown in the 1930s to make way for Union Station. See the live poultry shops, sniff the aromatic herbs, and come back at night when the restaurants are at their liveliest and the neon decorations glow, and you will find one of LA's major ethnic communities at its least Americanised (see also page 119).

A stronger reason to be in the area is the excellent Museum of Tolerance (see page 137), located on the southern fringe.

Chinatown has retained a distinct identity

A vibrant pot-pourri of races, religions, languages and cultures, Angelenos are a much more ethnically varied bunch than the stereotype of the well-off Anglo-American would suggest, with immigrant communities dotted around the city.

From Latin America Though visible all over the city, the vast majority of LA's 2.5 million Hispanic residents live in East LA; the third-largest Mexican community in the world, it is increasingly also home to Guatemalans and other immigrants from elsewhere in Central America. For a taste of local life, stroll among the exotic pet shops and botanicas (supplying the implements of the voodoo-like *Santeria*) of Brooklyn Avenue, and drop into the lively El Mercado indoor market at 3425 E. First Street.

From Asia Many Chinese railroad labourers settled in LA around the turn of the century. To make way for Union Station in the 1930s, the original Chinatown was moved a short distance north to the present Chinatown (see page 118) along North Broadway. Crowds spill ceaselessly out of the district's restaurants and shopping plazas, although many Chinese have moved from Chinatown to the suburban San Gabriel Valley.

LA's Japanese community, now numbering 100,000 and probably the city's most prosperous ethnic group, also has a long history but was devastated in 1942 when almost all its members were forced into internment camps for the duration of the war. Japanese LA's public face is within the traditional-Japanese-meets-modern-American architecture of Little Tokyo, where the Nisei Festival takes place each August and where the Japanese-American National Museum displays art and historical items.

Of the city's less populous Asian communities, many brightly painted buildings decorate the expanding Koreatown, based on Normandie Avenue, just south of Wilshire Boulevard; Vietnamese enclaves can be found within Chinatown and in Westchester; and a large Cambodian community is centred on Long Beach's Anaheim Street.

From Europe Armenians, Russians and Hungarians are evident around the Fairfax section of Wilshire Boulevard, also the heart of the second-largest Jewish community in the US, and many Greeks have settled in the area around St Sophia's Greek Orthodox Church.

From Africa Much of South Central LA is home to the bulk of the city's African-American population. A depressed area, it formed a natural starting point for the riots that shook the city in 1992. The violent images of those days, beamed around the world, were seen by some as an expression of the hopelessness many local residents were feeling. However, South Central has many successful community projects and has spawned 50 top rap stars.

CHICANO/LATINO/ HISPANIC
The precise meanings of the terms Chicano, Latino, and Hispanic have become blurred with use (and misuse) and you are likely to hear any one of them used to describe people or a person of Latin American origin or descent. Derived from the Aztec name for Mexico, 'Chicano' was first adopted by some U.S. citizens of Mexican origin during a 1970s political movement. Literally, 'Hispanic' means 'derived from the Spanish,' although many so-called Hispanics are actually of Indian blood. A more accurate term is 'Latino,' which refers to all people of Latin American origin.

119

Hard to believe though it may be, the origins of unrelentingly modern LA go back to 1781 and a farming community growing food for California's Spanish missions. The 44 original settlers – Native Americans, blacks, Spanish, mestizos and mulattos – relocated twice before basing themselves close to what is now El Pueblo State Historic Park, on the northern edge of Downtown.

The Old Plaza Funded in part by donations of cattle and whisky, the **Plaza Church▶▶**, on Main Street facing the **Old Plaza**, was commenced in 1818 but was not finished until 40 years later. Greatly modified over the decades, the church has a plain exterior that hides an interior rich with paintings and sacraments of the Catholic faith.

Also by the Old Plaza, the Italianate **Pico House▶** was the finest hotel south of San Francisco when it opened in 1870. It was financed by California's last Mexican governor, Pío Pico, who, so it is said, sat on a bench outside the building and wept after failing to meet the $30,000 mortgage payments.

No trace remains of LA's time as one of the West's most lawless towns – when cockfights were common along its shabby streets, and blood ran as freely as alcohol in its saloons – through the early days of US rule.

Olvera Street Running off the **Old Plaza▶▶▶**, Olvera Street was once the scene of much of the carnage. It has earned an honest living since the 1930s, however, as a would-be Mexican street market, where south-of-the-border arts and crafts are sold, and Mexican food is consumed from hole-in-the-wall cafés.

Once uncharitably described as 'the first Disneyland', Olvera Street nonetheless makes for enjoyable strolling, and at No. 10 enough remains of the 1818 **Avila Adobe▶▶** to justify its claim as the oldest house in LA – inside, reconstructed fittings suggest the local lifestyles as they were in the 1840s.

Film show To learn more about El Pueblo, watch the free film show in the information centre on Olvera Street, or join the walking tour from the Visitor Information Center, Sepulveda House, 622 N Main Street, facing the Old Plaza.

A street market in El Pueblo State Historic Park

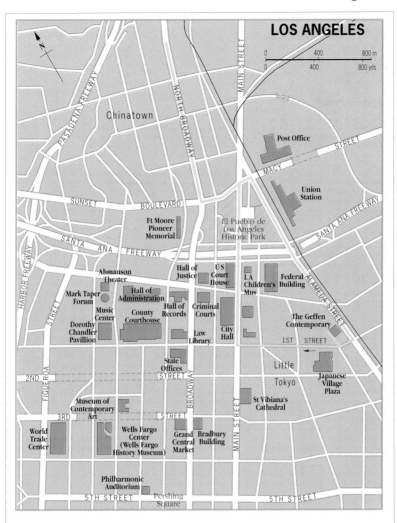

Downtown sights of Los Angeles

From the Japanese Village Plaza Mall go west along First Street, turning into Main Street for City Hall.
The observation deck in the 1928 **City Hall** has great views across LA.

Go north along Main Street for El Pueblo de Los Angeles (see page 120). Turn left into Macy Street then right onto Broadway for Chinatown. From El Pueblo, cross Alameda Street for Union Station.
Union Station has welcomed rail passengers to LA since 1939.

Walk south along Alameda Street, turn right into First Street and right again along Central Avenue for the Temporary Contemporary.
The **Geffen Contemporary** is a former police garage filled with oversized modern art works.

Return to First Street and turn right for Japanese Village Plaza Mall.

It may lack the tradition of European cities, but when it comes to architecture LA is no slouch. From playful gingerbread homes of the early 1900s to textbook examples of modernism, the city is filled with ingeniously designed buildings that, in some cases, are the finest examples of their kind.

WATTS TOWERS

As famous architects dotted the city with their masterworks and mistakes, one of LA's most enduring structures was being painstakingly assembled by an unknown tilesetter called Simon Rodia. Between 1921 and 1954, Rodia's 100-foot-high Watts Towers (1765 E 107th Street, Watts) evolved from bedsteads, bottletops and 70,000 shells. Working entirely alone and never giving any explanation for his creation, Rodia was to die in obscurity. Public support has, however, helped the towers survive several demolition threats, and recently restored, they remain as majestic and as mysterious as ever.

One of the many modernistic sculptures commissioned to decorate the otherwise stern plazas of Downtown's Financial District

Early structures LA's earliest buildings were flat-roofed, single-storey adobe (or mud-brick) structures. The heavily restored 1818 Avila Adobe in El Pueblo de Los Angeles is one example, though a broader sense of the style is given by Rancho Los Cerritos and Rancho Los Alamitos in Long Beach.

Many of the settlers from the eastern United States who arrived in LA at the start of the 20th century brought with them a liking for elaborate ornamentation. The desirable residences of the time were groups of richly decorative wood-built Queen Anne and Eastlake homes; the more turrets and twirls such a dwelling had, the more desirable it was. Some handsome survivors can be seen on **Carrol Avenue►►**, just west of Downtown.

California Bungalows Plainer wooden houses – the city's first low-cost urban housing – sprang up in a medley of styles but, characterised by balconies, porches and overhanging roofs, they became collectively known as California Bungalows. An expensive adaptation of the California Bungalow appeared in the suburb of Pasadena. Here, the firm of Greene & Greene took its inspiration from England's Arts and Crafts movement and made its definitive statement with the 1908 **Gamble House►►►** (see page 159), whose highly polished woodwork showcases the teak's natural pattern, joints are exposed and exaggerated, and every piece of furniture – from the tables and chairs to the lampshades – originated on the Greene & Greene drawing board.

Plentiful though the California Bungalows were in their various guises, it was the thick walls, open courtyards, arches and plushly landscaped gardens of the Spanish Colonial Revival that became more strongly associated with LA, and all of Southern California, which eventually acquired a Mediterranean look to match its climate.

The successes and excesses of the movie industry inspired further large, sometimes ludicrous imitations of European architecture. The symbol of LA's emergence as a modern city, however, was the art-deco explosion of the late 1920s and 1930s, whose aerodynamic contours, porthole windows and projecting wings were exuberant monuments to the technological age.

LA's outstanding art-deco buildings included the **May Co. Department Store►►** (6067 Wilshire Boulevard), with an immense finned cylinder joining the two exterior walls, and the **Coca-Cola bottling plant►►** (1334 S Central Avenue), thinly disguised as an ocean liner, complete with ship's bridge, hatch covers and portholes.

As weak art deco and Spanish Colonial Revival swamped the city, influential maverick Frank Lloyd Wright arrived and looked back to pre-Columbian times. In 1917, his **Hollyhock House**▶▶ (4800 Hollywood Boulevard) was an ambitious fusing of California Bungalow and Aztec temple. Unloved by its owner, the house and its grounds (the present Barnsdall Park) were given to the city. Wright refined his ideas and, in 1924, completed the **Ennis House**▶▶ (2607 Glendower Avenue).

Wright's assistant, the Austrian Rudolph Schindler, established his own modernist credentials with his home of concrete slabs and interlocking indoor and outdoor spaces in West Hollywood (833 N Kings Road), complete with open-air sleeping areas.

Encouraged by Schindler, fellow Austrian Richard Neutra arrived from Europe. In 1929, Neutra's **Lovell House**▶▶ (4616 Dundee Drive), with suspended balconies projecting from the hillside above Griffith Park, became LA's most acclaimed example of the international style.

More new styles From 1945 to 1964, the Case Study Program of experimental house building solidified LA's reputation as a centre of innovative architecture, though, by definition, the city's staggering postwar growth restricted new projects – as have the preservation orders that protect its architectural past.

In the mid-1970s, the glass silos of the **Westin Bonaventure Hotel**▶▶ (404 S Figueroa Street) heralded a spate of new Downtown development including Arata Isozaki's red sandstone mating of East and West, housing the **Museum of Contemporary Art**▶▶ (250 S Grand Avenue). When the billion-dollar Getty Center (see page 154) opened in 1997, it became LA's latest and perhaps most successful fusing of architecture and landscape.

CHARLES LUMMIS
Fear that the city's Spanish-Mexican architectural heritage might disappear encouraged a librarian, Charles Fletcher Lummis, to start the country's first preservation program in 1895, which saved LA's outlying Spanish missions (San Fernando Rey in the San Fernando Valley, and Mission San Gabriel Archangel in the San Gabriel Valley) from destruction.

123

From running stagecoaches across the wild west, Wells Fargo grew into one of the country's major financial institutions

The Autry Western Heritage Museum

Just one example of the countless statuary filling Malibu's J Paul Getty Museum

Index of museums in and around LA

Aerospace Museum
Open: daily, 10–5. Free. (See page 127.)

Armand Hammer Museum of Art and Culture Center
Open: Tuesday to Saturday 11–7, Thursday until 9; Sunday 11–5. Entry fee. (See page 136.)

Autry Western Heritage Museum
Open: Tuesday to Sunday, 10–5. Entry fee. (See page 126.)

Cabrillo Marine Museum
Open: Tuesday to Friday, noon–5; Saturday and Sunday, 10–5. Free. (See page 134.)

California Museum of Science and Industry
Open: daily, 10–5. Free. (See page 127.)

Getty Center
Open: Tuesday to Wednesday 11–7, Thursday to Friday 11–9, Saturday and Sunday 10–6. Free (fee for parking)

Hollywood Entertainment Museum
Open: Tuesday to Sunday 10–6. Entry fee.

Hollywood Studio Museum
Open: Saturday 10–4, Sunday 12–4. Entry fee. (See page 128.)

Hollywood Wax Museum
Open: Daily 10am–midnight. Entry fee. (See page 128.)

Huntington Art Collections
Open: Tuesday to Sunday 10:30–4:30; reduced hours in winter. Entry fee. (See page 155.)

LA County Museum of Art
Open: Tuesday to Thursday, 10–5; Friday, 10–9; Saturday and Sunday, 11–6. Entry fee. (See page 138.)

Laguna Beach Museum of Art
Open: Tuesday to Sunday, 11–5. Free. (See page 157.)

Los Angeles Maritime Museum
Open: Tuesday to Sunday, 10–5. Donation requested. (See page 134.)

Museum of Contemporary Art
Open: Tuesday to Sunday, 11–5; Thursday, 11–8. Entry fee.

Museum of Tolerance
Open: Monday to Thursday, 10–6; Friday, 10–1; Sunday, 11–6. Entry fee. (See page 137.)

Natural History Museum
Open: Tuesday to Sunday, 10–5. Entry fee. (See page 127.)

Newport Harbor Art Museum
Open: Tuesday to Saturday, 10–5. Entry fee. (See page 156.)

Norton Simon Museum
Open: Thursday to Sunday, noon–6. Entry fee. (See page 155.)

Pacific Asia Museum
Open: Wednesday to Sunday, noon–5. Donation requested. (See page 159.)

Richard M Nixon Birthplace and Library
Open: Monday to Saturday, 10–5; Sunday, 11–5. Entry fee. (See page 156.)

Southwest Museum
Open: Tuesday to Sunday, 10–5. Entry fee. (See page 158.)

In the realm of spectator sports, the work-hard, play-hard ethic in LA life shows its face as a passion for watching hard, and Angelenos take an avid interest in the exploits of the city's home teams.

National favourites LA has five professional teams, two each for baseball and basketball, and one for ice hockey.

The numerous college teams – the major ones being the Trojans (USC) and the Bruins (UCLA) – should not be considered second-rate. Many student athletes are on sports scholarships and destined for the professional leagues.

One of the biggest sporting events in LA, in fact, is the New Year's Day football clash between the student champions of the West and Midwest at Pasadena's 104,000-seat Rose Bowl stadium.

The season's regular events are listed in the phone book. Only tickets for major games, and any game by the LA Lakers, will prove elusive; use the phone numbers given below for detailed information.

Baseball The National League's LA Dodgers play at Dodger Stadium, on the edge of Elysian Park, off the Pasadena freeway (tel: 213/224–1500), while their American League counterparts, the California Angels, appear at Anaheim Stadium, in Anaheim, Orange County (tel: 714/634–2000). The season runs from April to October.

Basketball Most tickets to watch the fabled LA Lakers, who play at the Great Western Forum in Inglewood (tel: 310/419–3100), are snapped up before the November-to-April season even starts. The LA Clippers appear at the Sports Arena, just south of Exposition Park (tel: 213/748–8000).

Football Los Angeles football lovers are still recovering from the loss of both the city's professional teams – the Rams and the Raiders – in the mid-1990s. The search is on for replacements.

Horse racing Major meets are held at the LA County Fairgrounds in Pomona in September and October (tel: 714/623–3111); at Hollywood Park in Inglewood from April to July and during November and December (tel: 310/419–1500); and at Santa Anita Park in Arcadia from July to September and from December to April (tel: 818/574–7223).

Ice hockey The city's professional ice hockey teams are the LA Kings, who bully off at the Great Western Forum (tel: 310/673–6003), and Orange County's Mighty Ducks of Anaheim, based at Anaheim's Arrowhead Pond (tel: 714/704–2500). The ice hockey season lasts from October to April.

The strapping football players of UCLA's Bruins, who play their home games across the city at Pasadena's Rose Bowl stadium

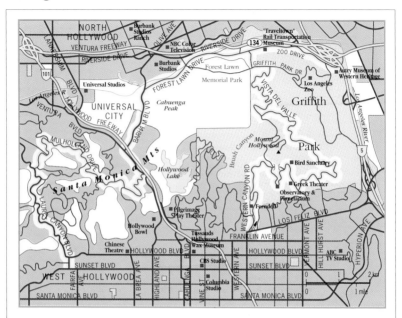

Drive

A tour around Griffith Park

Enter the park at the Western Canyon Road gate for the Ferndell.
A peaceful glade with a natural spring, the **Ferndell▶** is recommended for picnics.

Drive two miles further, then turn

Griffith Park Observatory

right along Observatory Drive for the observatory.
Griffith Park Observatory▶ ▶ allows the public access to its telescopes on certain nights; daytime views with the naked eye can also be spectacular. Other attractions include laser and star shows, and simulated space trips.

Descend from the observatory and turn right onto Western Canyon Road, continuing for a mile.
Pass the **Bird Sanctuary▶** on the left and the Greek Theater on the right.

At Vermont Avenue, turn left into Commonwealth Canyon Road and then follow Vista Del Valle for six miles, turning left into Griffith Park Drive and then right into Zoo Drive for the Autry Western Heritage Museum.
The **Autry Western Heritage Museum▶ ▶ ▶** earns its spurs by cogently portraying the settlement of the western United States. Close by, the **LA Zoo▶** is another busy attraction.

Drive back along Zoo Drive and head west along Forest Lawn Drive, leaving the park and crossing over the Hollywood Freeway to Mulholland Drive and Laurel Canyon Boulevard (see page 129).

It has been an open-air market and the site of horse- and camel-races. Its majestic LA Memorial Coliseum stadium was the site of the Olympic Games in 1932 and 1984. Now Exposition Park is best known for its museums and proximity to the USC campus.

Second in size only to the Smithsonian Institution in Washington, DC, the **California Museum of Science and Industry** grapples with the fundamentals of physics and chemistry with hands-on and interactive exhibits that can provide hours of fun for avid button-pressers of all ages.

The museum's Ahmanson Building houses several major large-scale working models, most impressively an almost too-realistic simulation of a major earthquake; if the shaking sets your pulse racing, give yourself a quick medical check-up in the Hall of Health.

A must for aviation and space fanatics, the **Aerospace Museum** is nonetheless an anticlimatic collection, mostly of intricate models of planes, satellites and space capsules suspended from the ceiling.

The echoing halls and galleries of the Spanish Renaissance-style **Natural History Museum** reveal a substantial collection of pre-Columbian artefacts, a multitude of fossils and the inevitable reconstructed dinosaur skeletons.

There is no excuse for not using the museum's California history collections to complete your understanding of the state's development. There are detailed

THE USC CAMPUS
The University of Southern California (USC) campus, which borders Exposition Park, will consume any time you have left after visiting the museums. The oldest building here (Widney Hall) dates from the 1880s; do not be misled by the cloistered courtyard and leering gargoyles of the Mudd Hall of Philosophy; they are intended to evoke a sense of medieval European academia.

127

Note, too, the George Lucas Film School, named after just one of its blockbuster director graduates – Steven Spielberg is another.

rundowns on indigenous Californians, the first European settlers, and the 1850s Gold Rush. The rapid growth of Los Angeles is chronicled, too, and its place as the first city built for the automobile is acknowledged with an exhibit of unusual old cars.

Finally, take a slow walk through the Hall of Minerals, which features some very, very precious stones, or visit the gardens, which have 150 different varieties of roses.

Built in 1921 and hosting the Olympic Games in 1932 and 1984, the LA Memorial Coliseum seats 91,000

Greta Garbo is just one of the celebrities remembered by Hollywood's Walk of Fame

DAY OF THE LOCUST
Given the number of accomplished novelists from all over the world who have arrived in Hollywood to try their hand at screenwriting, it is perhaps surprising that few have written about Hollywood itself as well as or as caustically as Nathaniel West, whose 1935 *The Day of the Locust* remains the classic satire of Hollywood in the boom years. Interestingly, the run-down rooming house in which West lived at the time of writing still stands, as shabbily as ever in the centre of Hollywood, at 1817 N Ivar Street.

▶▶▶ Hollywood   116B3

LA without Hollywood is impossible to imagine. For eight decades it has been the scene of the city's most public triumphs, disasters, scandals, and decadent extravagances – in short, it is everything that the city is famous for.

The beginning Hollywood as the world knows it began in the 1910s when a bunch of hard-up but ambitious film-makers came west in search of a warm climate, free natural backdrops, and an escape from the patent laws hindering their activity on the East Coast.

Within a decade, Hollywood seethed with directors, stars, would-be stars and opportunists, and all of Los Angeles became indelibly marked by the film industry as the unsophisticated early days grew into the prosperous decades of the 1940s and 1950s.

Seedy streets All but one of the major studios have moved out, so to today's Angelenos, Hollywood does not mean movies but seedy, low-rent neighbourhoods and streets that are best avoided after dark.

Hollywood's boundaries are hard to define but you will know you have arrived when the **Walk of Fame▶** appears beneath your feet: nearly 2,000 star-shaped brass plaques embedded in the Hollywood Boulevard sidewalk, each embossed with the name of an entertainment industry notable who did not mind paying $3,500 for the privilege.

Opened by Sid Grauman in 1927, **Mann's Chinese Theater▶▶** (6925 Hollywood Boulevard) draws 2 million gaping visitors a year, not for the intricacies of its mock-oriental architecture but for the hand- and footprints of screen idols who literally made their marks here when they were arriving for celebrity-packed movie premieres during the glory years. Some of them improvised: look for Betty Grable's leg-print, and the hoof-print of Gene Autry's horse.

Five years earlier, Grauman had celebrated the discovery of King Tut's tomb by erecting the **Egyptian Theater▶** (6704 Hollywood Boulevard), a plaster replica of the Temple of Thebes, now undergoing restoration and in its time among Hollywood's kitschiest excesses.

The **Hollywood Entertainment Museum** (7021 Hollywood Boulevard) reveals the flight deck from *Star Trek* and the bar from *Cheers* on its behind-the-scenes guided tours, and less impressively demonstrates editing techniques and outlines Hollywood's history.

Famous foundations As Max Factor supplied the make-up, Frederick's of Hollywood (6608 Hollywood Boulevard) supplied the high-fashion bras and corsets that held the famous flesh in place – numerous celebrity-donated examples are displayed in the store's Lingerie Museum.

The **Hollywood Wax Museum▶** (6767 Hollywood Boulevard) is popular but predictable; a better place to visit is the **Hollywood Studio Museum▶▶** (2100 N Highland Avenue), inside the barn where Cecil B De Mille directed *The Squaw Man*, Hollywood's first feature film, in 1913.

Just across Highland Avenue, the **Hollywood Bowl**, summer base of the LA Philharmonic, has staged music under the stars since the 1920s. The Bowl's acoustics were greatly improved by the so-called 'Shells', designed by the influential architect Frank Lloyd Wright and completed in 1928.

With $27,000 donated by local residents, the much decayed Hollywood sign was restored to its former glory in 1978

129

Cowboy lines From the 1910s, scores of would-be screen cowboys lined up at the junction of Sunset Boulevard and Gower Street for bit parts in B westerns – the modern Gower Gulch shopping plaza, thinly disguised as an Old West frontier town, is the only memorial to them. The **Hollywood Athletic Club▶** (6525 Sunset Boulevard) served as a watering hole for the likes of John Wayne and Charlie Chaplin.

The end The shady **Hollywood Memorial Cemetery ▶▶▶** (6000 Santa Monica Boulevard) provides a final resting place for Tyrone Power, Douglas Fairbanks and Rudolph Valentino, among many others. Immediately south is Paramount Studios, the last major film company in Hollywood.

As Sunset Boulevard crosses West Hollywood – packed with hip night spots and fashionable restaurants, and the base of LA's gay community – it briefly becomes the Sunset Strip, where enormous 'vanity boards' tout new films, new records and new faces.

Above Hollywood Laurel Canyon Boulevard and Mulholland Drive twist through the canyons of the Hollywood Hills where, over the years, innumerable stars have bought rambling mansions and gazed down on Los Angeles sprawling beneath their balconies.

It is seldom possible to catch more than passing glimpses or distant views of the most interesting homes (by the roadside, vendors sell photocopied and often out-of-date locator maps for the stars' homes), but among the highlights are Rudolph Valentino's 'Falcon Lair' (1436 Bella Drive), Harold Lloyd's 'Greenacres' (1740 Green Acres Place), and Errol Flynn's 'Mulholland House' (3100 Torreyson Place).

HOLLYWOOD SIGN
Erected in 1923 and illuminated with thousands of flashing light bulbs to advertise land sales in Beachwood Canyon (in the Hollywood Hills), the 50-foot-high Hollywood sign became famous throughout the world as the movie-making area's most enduring marker. Unhappy actress Peg Entwhistle committed suicide by jumping off it in 1932, but the closest anyone can legally get to the sign today is Beachwood Drive, which ends about 100 yards from its base.

Map labels

Long Beach Plaza
Long Beach Mural
4TH STREET
Post Office
3RD STREET
City Hall
LONG BEACH BOULEVARD
AVENUE
3RD STREET
BROADWAY
Public Library
BROADWAY
Civic Center
Lincoln Park
Greyhound Bus Depot
ATLANTIC AVENUE
OCEAN BOULEVARD
PACIFIC
Long Beach Heliport
World Trade Center & Long Beach Area Convention & Visitors Council
Visitors Center
Long Beach Museum of Art
OCEAN BOULEVARD
Pike Amusement
Convention and Entertainment Center
Catalina Cruises Terminal
Wilmore Park
California State University Headquarters
Shoreline Park
SHORELINE DRIVE
HARBOR SCENIC DRIVE
QUEENSWAY BRIDGE
Rainbow Lagoon
Shoreline Village
Long Beach Marina
Grissom Island
Queensway Bay
Helipad
QUEENS HIGHWAY
Harbor Pier
Queen Mary
San Pedro Bay
LONG BEACH
Londontowne

0 250 500 metres
0 250 500 yards

Walk

Long Beach walk

Begin on the Promenade, beside the Long Beach Mural.
Long Beach is now California's fifth-largest city. It grew rapidly in the 19th century as its popularity as a resort increased. Boat cruises to Catalina Island depart from the end of Golden Shore Boulevard and from Pier J (see later in this walk).

Funded by the Depression-era Federal Arts Project, the **Long Beach Mural▶** depicts 1930s Long Beach.

Walk south to Shoreline Park and turn left for Shoreline Village (on
Shoreline Village Drive).
With souvenir shops, specialty stores and lively restaurants, **Shoreline Village▶** stretches along the waterfront. There is a restored carousel and, from time to time, live entertainment on the boardwalk.

Walk through Shoreline Park and cross the Queensway Bridge, turning left along Queens Highway to Pier J.
This is where the **Queen Mary▶ ▶**, the last word in ocean-going luxury in the 1930s, is berthed. For a fee, the stately old liner can be boarded and its many restored staterooms and guest rooms – from the glamorous first-class compartments to the cramped third-class cabins – viewed, as can the crew's quarters and the engine rooms.

Return to the Promenade.

▶▶▶ Santa Monica   116A3

Groomed as a beachside resort beginning in 1875, Santa Monica enjoys cleaner air and cooler temperatures than the rest of LA and is the stamping ground of unconventional writers, artists and left-wing politicians. Santa Monica's pride and joy, however, despite pollution problems, is a white-sand beach wide enough to accommodate thousands of cyclists, joggers, sunbathers and swimmers. The wooden **Santa Monica Pier▶▶** has been around almost as long as the town, and displays a collection of fading monochrome snapshots from its youth. Along the pier are snack stands and a 70-year-old carousel – you may have seen it alongside Paul Newman in *The Sting* – that still gives inexpensive rides.

Away from the beach, the **Third Street Promenade ▶▶▶** attracts a daily procession of street musicians and artists, and has trendy sidewalk cafés. At the southern end of the promenade, **Santa Monica Place** is among the best shopping malls in LA for people-watching, and was designed by the archly individualist architect Frank Gehry, whose own distinctive former home stands at 1002 22nd Street.

Santa Monica's social profile rose greatly through the 1990s, when several luxury hotels were built beside the beach and their restaurants and public areas quickly drew the attention of LA and international celebrities. Another impressive development was the transformation of industrial warehouses into the collection of art galleries that make up **Bergamot Station**, 2525 Michigan Avenue, also the site of the **Santa Monica Museum of Art** with exhibitions focusing on modern and contemporary work from around the world.

Elsewhere, the **California Heritage Museum**, 2612 Main Street, fills an 1894 Queen Anne house with period rooms, while the **Museum of Flying**, 2772 Donald Douglas Loop N, explores aviation past and present with interactive displays.

MURALS
Murals are a distinctive feature of the cityscape in Santa Monica and Venice. Along Ocean Park Boulevard in Santa Monica are the *Whale Mural* and the 600-foot-long *Unbridled*, depicting horses escaping from the carousel. In Venice, look along Windward Avenue: inside the post office there is a large trompe l'oeil and, on the corner of Ocean Walk, the *Rebirth of Venus*, a witty parody of Botticelli.

VENICE
The name is all that remains from a doomed turn-of-the-century attempt to reclaim marshland and re-create the canals of the Italian city. These canals were soon turned into streets. The beachside boardwalk is now a menagerie of fire-eaters, tap-dancers, fortune-tellers, skateboarders and rollerbladers while musclemen pump iron in the open-air gym on Muscle Beach.

131

Santa Monica at night

These days it is not would-be film idols who walk the streets of Hollywood but would-be musicians, singers and song writers, all clutching demo tapes and hoping for at least a few minutes of fame.

LICENCE TO SERENADE
In 1838 a law was passed in Los Angeles banning the serenading of women without a licence.

Mike Love of the Beach Boys, whose music epitomised for many people around the world the California of sun, sea and surf

Home of La Bamba The base of several major record companies, LA is a magnet for aspiring rock musicians from all over the United States. Every night, hundreds of venues pulsate to the latest bands, and the city's place in rock history is only slightly less formidable than its role in the rise of the movies.

The first native Angeleno to make it big was Richie Valens (Richard Valenzuela), a 17-year-old Hispanic boy from East LA whose 'La Bamba' topped the charts in 1958 (and who, tragically, died a year later in a plane crash).

Surfin' Safari Predictably, it was not Valens's impoverished East LA but the coastal communities' idyllic surfing and hot-rodding lifestyles eulogised beginning in the early 1960s by The Beach Boys, Jan & Dean and their imitators, that gave the record-buying public a lingering image of LA.

Love and peace in the hills Later, while San Francisco was the undisputed world capital of flower-power, many of the psychedelic era's most influential bands were based in LA.

One was Buffalo Springfield (whose artists included future solo stars Neil Young and Stephen Stills); its 1967 debut single 'For What It's Worth' was a response to the 'Sunset Strip riot', when baton-wielding police attempted to move the hippies – hundreds of whom were arriving in the city – intent on taking over the Sunset Strip, then a collection of up market supper clubs.

Other seminal LA groups included Iron Butterfly and Love, but it was The Doors who garnered the most vociferous response, thanks in no small part to their iconoclastic lead singer, Jim Morrison, whose lyrics were considered poetry and whose drinking exploits around the LA bars became legendary.

As the hippies flooded Sunset Strip, the musicians retreated to Topanga Canyon, a patch of wild country in the hills just a few minutes' drive from the city's clubs and studios. The canyon saw many night-long parties and star-studded jam sessions, and one resident band, The Byrds, used the stables at the head of the canyon's horse trails on the cover of their 'Notorious Byrd Brothers' album.

LA lays back By the early 1970s, the idealism had waned and the profit-motivated music industry had, after earlier doubts, decided there was a fortune to be made from the embryonic rock culture.

The showcase clubs of the city became dominated by record-company-approved acts, and the easy-listening

rock of commercially mega-successful bands such as The Eagles and Fleetwood Mac, and singer-songwriters such as Jackson Browne, became the standard bearers of a cosy and complacent LA rock scene.

A new order With many of the most creative names of the 1960s gaining weight and drug habits in the Hollywood Hills, and music business executives too worried about losing their privileged positions to take risks, an artistic void had opened up by the mid-1970s, into which stepped the first LA punk bands – among them The Zeroes, The Plugz, The Dils, and X. In a city where façade usually counted for more than content, it was little surprise that the 1980s were dominated by the rise of glam-metal and the emergence of make-up wearing ear-crunchers such as Poison and Mötley Crüe.

A bit of everything The biggest 1980s success story, however, was the hard-rocking Guns 'n' Roses, carrying the rock-star-as-outlaw myth as far as it would go and becoming the role model for thousands of bandana-wearing hopefuls. Meanwhile, Los Lobos grew out of the bars of East LA and found an international audience appreciative of their mixing of corridos (Mexican folk songs) and rock-and-roll. As of the late 1990s the strongest sounds have been emerging from the ghettos of South Central LA, which have spawned globally acclaimed rap acts such as Ice-T and NWA. At the same time, LA has reflected the globalisation of music and its mixing of past and present with a scene diverse enough to include singer-songwriter Sheryl Crow and swing band revivals.

The Doors' singer Jim Morrison and keyboardist Ray Manzarek peer from the Downtown hotel, that gave the band's fifth album its title

LA JAZZ
Through the 1930s and 1940s, the predominantly African-American area of South Central LA was among the country's hottest jazz spots, with the likes of Dexter Gordon, Eric Dolphy, and Charles Mingus regularly appearing in various groups. Meanwhile, band leaders Stan Kenton and Gerry Mulligan, and trumpeter Chet Baker, were among the LA jazzsters credited with pioneering the laid-back style dubbed 'California cool'.

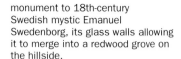

Drive

Coastal route from Marina del Rey to San Pedro

See map on page 135.

Begin at Fisherman's Village in Marina del Rey.
Owners and crews of the private yachts berthed in **Marina del Rey▶** fill the pricey seafood restaurants of **Fisherman's Village▶**, facing the world's largest artificial harbour.

Drive the quarter-mile from Fisherman's Village to Vista del Mar and turn left, continuing south to Manhattan Beach.
Nets on the sands signify **Manhattan Beach's▶▶** place as the home of beach volleyball, a strenuous sport whose professional participants can often be seen honing their skills here.

Drive south along Highland Avenue to Hermosa Beach, turn left into Pier Avenue.
The quintessential, quiet LA coastal community of **Hermosa Beach▶** honoured a local surfer of the 1960s with a statue at the end of Pier Avenue.

Continue south along Highland Avenue to Redondo Beach.
Redondo Beach, Fisherman's Wharf▶ holds souvenir shops, eateries, and stalls selling fresh seafood. Adjacent, the white-sand **Redondo State Beach▶** is popular with surfers.

Continue south, turn right along Palos Verdes Drive West, rounding the Palos Verdes peninsula.
Rising above the ocean, the tree-covered **Palos Verdes peninsula▶▶** has numerous secluded beaches, often reached only by steep footpaths down the cliff face.
Continue on Palos Verdes Drive South.
On the left, Frank Lloyd Wright's 1946 **Wayfarer's Chapel▶▶▶** is a monument to 18th-century Swedish mystic Emanuel Swedenborg, its glass walls allowing it to merge into a redwood grove on the hillside.

Continue to the end of Palos Verdes Drive South, turn right into Paseo Del Mar for Point Fermin Park.
A launch point for hang gliders, **Point Fermin Park▶** also has a 19th-century lighthouse.

Drive to the end of Paseo Del Mar and turn right along Stephen Wright Drive for the Cabrillo Marine Museum.
Well-stocked aquariums, large collections of shells and informative displays on marine ecology fill the **Cabrillo Marine Museum▶▶** (*Open*: Tuesday to Friday, noon–5; weekends, 10–5).

❏ Santa Monica's pier is easily the best of the bunch that exist along this section of LA's coast, a classic seaside addition dating from 1909. Farther south, Manhattan Beach's barren strip of concrete deserves an award for dullness; Hermosa Beach's pier draws the thickest concentration of patient anglers; while the Redondo Sportfishing pier is the departure point for fishermen with a more substantial catch in mind. The quaintest pier in the LA area, however, belongs to Avalon on Santa Catalina Island. ❏

Turn left into Pacific Avenue and enter San Pedro.
Originally a small fishing community, San Pedro quickly grew as the Port of Los Angeles was developed. Much of the seafaring flavour of bygone times remains strong around the short streets of **Old San Pedro▶**, and the **Los Angeles Maritime Museum▶** documents the growth of the town and the port. Close by, the overrated **Ports O'Call Village▶** has souvenir shops and restaurants.

Los Angeles

SNEAK PREVIEWS
Outside cinemas in
Westwood, and to a
lesser extent in other
parts of LA, you may be
offered free tickets to a
sneak preview of a new
movie or unfinished film,
screened to gauge
audience reactions before
final cuts are made.
These are offered only to
people who appear to be
members of the social
group expected to be
interested in the film.
After viewing, you will be
given a questionnaire to
fill out, which is used to
help plan the marketing of
the movie.

▶▶ **Westwood** *116A3*

Planned as a Mediterranean-style shopping village in the
1920s, Westwood is a network of narrow streets laden
with book, T-shirt and souvenir stores, and a variety
of informal restaurants catering to the crowds who flock
to the neighbourhood's first-run cinemas, eager to see
films still fresh from the studios' editing suites (see
panel, left). Marilyn Monroe is buried in Westwood
Memorial Park.

Westwood is one of the few places in LA intended for
walking, although it is also favoured by adolescents
(many from the adjoining UCLA campus) for bumper-
to-bumper car cruising; the evening traffic can be
intense, although a free minibus eases some of the strain.

A recent addition to Westwood is the **Armand Hammer
Museum of Art and Culture Center**▶▶▶, displaying
the ample fruits of 50 years of collecting by the
extremely rich oil magnate. The main gallery reads like a
Who's Who of European fine art – and includes an
outstanding set of lithographs by 19th-century caric-
aturist Honoré Daumier, while a separate gallery is
devoted entirely to the Codex Hammer, pages from the
notebooks of 15th-century genius Leonardo da Vinci. In
keeping with the history of the Codex's ownership,
Hammer renamed it after himself.

*Some of the many
cinemas in Westwood*

▶▶ UCLA   *116A3*

The Romanesque brick buildings around the central quadrangle of the University of California at Los Angeles (UCLA) form the heart of the oldest and most respected of LA's academic institutions, founded in 1929. The buildings are full of character and, together with their carefully tended gardens, they provide a welcome break from the corporate towers that fill much of the surrounding area.

There is plenty to see on the campus, but to find your way around it is essential to pick up a free map at one of the entrances.

Stop first at the **Powell Library▶▶**, for its grand staircase and imposing rotunda, and then enjoy the diverse folk art inside the neighbouring **Fowler Museum of Cultural History▶**. Cutting-edge American art is usually on show at the Wright Art Gallery, outside which the five-acre jacaranda-shaded **Franklin D Murphy Sculpture Garden▶** provides surprises of all shapes and sizes – not least works by Rodin and Matisse.

Non-academic Angelenos appreciate UCLA most of all for the Bruins, the university's sports teams whose huge success is recalled by wall-to-wall trophies glinting inside the **Athletic Hall of Fame▶**.

Take a look, too, at the Inverted Fountain, where 10,000 unseen gallons of recycled water re-create the sounds of a mountain stream.

▶ Wilshire Boulevard   *116B3*

Bearing the name of H Gaylord Wilshire, the socialist entrepreneur who, in the 1880s, purchased a row of bean fields and marked out its route, Wilshire Boulevard crosses between Downtown and the coast through 16 miles of ethnic diversity and landmark architecture, and passes by the city's major art collection.

At the turn of the century, the shovel of one-time gold prospector and future multi-millionaire, Edward L Doheny, struck oil and much of Wilshire Boulevard disappeared beneath a forest of oil derricks.

Royce Hall, on the UCLA campus

MUSEUM OF TOLERANCE
Just south of Wilshire Boulevard, the Museum of Tolerance (9786 Pico Boulevard) uses the latest multimedia and interactive technologies to present a thought-provoking and often harrowing examination of bigotry and racism, past and present. The $50 million museum is closely linked to the Simon Wiesenthal Center, known internationally for its human rights work, and its two main exhibits focus on the Holocaust and on prejudice in the US, including an exploration of the events surrounding the 1992 LA riots.

Miracle Mile As it turned out, the oil reserves were soon exhausted and a longer-lasting boom came in the 1920s and 1930s when Wilshire Boulevard acquired the fabulous art-deco department stores of the Miracle Mile – the first department stores in what were then the LA suburbs, and the first step on the way toward the city's decentralisation and dependence on the automobile; uniquely for the period, the stores were designed with their own parking lots.

Officially, the Miracle Mile extends between La Brea and Fairfax avenues, but the finest example of the art deco that dominates it is just east, with the (now closed) **Bullocks Wilshire Department Store►►** (No. 3050). Many of the other structures have aged less gracefully and are now surrounded by busy food shops serving one of the most varied quarters of the city: a melting pot of predominantly Mexican, Filipino and Korean settlers.

A forerunner of the Miracle Mile, the **Ambassador Hotel►** (No. 3400) cost a staggering $5 million and occupied 23 acres when it opened in 1921. Closed in 1989 and facing an uncertain future, the Ambassador's place in LA history is assured: besides the tales of Hollywood celebrities making fools of themselves in its legendary Coconut Grove nightclub, it was here in 1968 that Senator Robert Kennedy was assassinated.

The buildings of the Miracle Mile could hardly have a less architecturally inspiring neighbour than the **Los Angeles County Museum of Art►►►** (No. 5905). Within the vast museum's stern 1960s exterior, however, centuries' worth of European painting and sculpture, influential contemporary American works and countless treasures among the Asiatic collections provide several hours of enjoyable viewing.

Be certain to tour the museum's newest addition, the Japanese Pavilion, whose beautiful Edo-period paintings are greatly enhanced by the luminous qualities of the purpose-built pavilion.

Next door to the Museum of Art, several fiberglass mastodons partially sunk in tar frame the grounds of the **George C Page Museum►►** (No. 5801), which informatively annotates the fossils and reconstructs the skeletons of many of the creatures that came, literally, to a sticky end 2 million years ago in the **La Brea Tar Pits►**. The tar, once used by Native Americans to waterproof their homes, still seeps to the surface of streets in the area.

The **Craft and Folk Art Museum►** (No. 5800) has entertaining small temporary exhibitions of old and new folk art, and in a rough neighbourhood just south of Wilshire Boulevard, the **St Elmo's Village Art Center►** is an off-the-beaten-track art discovery: the community's success in creating and maintaining the mural-enshrouded art centre is celebrated in May with the Festival of the Art of Survival, which gets bigger and better with each passing year.

Community area The Fairfax Avenue section of Wilshire Boulevard passes through one of the United States' largest Jewish communities. Inside the Jewish Community Building (No. 6505), the **Martyr's Memorial and Museum►** of the Holocaust has stark reminders of

138

GARDENS IN THE CITY
Flowers, shrubs and trees fare surprisingly well in this city of freeways and smog in several caringly nurtured gardens. To escape the metropolis, take a picnic lunch to one of the following: the Rose Garden in Exposition Park; the grounds of Greystone Park (905 Loma Drive, Beverly Hills); the gardens of UCLA; the South Coast Botanical Gardens (26300 Crenshaw Boulevard in Rancho Palos Verdes); the Ferndell section of Griffith Park; or the Japanese Garden of the CSULB campus in Long Beach.

MACARTHUR PARK
Because singer Richard Harris had a hit in 1968 with a song named after it, MacArthur Park, bisected by Wilshire Boulevard west of Alvarado Street, enjoys a certain fame. However, few people realise this 32-acre green slab was the city's first public park, created in 1890. Enjoyed mostly by Latino mothers with toddlers by day, the park becomes a domain of drug dealers by night.

139

the horrors of Hitler's concentration camps and emotive paintings by some of those interned in them.

Just south of Wilshire Boulevard, the **Farmer's Market▶** began when a small group of farmers, poverty-stricken by the Depression, were allowed to sell their produce for free from a patch of open ground. Nowadays, it has grown into a curious mix of groaning fruit and vegetable stalls, tacky souvenir shops and food stands offering plenty of cheap, tasty snacks. Around 40,000 people visit Farmer's Market daily, many of them Angelenos enjoying the experience of shopping somewhere other than an air-conditioned mall.

Many prehistoric creatures, such as this mastodon re-created at the George C Page Museum, became trapped in the local tar pits, their remains first discovered in 1906

Bizarre merchandise is the stock-in-trade of shops on the West Hollywood section of Melrose Avenue

MARKETS
Some 30,000 people a day weave around the food stalls of the indoor Grand Central Market (317 S Broadway), where the noise level is not for the nervous. For very early risers (the action is over by 9am), sweet smells and bright colours abound at the Flower Market, between Seventh and Eighth streets.

PRODUCE MARKET
Mountainous piles of fruit and vegetables from the state's farms are unloaded at the Produce Market (on Eighth and Ninth streets near Central Avenue).

Shopping

Consuming passions run high in LA, and shopping is one of the city's favourite pastimes. Several areas, such as Farmer's Market, Fisherman's Wharf, and Ports O'Call Village are noted for their tourist appeal but actually offer little beyond standard souvenirs. However, there are many better and more interesting places – from luxury malls to thrift stores – to pursue the art of acquiring.

Something for everyone Few cities can equal LA's state-of-the-art shopping malls, gigantic air-conditioned shrines to consumerism. Two of the flashiest are The Beverly Center (bordered by Beverly and La Cienega boulevards), packed with stylish, refined shops that attract the affluent of West LA, and the Century City Shopping Center (10250 Santa Monica Boulevard). But the most architecturally imaginative place to shop is the Santa Monica Place (Fourth Street and Broadway) with all the usual retail outlets plus two department stores, spread across three floors and just a short walk from the beach.
Elsewhere, two smaller malls reflect contrasting ethnic groups. Little Tokyo's Japanese Village Plaza Mall (Central Avenue between First and Second streets) has numerous outlets for Japanese goods, food and clothes. Meanwhile, Latino East LA does its shopping at the lively El Mercado market (3425 E First Street).

Upmarket department stores All over the city, there are branches of fine stores such as Nordstrom, Neiman-Marcus, and Saks Fifth Avenue. Beverly Hills' Rodeo Drive and the Rodeo Center (see page 118) are the domain of the ultra-expensive.

Cheap clothing Substantially less expensive good-quality clothing can be found in Downtown's Garment District (centred on Los Angeles Street, between Seventh Street and Washington Boulevard), where a rake through the immense stocks of the Cooper Building (860 Los Angeles Street) will uncover many bargains. A few miles south, another outlet for top-name togs at wholesale prices is the Citadel (5675 E Telegraph Road).
As its name suggests, American Rag (150 S La Brea Avenue) stocks classic lines in American casualwear from the 1930s to the 1990s.

Accessories If money is no object, muster your credit and cruise the well-filled shelves of Hermès (343 N Rodeo Drive) or Luis Vuitton (307 N Rodeo Drive), seeking that perfect wallet, handbag or handmade silk tie. At the other extreme, NaNa (1228 Third Street, Santa Monica) is stuffed with daring hats, bizarre gloves and many other eccentric items.
The remnants of Downtown's once-thriving jewellery district are the best places to seek out wearable gems at the right price: try the St Vincent Jewelry Center (650 S Hill Street) or the International Jewelry Center. Alternatively, head to Santa Monica and investigate the wares of African Arts ect (1344 Third Street) and Indian Arts (1244 Third Street), featuring jewellery and more from Africa and South America respectively.

For the antique collector Searching for antiques and collectibles in this futuristic city may seem perverse, but the Santa Monica Antiques Market (1607 Lincoln Boulevard) makes for entertaining browsing with over 200 dealers sharing the space. Kitsch Americana fills Off the Wall (7325 Melrose Avenue), while delectable art-deco originals are the stock-in-trade of Thanks for the Memory (8319 Melrose Avenue). Devotees of Hollywood movie nostalgia should find something to tempt them at Chick-a-Boom (6817 Melrose Avenue).

For book lovers Impressively well-filled bookstores are found throughout LA The long-established Larry Edmunds (6658 Hollywood Boulevard) leads the field in movie and theater books and posters, although the Hollywood Book and Poster Company (6349 Hollywood Boulevard) is fast catching up.

For fiction, and everything else, allocate a day for scrutinising the endless shelves of Acres of Books (240 Long Beach Boulevard). Book Soup (8818 Sunset Boulevard) not only has the latest alternative, mainstream and classical fiction, but also attracts prestigious names to its regular author signings and readings, and has a knowledgeable crowd browsing its shelves nightly until midnight. Author readings are also a feature of the left-leaning political bookstore Midnight Special (1318 Third Street, Santa Monica), and the gay and lesbian orientated A Different Light (8858 Santa Monica Boulevard). Hard-to-find art and architecture volumes turn up in Arcana Books on the Arts (1229 Third Street Promenade, Santa Monica).

To turn browsing into meditation, visit the Bodhi Tree Bookstore (8585 Melrose Avenue), packed with New Age, healing, psychology, religious and philosophical titles.

141

A few of the basic essentials of life that are on hand for Beverly Hills shoppers

Food and drink

International flavour Gastronomically speaking, LA is at the crossroads of the world. Coffee shops, delis and burger joints are as common here as anywhere else in the country (if often in unusual forms, such as fancy hot dog stands and 1950s-themed diners), but overall American food is less prevalent than the scores of ethnic cuisines offered at anything from roadside stalls to reservation-only restaurants.

Angelenos and visitors alike enjoy a culinary choice that few cities can beat. What is more, you do not need to be rich to indulge.

Even the famously bizarre concoctions of LA's world-class chefs soon filter down from the temples of fine dining to affordable street-level outlets. Designer pizza, for example, with its exotic toppings, was born in the exclusive Spago's, but is now plied to the masses through the branches of California Pizza Kitchen.

The freshness of the fruit and vegetables raised on the state's farms heightens the flavours of many dishes, and salads are often full meals in themselves, with strawberries, orange sections and grapes alongside the more usual ingredients.

Having the Pacific Ocean for a neighbour keeps the quality high in LA's seafood restaurants which offer abalone, tuna, swordfish, and fist-size shrimps. Innumerable cafés along the coast offer tasty fish snacks as refreshments to accompany a day's tanning.

California cuisine Born from the free-wheeling spirit that characterises the Sunshine State, contemporary California cuisine combines fresh ingredients, bold flavours and culinary creativity to produce an exciting, vibrant style of cooking. Ask your waiter to describe the items on the menu, because, chances are, they will offer a few delicious suprises.

Mexican Most Mexican dishes served in the US are based on variations of the tortilla, a doughy pancake made from cornmeal or wheat, which can be baked or fried and then rolled or folded around food, or laid flat beneath it. Mashed or refried beans, rice, chilis, beef and cheese are the other staple ingredients. Fish tacos and the melted-cheese-filled tortilla called a *quesadilla*, are a couple of the meat-free alternatives.

Bowls of tortilla chips and spicy salsa are laid out as free hors d'oeuvres in Mexican restaurants; tortilla chips with melted cheese, known as nachos, make a good snack.

LA's Mexican menus also include the burrito – a large flour tortilla filled with beef, cheese, chilis and beans – which you will not find at all in Mexico.

Asian Not as cheap as Mexican but enticingly priced restaurants are all over the place; the most interesting are in Little Tokyo, where curry dishes are popular, and steaming sake is always on hand to help down the food.

Chinese food in its various forms comes best, not surprisingly, in the hundreds of restaurants filling Chinatown, and Korean cuisine is making steady headway from its Koreatown base.

MEAL COSTS
On average, you should budget for about $6 to $8 for breakfast in Los Angeles; $8 to $12 for lunch; and around $15 to $25 for dinner. Some establishments serve enormous helpings at mealtimes.

Italian food is not hard to come by in LA

European and North African The many sailors who have settled in San Pedro give rise to a globe-spanning group of eateries, including Greek, Moroccan and Eastern European, all of which can be found in the small harbourside town. Taken together, they're an easy way to learn about Mediterranean cuisine.

Italian Italian cooking is hard to miss. Pasta and pizza stops are everywhere, and in the classier places, top Italian chefs are inspired by the similarities in climate and natural produce between their homeland and southern California.

Drinks These are dispensed as eagerly as food. You may need to request a glass of ice water in these conservation-minded times, but rare is the coffee shop or diner that does not keep your coffee cup – choose between regular and decaf – filled to the brim. Ice tea is common and is the ideal coolant on a hot day; refills are usually free.

Most restaurants are fully licensed and some are regarded as places to drink as much as places to eat. Several Mexican eateries are better known for the strength of their margaritas – often available in fruit-flavoured forms besides the 'original' mix of tequila, Triple Sec and lime juice, with optional salt around the glass – than for the quality of their food.

Listings of recommended LA restaurants begin on page 272 of the Hotels and Restaurants section.

VEGETARIAN FOOD
A city where eating and health are both taken very seriously, it should be no surprise that LA has a generous number of vegetarian and wholefood eateries offering dishes free not only of meat but of almost anything remotely bad for you.

LA's Hard Rock Café, the first in what is now a worldwide chain, had to pay a Downtown diner with the same name for the right to use the title

eddie jacks

LUNCH • DINNER • VALET

1181 FOLSOM STREET (BETWEEN 7TH & 8TH)
SAN FRANCISCO, (415) 626-2388
CLOSED SUNDAYS

Nightlife

You could spend months exploring nocturnal LA and still only scratch the surface. For the latest on what's happening where, the best option is to read the listings in the *LA Weekly* newspaper.

Jazz, rock, and R&B These are the main fare of the city's innumerable live music venues.

The Troubador, 9081 Santa Monica Boulevard (tel: 310/276–6168), made its name as a folk venue and now features rock acts; the Roxy, 9009 Sunset Boulevard (tel: 310/276–2222), has hopeful new bands; and Whisky A Go Go, 8901 Sunset Boulevard (tel: 310/652–6402), is the archetypal long-running LA rock club. More recent, and since the death there of River Phoenix, more notorious, is the Viper Room, 8852 Sunset Boulevard (tel: 310/358–1880), usually with counterculture celebrities in the audience as well as on stage.

Harvelle's Blues Club, 1432 Fourth Street, Santa Monica (tel: 310/395–1675), presents top-rated blues and R&B artists in a replica of a Chicago blues bar; for similar music from local and national names in a mock Deep South setting, pay a visit to B.B. King's Blues Club, 1000 Universal Center Drive (tel: 818/6–BBKING), which really is owned by the legendary blues guitarist, or the House of Blues, 8430 Sunset Boulevard (tel: 213/848–5100).

Noted for their knowledgeable audiences and constantly good shows, the pick of the jazz clubs include: The Baked Potato, 3787 Cahuenga Boulevard (tel: 818/980–1615) and Catalina Bar & Grill, 1640 N Cahuenga Boulevard (tel: 213/466–2210).

Cabaret, comedy and magic These are all in plentiful supply in LA The Comedy Store, 8433 Sunset Boulevard (tel: 213/656–6225), is the main stage for proven comics; the Improvisation, 8162 Melrose Avenue (tel: 213/651–2583), features acts on the rise; the Groundlings Theater, 7307 Melrose Avenue (tel: 213/934–9700), has a well-deserved reputation for the very best improvised sketches. Upfront Comedy, 123 Broadway Avenue, Santa Monica (tel: 310/319–3477) is another likely venue.

Conjuring connoisseurs will love the Magic Castle, 7001 Franklin Avenue (tel: 213/851–3314), a building devoted to trickery where the strange happenings are not limited to the stage. The Castle is for members only, but your hotel receptionist should be able to arrange entry.

Theatre, dancing, and music If you simply want to dance, go to the Crush Bar, 1743 N. Cahuenga Boulevard (tel: 213/463–9017), and join the not-quite-fashionable crowd gyrating 60s-style across two spacious floors; The World, 7070 Hollywood Boulevard (tel: 213/467–7070), has a different musical theme nightly. If you want to be seen with the LA jet-set, try to look fashionable and show up at The Room, 1624 Cahuenga Boulevard (tel: 213/694–1813).

Classical music centres on the Music Center, located on 135 N Grand Avenue, whose Dorothy Chandler Pavilion is the venue for the Los Angeles Master Chorale (tel: 213/626–0624), Los Angeles Opera (tel: 213/972–7219) and Los Angeles Philharmonic (tel: 213/850–2000), which also plays a summer season at the Hollywood Bowl, 2301 N Highland Avenue. Also at the Music Center, the Mark Taper Forum (tel: (213/972–0700) runs contemporary plays, and the Ahmanson Theater (tel: (213/972–7200) hosts Broadway blockbusters. The Shubert Theater, 2020 Avenue of the Stars (tel: 310/201–1500) also mounts touring productions of New York shows.

Scores of smaller theatres are found all over LA and, not surprisingly, given the level of dramatic talent in the city, often feature plays written and acted to exceptionally high levels. Locations and productions change frequently; check the papers for listings and reviews.

Bars There are few of the smoky bars that predominate in many US cities; if you're seeking local colour, try Barney's Beanery, 8447 Santa Monica Boulevard (tel: 213/654–2287), with its pool tables and dozens of imported brews, or Al's Bar, 305 S Hewitt Street (tel: 213/625–9703), supplying beer and arty music to a bohemian crowd.

Hotel choice Among the distinctive hotel bars are the Biltmore Hotel's Gallery Bar, 506 S Grand Avenue (tel: 213/624–1011), with its marble columns and Mies van der Rohe chairs, the revolving Bonavista Lounge of the Westin Bonaventure, 404 S Figueroa Street (tel: 213/624–1000), and the most famous place in Los Angeles for an overpriced tipple, the Polo Lounge of the Beverly Hills Hotel, 9641 Sunset Boulevard (tel: 213/276–2751).

COFFEE BARS
The last few years have seen LA's nightlife enriched by an influx of coffee bars. As their name suggests, such places serve coffee (usually a wide variety, all available with or without caffeine) rather than alcohol, and they range from stylish haunts such as Highland Grounds, 742 N Highland Boulevard, West Hollywood (tel: 213/466–1507), to wackily decorated hangouts of would-be avant-garde writers and poets such as The Kindness of Strangers, 4378 Lankershim Boulevard, Universal City (tel: 818/752–9566).

145

Taking its name from the 'strip' of glamorous nightclubs that lined this mile-long section of Sunset Boulevard from the 1940s, Sunset Strip is still a major nightlife area as well as a prime site for large and colourful billboards, usually advertising new films or record releases

Accommodation

From whirlpool-equipped luxury suites to dependable no-frills motel rooms and budget-priced beds in youth hostel dormitories, there is no shortage of places to stay in LA.

Book in advance Wherever you plan to stay and however much you plan to spend, it is wise to book as far in advance as possible. Many hotels have toll-free 800 phone numbers enabling you to call them free of charge from anywhere within the United States.

If you do not have a reservation, any of the visitor information offices listed on page 149 can help find a place to stay; each has shelves laden with hotel, motel, and hostel brochures, which sometimes offer a few dollars' discount on the regular price.

Getting around LA is nearly impossible without a car, which means location is of less importance when seeking accommodation than ease of access to the city's freeways. If you are not using a car, spread your stay across several areas to avoid long hours riding the LA buses. Location does make a difference to the cost, however, and you should also note that very few parts of LA are safe to walk around in after dark.

The five mirrored cylinders of LA's Bonaventure Hotel became a futuristic addition to the Downtown landscape in 1978

A price to suit every pocket Downtown accommodation spans everything from low-rent flophouses to architecturally inventive hotels for business travellers. Between these extremes, a growing number of hotels ($70 to $90) offer solid value and make a good base for exploring the area – a rare instance of an LA district geared, in daylight, to walking.

Promising Old World elegance in the heart of Beverly Hills, the Beverly Wilshire Hotel has hosted the rich and famous since 1928

Moving west, central Hollywood, holding the main remnants from the movie industry's golden years, has a dozen or so comfortable hotels ($85 to $105) close to Hollywood Boulevard; just south, numerous motels ($70 to $100) of varying quality can be found along Sunset Boulevard.

Standards and prices rise in unison as you continue west into West Hollywood, Beverly Hills, and Westwood. It is here that you will find plush hotels with fitness facilities and rooftop tennis courts intended to help visiting entertainment industry moguls unwind. Prices begin at around $150 and increase swiftly; this is a very refined area in which to stay, and several sections are safe for evening strolling.

At the coast The building of new ocean-view hotels and renovations of older establishments has made Santa Monica one of LA's best areas for quality accom-modation. There are still a few shabby but serviceable motels (upwards of $60) on the periphery, but the town itself boasts stylish mid-range options (around $110) and several full-service resorts (upwards of $150). To the south, through rowdy Venice Beach and on to the quieter communities of Manhattan Beach, Hermosa Beach and Redondo Beach, there is a wide choice of medium-priced hotels and motels ($60 to $90). A good way to save money is to seek out accommodation a few blocks inland where you will often pay $10 or $20 less than at a hotel facing the beach.

Around the Palos Verdes peninsula San Pedro has a good mix of modern chain hotels and trusty motels (from $80 and $50 respectively), as does, to a lesser extent, nearby Long Beach.

Flying in very late or flying out very early are the only reasons to opt for one of the pricey hotels surrounding the airport. Many hotels in other areas provide free airport transportation; even if they do not, airport shuttle buses are plentiful.

Listings of recommended LA accommodation begin on page 271.

YOUTH HOSTELS
Youth hostels are much less expensive than hotels and motels, and there are several in Hollywood, one in San Pedro, and two in Santa Monica; as well as a number of backpacker-patronised hostels in and around Venice Beach, where nightly stays in small dormitories cost from $12 to $18.

BED AND BREAKFAST
Not surprisingly, this sprawling metropolis has no campgrounds within its boundaries, although some of the most atmospheric accommodation is offered by a tiny band of bed-and-breakfasts ($75 to $150) scattered across the city, usually graciously appointed Victorian homes with a limited number of guest rooms. To stay in one of these popular hideaways, you will need either a lot of luck or a six-month advance booking.

Los Angeles

What might look like a futuristic air traffic control centre is actually the Theme Building at LAX, Los Angeles International Airport, mostly visited for its restaurant

Practical points

Arriving by plane All international flights and most domestic flights land at Los Angeles International Airport (LAX, tel: 310/646–5252), 15 miles south-west of Downtown and a mile east of the coast. Some domestic airlines also land at Burbank (tel: 818/840–8840) and Orange County (tel: 714/252–5200) airports: these can be much more convenient than LAX, especially for Disneyland or Burbank.

To get from the airport to other parts of the city, use one of the shuttle buses (there are dozens, run by private firms) that pick up passengers from the airport concourse and deliver them to almost any address in LA The shuttle buses charge according to how far you are going: most fares are between $12 and $20. Local buses (see below) are cheaper, but LA's bus network can be bewildering for first-time arrivals. Taking a taxi from the airport is likely to cost in excess of $30.

Airlines All the major airlines have several offices around LA. Their main phone numbers are: American Airlines (tel: 800/433–7300); British Airways (tel: 800/247–9297); Continental (tel: 800/525–0280); Delta (tel: 213/221–1212); Northwest (tel: 800/225–2525); United (tel: 800/241–6522); Virgin (tel: 800/862–8621).

Arriving by bus or train All long-distance buses into LA stop in Downtown at 1716 E Seventh Street (tel: 213/629–8400); some services also run to Hollywood, 1409 Vine Street (tel: 213/466–6382) and Santa Monica, 1433 Fifth Street (tel: 310/394–5433).

LA's railroad station is Union Station, 800 N Alameda Street in Downtown (tel: 800/872–7245).

Getting around As mentioned earlier, it is easiest to get around LA by car. The bus system, however, is comprehensive, and there are taxi services.

Car hire – If you have arranged car hire ahead of arrival, your car can be picked up at the airport; just look for the appropriate car hire firm's desk. You can also hire on arrival at the airport, or elsewhere in LA, by phoning one of the numerous car-hire firms (whose offices are all over the city) at one of the following numbers: Alamo

SAFETY
Despite the globally publicised riots of 1992, LA is no more dangerous than any other major US city. As elsewhere, it is sufficient to take simple precautions: keep your bags close at hand and difficult to snatch, avoid run-down areas (following advice from your hotel), and keep car doors locked.

(tel: 800/327–9633); Avis (tel: 800/331–1212); Budget (tel: 213/527–0700); or Hertz (tel: 800/654–3131).

Local buses – Contrary to popular belief, LA has the largest bus service in the country. Given the sheer size of the city, however, getting from place to place by bus can be extremely time-consuming.

Most services are run by the MTA (for information, tel: 800 COMMUTE) and have a flat single-journey fare, payable with exact change when boarding.

Buses run every 10 minutes (less frequently at night) along the main streets linking Downtown and the coast, passing through Hollywood and Beverly Hills before reaching Santa Monica or Venice. Useful routes are 1 (along Hollywood Boulevard); 2 (along Sunset Boulevard); 4 (along Santa Monica Boulevard); 11 (along Melrose Avenue); and 20, 21 and 22 (along Wilshire Boulevard).

Taxis – LA's taxis charge a fee at the flag (that is, when your trip commences) and then a further fixed charge per mile. They need to be phoned for rather than hailed from the curb: Checker Cab (tel: 213/221–2355) and LA Taxi (tel: 310/715–1968) are two major firms; others are listed in the phone book.

Useful phone numbers

Dentist referral service (tel: 310/620–1728)
In-Hotel Medical Care (tel: 800/362–2791)
Emergency services 911
Time (tel: 213/853–1212)
Traveller's Info Line (tel: 213/686–0950)
Weather (tel: 213/554–1212).

Visitor information The biggest source of tourist information in the city is the Visitor Information Center, 685 S Figueroa Street, Downtown (tel: 800 CATCH–LA).

Smaller but equally useful offices in other areas include Beverly Hills Visitors Bureau, 239 S Beverly Drive, Beverly Hills (tel: 310/271–8174); the Janes House, 6541 Hollywood Boulevard, Hollywood (tel: 213/236–2331); Santa Monica Convention & Visitors Bureau, 520 Broadway, Santa Monica (tel: 310/319–6263); Long Beach Visitor and Convention Council, 1 World Trade Center, Suite 300, Long Beach (tel: 310/436–3645); and San Pedro Peninsula Chamber of Commerce, 390 W Seventh Street, San Pedro (tel: 310/832–7272).

THE LA SUBWAY

After years of planning and the spending of many millions of dollars, Los Angeles set about reducing its dependency on the car by opening the first section of the Metro Rail subway system in 1990. The still-growing network of colour-coded lines link Downtown and Longbeach (Blue Line), Downtown and Redondo Beach via LAX (Green Line), while work continues on the Red Line, which will eventually connect Downtown, Hollywood and the San Fernando Valley.

149

Among many taxi companies, LA has its share of Yellow Cabs. Their colour was chosen after a report suggested that yellow was the colour most easily spotted on the street

Map legend / labels:

Six Flags Magic Mountain, Valencia, Mt Gleason 1991m, Santa Susana Mts, Veterans Memorial Park, Strawberry Peak 1879m, San Gabriel Wilderness, Mt Baden-Powell 2865m, Mt San Antonio (Old Baldy Peak) 3068m, San Fernando Mission, San Fernando, Angeles National Forest, Calif St Univ Northridge, Burbank, La Crescenta, Mt Wilson Observatory, San Gabriel Peak 1879m, San Gabriel Res, Claremont, Motion Picture Country House & Hospital, Canoga Park, Los Encinos SHP, Descanso Gardens, Forest Lawn, Glendale, Altadena, Monrovia, Duarte, Pasadena, Arcadia, Glendora, Santa Monica Mts, Nat Rec Area, Getty Center, J Paul Getty Museum, Beverly Hills, Huntington Art Gallery & Library, Southwest Museum, Arboretum, Covina, Bonelli Reg Park, Upland, Malibu, UCLA, West Hollywood, Alhambra, Mission San Gabriel Arcangel, Will Rogers SHP, Malibu Lagoon State Beach, Santa Monica, Culver City, Exposition Park, LOS ANGELES, East Los Angeles, La Puente, Romona, Chino, Marina del Rey, Inglewood, Montebello, Pico Rivera, Whittier, San Juan Hill 543m, Los Angeles International Airport, Lynwood, Bell Gardens, La Habra, Chino Hills SP, Santa, Hawthorne, Compton, Norwalk, La Mirada, Calif St Univ Fullerton, Yorba Linda, Monica, Manhattan Beach, Gardena, Movieland Wax Museum, Bay, Redondo Beach, Carson, Lakewood, Knott's Berry Farm, Anaheim, Cleveland National Forest, Palos Verdes Estates, Torrance, Disneyland, Anaheim Stadium, Orange, Lunada Bay, South Coast Botanic Gardens, Long Beach, Rancho Los Alamitos, Westminster, Garden Grove, Bowers Museum, Tustin, Pt Vicente, Rancho Palos Verdes, San Pedro, San Pedro Bay, Seal Beach, Santa Ana, Pt Fermin, Bolsa Chica St Beach, Sunset Beach, Movieland of the Air, Huntington Beach, Irvine, Lion Country Safari, El Toro, Newport Beach, Balboa, Corona del Mar State Beach, Crystal Cove SP, Laguna Beach, San Juan Capistrano, Mission, San Pedro Channel, West End, Santa Catalina Island, Dana Point, Doheny State Beach, Outer Santa Barbara Channel, Mt Orizaba 648m, Avalon, Seal Rocks

AROUND LOS ANGELES

| 0 | 10 | 20 | 30 km |
| 0 | 5 | 10 | 15 miles |

150

The beauty of Malibu: a beach nearby, on the Pacific Coast Highway

FRANTIC GROWTH During the last fifty years Los Angeles has spread across hills, through valleys and along the coast, absorbing entire communities and turning former farmland into a uniform suburbia stretching as far as the eye can see.

But there are a few stops of note for visitors. Several older towns have retained their character in this commuter-dominated territory, and it is also around LA that some of the state's very best art collections are stashed. Here, too, Disneyland blazed a trail for theme parks throughout the world, and the coastline spans everything from broad sandy beaches to towering rocky bluffs.

Beside the ocean just north of LA, Malibu draws visitors in search of California's rich and beautiful people. Much more apparent, however, are the surfer-dominated sands and, just inland, rugged canyons that shelter secluded hamlets and provide boundless scope for wilderness hiking.

To the south, the Orange County shoreline is sculpted into numerous coves and inlets, along which several distinctive and personable communities stand in marked contrast to inland Orange County, a network of middle-class suburbs (among the most affluent and conservative places to live in the US) pockmarked by theme parks – most famously Disneyland – the only reason for most people to penetrate the area's blandness.

Beyond the hills on LA's northern edge, an immense population fills the flat floors of the San Gabriel and San Fernando valleys. The luckiest of the valley dwellers are those who live in long-established settlements such as Pasadena – with a clutch of museums and a pleasingly restored downtown area, the only valley town worth spending time in, and a useful base for exploring several historic sites scattered through the valleys.

Around Los Angeles

The seemingly ramshackle nature of these beachside homes in Malibu belies the fact that some of their owners are extremely wealthy and some are household names. With hills so close to the beach, many Malibu homes are damaged each year by the landslides that follow heavy rains, a feature of the LA winter

▶▶▶ **Malibu** 150A3

Many of LA's – and the world's – richest and most glamorous people own million-dollar homes in Malibu, immediately north of Santa Monica. However, it is the dramatic Malibu hills, twisting canyons and inviting beaches that impress.

A century ago, a well-off settler called Frederick H. Rindge bought the Mexican rancho which, at that time, covered Malibu. As LA expanded, Rindge (and later, after his death, his widow, Mary) fought tooth and nail against state plans to put a road through their land, only to be defeated in the Supreme Court and subsequently to see their fortune vanish in the Wall Street Crash.

The Malibu Beach Colony From the 1920s, a secluded beachside enclave of Hollywood notables, which included Clara Bow, Barbara Stanwyck and Gloria Swanson, began turning Malibu into a desirable address. Even today, Malibu's rock stars, TV personalities and sports stars carefully (if illegally) prevent public access to the beaches close to their homes.

Approaching Malibu from the south brings you first through Pacific Palisades, where the **Will Rogers State Park**▶▶ holds the former home of the 'Cowboy Philosopher', whose homespun wisdom and one-line witticisms kept Americans amused through the 1920s and 1930s. Old-West artefacts are piled high inside the humorist's former home, and the 187-acre grounds include numerous picnic spots, walking and hiking trails, and a still-used polo field where Rogers indulged in his favourite pastime.

A mile to the north, the **Self-Realisation Fellowship**▶, founded in 1950, seeks to express the universality of the world's major religions. Arranged around a swan-filled lake, the fellowship evokes a suitable mood of serenity and contemplation, and a replica Dutch windmill conceals a small, atmospheric chapel.

Health and nature In the psychedelic 1960s, a hippie colony arrived in **Topanga Canyon** and established a base for alternative lifestyles and exploring the inner self. In the 1990s, most people come for the untamed natural beauty, but there is still a strong sense of the

THE GRUNION RUN
Between March and August on nights following high tides, small fish called grunion come ashore for a frantic three-hour bout of spawning and egg-burying known as the Grunion Run. Seeing the beach crawling with thousands of these squirming fish, the only kind to lay their eggs on land, is an amazing sight that pulls big crowds. Any beach in the LA area is a likely vantage point for this only-in-California phenomenon.

1960s and the 1980s New Age movement, most evident in the health food restaurants, handicraft shops and bookstores.

A network of hiking trails weaves across the chaparral-covered slopes of the 9,000-acre **Topanga State Park▶ ▶**, emerging to breathtaking views of ocean, mountains and sprawling LA.

Similar terrain fills **Malibu Creek State Park▶**, a few miles north, once used by 20th-Century Fox as the setting of *M*A*S*H*, among many film and TV productions, and where wildflowers brighten the spring meadows.

The town of Malibu is surprisingly nondescript, and it has been the local beaches that have pulled the crowds since Surfrider Beach provided the setting for the low-budget beach party movies of the late 1950s.

Surfrider Beach, now renamed Malibu Lagoon State Beach, has been overlooked for almost a century by the 700-foot **Malibu Pier▶**. Besides making a prime vantage point for watching the surfers, the pier (built by Frederick Rindge to unload supply ships) also marks the site of the **Adamson House▶ ▶**, built in 1929 and inhabited by a member of the Rindge family until 1964. Touring the house – whose Spanish colonial design is enhanced by the colourful ceramics known as 'Malibu tiles', hand-carved teakwood doors and a fine assortment of decorative ironwork and murals – and the adjoining museum gives an intriguing peep into Malibu's past.

Las Tunas and Corral beaches are noted for their scuba diving, Paradise Cove is ideal for beachcombing, the picnic tables and snack stands of Zuma Beach attract thousands of San Fernando Valley dwellers every weekend, and **Leo Carrillo State Beach▶** (which takes its name from the actor who played Pancho in the *Cisco Kid* TV series) is split in two by Sequit Point, a bluff through which wave action has gouged a large tunnel.

UNDERWATER ADVENTURE
Surfing, swimming and sunbathing are not the only activities enjoyed along the LA area's coastline. From Malibu in the north to San Clemente in the south, there are ample opportunities for snorkelling and scuba diving. Explorable underwater caves are plentiful, rich kelp beds attract shoals of brightly coloured fish, and the deep water on the ocean side of Santa Catalina (see page 162) has several submerged wrecks. Equipment rental outlets are easy to find anywhere where conditions are suitable.

153

Many beaches around LA have ideal surfing conditions

Three exceptional but very different art museums lie within the Los Angeles area. One of them, the Getty Center, should be seen for its setting alone: high above West LA, occupying what is said to be the most expensive building ever built in the United States. The Norton Simon and the Huntingdon also hold important collections.

154

The impressive purpose-built Getty Center houses an incredible display of art and antiquities from all round the world

Building for beauty Designed by architect Richard Meier at a cost of a billion dollars, the Getty Center sits with considerable aplomb in a magnificent hillside site. Opened in December 1997, the centre is the latest and grandest addition to the Getty holdings. These began with the Greek and Roman antiquities, French furnishings and European paintings collected by the immensely rich oil tycoon John Paul Getty and first publicly displayed in 1974 in a re-creation of a Pompeiian villa (see panel), and continued after the man's death with a $700 million endowment that made this art museum the richest in the world.

Only a part of the Getty Center is a museum: sharing the site are the offices of the Getty research, conservation and education institutes, all as well financed as the museum itself.

Almost inevitably, the building – arranged in a series of pavilions linked by plazas and terraces that provide stunning panoramas across LA – completely steals attention from the art exhibited inside.

THE GETTY VILLA
In a hilltop location in Malibu overlooking the ocean, the Getty Villa, formerly the site of the Getty collections, is a replica of the Villa del Papiri, an Italian villa destroyed by the eruption of Vesuvius in AD 79. Currently being remodelled, the villa will reopen in 2001 as the home of Getty's Greek and Roman antiquities and as a research centre for studies in comparative cultures and archaeology.

The exhibits Appreciating the collections, chiefly European art from the Renaissance to the Post-Impressionists, is aided by the excellent Art Information Rooms, with books and interactive multimedia screens enabling visitors to discover more about the art and artists whose work is displayed. Temporary exhibitions are of exceptional standard, and among the highlights of the permanent display are paintings such as Van Gogh's *Irises* and Monet's haystack series, the Drawings Collection with works from 1400 onward, and the many masterpieces of medieval artwork in the Illuminated Manuscripts Collection.

The Norton Simon Museum It may be less famous and much less rich, but the quality of the paintings within the Norton Simon Museum in Pasadena surpasses those of the Getty. Here, Rubens, Rembrandt, Raphael and Brueghel delight among the Old Masters; Cézanne, Renoir and Van Gogh shine out in well-filled Impressionist and Post-Impressionist galleries; a Degas collection includes a set of small, sculpted dancers; and the 20th-century collection features works by Picasso, Matisse and the German Expressionists.

The European displays are matched by the museum's stunning Asian collections, spanning 2,000 years of North Indian Buddhist art and Hindu sculpture, and South Indian, Himalayan and Southeast Asian art.

The Huntington Art Collections Just a few miles east of the Norton, the Huntington Art Collections house an extraordinary stock of English 18th-century portraiture and 19th-century landscapes.

In the former home of railroad tycoon Henry E Huntington, who instigated LA's first (and last) efficient mass transit system during the early 1900s, the ornately furnished gallery rooms hold works by Hogarth, Turner and Constable, and lead to the prized exhibits: Gainsborough's *Blue Boy*, Sir Thomas Lawrence's *Pinkie*, and Reynolds' *Mrs Siddons as the Tragic Muse*.

Other sections of the house contain Renaissance paintings and 18th-century French sculpture, and the adjoining Virginia Steele Scott Gallery shows American art from colonial times to the present, and includes a section on the architectural firm of Greene & Greene.

Rare books and manuscripts Elsewhere on the Huntington estate, 2 million manuscripts and 600,000 rare books are housed in the **Huntington Library** – among them the *Ellesmere Chaucer*, believed to be the most complete and reliable manuscript of the *Canterbury Tales*, and dated to 1410. Other highlights include a *Gutenberg Bible*, one of 12 surviving copies printed on vellum, and Shakespeare's **First Folio**, the first edition of the bard's plays, printed in 1623.

NORTON SIMON
Compared to the flamboyant and controversial J Paul Getty, Norton Simon is a relatively unsung patron of the arts whose personal collection – forming the Norton Simon Museum – was financed by the vast wealth accruing from his large and diverse business empire. Already a long-established collector of European Old Masters, Simon allegedly acquired his taste for art from the subcontinent during a visit to India's National Museum in 1971.

An exhibit at the J Paul Getty Museum

THE HUNTINGTON GARDENS
After filling your head with the Huntington Collection's art and books, unwind with a lengthy stroll through the immaculately groomed Huntington Botanical Gardens.

The northern section of 3-mile-long Balboa Beach, overlooked by luxurious ocean-view homes

THE CRYSTAL CATHEDRAL
Made entirely of glass, save for its white steel trusses and wooden fittings, the multimillion-dollar Crystal Cathedral (12141 Lewis Street, Garden Grove) was built in 1980 at the behest of TV evangelist Robert Schuller. In 1955, Schuller's preaching career began in an abandoned drive-in cinema, later moved to the world's first drive-in church, and now centres on showbiz-style sermons delivered from the Crystal Cathedral's pulpit, which are broadcast live on cable TV.

Orange County

Aside from cutting inland to visit Disneyland and a few other theme parks, the best way to take in Orange County – characterised by plain shopping malls, identical houses and freeway interchanges – is by sticking to its coast.

One place warranting a detour deep in suburbia, however, is the **Richard M Nixon Birthplace and Library**▶▶ at Yorba Linda, which records in a lavish (and entirely uncritical) manner the extraordinary career of the nation's 37th president (who is also buried here).

The first of the coastal towns, **Huntington Beach**▶ has been a surfing hot spot since the 1920s when California's earliest surfing contests were held beside its pier. In the evening, the action moves ashore with dozens of impromptu barbecues held around the beach's firerings. By contrast, well-heeled yacht owners help make neighbouring **Newport Beach**▶ a shrine to moneyed living, with only the three-mile-long **Balboa Peninsula**▶▶ offering any inducement to visitors.

A fine-sand beach lines the peninsula, whose southern end holds the wooden Balboa Pavilion, a ritzy dance hall from 1905 that is now filled with souvenir shops and amusement arcades. Pleasure craft cruise the harbour from the nearby marina, and another short boat trip is the 35¢ ride offered by the Balboa ferry, which has plied the almost jumpable gap between the peninsula and Balboa Isle – an artificial island packed with expensive homes – since 1909.

Away from the beach, local life revolves around the high-fashion clothing stores of the primly landscaped Fashion Island shopping centre, and the **Newport Harbor Art Museum**▶▶, justly acclaimed for its displays of contemporary southern Californian art.

South of Newport Beach, **Crystal Cove State Park**▶ has a refreshingly unkempt and underused beach, while hiking trails through the inland section of the park lead into the San Joaquin Hills, once a grazing place for the cattle of Mission San Juan Capistrano.

Powdery-sand beaches, rocky outcrops and secluded inlets make the **Laguna Beach**▶▶ shoreline the most attractive in Orange County. Such visual appeal has also turned the town into an artists' colony, with a liberal reputation not shared by its Orange County neighbours.

Art galleries and handicraft stalls line Laguna's short streets. Dropping into the **Laguna Beach Museum of Art▶** reveals the best works of the local artists, and during July and August, thousands flock to the Pageant of the Masters arts festival (see page 158). South of Laguna Beach, the dramatic headland of **Dana Point▶** rises high above the ocean. It was named after Richard Henry Dana, who described how cowhides were flung over the cliffs to be loaded onto boats below in *Two Years Before the Mast*, his 1840 classic of pioneer writing.

At the southern tip of Orange County, **San Clemente▶** is a likable if unexciting resort town, with a cliff-walled beach. To Californians, the town is best known as the location of Richard Nixon's 'Western White House', the estate overlooking the ocean where the disgraced ex-president sat out his post-resignation years.

Mission San Juan Capistrano▶▶▶ was completed in 1806; its **Serra Chapel** is believed to be the state's oldest building. A replica of the Great Stone Church, an immense structure with seven domes and a 120-foot high bell tower that stood in the mission until destroyed by an earthquake in 1812, stands to the north along El Camino Real and serves the local Catholic community. Follow El Camino Real south downhill and turn right onto Verdugo Street to see the **Capistrano Depot▶**, still the railway terminal, with Spanish arches and decorative tiles. Nearby, on Los Rios Street, is the **O'Neill Museum▶**, which shows the locations of 19th-century adobe homes in the adjacent **Los Rios Historic District▶**.

SWALLOW SONG
Since Spanish times, swallows have nested at Mission San Juan Capistrano. Legend has it that they return from their winter migration each March 19, St Joseph's Day. In fact, the swallows return throughout the spring. Nonetheless, crowds of visitors arrive on March 19 for the Fiestas de la Golondrinia, a welcome-home carnival that takes place with or without the swallows, and October's Adios de las Golondrinias, a smaller event marking the swallows' winter departure.

157

Mission San Juan Capistrano. Around the courtyard are a small museum and re-created workshops in the style of the Spanish era

158

In the distance, the slopes of the San Gabriel Mountains rise sharply above the tree-lined streets of Pasadena

San Gabriel Valley

In the 1920s, the San Gabriel Valley was a verdant landscape of walnut, orange and lemon groves, dotted with small settlements to which Angelenos repaired to improve their health. Today, the valley communities have blurred into an almighty slab of suburbia and suffer in the summer months from the infamous LA smog, often thick enough to obscure the nearby mountains, and noxious enough to warrant health warnings.

Conditions permitting, the best base for seeing the valley is **Pasadena►►►**, within easy reach of the Gamble House (see page 159), the Norton Simon Museum, and the Huntington Art Collections (see page 155), and a section of Colorado Boulevard that has been transformed into a very attractive 'Old Town'.

A few miles south, the first fixed settlement in the valley grew up around **Mission San Gabriel Arcangel►** (537 West Mission Drive, San Gabriel), founded in 1771. Its citrus groves, livestock and high-yield vineyards made it the most prosperous of the California missions.

Within the five-foot-thick buttressed walls, the mission's original altar remains, and many smaller original items, including some of California's earliest winemaking equipment, are gathered in the museum. Outside, the well-tended gardens invite a stroll.

Reminders of the valley's green past are provided by the **LA Arboretum►** (301 N Baldwin Avenue, Arcadia), filling 127 acres of a former Mexican rancho with an exotic array of over 30,000 plants collected from every continent, and by **Descanso Gardens►** (1481 Descanso Drive, La Canada), with more flowers, and boasts an oriental teahouse dispensing refreshments.

Don't miss the **Southwest Museum►►** (just off the Pasadena Freeway at 234 Museum Drive, Highland Park), the brainchild of Charles Lummis, an early protector of LA's architectural heritage (see pages 122–3). Together with a reconstruction of an 1850s adobe building, typical of Mexican California, it offers a record of American cultures and the museum is the oldest museum in LA, opened in 1907.

Map

```
Rose Bowl          210        PASADENA              SIERRA MADRE BLVD
Stadium
Brookside                  Pacific Asia        FOOTHILL  FREEWAY
Park              Museum
134  VENTURA  Gamble House  City Hall  COLORADO  BLVD    210    Santa Anita
FREEWAY                                                              Park Race
Carmelita Gdns   Civic Auditorium  EAST                L A State    Track
& Norton         Kidspace       PASADENA              & County    Arcadia
Simon Art Mus                                          Arboretum   Country
CALIFORNIA  BLVD        CHAPMAN                                     Park
Huntington Library,    WOODS
Art Gallery and                                                     ARCADIA
YORK BLVD        Botanical Gardens      DRIVE
PASADENA  FREEWAY  El Molino Viejo
HIGHLAND                                  SAN MARINO
PARK        110
Southwest        SOUTH PASADENA
Museum                      Mission       LAS  TUNAS  DRIVE  0        2 km
Arroyo Seco Park            San Gabriel
Casa de Abobe               Arcangel    SAN  GABRIEL        0    1 mile
```

Drive

The San Gabriel Valley

Begin at the Southwest Museum in Highland Park. Drive north on the Pasadena Freeway, exiting on to Arroyo Boulevard and continuing north to the Rose Bowl Stadium.
The **Rose Bowl Stadium▶** has staged the New Year's Day Rose Bowl since 1923.

Go along Rosemont Boulevard and follow signs for the Gamble House.
The **Gamble House▶▶▶** is a definitive example of the California Arts & Crafts architectural movement.

Drive half a mile south on Prospect Street before turning left on to Colorado Boulevard, continuing for six miles to Santa Anita Racetrack.
Birthplace of the photo-finish, the **Santa Anita Racetrack▶** is a famous horse-racing venue.

Backtrack briefly and turn south on to Rosemead Boulevard. After three miles exit west on to Las Tunas Drive, following signs for Mission San Gabriel Arcangel.
Once the only permanent settlement in the valley, the heavily restored **Mission San Gabriel Arcangel▶** is now engulfed by suburbia.

Walk

Pasadena

Begin at the public library, 285 E Walnut Street.
The Renaissance-style **public library** was completed in 1927.

Walk south along Garfield Avenue for Pasadena City Hall.
The courtyard of the Spanish baroque-style City Hall surrounds a fountained garden, and a staircase provides access to the dome.

Continue along Garfield Avenue, shortly turning right along Colorado Boulevard and crossing Raymond Avenue for the 'Old Town'.
Pasadena's **'Old Town'** has numerous restored shop façades from the 1910s and 1920s.

Continue along Colorado Boulevard for the Norton Simon Museum (see page 155). Backtrack along Colorado Boulevard to Los Robles Avenue, turning left for the Pacific Asia Museum.
Housed in a 1924 re-creation of a Chinese palace, the **Pacific Asia Museum** exhibits the arts of the Far East and Pacific Rim.

Continue along Los Robles Avenue to Walnut Street, turning left to the library.

159

In a perfect example of LA's contrasts and extremes, the city's environs contain not only three world-class art collections (see pages 154–5) but also three enormously popular theme parks, including Disneyland, the world's very first theme park.

Kids love California's theme and amusement parks, even though the state has been overtaken by Florida as the provider of the world's most innovative entertainment parks

Disneyland►►► More than 300 million people have visited Disneyland (1313 South Harbor Boulevard, Anaheim) since it opened in 1955, and very few of them have left disappointed. Whether you're shaking hands with Mickey Mouse or flying through outer space, Disneyland offers escapism at its most innovative in a multitude of constantly updated rides and shows.

Extraordinary though it may seem now, visionary animator Walt Disney had to struggle to convince his business partners of the viability of Disneyland, which he described as 'a place for people to find happiness and knowledge'. Disney had the last laugh when a million visitors arrived in the first seven weeks and the park paid off its $9 million debt within a year.

The jungle of tourist hotels and restaurants that now surround it are proof that Disneyland is never deserted, but being selective about when you come may well save hours of standing in line for the most popular attractions: if possible, come midweek between mid-September and mid-June.

In the park, head first for **Tomorrowland**, which holds the most imaginative and popular rides. Here you can go into orbit on a Saturn rocket, venture underwater on the Submarine Voyage, fasten your seatbelt for Star Tours (a space trip based on the *Star Wars* film), and enjoy a nerve-jangling 'flight' through Space Mountain, a darkened indoor roller coaster. In nearby **Adventureland** you can explore an ancient temple in the company of Indiana Jones.

Many early Disney characters appear in the less hair-raising rides of **Fantasyland**, among them Snow White's

MEDIEVAL TIMES
A four-course banquet inside a mock 11th-century castle, complete with javelin-throwing contests, sword fights and jousting knights on horseback, is just the ticket after a day spent wandering through a theme park. And that is precisely what is offered at Medieval Times (7662 Beach Boulevard, Buena Park). Reservations are a good idea (tel: 800/ 899–6600).

Scary Adventures, Peter Pan's Flight, Mr Toad's Wild Ride, and Pinocchio's Daring Journey. Pioneer-period **Frontierland** puts you aboard a runaway train, the Big Thunder Mountain Railroad, and next door, beneath the iron balconies of New Orleans Square, you can cast off with the Pirates of the Caribbean or count the ghosts in the Haunted Mansion.

When you tire, take a ride on the **Disney monorail**, looping from the entrance to Tomorrowland and back, or on the Santa Fe & Disneyland Railroad, which circles the park, negotiating the Grand Canyon on the way.

Knotts Berry Farm▶ Smaller and far less slick than Disneyland, Knotts Berry Farm (8039 Beach Boulevard, Buena Park) grew from an 1848 gold-rush town re-created during the Depression by farmer John Knott to entertain customers arriving for his wife's 65¢ dinners.

The ghost town section still remains, although millions of dollars have been pumped into the park since Knott's time. Today's thrills include the Windjammer and Hammerhead roller coasters, themed on Southern California beach culture, and the thrills-a-minute boat trip through Big Foot Rapids. Elsewhere, **Camp Snoopy** entertains youngsters with characters from the *Peanuts* cartoon strip, and Fiesta Village showcases sentimentally south-of-the-border life.

Six Flags Magic Mountain▶▶ (26101 Magic Mountain Parkway, Valencia) has 200 acres that are almost entirely devoted to scaring people witless on roller coasters and other attractions.

UP AND DOWN AT SIX FLAGS
At Six Flags, the Colossus is said to be the fastest and biggest wooden roller coaster ever built. Not to be outclassed, the Revolution dips and dives on its steel tracks before hurling its passengers around a vertical loop, and the aptly named Shock Wave lets you experience high-speed twists and curves while standing up. Even more thrilling is Superman: The Escape, which accelerates from zero to 100mph in seven seconds and includes a 100 mph backward fall from a 41-storey tower.

161

This roller coaster thrills riders at Knotts Berry Farm

A MOUSE IN HOLLYWOOD
Wearing a bright red bow tie and with $40 in his pocket, the 22-year-old Walter Elias Disney arrived in Hollywood in 1923, soon opening his own studio to develop his groundbreaking animation ideas. The advent of talkies paved the way not only for speaking actors but also for cartoon characters with a voice. In 1928, Walt premiered his masterpiece, a talking mouse originally called Mortimer but quickly renamed Mickey by Walt's wife.

CATALINA CREATURES
Separation from the mainland has enabled Catalina to support a variety of unique flora and fauna. Among the latter is the Catalina shrew, so rare it has only been officially sighted twice, and the more commonly seen Catalina mouse, a species larger and happier than its mainland cousins due to the extinction of its natural enemies and an abundance of food amid Catalina's vegetation, which includes coreopsis, blue-eyed grass, western thistle, cholla cactus, snake cactus and trees such as island cherry, island oak and ironwood.

Looking north over the colourful rooftops of Avalon which, with 2,000 inhabitants, is Santa Catalina's main town. The art-deco Avalon Ballroom is easy to spot at the edge of the bay

Santa Catalina

The best day-trip in the LA area starts with an hour-long ferry crossing to Santa Catalina, an island 26 miles off the Orange County coast. An enticing mix of romantic vacation hideaway and wild backcountry, Catalina also holds the only city in California (Avalon, population 2,000) where nobody travels by car.

Practicalities Several sailings to Santa Catalina depart daily from San Pedro, Long Beach and (in summer) Newport Beach and Redondo Beach. Operators are Catalina Cruises (tel: 800/538–4554), Catalina Express (tel: 800/464–4228) and Catalina Passenger Service (tel: 714/673–5245). Once ashore, visitors can see the sights of Avalon by bicycle or electric cart, both available from stands on Crescent Avenue. Trekking into the interior requires a permit from the Visitor Information Center, which faces the pier.

History A 4,000-year occupancy of the island by the Gabrieleño was ended in the early 1800s when white fur-trappers arrived and the tribe was forcibly resettled on the mainland. Catalina became a haunt of smugglers and pirates until William Wrigley, Jr (of the Wrigley chewing-gum dynasty), bought it in 1911, discovered a loophole in the state's antigambling laws and opened the Avalon Casino to entice moneyed mainlanders.

With its art-deco features restored to their original glory, the casino is now known as the **Avalon Ballroom**▶▶ and demands to be toured. More about the island's unusual history can be gleaned inside the adjacent **Catalina Museum**▶.

Besides the casino and museum, Avalon also has an enjoyable pier, glass-bottomed boat trips, a small sandy beach, whimsical residential architecture galore, and the curious sight of islanders weaving around on electrically powered carts (to prevent pollution; cars are as good as banned).

Outside Avalon To see the rest of Catalina, you need to venture into the pristine interior. The only road, actually a narrow track, runs to the island's airport, passing the flat-topped **Mt Orizaba**, Catalina's highest point, with fabulous views over the ocean.

William Wrigley, Jr, ploughed some of the casino's profits into the Santa Catalina Conservancy, which has restricted commercial development and protected much of the island's unique flora and fauna – including an extraordinary variety of wildflowers – easily appreciated at the **Wrigley Memorial Gardens▶** (1400 Avalon Canyon Road).

The former Wrigley mansion (on Wrigley Terrace Drive), a summer home of the family, is now a guest house, as is the pueblo-style former dwelling of Western author Zane Grey (The **Zane Grey Hotel▶▶**, 199 Chimes Tower Road), who arrived in Catalina for the filming of his book, *The Vanishing American*, and liked it here so much he never left. It is possible to tour both ex-homes.

San Fernando Valley

The ultimate dormitory community for the ultimate metropolis: 1.8 million people fill the 177 square miles of the San Fernando Valley, occupying a vast expanse of identical stuccoed bungalows and doing their shopping in malls haunted by the legendary Valley Girls, who added tidbits such as 'gag me with a spoon', to America's vernacular.

Like the San Gabriel Valley to the east, white settlement in the San Fernando Valley began with a Spanish mission and later, through the Mexican period, was divided into gigantic landholdings roamed by herds of cattle.

Expansion Not until water began pouring along the Owens Valley Aqueduct in 1913 and the San Fernando Valley joined itself administratively to LA, did growth truly begin. Film companies arrived to escape the high rents and confined spaces of Hollywood, heavy industries followed, and the advent of freeways made the valley a viable LA commuter base.

The sights All that most tourists see of the valley are the film and TV-studio tours in North Hollywood and Burbank (see panel), the roller coasters of the Six Flags Magic Mountain theme park (see page 161), and Glendale's Forest Lawn Cemetery (see page 165). Yet while first appearances may suggest otherwise, the San Fernando Valley does a pretty good job of preserving its past.

Now unceremoniously skirted by freeways, the focal point of valley life at the turn of the 19th century was **Mission San Fernando Rey▶** (15151 San Fernando Mission Boulevard), whose church, bell tower and monastery have been completely rebuilt and many of the original workshops and storerooms re-created to give visitors a sound grounding in the fundamentals of mission life.

In Brand Park, facing the mission, a selection of various plants and shrubs from California's other missions are grown and, a few streets away, the San Fernando Historical Society mounts temporary exhibitions inside the Indian-built **Andres Pico Adobe▶** (10940 Sepulveda Boulevard), LA's second-oldest home, dating from 1834.

STUDIO TOURS
The stunt-filled Universal Studios Tour (tel: 818/508–9600), which puts on a saloon bar shoot-out, a meeting with Jaws, and the parting of the Red Sea for its visitors, is the most spectacular of the film and TV studio tours available in the San Fernando Valley. To learn about actual production techniques, reserve a place on the Warner Brothers Studios VIP tour (tel: 818/954–1744), which includes visiting in-use sound stages and editing suites.

WATER WARS
When water arrived in the San Fernando Aqueduct, a feat of engineering that took six years and cost $25 million, it controversially robbed the people of Owens Valley of their own water supply. Controversy was followed by disaster in 1928, when the aqueduct's St Francis Dam collapsed, killing 400 people.

The 8 million vehicles driven by the 8.6 million residents of metropolitan LA keep roads busy night and day

TUJUNGA WASH
Half a mile long and still growing, the *Tujunga Wash* mural is the longest such artwork in the world, and the account of California history it depicts does not spare the murkier episodes staining the state's back pages. You will find the mural, a collaborative project overseen by the Venice Arts Center, on Coldwater Canyon Boulevard, between Burbank Boulevard and Oxnard Street.

Encino▶ Several further points of historical appeal lie in Encino, a leafy well-to-do district on the western side of the valley. Here, the nine-acre **Los Encinos State Historic Park▶** is filled with eucalyptus trees and contains a natural spring that quenched the thirst of a Spanish discovery party in 1769, and also the nine-room Osa Adobe built in 1849. A less expected sight in the park is a limestone French-style house, the work of two Basque brothers in 1872.

Calabasas▶ The cobwebs are kept off two more aging homes in Calabasas, an Old West–flavoured town making much of its past as a stagecoach stop. The **Leonis Adobe▶** (23537 Calabasas Road) had its second storey added by Miguel Leonis, a smuggler turned sheep farmer, in imitation of the Monterey style in vogue during the 1840s. The **Plummer House▶**, dating from 1879, now forms the entrance to the Leonis Adobe and has displays on the valley's rancho period.

At the northern end of the valley, the mansion and grounds of the hilltop **William S. Hart County Park▶▶** (24151 San Fernando Road) belonged to a silent-era movie cowboy, who became the role model for all subsequent celluloid western heroes. Packed with Old West furnishings and ornaments, and intriguing bits and pieces from Hart's acting career, the home is set at the heart of a 260-acre park, and watched over by the grazing bison.

Forest Lawn cemetery has several branches around LA, but the most famous of them – and the one that inspired Evelyn Waugh's satirical novel The Loved One *– fills a 300-acre hillside site on the edge of the San Fernando Valley (1712 S Glendale Avenue, Glendale).*

A unique concept Founded in 1917, Forest Lawn was designed to create a fusion of art and landscaping to uplift the living as much as to remember the dead. To this end, the cemetery boasts almost 1,000 pieces of classical statuary, including replicas of all of Michelangelo's most noted works, a huge stained-glass replica of da Vinci's *The Last Supper,* and a 500-square-foot mosaic based on the *Signing of the Declaration of Independence.*

Forest Lawn's small amount of original art is no less grandiose. In the **Hall of the Crucifixion-Resurrection►►**, Jan Styka's 195-foot-by-45-foot *Crucifixion* is claimed to be the world's largest religious work on canvas, and it partners Robert Clark's only slightly smaller *The Resurrection.* Meanwhile, funeral services (and, surprisingly perhaps, a large number of weddings) take place in the cemetery's churches:

Forest Lawn statuary

painstaking re-creations of 10th- and 14th-century English and Scottish buildings.

Last stop for the rich and famous
The fame of the cemetery itself tends to eclipse the stature of the many movie idols spending eternity within its grounds. The tombs of Clark Gable, Carole Lombard, Jean Harlow, and W C Fields are inside the **Great Mausoleum►►**, while Clara Bow, Chico Marx, Alan Ladd and Nat King Cole are among those interred in the **Freedom Mausoleum►**, just outside of which lies Errol Flynn – allegedly sharing his coffin with six bottles of whisky.

The other main branch of Forest Lawn is in the Hollywood Hills on the edge of Griffith Park (6300 Forest Lawn Drive) where, besides another batch of imitation European sculpture, the roll call of the deceased includes greats such as Buster Keaton, Stan Laurel, George Raft and Liberace.

Map labels:

Temecula · Radec · see Drive page 177

Camp Pendleton Marine Base · Aguanga · Iron Springs Mt 1754m

4 · Santa Margarita

Margarita Mts · Rainbow

Fallbrook · Pala · Pala Mission · Cleveland · Oak Grove

Pala Mesa · Palomar Mountain · Palomar Observatory · Hot Springs Mt 1991m

Pala Indian Res · National · Birch Hill

San Diego Aqueduct · San Luis Rey

5 · Guajome Regional Park · Rincon · Lake Henshaw · Warner Springs

3 · San Luis Rey · Mission San Luis Rey de Francia · Vista · Forest

Oceanside · Pine Mt 1287m · Volcan Mts

Carlsbad · San Marcos · Mesa Grande

Lake San Marcos · Escondido · San Diego Wild Animal Park · Sutherland Lake · Santa Ysabel · Whispering Pines

Santa Ysabel Cr · Ballena Valley · Julian

San Pasqual Battlefield St Hist Park

Leucadia · Escondido · Lake Hodges · Ramona · Julian Pioneer Museum

Encinitas · Rancho Santa Fe · Rancho Bernardo · Harrison Park · Cuyamaca Res

Cardiff-by-the-Sea · San Dieguito · Fernbrook · Cleveland · Cuyamaca · Cuyamaca Peak 1888m

Solana Beach · Los Penasquitos Canyon · Poway · San Vicente Res · Cuyamaca Mts · Rancho S P

Del Mar · 15 · Barona · El Capitan Res · Green Valley Falls

2 · Miramar

Scripps Aquarium · Lakeside · 8 · Alpine · National

La Jolla Museum of Contemporary Art · San Diego · Pine Valley

805 · La Jolla · Clairemont · Mission San Diego de Alcala · Santee · Flinn Springs · Suncrest · Pine Valley Cr

Pacific Beach · Mission Beach · Mission Bay · Old Town · El Cajon · Loveland Res · Forest

Sea World · Zoo · La Mesa · Spring Valley · Sweetwater

Ocean Beach · Balboa Park · Lemon Grove

SAN DIEGO · La Presa · Jamul · Barrett Lake · Morena Village

Point Loma · Villa Montezuma · Sweetwater Res

Cabrillo Nat Monument · Coronado · National City · Cottonwood Cr

SAN DIEGO · Silver Strand St Beach · Chula Vista · Lower Otay Res · Campo

0 · 10 · 20 km · Imperial Beach · 5 · Tecate

0 · 10 miles · San Ysidro · Otay · MEX

A · B · C

JUAN CABRILLO
A Portuguese soldier who rose to the command of a Spanish ship and was charged with exploring the California coastline, Juan Cabrillo and his crew sheltered from a storm in what became San Diego Bay on September 1542, making the first European sighting of the California mainland. Cabrillo died later in the voyage and the expedition was regarded as a failure, despite its lasting place in California's history.

DAILY SUNSHINE Affluent and comfortable, San Diego is as close to the ideal vacation destination as it is possible to get. While lacking the romance of San Francisco and the glamour of Los Angeles, San Diego is free of smog and inner-city social problems, and nobody who lives there – whether they are basking on the best beaches in California or making their fortune in the city's international banking market – would trade California's second-biggest city for any other.

Sheltering from a storm in 1542, Juan Cabrillo and crew dropped anchor in what is now San Diego Bay. Yet it was not until the building of California's first mission in 1769 that San Diego's settlement began, in what is now the Old Town, six miles north-west of today's Downtown.

DOWNTOWN itself came into being only a few decades after US rule was established, the centre of a classic rough-and-ready frontier town. San Diego did itself a power of good by staging the 1915 Panama–California Exposition. This brought international prestige, and turned Balboa Park – a mile north of Downtown – into a nationally known showcase of Spanish-style architecture and landscape gardening.

Another economic boost came in the 1940s when San Diego became the base of the US Navy's Pacific fleet. Aircraft carriers and frigates became a common sight, and the military presence fuelled the city's reputation for conservatism.

Today's San Diego knows how to look after itself. Restoration programmes have kept many of the historic areas intact and accessible, numerous parks and waterways are set aside for recreational use, and the investment of $165 million in a sparkling Convention Center, which opened in 1989, proved the city's intention to be among the nation's most up-to-date and user-friendly cities.

AROUND SAN DIEGO There is a sharp distinction between the heavily populated suburban communities lining the coast and the sleepy rural towns dotting a sparse inland area, which is flanked by pine-coated hills.

San Diego is also on Mexico's doorstep: the city's public transportation runs to the border, and Tijuana, just over it, can easily be toured as a half-day excursion. It is also enjoying an economic boom thanks to 1994's North American Free Trade Agreement, increasing the level of commerce with nearby Mexico.

San Diego

▶▶▶ REGION HIGHLIGHTS

Balboa Park *page 168*

Mission Beach
page 174

Hotel Del Coronado
page 169

Gaslamp Quarter
pages 170, 171

Point Loma *page 173*

Old Town San Diego
page 172

La Jolla *page 179*

Julian *page 178*

Mission San Luis Rey de Francia *page 181*

Ocean Beach *page 174*

A San Diego street

San Diego

MUSEUM COSTS
Entry to almost all the Balboa Park museums is free on the first Tuesday of every month, otherwise admission ranges from free to $5. Buying a Balboa Passport allows you into any nine museums during any week. Most of the museums are closed on Mondays.

Saturdays on El Prado in Balboa Park find street performers, often of Central or South American origin, entertaining the crowds

▶▶▶ Balboa Park

Leasing a section of the rattlesnake-infested scrubland on the northern outskirts of late-1800s San Diego paid off for the local authorities. Planting trees in lieu of houses, a local botanist started what officially became Balboa Park in 1911 – 1,000 green acres of lush, tropical landscaping only a mile from Downtown. The park is sprinkled with Spanish baroque-style buildings, erected for the Panama–California Exposition of 1915 and the California–Pacific International Exposition 20 years later; they constitute one of the largest groupings of museums in the country.

In the northern half of the park, the **San Diego Museum of Art▶▶** draws its ample collection from near and far: floors of European Old Masters adjoin rooms of squatting Buddhas and gleaming jewels from all points east, and vigorous American pop art fills the final spacious halls.

The smaller **Timkin Museum of Art▶▶▶** is more selective, with an outstanding grouping of Russian icons taking pride of place amid a scattering of Old Masters and some quality 19th-century American paintings. Nearby, the Mengei International Museum has excellent folk art exhibits, and the temporary exhibitions at the **Museum of Photographic Arts▶** are rarely dull.

Away from art, there are entertaining and informative hands-on exhibits in the **Museum of Natural History▶**, and at the **Reuben H. Fleet Space Theater and Science Center▶▶** the IMAX films, projected onto a gigantic screen, make the shows – ranging from space trips to mountain ascents – breathtakingly realistic.

The Museum of Man▶ reveals something of the Native American cultures of the south-west and the efforts of anthropologists to examine them, though the overall effect is slightly shallow. The **Museum of San Diego History▶** is

THE OLD GLOBE THEATER
The 500-seat Old Globe Theater (in Balboa Park), an approximate replica of London's 15th-century original, is one of three theatres forming the Simon Edison Complex for the Performing Arts. To find out what is playing, tel: 619/239–2255.

more enjoyable, recording the rise of the city. In the centre of Balboa Park, the open-air Spreckels Organ Pavilion houses the world's largest pipe organ (there is a free recital each Sunday afternoon), and each of the cottages of the House of Pacific Relations has a few cultural knick-knacks from foreign countries. Green-thumbed visitors are better advised to spend time amid the ferns, orchids and begonias in the **Botanical Building▶▶**.

At the southern section of the park (reached on foot or aboard a free trolley), the **Aerospace Museum▶▶▶** showcases entertaining collections related to flight and fliers from the beginnings of manned flight to the conquest of space. Next door, the **Automotive Museum▶** does a less thorough job for land-based transport, via rows of the streamlined 1940s and 1950s cars.

▶▶ Coronado

Across the curling Coronado Bridge from Downtown, and also accessible by the ferry from San Diego Harbor, the tidy community of Coronado grew up around the **Hotel Del Coronado,** a whimsical Victorian pile of wooden turrets and towers built to lure wealthy, ailing Easterners to the balmy southern climate.

The hotel has been spoiling its guests since the 1880s, the most notable of whom – including the future Edward VIII and Mrs Simpson, who allegedly met here in 1920 – are remembered inside the hotel's small museum. You will also spot memorabilia from the 1950s movie *Some Like It Hot,* which found Marilyn Monroe, Jack Lemmon and Tony Curtis cavorting around the hotel's grounds.

Other than the hotel, there is little else to see in Coronado, though the Trackless Trolley finds enough to fill a 20-minute narrated tour; it leaves from the ferry dock and includes a stop at the hotel.

FESTIVALS
Festivals are a dime a dozen in San Diego, but the following are the most enjoyable: the Mexican Cinco de Mayo (May 5) celebration in the Old Town; the Cabrillo Festival, centred on Point Loma, a re-enactment of the first European landing in California (late September); the Michelob Street Scene, open-air rock music in Downtown's Gaslamp Quarter (September); and the Over-the-Line softball tournament contested by 1,000 teams on the city's beaches every July. Around San Diego, the major event is the Del Mar Fair, a three-week-long re-creation of an old-time state fair, running from mid-June.

169

When it opened in 1888, the Hotel Del Coronado had more indoor toilets, 75 for its 399 guest rooms, than any other building in the US

Hotel del Coronado

Few California cities have been as careful or as successful as San Diego in protecting and restoring their architectural heritage. From the squat adobe homes of pioneer settlers to the streamlined office blocks of contemporary San Diego, the city's buildings are seldom individually striking, but collectively they provide a lucid insight into the community's development.

Old Town Many cramped but comfortable adobe homes were built in what is now the Old Town, with thick mud-brick walls to keep the rooms cool in summer while improvised carpets of straw softened the rough floors. Several good examples remain, their survival largely due to the relocation of the city to the present Downtown during the late 1800s.

170

❏ Tijuana is only 23 miles from San Diego and a visit does give a taste of south-of-the-border life. There are no customs or immigration formalities but, to re-enter the US, passport holders who are not US citizens and who require a visa for entry into the US will need to meet the usual requirements. ❏

Santa Fe Railroad Depot, a fine example of Spanish-Moorish style

The Gaslamp Quarter Downtown, the boom years are remembered by the tidied, turn-of-the-century commercial brick buildings of the Gaslamp Quarter, whose owners grew rich and secreted themselves in picturesque Queen Anne homes, many of which still stand a few miles north in the Hillcrest area.

Expo Although San Diego originally grew around a Spanish mission, it was not until 1915 that the city made a fuss about its roots, erecting half a dozen Spanish baroque-style buildings in Balboa Park for the Panama–California Exposition.

Few of these buildings were intended to last, but the success of the Exposition in putting San Diego on the map, and the popularity of the buildings – with their elaborate facades and sculpture-filled courtyards – among local people was impossible to ignore. Strengthening and rebuilding took place, and a second Exposition was held in 1935, this time signalling the city's emergence from the Depression. The spacious Spanish-Moorish Santa Fe Railroad Depot, on Broadway in Downtown, was also designed for the 1915 Expo and continues to be a pleasing sight for train travellers. Now the station is overshadowed by the black, bronze and silver exteriors of American Plaza, a complex of stores and offices rising up to proclaim the city's present-day role as a centre of US–Far East high finance.

▶▶▶ Downtown

A frantic swirl of bankers, beggars, locals and tourists, Downtown San Diego's easily walked **Gaslamp Quarter▶▶▶** should not be missed. It comprises 16 short blocks lined by restored buildings just south of Broadway between 4th and 6th avenues.

Patterned red-brickwork and other Romanesque revival trimmings decorate many of the district's structures, which went up between the 1860s and 1920s, though the best place to begin is at the **William Heath Davis House▶** (410 Island Avenue; also the departure point for Saturday walking tours), a simple wooden dwelling dating from 1850.

▶▶ Mission Bay

The marshland that once filled the gap between Downtown and Mission Beach has been transformed into the sculptured lagoons and beaches of Mission Bay Park, offering rich pickings for watersports fans. Mission Bay is also the home of **Sea World▶▶▶**, whose theatrical shows by killer whales and dolphins draw thousands of people; the penguin and shark exhibits are among the best of their kind. Equally good is **Wild Arctic,** a simulated journey to an abandoned polar research station that begins with a helicopter flight though a blizzard and concludes at a series of replicated habitats housing seals, walruses, polar bears, beluga whales and residents of the world's coldest region.

▶ Mission Valley

From 1769, California's first Spanish mission sat on the hilltop overlooking what is now the Old Town, where San Diego began. Half a decade on, the mission was moved six miles north, and the Old Town almost disappeared when the new San Diego (the present Downtown) was founded.

The restored buildings of the Old Town merit a stroll, though for atmosphere, few match the reconstructed **San Diego Mission▶▶** (10818 San Diego Mission Road), still serving a spiritual function but now in the urban sprawl of Mission Valley.

The social scene at Mission Beach, a San Diego community almost entirely devoted to sun, sand and surf

VILLA MONTEZUMA
San Diego in the late 19th century was better known for its saloons and brothels than its culture. Endeavouring to change things, a band of wealthy settlers banded together and built an irresistible mansion – the Villa Montezuma (1925 K Street) – to lure a renowned English-born aesthete and entertainer, Jesse Shepard, to the fledgling city. Shepard's effect on the community, and his penchant for stained glass and spiritualism, can be assessed on guided tours of the lovingly restored abode.

San Diego

OLD TOWN TROLLEY
One way to reach the Old Town is aboard an Old Town Trolley, one of several buses that link Old Town with Balboa Park, Coronado, and Downtown, on a two-hour loop route. It is a stress-free way to see the city, and the amusing spiel of the drivers will keep you entertained and informed. Tickets can be used repeatedly all day (for details, tel: 619/298–8687).

Shielded from the southern California sun, diners sample Mexican fare offered at Bazaar del Mundo, adjacent to Old Town State Historic Park

▶▶▶ Old Town

San Diego's first permanent settlement mostly comprised presidio (the military fort protecting the mission) personnel and their families living at the foot of the hill beneath the mission. Within the Old Town State Historic Park, several of San Diego's earliest buildings have been restored, and many more are devoted to preserving the memory of bygone times.

The adobe structures of the early 1800s are by far the most interesting buildings. The largest of them, the **Casa de Estudillo**▶▶, belonged to José Estudillo, the first commander of the presidio. Following Estudillo's death, the structure proved large enough to accommodate Estudillo's son, his wife and their 12 children.

José Estudillo's son-in-law, Juan Bandini, was another significant figure in early San Diego, who turned his home – Casa de Bandini – into a noted social gathering place. When Bandini fell on hard times, the house was sold and turned into a hotel; it is now an enjoyable Mexican restaurant.

San Diego came under US rule in 1846, an era evoked by several things: the single-classroom **Mason Street School**▶▶; the Western memorabilia inside the Seeley Stables; the **San Diego Union Building**▶, where the first edition of what is still the city's main newspaper was assembled in 1868; and the **Whaley House Museum**▶ (just outside the park at 2482 San Diego Avenue), San Diego's first brick-built house, stuffed with the fixtures and fittings typical of a well-to-do settler of the 1850s. The Whaley House, incidentally, is one of only two in California officially recognised by the state government as being haunted: the spirits are thought to be former residents Thomas and Anna Whaley.

One edge of the park is consumed by Bazaar del Mundo, an entertaining if upmarket imitation of a Mexican street bazaar, whose tiled courtyard is lined with restaurants and crafts shops.

▶▶▶ Point Loma

Wealthy residential areas, naval bases, thick woodlands and coastal bluffs reminiscent of the state's Central Coast characterise the 10-mile-long Point Loma peninsula that divides San Diego Bay from the Pacific.

At Point Loma's southernmost point, the unspectacular **Cabrillo National Monument▶** marks the landing of Juan Cabrillo, a Portuguese adventurer. In September 1542, he was the first European to arrive in California.

The view over the bay to the San Diego skyline is sufficient reason to come here, however, and there is also a 19th-century lighthouse to explore and footpaths leading to the tidal pools beneath the bluffs.

▶ Presidio Park

In a faithful reconstruction of the original mission, and close to its original site at the crown of Presidio Park, the Junípero Serra Museum provides a modest insight into Spanish mission life in California. More dramatically, the contrast of early photos and the current view through the windows makes plain the incredible recent growth of the city: quiet orange groves have become traffic-clogged freeways in just a few decades.

▶ San Diego Harbor

The departure point for numerous sailings and the site of a sea-oriented museum, San Diego Harbor is where the city displays its nautical connections. The pick of three vintage vessels moored in the **Maritime Museum▶** is the *Star of India*, a fully equipped three-mast sailing ship that plied the seven seas from 1863.

The nearby piers are the embarkation points for harbour cruises, whale-watching trips and the ferry to Coronado (see page 169). If dry land holds more appeal than water, however, follow the **Embarcadero▶▶**. On this pleasant walkway, which winds south from the harbour, you will pass kite-flyers, joggers and roller-skaters before reaching the browsable souvenir shops of **Seaport Village▶**. The Embarcadero continues past the city's gleaming convention centre and ends at the edge of the Gaslamp District.

▶▶▶ San Diego Zoo

To the north of Balboa Park, San Diego Zoo got started with animals left over from the 1915 Panama–California Exposition. It has since grown into one of the world's leading zoos, re-creating a range of habitats – from deep canyons to equatorial rain forests. Wherever possible, moats and other natural obstacles are used instead of cages.

Among nearly 4,000 inhabitants on the 128 acres of lushly vegetated grounds is the nation's largest gathering of koalas, some flourishing Galapagos turtles (like koalas, an endangered species), and an excellent collection of primates. Many other smaller, strokable creatures reside in the **Children's Zoo▶**.

These inhabitants of the Flamingo Lagoon are among the 800 animal species resident at San Diego Zoo

173

ON THE BAY
Whenever schedules permit, the US Navy berths one or more of its vessels at the end of Broadway Pier for free public viewing. Nearby are the departure points for civilian ferries and pleasure boats, such as the San Diego Bay Ferry (also called the Coronado Ferry) to Coronado, numerous sightseeing trips around the bay and all-day cruises to the Mexican coastal town of Ensenada.

San Diego is great news for sea and sand addicts. Whether you want to surf, swim, sunbathe, snorkel, or strip completely, you will find the perfect spot somewhere along the 70 miles of coastline in and around the city.

WATER SPORTS

In a city almost surrounded by water, it should be no surprise that water sports are big news in San Diego. Yachting is favoured by the jet set, but it is surfing that captures the imagination and there is no better place in the state to try your luck. Boards can be rented for around $18 a day from any of the numerous shops around Ocean Beach and Mission Beach. If you prefer, sit back and watch accomplished exponents of the art in action at Tourmaline Surfing Park and Windansea Beach in La Jolla.

174

Imperial Beach▶ Quiet and secluded (not least because of fears of sewage spills from Mexico), Imperial Beach is an inauspicious beginning at San Diego's southern extremity, but its northern edge meets the more promising Silver Strand State Beach, a 15-mile-long sliver of sand dividing San Diego Bay from the Pacific Ocean.

Silver Strand State Beach▶▶ Some parts of Silver Strand are high-grade beachcombing territory (indeed, its name is derived from the millions of tiny silver seashells that are washed up on it). Other sections of the beach are equipped with picnic tables and fire rings that attract families on weekends. Silver Strand also provides the sole link between the mainland and Coronado, where a lack of strong currents makes Coronado Shores Beach an ideal base for a swim.

Ocean Beach▶▶ Across the bay, sheer-sided cliffs are typical of the Point Loma shoreline. A notable exception, though, is Ocean Beach, a haunt of surfers and beach revellers, if much less the all-out party venue today than it was a few years ago. At the nearby northern end, in a very California gesture, Dog Beach is reserved for untethered canines and their owners.

Mission Beach▶▶▶ You should not miss Mission Beach. Seething with surfers and barely covered tanning flesh, and buzzing with impromptu games of beach volleyball, Mission Beach is a perfect example of the southern California beach strip. Beside the beach a restored vintage carousel began turning once again in 1991, and the chic shops and fitness centre of Belmont Park replaced what used to be a crumbling roadway. All of these things have encouraged more families to visit Mission Beach but have done little to dent the pervading sense of youthful hedonism.

Pacific Beach▶▶ Directly north of Mission Beach, Pacific Beach is calmer and more refined. Nevertheless,

Residents and locals enjoy a section of the 3-mile-long beachside boardwalk running between Mission and Pacific Beach

it's here you'll find most of the bars and clubs favoured by Mission Beach revellers after dark. It also eases the transition from San Diego into La Jolla, where **Tourmaline Surfing Park**▶▶ and **Windansea Beach**▶▶ are legendary among skilled surfers (novices are welcome only as spectators). Also in La Jolla, the crystal-clear waters of **La Jolla Cove**▶▶▶ cover a marine park and a series of caves, which are enjoyable to explore with the aid of a snorkel, and **La Jolla Shores**▶▶, an inviting swath of sand where well-heeled locals parade their designer swimwear.

For a complete tan, make for the soft sands of **Black's Beach**▶, a few miles north of La Jolla, where all-nude volleyball games are played (although nudity was out-lawed in 1971). Perhaps the authorities turn a blind eye since the beach is shielded from prying eyes by 1,000-foot-high sandstone cliffs, with the beach accessible only by a treacherous pathway.

Star-spotting This plays a key part of the activity on **Del Mar Beach**▶, though often the film, TV and sports celebrities who live in the town take the rays from the privacy of their poolside. A few miles north, **Solana Beach**▶ has a more egalitarian mood, as does **Moonlight State Beach**▶▶, between Leucadia and Encinitas, the start of a surfer-dominated strand stretching for 10 miles to **Carlsbad**▶ where the classic Beach Boys' songs still ring true and board-clutching blonds appear whenever the surf's up. The bars and diners here also retain a laid-back ambience.

Camp Pendleton Marine Base Here, except for a nuclear power station, no buildings blot the landscape and **San Onofre State Beach**▶▶ offers what is generally acknowledged as the best surfing in the United States; check first because the beach is only open to the public on a few specific days.

The placid lagoon of Mission Bay enables San Diegans to enjoy water sports safely; on its edge are man-made beaches and moorings for 2,500 boats

SEEING GRAY WHALES
The much-loved California gray whales head south from the Arctic Ocean to the warm waters off Baja California from mid-December to March. With luck, you will catch sight of them from the viewing platforms close to the Cabrillo National Monument on Point Loma, or from Whale Point in La Jolla. For a closer look, numerous companies run boat tours, advertised along San Diego Harbor.

TORREY PINES STATE PRESERVE

The tall bluffs that divide La Jolla from Del Mar are covered by the 1,000-acre Torrey Pines State Preserve, holding one of the world's two surviving stands of the Torrey pine tree. Because of salty soil, the pines here grow as little as 10 feet in 100 years, while ocean winds force them into strange, stumpy shapes that make any of the short walking trails a memorable experience.

The Indian Museum at Cuyamaca Rancho State Park. The word Cuyamaca, meaning 'rainy region', comes from Diegueño native dialect

Around San Diego

▶ Carlsbad

Among the more distinctive of the coastal communities in the San Diego hinterland, Carlsbad is also one of the nicest for strolling. The tourist-friendly shops of the downtown area include the **Alt Karlsbad Hanse Gift Shop**, which doubles as the entrance to a small museum recording the stroke of luck that allowed the town to prosper from the late 1800s: a natural well, the waters of which became famous for their healthful qualities.

▶ Chula Vista

Striving to forge an identity of its own within the metropolitan San Diego area, Chula Vista benefits from a bayside location: its enjoyable harbourside walk meanders beside a multitude of yachts and fishing boats, and the **Nature Interpretive Center▶▶** (1000 Gunpowder Point Drive) provides a solid introduction to the diverse and interesting ecological zones of California's wetlands; some of the 130 species of bird that inhabit them can be spied from the observation tower and foot trails.

▶ Cuyamaca

Often neglected by visitors making for the neighbouring Anza-Borrego Desert, Cuyamaca and its enormous **Cuyamaca Rancho State Park▶▶** offer landscapes ranging from forests of oak and pine to upland meadows riven by mountain streams. It is a place best appreciated by hiking and camping: this is easily done, as hundreds of miles of trails criss-cross the park's 26,000 acres, and campsites are plentiful.

Near the information centre there is also a small museum recording the resistance of the local Native American tribes to 19th-century white settlers' attempts to plunder the region of its native oak and pine tree stocks.

▶ Del Mar

Actor Bing Crosby and singer Pat O'Brien took a shine to the seaside resort of Del Mar during the 1930s and pumped money into the local racetrack, which soon became a palm-bordered architectural masterpiece and helped solidify the town's reputation as a playground for Hollywood's rich and famous. Many names still have vacation homes here, though the real draws are the beach and the shops and restaurants along 15th Street.

Drive

Highway 76 and Highway 78

(See map on page 166.)

Leave Oceanside on Highway 76; drive for five miles to San Luis Rey.
On the left, **Mission San Luis Rey de Francia►►** dates from 1798, and is the largest of the California missions (see page 181). The ruins of the guards' barracks are on the right.

Continue for three miles.
On the right, the **Guajome Adobe►** was at the centre of Rancho Guajome (see panel, this page), a major landholding during Mexican rule in the 19th century; it now sits at the heart of the 500-acre **Guajome Regional Park►**.

Continue on Highway 76, entering the Pala Indian Reservation.
On the left, the small **Pala Mission►►** was founded in 1816 and serves the spiritual and educational needs of reservation dwellers. The interior of the **chapel** is decorated by Pala murals (see page 180).

Continue for 24 miles and turn left along Road S6 for the Palomar Observatory.
Since the 1940s, the 200-inch telescope in the **Palomar Observatory►►** has tracked and photographed galaxies at the edge of the known universe. The museum has photos and explanatory displays, and the mighty telescope can be viewed from the visitors' gallery.

Return to Highway 76 and continue for 30 miles to the intersection with Highway 78 at Santa Ysabel.
Just before the intersection, the tiny **Mission Santa Ysabel►►** stands on the left, with a one-room museum and a large Native American cemetery.

Drive west for 32 miles on Highway 78, passing Ramona and San Diego

❏ Following Mexican independence from Spain, large chunks of mission-owned land were granted to Spanish-Mexican settlers, the so-called Californios, for farming. One of these major farms became Rancho Guajome, at the centre of which was the 20-room Guajome Adobe, now rated as one of the finest examples of the period's domestic architecture. Eight miles from Oceanside on Highway 76, the adobe is best appreciated by joining the guided tour (for further details, tel: 619/565–3600). ❏

Wild Animal Park, to Escondido.
Escondido► is best known as the former home of Lawrence Welk, whose museum, recording the growth of his 'champagne music', and golf-based resort consume the northern edge of town.

Continue for 24 miles on Highway 78, to Carlsbad.
The surfer-packed beach at **Carlsbad►** is typical of San Diego's coastal towns, but its past glory as a spa resort makes it one of the more historically distinguished (see page 176).

The Palomar Observatory

The grounds of Bernardo Winery, near Escondido, one of the oldest of several noted San Diego area wineries

▶ Escondido

A quiet residential community, Escondido is also the former home of entertainer Lawrence Welk, whose **Lawrence Welk Village▶**, containing a dinner theatre and a museum devoted to his career, sits on the edge of town. Many consider him a symbol of bad music and sanitised culture and visit to make fun of his image.

Close by are a couple of commendable wineries – Bernardo and Orfila – both of which offer free tastings and tours. A bigger attraction is the expansive **San Diego Wild Animal Park▶▶**, six miles east, which re-creates African and Asian terrains and fills them with the appropriate creatures.

▶▶▶ Julian

First settled by gold miners in the 1860s, Julian swiftly became one of the biggest towns in San Diego County. The present population is just 500, with locals outnumbered on weekends by visitors enjoying Julian's setting in thickly forested mountain foothills. Many San Diegans bring their children to Julian during the winter for their first sight of snow. The **Pioneer Museum▶▶** forges a strong impression of the town's rough-and-ready early days.

Inside the **Julian Cider Mill▶**, a right turning off Main Street, you can inspect the process of turning apples into cider, see peanut butter being made, and sample honey produced by the mill's own beehive. Across Main Street and B Street, the **Julian Hotel▶**, founded by freed slaves, has been offering accommodation since 1899, but keeps its quaintly furnished interior for viewing by guests only. Back along Main Street and to the right along C Street are signs showing the way to the **Eagle and High Peaks Mine Museum▶▶**, which stores the last vestiges of Julian's gold-mining industry and has a former mineshaft open for public scrutiny.

A BOUNTIFUL HARVEST
The comparatively cool climate and fertile soils found in the foothills of the mountains dividing San Diego County from the inland deserts allow the cultivation of apples, peaches, pears and other fruit that are otherwise in short supply. Drive anywhere close to Julian and you will find roadside stalls offering locally grown fruit and jam, and each October the town lets its hair down for the month-long Apple Harvest Festival.

San Diego's priciest homes, most expensive stores and smartest restaurants are along the hibiscus-lined lanes of La Jolla (pronounced 'La Hoya'), a hillside community rising high above the Pacific directly north of the city.

Chic and non-conformist Its showpiece Prospect Street and Girard Avenue filled with trendy art galleries, expensive boutiques, members-only fitness centres, and chic top-notch eateries, La Jolla is a place with pretensions. However, it also has streak of non-conformity, stemming from its many resident artists and writers and its proximity to the sprawling campus of the University of California.

The town, whose name either means 'the jewel' (from the Spanish) or 'cave' (from Native American legend) depending on who tells the tale, also boasts a picturesque coastline, a fine modern art museum, and fancy wrought-iron benches that are a welcome sight when you're in need of a breather.

Modern art After admiring the contours of the coast from **Scripps Park►►**, a small and tidy green patch flanked by palm trees above La Jolla Cove, look into the **Museum of Contemporary Art►►**, which specialises in modern works from the California minimalist and pop art genres. Most of the museum itself is a modern work, too, designed by renowned San Diego architect Irving Gill, although its origins go back to 1915 and an oceanside villa belonging to Ellen Browning Scripps, wealthy sister of a publishing magnate, who poured money into La Jolla throughout her life.

Marine research Scripps is to be thanked for keeping much of La Jolla free from developer-led devastation, most spectacularly the Torrey Pines State Preserve (see page 176). Her money financed the **Scripps Oceanographic Institute** and the **Stephen Birch Aquarium Museum►►**, in which stunning

re-creations of marine habitats illuminate the mysteries of the deep, and perched above the ocean, the **Salk Institute**, an extremely well-equipped biological research centre occupying an imposing concrete structure (intended to stimulate original thought).

Folk art One further sight of note in La Jolla, though oddly placed in the University Town Center shopping mall, is the **Mengei International Museum►**, whose stimulating exhibitions are drawn from native cultures around the globe; another branch is in Balboa Park.

179

A university campus sculpture

RANCHO SANTE FE
One of southern California's most exclusive communities lies five miles inland from Solana Beach on Road S8. Here, in the 1920s, Hollywood's favourite couple, Douglas Fairbanks and Mary Pickford, bought a ranch and soon turned the area into a millionaires' playground known as Rancho Sante Fe. Many fabulous hillside mansions are obscured from public view by trees, though anyone can walk around the town's ultra chic Rancho Sante Fe Inn in the hope that some of the glamour may rub off on them.

The Pala-Indian Culture Center. The Pala Indian reservation is one of three in California predating US rule

▶ Oceanside

The town has a decent strip of beach and anglers line the wooden pier, but most of Oceanside is dominated by the Marines from the neighbouring Camp Pendleton base, the US military's main centre for amphibious-landing training, and the reason why 125,000 acres along the coast north from Oceanside are totally free of development. There is a Landing Vehicle Track Museum inside the base where you can learn about the tricks of the amphibious landing trade. Back in town, the pier's **Surf Museum** displays vintage boards and other memorabilia of the area's most popular recreational pursuit.

▶ Pala

The tiny community of Pala sits just inside the Pala reservation and is the site of the only mission in California still serving Native Americans as a place of worship and education.

Built in 1816 as a branch of Mission San Luis Rey, the **Pala Mission▶▶** (known formally as Mission Assistencia de San Antonio de Pala) had suffered considerable deterioration by the time the Cupeño tribe was forcibly moved to the area in 1903. Some parts of the mission have been finely restored and the interior walls of the chapel are covered with intriguing frescoes, but the bumpy brick floors and the splintered beams give the whole place a rustic appearance, something which is matched by the hand-made wooden crosses marking the tombs of the Native American cemetery, just outside.

►► San Luis Rey

Once described as 'the most beautiful, most symmetrical, and the most substantial mission in California,' the **Mission San Luis Rey de Francia►►** had 3,000 Native Americans (more than any other California Mission) under its jurisdiction during the early 1800s, and even today is an impressive sight as it emerges from the anonymous suburbia that fills the five miles between it and uninteresting, military-dominated Oceanside.

While only the 1807 church is original, the mission has been kept in good repair by the order of Franciscan monks who have occupied it since 1893. The museum gives an instructive account of mission-era life, and there are numerous pieces from the time of the mission's founder, Padre Fermin de Lasuén.

In mid-July, a fiesta based around the traditional Blessing of the Animals ceremony takes place in the mission's grounds.

► Santa Ysabel

Most people visit Santa Ysabel, a community of a few hundred people around the intersection of Highway 78 and Highway 79, only long enough to buy bread from **Dudley's Bakery►**, where the choice of still-warm loaves spans jalapeño, onion, potato, Irish brown and German pumpernickel.

A short way along Highway 79, the minuscule **Mission Santa Ysabel►►** is of historical significance and interest, founded in 1818 as a branch of the San Diego Mission. The small church that stands here now dates from 1924, and is not as interesting as the mission's one-room museum, which is packed with historic photos and objects, and carries a text describing the mystery of the mission's missing bells. There is a box inside the museum for your dollar donation, and a sign reminding you to switch off the light when you leave.

If you visit in November, you will see the mission's Native American cemetery bathed in candle-light; traditionally at this time, a candle is placed on every grave.

Mission San Luis Rey de Francia, the eighteenth of California's missions, was also the largest, originally covering 6 acres with space for 1,000 worshippers inside its church

FLOWER POWER
From May to September, the hillsides of Encinitas, halfway between Del Mar and Carlsbad, are covered with a colourful carpet of blooming flowers – an indication of the town's place as a major flower-producing centre. To revel in the sights and fragrances, stop at the Quail Botanical Gardens (230 Quail Gardens Drive) and follow the self-guided walking tour.

THE DESERTS

0   40   80 km
0   20   40 miles

Inyo Nat Fotest
Scotty's Castle
Ubehebe Crater
Death
Independence
2799m
Owens Lake
4 Lone Pine
Darwin
Olancha
Mahogany Flat
Coso Peak 2487m
Little Lake
Trona
Searles Lake
Inyokern
Ridgecrest
Randsburg
Red Rock Canyon S P
3
Mojave
Rosamond
Boron
Four Corners
Fremont Peak 1397m
Barstow
Daggett
Antelope Valley
Lancaster
Palmdale
Adelanto
Victorville
Apple Valley
Angeles Nat Forest
San Bernardino Mountains
2 Glendale
San Bernardino
Redlands
Pasadena
Cherry Valley
LOS ANGELES
Riverside
LONG BEACH
Glen Ivy Hot Springs
Palm Springs
Anaheim
Santa Ana
Huntington Beach
San Juan Capistrana
Rancho California
Laguna Beach
San Clemente
5
Palomar Observatory
Oceanside
Carlsbad
Encinitas
Escondido
Cleveland
1 Gulf of Santa Catalina
Solana Beach
La Jolla
El Cajon
Coronado
Chula Vista
SAN DIEGO
Campo

Stovepipe Wells
Death Valley (Furnace Creek)
Death Valley
National
Badwater Basin -860
Monument
Death Valley Junction
Shoshone
Tecopa Hot Springs
Kingston Peak 2232m
Baker
15
Nipton
Soda Lake
East Mojave Nat Rec Area
Kelso
Hackberry Mtn 1643m
Calico Ghost Town
Devil's Playground
Providence Mts S R A
Essex
Ludlow
40
Amboy
Bristol Lake
Cadiz
Old Woman Mts
Needles
Chemehuevi Valley Indian Res
Joshua Tree
Twentynine Palms
Danby Lake
Rice
Sonora
Vidal Junction
Desert Hot Springs
Joshua Tree National Monument
Granite Mts 1327m
Desert
Midland
Cathedral City
Indio
Coachella
Desert Center
10
Blythe
Hemet
Agua Caliente Ind Res
Mecca
Palo Verde
Rainbow
Salton Sea S R A
California Canal
Chocolate Mts
Borrego Springs
Salton Sea
Brawley
Anza-Borrego Desert State Park
Julian
Glamis
Picacho S R A
Pine Valley
Manzanita Ind Res
231m
Imperial Valley
El Centro
Holtville
Winterhaven
8
Calexico
MEX

Owens River
Fork Kern
Los Angeles Aqueduct
Panamint Range
Mahogany Flat
Amargosa Range
Granite Mts
Mojave Desert
N E V A D A
A R I Z O N A
Colorado River
Colorado Aqueduct

STUNNING VISTAS Far from being the barren wastelands many people expect, the three deserts that occupy the southern and eastern parts of the state provide some of the most striking panoramas in all of California.

FLORA AND FAUNA These climatically extreme but ecologically delicate regions teem with exotic plant and animal life, and contain often monotonous – but sometimes spectacular – landscapes of rippled sand dunes, weather-sculpted rocks and eerily shaped trees, interspersed with palm-filled oases and bordered by snow-capped mountain ranges.

The high elevation of the northernmost desert, the Great Basin, pushing into the Owens Valley from Nevada, limits its vegetation to the bush shrub – making for the least interesting of the three deserts. Immediately south is the Mojave Desert, the site of Death Valley, one of the natural world's most remarkable places, and the more subdued but equally haunting Joshua Tree National Monument.

South of the San Jacinto Mountains, the mild winters of the Colorado Desert support a multitude of desert vegetation, best examined in the Anza-Borrego Desert, an area steeped in pioneer-period history, whose higher points give views to the Salton Sea, a vast inland lake created, bizarrely, by human error.

GHOST TOWNS AND RUINED GOLD MINES Particularly plentiful in the Mojave, these are testament to the fact that desert life has never been easy (even today; see the tips on pages 194–5), although Native American habitation of these fierce regions goes back thousands of years, and there are many markers to aboriginal culture – most impressively the ancient rock drawings called petroglyphs.

While large towns such as Riverside occupy the fertile lands on the extreme western edge of the deserts, other substantial communities have grown up as health resorts at the numerous natural hot springs. And in the oases towns of the Coachella Valley, most famously Palm Springs, desert living means luxury living for the nation's highest rollers. Also rife are reminders of the 19th-century travellers who sought a route through the deserts to the ocean as the US embraced westward expansion. Their failure became the stuff of legend and gave Death Valley its name.

▶▶▶ REGION HIGHLIGHTS

Desert vegetation silhouetted against the twilight sky in Anza-Borrego State Park

Colour in the wilderness: Anza-Borrego Desert

184

▶▶ Anza-Borrego Desert

Named after Juan Bautista de Anza, a Spaniard who made the first recorded crossing of it in 1774, and for the bighorn sheep (or borrego) who once roamed it in force, the 600,000-acre Anza-Borrego Desert is a mixture of sun-scorched lowlands and narrow, twisting canyons, and forms the largest state park in the United States.

Holding the only accommodation (other than basic hikers' campsites), the mountain-ringed oasis town of **Borrego Springs** is an obvious base for touring Anza-Borrego – though even here, summer temperatures frequently rise above 100° F (38° C).

The park's visitor centre, set into the mountainside two miles west of Borrego Springs at **Palm Canyon▶▶**, carries essential maps and information, and mounts displays on desert history, geology and climate. Outside, a cactus garden and a simple nature trail will whet your appetite for what lies beyond.

Sandstone formations warped by millions of years of erosion are a common and evocative sight throughout the park, but the most striking views come at **Font's Point▶▶**, off Road S22, which overlooks the bone-dry creek beds and steep-sided ravines of the Borrego Badlands, a vegetation-free mass inhabited only by lizards and snakes.

Through the southerly sections of the park, 1840s gold prospectors hacked out the only snow-free route into California, a trail later followed by Mormons on the journey that led to the founding of Salt Lake City and by the Butterfield Overland Mail company, whose stagecoaches carried passengers and post to the infant communities of Los Angeles and San Diego. From **Box Canyon Monument▶** on Road S2, a path leads to a lookout point above the old trail.

The barren vistas may suggest otherwise, but desert ecology is a fragile affair, and its subtleties are highlighted from March to May as wildflowers bloom across the Anza-Borrego hillsides, bringing tens of thousands of Californians to enjoy the colours and sweet smells.

By contrast, frustrated rally drivers power off-road vehicles over the dunes and the dry riverbeds of the **Ocotillo Wells Recreational Area**, on the park's eastern edge.

▶ Barstow

Most visitors to Barstow are bus passengers on their way to or from Las Vegas, or shoppers from LA driving out for the discounted designer-label clothes and the range of goods sold at the town's **Factory Merchants' Outlet Plaza▶**.

More edifying matter fills the **California Desert Information Center▶▶** (831 Barstow Road; tel: 619/256–8313), packed with exhibits on desert ecology and practical information about the area.

▶ Big Bear Lake

High in the San Bernardino Mountains, the seven-mile-long Big Bear Lake, formed by a dam in 1883, is a centre for water sports and horseback riding in summer, for skiing in winter. You can tour the lake on a paddle wheeler, Big Bear Queen, between May and October.

► Blythe

A blink-and-you-miss-it town on the Arizona border, Blythe is slowly transforming itself into a desert health resort, although as yet local interest begins and ends with the giant-sized **rock drawings** on the Colorado River Indian Reservation, immediately to the north-east.

► Calico

Since 1968, archaeological excavations close to Calico have revealed more and more of a 'tool factory' claimed to be 200,000 years old. If such advanced age can be proven, this is both the oldest known site of human habitation in the United States and one that overturns all the established theories concerning the earliest Americans. The dig site can be viewed, although the visitor's centre is more informative.

The town of Calico flourished a century ago because of silver and borax mines that yielded millions of dollars' worth of the metals. Like other Califonia mining towns, the community declined when the mines were exhausted – unlike other abandoned mining settlements, Calico was reactivated in the 1950s as a tourist attraction. The walk-through mine, steam railway and wooden buildings, now mostly holding stores – linked by raised wooden sidewalks – are the main attractions, along with pseudo-miners who merrily strum banjos. Still, while Calico can provide a welcome break from driving, only the pervading heat seems at all authentic.

185

A vision of the past: Calico rebuilt

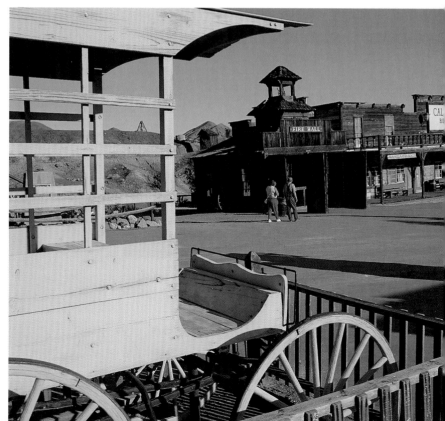

▶ Cherry Valley

An unlikely find in apple-filled Cherry Valley, near San Bernardino, is a gathering of furniture and 17th- to 19th-century European and Asian art at the **Edward-Dean Museum of Decorative Arts**▶ (9401 Oak Glen Road).

▶ Daggett

In Daggett, just east of Barstow, hundreds of mirrors protruding at odd angles from the ground are actually the heliostats of the **Solar One Power Plant**▶, busy producing energy from the sun's rays. A visitor centre explains the technology of the process. Also in town, the **Stone Hotel**▶ has provided shelter for desert travellers since 1875.

▶ Darwin

Darwin is just one of several short-lived silver prospectors' communities that now stand in ruins close to the junction of Highway 395 and Highway 190 on the approach to Death Valley. A dirt track south leads to the secluded beauty of Darwin Falls, a waterfall fed by a natural spring.

186

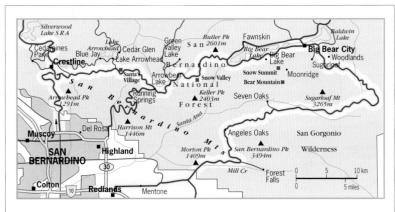

Drive

'The Rim of the World'

Drive north from San Bernardino on Road 18 to Crestline, then join Road 138 for 10 miles to the Silverwood Lake State Recreation Area.
Picnicking, hiking, swimming and varied birdlife are the primary attractions here.

Return to Road 18 and drive east for 15 miles to Lake Arrowhead.
LA's wealthy socialites pass leisurely weekends in luxury homes at **Lake Arrowhead**▶▶.

Continue three miles east on Road 18 for Santa's Village.
Santa's Village▶ is a tacky but entertaining collection of amusement rides aimed at kids.

Continue for 30 miles on Road 18 for Big Bear Lake.
LA residents who cannot afford to weekend at Lake Arrowhead make the most of **Big Bear Lake**▶ (see page 184).

Continue east on Road 18 for 12 miles, joining Road 38 at Big Bear City and then make a 50-mile winding descent to Redlands (see pages 192–3).

Filled by a larger-than-life landscape of sand dunes, volcanic craters, salt flats, and multi-coloured mountain walls, Death Valley is one of the hottest and driest places in the world – yet also one of the most misleadingly named.

Life in Death Valley Death Valley's seemingly inhospitable environs actually support a rich diversity of life. A unique species of tiny fish lives in its ponds, wild asses and bighorn sheep roam the hillsides, and mesquite and bristlecone pines are among the 900 varieties of plant life here.

Signs of human habitation have been dated to 5000 BC, when much of the valley was filled by a lake. The most recent permanent inhabitants were the Shoshone, here during the 1880s when the first white men arrived to mine a rich strain of borax. A few hours of carefully planned driving will reveal sights to linger in the memory for years, although seeing all of Death Valley on anything less than a lengthy hiking expedition is impossible – and even short hikes should be undertaken with care (see pages 194–5).

Points of interest Signposted viewing points on the nine-mile **Artists Drive**▶▶▶ make clear the varying colours of the valley's rock walls, caused by the presence in the rock of oxides, copper and mica.

Barren beauty in Death Valley

❑ Chicago millionaire Albert Johnson lived in an unfinished Spanish-Moorish mansion at the northern edge of Death Valley with a con man called Scot. Johnson died in 1948, and Scot followed him in 1954. Scotties Castle, as it's known, is now a regular part of Death Valley tours. ❑

187

To the north, a turnoff leads to **Golden Canyon**▶▶, whose metallic tints make it live up to its name at sunrise and sunset. On the northern side of Road 198, just east of **Stovepipe Wells**▶▶▶, sand dunes form a 14-square-mile rippled yellow carpet.

Deposited between 2 million and 12 million years ago, the mud flats of **Zabriskie Point**▶▶▶ (reached with Road 190) are legendary for the almost hypnotic effect they have on visitors. **Dante's View**▶▶▶ (reached off Road 190) overlooks the entire valley and makes visible two of the highest and lowest points in the United States: Badwater, 282 feet below sea level and, 60 miles distant, 14,495-foot-high Mount Whitney.

The Deserts

LOST HORSE MINE

The Joshua Tree National Monument area has been prized not only for its trees but also for its deposits of gold. Between 1896 and 1899, the Lost Horse Mine produced gold worth around $3,000 a day. Marked on maps distributed at the visitor centre, the mine is easily accessible and is only a short walk from the road. The old stamp mill and other mining implements can be seen.

Growing up to 50 feet tall, Joshua trees are found in California's desert regions at altitudes of 3,000–5,000 feet

▶ Desert Hot Springs

In Desert Hot Springs, a health resort community close to Palm Springs, **Cabot's Old Indian Pueblo Museum** has an intriguing collection of pioneer-era desert relics and Native American artefacts, including a 20-ton monument carved from a sequoia tree that fills the spacious four-storey former home of Cabot Yerka, one of the area's first settlers.

▶ Indio

The National Date Festival has been held each February in Indio since 1921, and the celebrations of the town's best-known product include ostrich and camel races. Meanwhile, the **Coachella Valley Museum and Cultural Center** fills a building only slightly younger than the Date Festival with memorabilia spanning 70 years of local life.

▶▶ Joshua Tree National Monument

High and low desert meet in the 850 square miles of the Joshua Tree National Monument, whose name comes from the trees, a species of yucca growing up to 50 feet tall that were christened by west-bound Mormon travellers who saw their upraised branches as the arms of the prophet Joshua, pointing the route west.

The weird look of the trees and the huge quartz boulders nearby endow the western section of the monument with an eerie quality, particularly when bathed in the red glow of sunrise or sunset – it is easy to understand why many Californians attribute mystical qualities to the area. (The eastern half is best left to seasoned desert adventurers.)

More prosaically, the irregular formations of the granite slopes are prized by climbers, many hiking trails crisscross the wild landscapes, and there is plenty to be appreciated by car – but do not undertake any kind of visit without first stopping to pick up maps and advice from the visitor centre at Oasis, just south of Twentynine Palms (or from the other centres at Cottonwood and Blackrock Canyon).

Within the monument, **Key's View▶▶** is an essential stop: a high vantage point with panoramic views over the Joshua Tree area and, on a clear day, to Palm Springs and the Salton Sea, 40 miles away.

A signposted side road, nine miles south of the Oasis visitor centre, leads to the **Cholla Cactus Garden▶**, where a foot trail passes a variety of plants – and also quite a few of the creatures – which have adapted themselves for desert survival.

The Geology Tour Road▶▶▶ runs through 18 miles of strange terrain, and a free brochure from the visitor centre aids understanding of the subterranean upheaval that gave rise to these spectacular scenes.

Gold mining flourished here from the 1880s and continued into the 1940s. Of the disused mines strewn across the area, the Lost Horse Mine, said to have produced $3,000 worth of gold a day (see panel), repays a 1.5-mile hike, while another, the Desert Queen Ranch, can be reached only with a ranger-led tour, usually weekends only, more frequent tours in summer.

A Palm Springs palm tree. Close to the town, the canyons of the San Jacinto mountains hold the world's largest gathering of Washington palms, the only palm type native to California

189

▶▶ Palm Springs

The best known and by far the nicest of half a dozen shoulder-to-shoulder towns (collectively known as the 'desert communities') lining Highway 111, which loops off Interstate 10 in the Coachella Valley, Palm Springs attracts 2 million visitors a year, many of them drawn by the glamorous reputation of the country's most famous resort.

The healthful qualities of the local mineral springs encouraged efforts to market Palm Springs as a spa town as early as the 1890s, but it was not until actors Charlie Farrel and Ralph Bellamy founded the Palm Springs Racket Club in 1931 that Palm Springs really took off. They lured their Hollywood celebrity chums – Humphrey Bogart, Clark Gable and Marlene Dietrich among many – with the promise of inexpensive luxury homes, a balmy winter climate, and relaxation far from the madding crowds.

Comedian Jack Benny's broadcasts from the town's Plaza Theater and the arrival of many more show-biz names (and later, political ones, including former president Gerald Ford and his wife, Betty, who put her name to the nation's best-known detoxification clinic) helped cement the town's links with affluent and influential high society.

Surprisingly perhaps, for all its upmarket trappings, Palm Springs is small (with only 30,000 residents) and very affable and street crime is virtually unknown.

THE EASTERN MOJAVE
Known to locals as the 'lonesome triangle', the eastern Mojave desert lies mostly between Interstate 15, Interstate 40 and the Colorado River. One of the rewards for braving its 1.5 million acres of arid and unyielding terrain is the Mitchell Caverns in the Providence Mountains State Recreation Area, about 80 miles east of Barstow. They are filled with strange limestone formations and their smoke-blackened walls indicate 500 years of Native American use.

INDIAN CANYONS
Drive five miles from the centre of Palm Springs along South Palm Canyon Drive and you reach a toll road leading into the Indian Canyons, once the domain of a large group of Cahuillas. The easiest to explore is Palm Canyon, lined for its first seven miles by native Californian palms, their greenery providing a vivid counterpoint to the stark canyon walls. Beyond its parking lot, Palm Canyon – like the other canyons – can be investigated further on foot or horseback.

Strange territory Palm Springs has many curious features. Its dozens of golf courses are sprayed with a million gallons of recycled water per week; palm trees cover the tops of street lights to prevent their glare from diminishing the clarity of the star-filled night sky; and the town's major landowners are the Agua Caliente, from whom businesses rent land on 99-year leases.

Favourite Palm Springs pastimes are poolside tanning, shopping in the air-conditioned malls, and eating in the restaurants along Palm Canyon Drive, where micromist systems spray fine clouds of water to cool patio diners.

Other possible activities include exploring **Moorten's Botanical Garden►►** (1701 S Palm Canyon Drive), a jungle-like collection of cacti and other imposing desert vegetation, whose creator also landscaped a section of Disneyland. Equally recommended is the **Desert Museum►►** (101 Museum Drive), which crowns its 20-acre sculpture-filled grounds with imaginative indoor exhibitions of desert-related art, natural history and anthropology, and fields a strong winter programme of performing arts in the adjoining Annenberg Theater.

Vestiges of Palm Springs' earlier times are maintained at the **Village Green Heritage Center►** (221 S Palm Canyon Drive), where you can visit the 1884 McCallum Adobe and the 1893 Cornelia White's House. More entertaining is a rake through the 1930s consumer durables inside the re-created Ruddy's General Store.

When the heat becomes too much, rise 6,000 feet up into cooler climes on the **Aerial Tramway►►►**, watching the desert scene turn alpine as you reach San Jacinto State Park. The views alone make the ascent worthwhile, even if you do not plan to use the park's 50 miles of hiking and horse trails, which become cross-country ski trails in winter.

Climbing 6,000 feet in 14 minutes, this cable car on the Park Springs Aerial Tramway gives its passengers views of the broad and flat Coachella Valley and the distant Indio Hills as it ascends into the San Jacinto Mountains

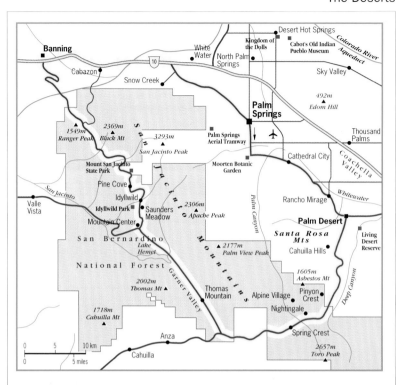

Drive

Around Palm Springs

Drive south from Palm Springs on Road 111 to Rancho Mirage.
Many of the wealthy who supposedly live in Palm Springs actually live among the golf courses and country clubs of **Rancho Mirage▶▶**.

Continue to Palm Desert.
The ultra-rich of the desert communities do their shopping along the pricey **El Paseo▶▶** in Palm Desert. A less costly stop is the 900-acre **Living Desert Reserve▶▶**, where a stroll along the foot trails will reveal much about desert ecology.

From Palm Desert, take Road 74 and climb for 54 miles into the San Jacinto Mountains; at the junction with Road 243, turn right on to Road 243 for Idyllwild.
A mile high and surrounded by tall pines, **Idyllwild▶** is a mountain resort that is also noted for its School of Music and Arts.

Continue on Road 234 for 21 miles to Interstate 10; drive east on Interstate 10 for 12 miles before exiting onto Road 111 and returning to Palm Springs.

❏ The first date-palm seeds in North America arrived with the Spanish in the late 1700s, but only this century did the US Department of Agriculture develop a strain suited to life in the California desert, the only place in the United States where climate and soil are right. The most productive area is around Indio, where 4,000 acres of date palms annually produce $30 million worth of the fruit. ❏

Although it might look an inviting place for a dip, the Salton Sea developed from a salt marsh and its heavily saline waters make swimming uncomfortable; it also holds high levels of selenium

▶▶ Rainbow Basin

At the heart of the Rainbow Basin, 15 miles west of Barstow, you will find a steep gorge with colourful, striped sides – an effect caused by different layers of sediment. The rock walls are also packed with the fossils of three-toed horses, dog-bears, mastodons and other prehistoric creatures which inhabited this once lake-filled area.

▶ Randsburg

Many buildings dating to the 1890s – when the discovery of gold brought the town a 3,000-strong population and made it a stop on the Santa Fe Railroad – have been carefully preserved in Randsburg, and the **Desert Museum** (161 Butte Avenue) is filled to its rafters with unusual remnants from mining days.

▶ Redlands

Earning its name from the colour of its soil, Redlands flourished as a citrus farming centre thanks to the diverting of water from Big Bear Lake in the 1880s. At the same time, the town found favour with wealthy wintering Easterners, whose money financed the ornately gabled and turreted wooden homes still standing along Olive Street, although these are outdone in grandeur by the chateau-style **Kimberly Crest** (1325 Prospect Street), which is sometimes open for tours.

In Smiley Park in the town centre, the Redlands Bowl auditorium is known throughout the state for its summer ballet and opera programmes, and, nearby, the **Lincoln Memorial Shrine**▶ ranks among California's most obsessive historical collections, completely devoted to President Abraham Lincoln and his role in the Civil War.

On the fringes of Redlands, the wide-ranging collections and displays of the **San Bernardino County Museum**▶▶ (2024 Orange Tree Lane) provide an overview of the growth of the area, though more evocative of life in the early 1800s is the two-room museum at the restored **San Bernardino Asistencia**▶ (26930 Barton Road), a branch of Mission San Gabriel Arcangel.

Ridgecrest

The sole redeeming feature of Ridgecrest, a large community mostly composed of military personnel from the China Lake Naval Weapons Center, is the **Mutarango Museum**▶▶, with a small but engaging collection of the native art and culture of the eastern Mojave, and a special display on the rock inscriptions found in the China Lake area.

▶▶ Riverside

The California orange – the navel – was born in Riverside in the 1870s, and the town's resultant affluence saw the building of the **Mission Inn** (3649 Seventh Street), a Spanish-style exercise in luxury whose bedrooms, music rooms, terraces and patios were decorated by $1 million worth of antiques. Guided tours of the inn, now restored, are occasionally offered.

A busy industrial centre as well as an agricultural base, Riverside also has the **Municipal Museum**▶ (3720 Orange Street), which preserves copious relics of the city's past.

Just east of the town, the local branch of the University of California looks after the 39-acre **Botanical Gardens**▶, which specialise in winter-blooming, dry-climate plants and feature a formidable batch of cacti. To the west, the **March Field Museum**▶▶ (16222 1–215) displays mostly military aircraft from 1918 onward.

Wild cacti cover much of **Mount Rubidoux**, to the west of Riverside, the 1,300-foot summit of which can be reached by a twisting lane. At the top, there are impressive views and the Serra Cross, the venue for Easter sunrise services since 1909.

▶ Salton Sea

One of the largest inland seas in the world, the Salton Sea was created in 1905 by an engineering blunder and a severe winter, which caused the Colorado River to breach the canals directing it to the Imperial Valley, and to flood a dried-up lake bed just east of the Anza-Borrego Desert.

Enormous but very shallow, the Salton Sea was stocked with ocean fish when its water turned saline, and anglers were quick to take advantage of the marinas and campgrounds of the Salton Sea Recreation Area created on its eastern bank. Nowadays you'll also find watersports fans.

Meanwhile, bird-watchers arrive in search of herons and egrets, among a host of much rarer winged creatures who are regular visitors to the Salton Sea Wildlife Refuge, on the sea's southern edge.

▶ Twentynine Palms

Ignored by many travellers speeding through on their way to the nearby Joshua Tree National Monument (see page 188), Twentynine Palms is worth a stop for the **Historical Society Museum**▶ (6136 Adobe Road), charting the origins and growth of this little desert settlement.

GULF AND PALM SPRINGS
Seventy courses have earned Palm Springs and the desert communities the title of 'Golf Capital of America'. Many top tournaments are held here and famous names – be they golfers, entertainers, or ex-presidents – are familiar figures on the fairways. Many courses are members-only or very expensive, although local municipal courses (listed in the phone book) are always cheap and open to all. Interestingly, to conserve water, new courses have to be laid on a bed of tile; this enables precious water to be collected after irrigating the greens, and then recycled.

193

DESERT HOT SPRINGS
California's desert regions are sprinkled with hot springs, whose thermally heated, mineral-rich water bubbles up through the earth's crust. Opportunities to sample the waters, and put their alleged health-improving qualities to the test, are numerous and range from the whirlpool- and sauna-equipped spa resorts such as Murrieta Hot Springs, about 25 miles south of Riverside, to the free mineral baths at Tecopa Hot Springs County Park, close to Road 127, just east of Death Valley.

By world standards, California's three deserts are lush and young, formed 1 million to 5 million years ago, primarily because rain-bearing clouds could not cross the Sierra Nevada mountains. Their landscapes are extremely varied, as are their flora and fauna, some of which are unique and all of which have been able to adapt to desert conditions in a variety of inventive ways.

194

Desert flora The cactus is the most obvious example of the succulent desert plant, one that stores water whenever it is available, using a shallow but extensive root system.

Some non-succulent plants can become dormant in the absence of water, while others – such as the brittle bush and creosote bush – can reduce the size and density of their leaves to reduce water loss, and, when necessary, shed all their leaves and branches to protect their root system.

Other than the Joshua trees of the Joshua Tree National Monument, the plants that bring most people to the deserts are the springtime wildflowers. These grow from seeds that germinate only in response to a precise amount of rainfall, which ensures the survival of the plant.

Desert fauna Desert animals are no less inventive. The kangaroo rat never drinks but creates water inside its body after eating dry seeds and is able to condense moisture while exhaling air; the red-spotted toad can absorb its own urine; and desert insects respond to unfavourable conditions by entering a form of suspended animation called aestivation.

Aside from cold-blooded reptiles such as lizards, which scamper from sunlight to shade to regulate their body temperature, and a multitude of birds ranging from turkey vultures to scrub jays, most desert creatures are nocturnal and spend time in the heat of the day sleeping behind rocks or plants.

Desert animals that you are most likely to encounter are the chipmunk-like antelope ground squirrel and the large desert tortoises, most commonly found chewing on grasses and wildflowers in spring. With luck, training your binoculars on distant slopes will bring a glimpse of the rarely sighted bighorn sheep.

Desert travel tips Careful preparation will help you to experience the desert comfortably and safely – and may even save your life.

The only sensible time for desert travel is between November and April, when daytime temperatures are warm but bearable (though the nights can be freezing), and well short of the roasting heat of the summer, when tourist services such as visitor centres are likely to be closed.

FLOWERS OF ANTELOPE VALLEY
You will not see any antelopes in Antelope Valley, but arrive between March and May and you will see millions of orange and purple wildflowers brightening the hillsides that rim the western edge of the Mojave Desert. And at the Antelope Valley California Poppy Reserve, 2,000 acres are set aside for the careful nurturing of California's state flower – the subtleties of which are explained inside a specially built, energy-conserving visitor centre.

Desert driving Before setting out, ensure that your vehicle is in perfect condition, and stock up with ample food and – most crucially of all – at least a gallon of drinking water per person per day.

You should also take around five gallons of spare fuel – desert driving means fewer miles per gallon than on regular roads – and a similar amount of spare water for the radiator.

In the desert, never drive off the marked roads – doing so causes environmental damage. If you intend to travel on one of the isolated side roads, inform a park ranger, or other relevant authority of your plans.

If your car breaks down, do not leave it. Wait until another car passes and signal for assistance. This may involve a long wait.

Other useful tools include a first-aid kit, a flashlight, and waterproof matches.

Desert hiking and walking Many trails can be easily hiked in a few hours, but do not embark on one without a detailed map and some water.

Even on a short walk, be sure to drink water regularly even if you do not feel thirsty. Keep in the shade whenever possible, and stop for a rest at the first sign of dizziness.

Wear loose, light-coloured clothing, dark glasses of good quality, and a wide-brimmed hat, and apply sunscreen liberally. At night the desert is a cold place, so plan accordingly. On your feet, wear sneakers or hiking boots with socks – do not wear sandals.

Be careful where you put your hands and feet, and be wary when turning over rocks. These precautions will help avoid potentially fatal contact with black widow spiders, scorpions and rattlesnakes, and the less harmful tarantulas and centipedes.

Know what to do if you are bitten by a desert creature – details are available from any desert visitor centre or rangers' office.

BORAX MINING
In the California of the late 1800s, gold mining was more glamorous but less lucrative than borax mining. Rich deposits of borax – used in the manufacture of glass and in glazes for ceramics – were discovered in Death Valley (see page 187). Getting the mineral out of the ground proved a lot easier than getting it out of Death Valley, however, and it took 20-strong mule teams 10 days to haul their loads to the nearest train station. Nowadays, most of the world's borax comes from the Boron area, about 80 miles west of Death Valley.

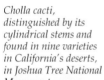

195

Cholla cacti, distinguished by its cylindrical stems and found in nine varieties in California's deserts, in Joshua Tree National Monument

A GREAT DIVIDE You might be a geological ignoramus when you arrive in the Sierra Nevada region, but you will leave with a much surer knowledge of earthly forces and how they have shaped – and continue to shape – California. An expanse of granite domes, pinnacles and ridges some 450 miles long and up to 80 miles wide, the Sierra Nevada mountains give the region its name and divide the state's fertile Central Valley from the arid eastern deserts.

HOT STUFF Despite the feelings of permanence evoked by the colossal peaks, the Sierra Nevada is one of North America's most geologically volatile regions; the hot springs that litter the area are merely the most benign manifestation of the tensions lying deep underground.

Historically, the Sierra Nevada provided one of the major obstacles for would-be settlers approaching by land. Now, travellers still have to plan carefully how – and when – they tour the area.

Approaching from the west, it is tempting to make a beeline for the national parks at the heart of the region – world-famous Yosemite, and less visited but equally worthwhile Sequoia and Kings Canyon – and not worry too much about pressing further east.

EASTERN PLEASURES It is in the east, however, that the sheer-sided Owens Valley forms a slender and visually spectacular corridor, linking the Sierra Nevada's wealth of strange geological phenomena – such as the eerie tufa formations around Mono Lake, a heavily saline body of water at the heart of a long-running ecological dispute, and the geometrically precise basalt colums of the Devil's Postpile Monument – while giving access to scores of sparkling alpine lakes, including stunning Lake Tahoe, on the region's northern edge.

Unfailingly, the Sierra Nevada's natural sights exert greater appeal than its towns. A few bear witness to the region's pioneer days (and one, Bodie, is a genuine Gold-Rush ghost town) but most of the modestly sized settlements are geared to serving the hikers and climbers who are the lifeblood of local economies.

In winter, mountain roads are closed and hiking routes inaccessible, rendering the most pristine sections of the Sierra Nevada's magical icy landscapes off-limits. The bulk of the region's visitors at this time of the year are skiers – and increasing numbers of snowboarders – who turn Lake Tahoe and Mammoth Lakes into the country's busiest winter sports centres.

Winter transportation in Mammoth Lakes

OLDEST LIVING THING
Research during the 1950s by Professor Edmund Shulman of the University of Arizona dated the oldest of the bristlecone pines at 4,600 years, the prelude to much hullabaloo over the discovery of the world's oldest living things. In 1980, however, the bristlecones were made to look like mere infants by a desert shrub, the creosote bush, one of which was found by a botanist to have lived to the ripe old age of 11,500 years.

198

▶ **Bass Lake** 196A3

A large reservoir in the pine-covered foothills on the western approach to Yosemite National Park (see pages 208–9), Bass Lake is one of the state's busiest recreational areas. Speedboats and water-skiers skim across the surface, anglers are tempted by the spiny-finned fish that give the lake its name, and a series of trails pick through the surrounding countryside, offering some respite from the crowds that pack the lakeside cottages and campsites throughout the summer.

▶ **Big Pine** 196C3

Like most Owens Valley towns, Big Pine offers little other than food, lodging and access to spectacular natural areas. Above the town, the Palisades Glacier – North America's most southerly ice sheet – draws expert ice climbers to its tricky slopes. The world's oldest living trees are at the **Ancient Bristlecone Pine Forest▶▶**, 12 miles east and reached by State Road 168.

The **Visitor Center at Schulman Grove▶▶▶** provides an introduction to the strange, warped forms of the 4,000-year-old bristlecone pines, which dominate this extraordinary landscape, each one growing barely an inch per year and looking more dead than alive. The pines survive due to a widely spread root system, which enables them to draw in whatever moisture is available; the distance between the pines reduces the risk of forest fires.

Alabama Hills, near Bishop

The most evocative section of the forest is 11 miles further on and 1,000 feet higher at **Patriarch Grove▶**, where a scattering of bristlecones bestow a weird beauty on an uncompromising terrain – an area selected by NASA for the testing of its lunar rover before it was sent to the moon.

▶ **Bishop** 196B3

Nestling among the motels, restaurants and adventure sports shops that fill Bishop, 15 miles north of Big Pine, the **Paiute-Shoshone Indian Cultural Center and Museum▶▶** (2300 W Line Street) provides an opportunity to discover something of the lifestyles and handicrafts of the valley's native dwellers.

In the Sierra Nevada, as elsewhere in the state, canoeing and white-water rafting are available wherever conditions are right, along with downhill and cross-country skiing, snowboarding, climbing and mountain biking: the region fully lives up to its reputation as California's most sports-crazy area. There are plenty of schools to help beginners master the basic skills.

Skiing A November-to-May snow covering facilitates some outstanding downhill skiing in the region, although cross-country (or Nordic) skiing is also popular – most area hiking trails (and there are many) can be skied as soon as the snow falls.

Venue of the Winter Olympics in 1960, Lake Tahoe has dozens of ski resorts; Tahoe Donner (tel: 916/587–9444) is the best bet for beginners.

Further south Mammoth Lakes is no less busy, with activity centres on the enormous Mammoth Mountain Resort (tel: 619/934–2571), while the Tamarack Cross-Country Ski Center (tel: 619/934–2442) organises a web of backcountry routes.

In Yosemite National Park, the gentle slopes of the Badger Pass Ski Area are ideal for novices – and the setting is spectacular. Also in the park, the Yosemite Cross-Country Ski School (tel: 209/372–8444) runs overnight and three-day guided cross-country trips to Glacier Point. For skiing with a spectacular view, try Bear Valley (tel: 209/753–2301), where the slopes overlook California's deepest canyon.

Climbing Sheer, near-vertical granite rock faces, such as Yosemite's El Capitan, have forced the world's mountaineering fraternity to devise entirely new techniques to conquer them. The region's climbing schools pass on such skills, and also instruct beginners in the rudiments of rock and ice climbing.

The main climbing schools are Yosemite Mountaineering School (June–Aug tel: 209/372–1335; otherwise 209/372–1244), based in Yosemite National Park, and Alpine Skills International (tel: 916/426–9100), based at Donner Pass, which arranges classes on all aspects of climbing and runs trips suited to differing skill levels.

Mountain biking Another thrilling way to explore the ups and downs of the Sierra Nevada is by mountain bike. Many sports shops throughout the Owens Valley and around Lake Tahoe rent mountain bikes for a charge of around $30 a day. And in summer, some of the ski slopes around Mammoth Lakes become the **Mammoth Mountain Bike Park** (tel: 619/934–0606), offering fifty miles to suit all levels of experience. Each July, the slopes host the World Cup Kamikaze Downhill race (see page 202).

WHITE-WATER RAFTING
During April and May, when the melting snow of the High Sierra mountains sends rivers cascading through the foothills, white-water rafting comes into its own along the American and Tuolumne rivers. Most Gold Country towns have companies offering guided river runs, which range from white-knuckle beginners' specials to death-defying experts-only trips. Operators include OARS in Angels Camp (tel: 209/736–4677), and CBOC white-water rafting in Coloma (tel: 800/356–2262).

199

GUIDED TREKKING
An unusual way to soak up the beauty of the Sierra Nevada – and learn a great deal about what you are seeing – is on a pack trip, allowing a mule or a llama to carry your backpack while you ride shank's mare and the guide (usually a qualified naturalist) provides a commentary. Many companies – widely advertised in the area – operate pack trips from the main trailheads. More information is available from the Eastern Sierra High Packers Association, operating through the Bishop Chamber of Commerce (tel: 619/873–8405).

Sierra Nevada

BODIE

Bump over the potholes of Bodie Road, off Highway 395, 20 miles south-east of Bridgeport, and you will enter Bodie Ghost Town State Park. A century ago nearly 10,000 people lived in the Gold-Rush town; their buildings are now too rickety to enter, save for the Miner's Union Hall, which houses a museum. The last three miles of road may be closed in winter.

THE DONNER PARTY

One of the gorier tales of early California concerns the Donner Party of 1846, a wagon train of 89 men, women and children following the Emigrant Trail into California. A series of errors of judgement by their leader culminated in the party being trapped by snow and forced to spend the winter without supplies in what is now the Donner Pass, just west of Truckee. Only 47 people survived the ordeal, some of them having resorted to cannibalism to stay alive.

Grover Hot Springs State Park in summer. In winter, the area is used for Nordic skiing

▶ Bridgeport   196B4

These days little more than a collection of supply stores, Bridgeport's elegant 1880 **County Courthouse▶** reflects the community's boom years when, as the county seat, it grew wealthy from nearby Bodie's gold strikes. If you need proof of former glories, explore the **Mono County Museum▶**, inside the town's former schoolhouse, which stores artefacts from the halcyon decades.

▶▶ Grover Hot Springs State Park   196A5

Set in a divine alpine meadow, the bubbling waters issuing from the earth at Grover Hot Springs State Park have been credited since California's pioneer days as a cure for whatever ails. More recently, the mineral-rich spring water has meant bliss for aching hikers, who enjoy a soak in one of the park's two temperature-regulated bathing pools.

▶ Independence   196C2

Besides rest and nourishment, Independence, 28 miles south of Big Pine, offers the excellent **Eastern California Museum▶▶** (155 Grant Street), covering the geology, history and ecology of the region. The museum includes a striking collection of Paiute and Shoshone crafts, and a thought-provoking exhibit on **Manzanar Camp** (for tours, tel: 760/878–2932), a few miles south of the town, where 10,000 Japanese-Americans were interned following the outbreak of hostilities between the United States and Japan in 1941.

Some of the town's older buildings have been moved to the museum's grounds, together with a large number of aging farming and mining machinery, where they have been assembled as a pioneer village. One that has not been relocated is the former home of author and naturalist Mary Austin (ask directions from the museum), who lived from 1896 in Independence, and described Owens Valley life evocatively in *This Land of Little Rain*, a book of essays published in 1903.

Drive

Sequoia and Kings Canyon National Parks

Enter Sequoia National Park on Highway 198.
Sequoia National Park►► is home to thousands of giant sequoia trees.

Continue on Highway 198, the General's Highway, to Giant Forest Village, turning right on to Crescent Meadow Road.
The road passes famous trees, such as the **Auto Log►**, and foot trails lead into the groves, one of which contains the largest, the **General Sherman Tree►►**.

Turn off Crescent Meadow Road for Moro Rock.
There are fantastic views from the top of **Moro Rock►►►**.

Return to the General's Highway, continuing to Grant Grove.
At **Grant Grove** an excellent **Visitors' Center►►** describes the lives of giant sequoias.

Join the Kings Canyon Highway and drive toward Cedar Grove.

❑ California's coastal redwoods may be taller, but in terms of bulk the giant sequoia tree – which grows only on the western slopes of the Sierra Nevada – is the world's second largest living thing (the largest is an underground-dwelling fungus). The biggest of the trees, the General Sherman Tree in Sequoia National Park, boasts a circumference of 102 feet. The largest sequoias have lived for over 3,000 years, their longevity aided by fire-resistant bark. ❑

The giant sequoia tree

Part of **Kings Canyon National Park►►**, the highway makes a spectacular, winding descent through Kings Canyon.

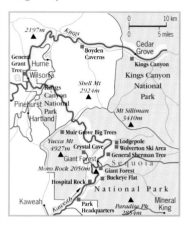

Turn off Kings Canyon Road for Boyden Caverns, signposted near the canyon's floor.
See the fabulous stalagmites and stalactites inside the deep **Boyden Caverns►►►**.

Continue along Kings Canyon Highway, passing Cedar Grove Village for Zumwalt Meadow.
A one-mile walking trail crosses the Kings River by a suspension bridge as it winds above and around loose **Zumwalt Meadow►**.

Beyond Zumwalt Meadow, only hiking trails enable you to penetrate further into the Kings Canyon backcountry.

You do not need to be in California for long to realize that the state sits on a very fidgety portion of the earth's crust. Not only are earthquakes an almost daily phenomenon (the vast majority of them are too small to cause any concern), but natural forces are still molding what may at first appear to be a solid geographical region: the Sierra Nevada mountains.

MOUNTAIN BIKE RACING
Mountain bikes are ridden at breakneck speed up and down the tortuous terrain for which they were designed in the World Cup Kamikaze Downhill Mountain Bike Race, which pushes the machines and their riders to the limit. The event is held at Mammoth Mountain during July.

The formation of the Sierra Nevada Around 200 million years ago, the Pacific plate was gradually slipping under the North American continental plate and what is now California began emerging from the ocean as immense pressures in the earth's crust caused the seabed to buckle and rise. This in turn formed the earliest outline of what were to become the Sierra Nevada mountains.

Between 250 million and 80 million years ago, the surface rock had eroded sufficiently to allow hot magma within the earth's crust to push upward (owing to the reduction of the pressure from above). This magma eventually burst through the surface as volcanoes or, more often, cooled beneath the surface to form huge granite intrusions known as batholites.

Combining with minerals in liquid form on its upward journey, this molten rock provided California with its deposits of gold, silver and other precious metals.

A subsequent process known as exfoliation, when surface rock expands as a result of underground heat, caused the outer layers of the granite monoliths to fracture and break away, eventually creating the bare domes that are characteristic of the Sierra Nevada ranges. Prime examples are El Capitan and Half Dome in Yosemite Valley.

Around 70 million years ago, the rising of the coastal mountains caused the Sierras to tilt westward, a process that increased the erosive power of its rivers and proceeded to carve great valleys through the hillsides.

FIRST SIGHT
The first white people to see the Sierra Nevada are thought to have been the Spanish military captain, Pedro Fages, and Franciscan missionary Juan Crespi in 1772. Both men had been part of the Portolá expedition which three years earlier made the first European sighting of San Francisco Bay.

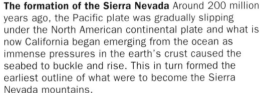

During three separate periods, the latest around 30,000 years ago, falling global temperatures caused glaciers to form in the Sierras. The moving ice sheets wore away the weaker rock (leaving spindly towers and pinnacled ridges), smoothed the harder rock surfaces, and chiseled out the rock bowls that later filled with crystal-clear water and became alpine lakes.

Yosemite Valley's U-shape (river-formed valleys have a V-shape) was formed by the action of ice. Lake Tahoe is the country's largest example of a glacial lake, with many smaller ones lying close to Mammoth Lakes.

The Sierra Nevada today The eastern and western sides of the Sierra Nevada are markedly different nowadays. In the west, the forested foothills composed of older rocks rise steadily upward from the immense flat expanse of the Central Valley toward the region's big peaks. In the east, however, the mountains fall off sharply, forming a spectacular wall to the slender corridor of the Owens Valley with a 400-mile-long fault-line along their base considered by many experts to be the most geologically active place in the United States.

An earthquake here in 1872, one of the strongest ever in North America (estimated at 8.3 on today's Richter scale), demolished the town of Lone Pine and instantly added 13 feet to the height of the surrounding ridges. Drive along Highway 395 close to the Alabama Hills and the scarps created by this quake are still clearly visible. More evidence – often bizarre, and often beautiful – of violent upheaval is everywhere, from the columns of cooled lava at the Devil's Postpile Monument to the valley's innumerable hot springs.

Curiously, though, while the Sierra side of the Owens Valley is a comparative infant, the White Mountains, which form the valley's east wall, are composed of some of California's oldest rock and dotted throughout with the world's oldest living things, the bristlecone pine trees, which are thousands of years old.

As geysers gurgle far below, the Palisades Glacier continues to creep steadily through the mountain canyons above Big Pine, a constant reminder of the region's geological extremes – and the fact that the formation of the Sierra Nevada is a process that is far from complete.

CLIMBING MOUNT WHITNEY
The highest point in the contiguous United States, 14,494-foot Mount Whitney can be seen from many places, but its summit can be reached only by trekking up a stiff 10-mile trail from the end of the Whitney Portal Road, which branches from Lone Pine. The trail is usually snow-free only for a few weeks in summer, when hundreds of visitors jam the parking lot at the trailhead before commencing the climb.

JOSIAH DWIGHT WHITNEY
While John Muir is a name many in California associate with the Sierra Nevada, fewer are aware that it was Josiah Dwight Whitney after whom Mt. Whitney was named. Appointed California's state geologist in 1860, Whitney was assigned to map the Sierra Nevada and assess its mineral wealth. Among many controversies of Whitney's tenure was his belief that he had discovered the 'missing link' between man and the apes, with a skeleton found in Calaveras county.

An alpine lake in the Sierra Nevada. Lakes of this kind result from Ice-Age glaciers leaving indentations in the rock that fill with melting snow

THE PETROGLYPH LOOP TRAIL

Native Americans – some of them predating known tribes – carved colourful figures, or petroglyphs, on to many of California's hillsides. Just outside Laws, a 50-mile Petroglyph Loop Trial through the Chalfont Valley has six marked stops where some of these unusual – and dateless – works can be seen.

Although existing for thousands of years, these tufa formations reflected in the still waters of Mono Lake broke surface only when the water level fell following the draining of tributary rivers to provide drinking water for Los Angeles

▶ **Laws**   *196C3*

Being a stop on the railroad line was a blessing during the frontier days, when Owens Valley farm produce needed transporting to the state's mining areas. One such stop was at Laws, six miles from Bishop, which has been partly re-created in its 1880s form as the **Laws Railway Museum and State Historic Site**▶▶. The train terminal is an impressive restoration, as are several of the town's other early buildings: your tour around them might well be in the company of local history enthusiasts, dressed in period costume.

▶▶ **Mono Lake**   *196B4*

Almost a million years old and 9,000 feet above sea level, few sights in the Sierra Nevada can match the otherworldly vistas seen at Mono Lake. Gazing across the 13-mile-wide saltwater expanse (often called California's Dead Sea), the eye comes to rest on the bizarre **tufa formations**▶▶▶, mostly on the south side, which sprout above the surface in mysterious shapes, each one a pillar of limestone created by the alkaline lake water mingling with fresh spring water. The tufa formations have existed for thousands of years, but surfaced only when the lake level fell when its tributary rivers were drained to provide water for Los Angeles (see panel, page 206).

The falling water level caused by the Owens Valley aqueduct has greatly affected a finely balanced

ecosystem for which the lake is the linchpin. One consequence was to turn Niget Island, in the centre of the lake, into a peninsula, allowing hungry coyotes to reach what was previously a secure nesting place for California gulls, where 90 per cent of their population breed. In 1994 decisive action finally began to raise the water levels. One effect so far has been to make Niget Island once again an island. Beside Highway 395, just north of Lee Vining, the **Mono Basin Scenic Area Visitor Center** explains the lake's evolutionary history and the various threats that it is currently facing.

Fringed by thick forests and overlooked by snow-capped mountain peaks, Lake Tahoe holds enough water to flood the entire state. To most Californians the lake means water sports, skiing or gambling (the eastern third of the lake lies in Nevada, where gambling is legal), but there are many other attractions for visitors.

Commercialism Such is the scale of recreational tourism that the area's natural beauty is always threatened by motels, fast-food outlets and ski lifts. The blight is most pronounced at South Lake Tahoe, an eight-mile sprawl of hotels and restaurants beside Highway 50, which merges into Stateline, a Nevada town dominated by high-rise casinos.

Enjoyable lake cruises These are a more positive feature of South Lake Tahoe, and the **Lake Tahoe Historical Society Museum▶** (3058 Highway 50) gives background on the formation of the lake and its cultures. The prettiest section of the lake is the south-western corner, where the steep, conifer-fringed and boulder-strewn slopes of **Emerald Bay State Park▶▶** (on State Road 89) reach down to a secluded inlet. Here, a mile-long trail leads to **Vikingsholm▶▶▶**, an approximation of a 9th-century Nordic castle designed in the 1920s by a Swedish-born architect, Lennart Palme, whose goal was to create a 38-room lakeside home without disturbing a single tree. Another short trail leads to cascading **Eagle Falls▶**.

Thirty miles north are some enjoyable sandy beaches at **Sugar Pine Point State Park▶▶**; the 1903 **Erhmann mansion▶▶**, built of local wood and stone for a San Francisco banker, now serves as the visitor centre. Similar properties have been renovated at the **Tallac Historic Site▶▶**, near Fallen Leaf Lake.

North of Lake Tahoe, **Truckee▶** appeared with the building of the transcontinental railroad in the mid-1800s, which linked the rest of the nation to Sacramento, 80 miles west. The difficulties that the local terrain presented to travellers prior to the opening of the railroad are outlined inside the **Emigrant Trail Museum▶▶**, at Donner Memorial State Park, a few miles west of Truckee on Interstate 80.

205

❏ The *Tahoe Queen* (tel: 800/23–TAHOE) operates daily sightseeing trips and, after dark, a dinner cruise. The *MS Dixie* (tel: 702/588–3508) makes a sightseeing excursion from Zephyr Cove as far as Emerald Bay. ❏

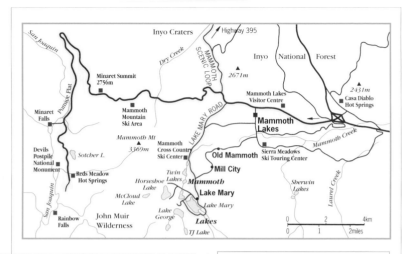

Drive

Mammoth Lakes

Leave Highway 395 between Lee Vining and Bishop, taking State Road 203 until you come to Mammoth Lakes.
With a population of 4,000 and hotel beds for 40,000, **Mammoth Lakes**►► is one of the United States' most popular ski areas.

Alongside State Road 203, look for the combined Ranger Station and Visitors' Bureau.
The volatile geology of Mammoth Lakes is explained inside the excellent **Visitors' Bureau**►.

Continue on State Road 203 for eight miles, reaching the Minaret Vista Picnic Area.
Jagged peaks and ridges rise high above the **Minaret Vista Picnic Area**►►; far below, the San Joaquin River negotiates a deep canyon.

Continue on State Road 203 for 14 miles, for the Devils Postpile Monument.
The extraordinary hexagonal basalt columns of the **Devils Postpile Monument**►►► formed as

❏ The Owens Valley Aqueduct was completed in 1913 to siphon water from the Owens Valley to the growing metropolis of Los Angeles. Despite the harm the scheme caused to the valley, the aqueduct was extended to Mono Lake in 1941, and a second aqueduct was built in 1970. ❏

molten lava flow cooled and was polished by passing glaciers.

Retrace your route along State Road 203, after 17 miles turning right on to Lake Mary Road and continuing for six miles to the Lake Mary Loop Road.
The Lake Mary Loop Road circles **Lake Mary**►, the largest of several glacial lakes in the vicinity.

Return to State Road 203 and turn left, after a mile turning right to come on to the Mammoth Scenic Loop.
Constructed in the 1970s as an evacuation route in the event of a major earthquake, the **Mammoth Scenic Loop**►► passes several examples of volcanic upheaval, including the water-filled **Inyo Craters**►, to the left.

Continue on the Mammoth Scenic Loop to rejoin Highway 395 eight miles north of the State Road 203 junction.

Excellently laid out and well-maintained short trails put some of the Sierra Nevada's most unforgettable scenery within reach even of those people who consider it a major expedition to get out of their cars. The best of the easier walks lie in the Yosemite Valley (described on pages 208–9) and around the giant trees of Sequoia National Park (see page 201). Longer walks (such as the John Muir trail) often branch from simpler foot trails, allowing longer and more arduous forays into the rugged Sierra backcountry.

Exploring on foot Some hikes, travelling far from roads and motels, might take a few hours or a few days (with camping at undeveloped sites), and often connect with longer routes such as the 250-mile **John Muir Trail**, between Mount Whitney and Yosemite Valley, itself part of the enormous Pacific Crest Trail that runs all the way from Mexico to Canada.

Aside from being a starting point for the John Muir Trail, Yosemite National Park has many other hikes that demand fitness and determination. Of them, the most rewarding is the eight-mile route to the summit of Half Dome from the Holiday Isles campsite, steep enough in some sections that hikers are forced to use steel climbing cables fixed to the smooth granite surface.

Many other hikes radiate from Yosemite's Tuolumne Meadows; among them is the High Sierra Loop Trail, which bobs and weaves around waterfalls, meadows and steep-sided river creeks,for a distance long enough to have six well-equipped overnight huts at eight-mile intervals on its course. Reservations are essential at these.

The High Sierras After viewing the big trees of Sequoia National Park, drive the 100-mile winding road through the secluded southern section of the park and you will reach Mineral King, a hauntingly quiet valley, 7,500 feet high. Some of the greatest views of the High Sierras – peaceful alpine lakes lined by fir trees and surrounded by forbidding granite peaks – are within reach of Mineral King on short (but often steep) trails. Here, the intrepid walker can also join the 50-mile High Sierra Trail, which affords unmatched high-country views and links with the John Muir Trail.

On the trail in the Sierra Nevada

Guaranteed to stir the soul, Yosemite Valley's granite cliffs topped by tumbling waterfalls and lake-studded alpine meadows all help to make this venerable national park one of the world's most beautiful places.

WATERFALLS
Do not be surprised to find the waterfalls of the Sierra Nevada – and especially those in Yosemite – more closely resembling dripping faucets than the gushing torrents of popular description. The falls are only fully active during the spring, when they are fuelled by melting snow.

When to visit The park can be visited year-round, but arriving in spring or autumn avoids winter snows and summer's tourist crowds, which have led to plans to ban cars from Yosemite Valley, the park's single most spectacular section. You have not seen Yosemite until you have seen Yosemite Valley, but it is only a seven-mile long section of the 1,000-square-mile park and you should also explore other parts, such as Tuoloumne Meadows on the park's eastern side, and Wawona and the Mariposa Grove, south of the valley.

The numerous accidents caused by distracted drivers prove that there is much to admire even from a car window. Simple foot trails make much more of it accessible, while a network of hiking trails through Yosemite's many undeveloped portions link with marathon trans-Sierra treks (see page 207).

Yosemite Valley A natural sculpture on an infinite scale, Yosemite Valley has been filling arrivals with awe since the first non-natives entered it in the mid-19th century. After the valley was carved by glaciers, a lake covered its floor. The lake slowly silted up and became today's lush meadow, dotted with fir trees and enclosed by enormous granite peaks.

The spring sunshine catches the face of Yosemite's El Capitan. The steadily rising temperatures cause a gradual melting of the winter snows that will soon lead to the national park's waterfalls being at their most spectacular

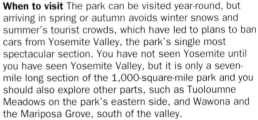

The 8,842-foot **Half Dome**▶▶, its missing half crushed beneath the ice fields, is a vivid reminder of the incredible forces that shaped Yosemite Valley. There is a good view of Half Dome and exceptional views across the valley, from **Glacier Point**▶▶, at the top of a 3,200-foot-high rock wall on the valley's south side, accessible via a winding road and by a steep four-mile trail.

Try to visit Glacier Point at sunset, when Half Dome glows with orange hues, or at night, when moonlight illuminates the valley and millions of stars twinkle above the Sierra Nevada peaks.

From Glacier Point you also get a sense of the mind-boggling scale of **El Capitan**▶▶ at the valley's western end, the world's tallest exposed granite monolith, rising three times higher than the Empire State Building.

A common sight at El Capitan's foot are binocular-wielding visitors, who hope to watch the climbers – almost invisible from the ground – as they seek out the challenging peak's few cracks and fissures.

After enjoying the grand views, explore the walking trails. These reach waterfalls, such as **Lower Yosemite Falls**▶ (the more impressive **Upper Yosemite Fall**▶▶ is at the end of a three-mile uphill hike) and **Bridalveil Falls**▶, opposite El Capitan. With a day to spare, tackle the longer trek to **Vernal Falls**▶▶ and **Nevada Falls**▶▶, reached via the steep but rewarding Mist Trail.

Also on the valley floor, Yosemite Village has shops, services and the **Indian Cultural Museum**▶, giving a brief account of Yosemite's Miwoks and Paiutes.

Close by, the stone-and-concrete **Ahwahnee Hotel**▶▶, the most upmarket accommodation in the park, has fit neatly into its surrounds since 1927; step inside to peek at the gorgeous dining room and to admire the lounge's mammoth stone fireplace.

Tuoloumne Meadows Close to the park's eastern entrance but better reached from the west by the vista-rich **Tioga Road**▶▶, the vivid green Tuoloumne Meadows – the Sierras' largest alpine meadow – forms a striking contrast to the bald granite peaks all around.

Primarily a base for hardened hikers and experienced climbers, Tuoloumne Meadows is also one of the most quietly beautiful sections of the park, with plenty to reward a day's rambling.

Wawona and the Mariposa Grove After the crowds and visual drama of Yosemite Valley, Wawona, surrounded by dense forests and bordered by meadows and gushing streams, is the picture of pastoral tranquillity. The white, wood-framed **Wawona Hotel**▶▶, opened in 1879 to house stagecoach travellers, adds to the rural charm.

Near the hotel, the **Pioneer Yosemite History Center**▶ remembers, with exhibits and restored buildings, the region's early white settlers. One of them, Glen Clerk, is credited with the discovery of the **Mariposa Grove**▶▶, the thickest of the park's three stands of giant sequoia trees. If you are not visiting Sequoia National Park (see page 201), be sure to explore these fascinating trees on the grove's narrated tram tours.

209

JOHN MUIR'S VIEW
On the way to spending his first summer in the Sierra Nevada, John Muir wrote, in typically lyrical style: 'Along the eastern margin rises the mighty Sierra, miles in height, reposing like a smooth, cumulus cloud in the sunny sky, and so gloriously coloured and so luminous, it seems not to be clothed with light, but composed of it, like the wall of some celestial city'.

JOHN MUIR
Scottish-born John Muir arrived in San Francisco in 1868 and allegedly asked for directions to 'somewhere wild'. Accompanied only by a mule, Muir spent many summers exploring the Sierra Nevada. The eulogistic writings that resulted from these trips, and his tireless efforts to have the Yosemite area put under federal protection, led to the formation of the still-influential Sierra Club, and the creation of Yosemite National Park in 1890 (for more on Muir, see page 81).

GOLD COUNTRY AND FAR NORTH

O R E G O N

0 25 50 75 km
0 25 50 miles

Yreka

Goose Lake

Clear Lake Res

Upper Alkali
Lake (Dry)

Modoc

Lava Beds
National
Monument

National

XL Ranch
Ind Res

Alturas

Warner Mts

Middle
Alkali
Lake

Mt Shasta 4317m

Klamath

Canby

Weed

Forest

National

Pit

Eagleville

Lower Alkali
Lake (Dry)

Callahan

Mt Shasta

Mt Shasta Ski Park

Castle Crags

McCloud

Forest

Ahjumawi Lava
Springs S P

Adin

South Fork

Trinity

Whiskeytown-Shasta-Trinity
National Recreation Area

McArthur Burney
Falls Memorial S P

Termo

see Drive
page 214

Claire
Eagle
Lake

Shasta
Lake

Lake Shasta Caverns

Lassen

Eagle
Lake

Bridge Bay

Whiskeytown
Lake

Shasta S H P

Shasta

Redding

Shingletown

Lassen Pk
3187m

National

Lassen Volcanic
National Park

Susanville

N E V A D A

Anderson

Lassen
Np Ski Area

Forest

Westwood

Paynes Creek

Mt Meadows
Reservoir

Honey
Lake

Red Bluff

Wm B Ide Adobe S H P

Lake
Almanor

Mendocino

Mill

Plumas

Corning

Wooden Bridge S R A

Belden

Feather

National

National

Quincy

Forest

Orland

Paradise

Lake
Oroville

Plumas
Eureka S P

Plumas-Eureka
Ski Bowl

Portola

Forest

Elk Creek

Chico

Lake Oroville
S R A

Butte

Sierra
City

Willows

Oroville

Downieville

Malakoff Diggins
S H P

Tahoe National Forest

Colusa
Ind Res

Nevada
City

Truckee

Williams

Rough and Ready

Grass
Valley

80

Donner
Memorial S P

Lake
Tahoe

Clear
Lake

Yuba
City

Marysville

Bear

Tahoe
City

Lower Lake

Sacramento

Auburn

D L Bliss S P

South Lake
Tahoe

Eldorado
Coloma

Marshall Gold
Discovery S H P

3055m

Healdsburg

Lake
Berryessa

505

Roseville

Folsom
Lake

Placerville

National

Grover Hot
Springs S P

Woodland

Folsom

Davis

Cosumnes

Forest

Santa Rosa

Vacaville

SACRAMENTO

Plymouth

Volcano

Indian Grinding Rock S H P

Napa

80

Lodi

Amador City

Jackson

Petaluma

Fairfield

San Andreas

Mokelumne Hill

Mercer
Caverns

Calaveras Big Trees S P

Novato

San
Pablo
Bay

Vallejo

Angels Camp

Murphys

Moaning Caves

San Rafael

Antioch

New Melones
Lake

Columbia S H P

Yosemite

Muir Woods
Nat Mon

680

Concord

Stockton

Columbia

National

SAN
FRANCISCO

Golden Gate N R A

Oakland

Mt Diablo S P

205

Jamestown

Chinese Camp

Sonora

Park

San
Francisco
Bay

580

Livermore

Hetch Hetchy Aqueduct

Don Pedro
Lake

Coulterville

San Mateo

Hayward

Fremont

880

5

San Joaquin

Modesto

Lake
McClure

Merced

Mariposa

A

B

C

BOUNDLESS WEALTH In 1848, the discovery of gold changed California forever. Previously a remote farming outpost, California suddenly became the place to be, and for the first time (and certainly not the last) its very name exuded the promise of instant and unbridled riches. With no easy links to the rest of the country – the Sierra Nevada mountains, whose hillsides held the gold that the rivers had washed to the lowlands, were then as now a formidable natural barrier – it was not until 1849 that the first huge influx of wealth-seekers arrived, the so-called Forty-niners. Three years later, 100,000 people had settled in the hastily built wood and brick towns of what was being called the Gold Country.

Most gold-rush fortunes were made by merchants and storekeepers rather than the hopeful prospectors; none became more successful or as influential in shaping the future as the so-called Big Four (see page 221). Many of the prospectors wound up as labourers in the company-owned mines that came to dominate the industry as the stocks of river gold were exhausted.

As mining machinery arrived by ship, port towns such as San Francisco and Sacramento flourished; the latter became the state capital in 1854. The only Gold Country settlement still of appreciable size, Sacramento lost its prestige when California's influential figures departed for the coastal cities. Today it makes the most of its history and is slowly shedding the staid image impressed upon it by its army of state bureaucrats.

EAST OF SACRAMENTO The appropriately numbered State Road 49 links many of the smaller Gold Country towns, which pepper a 200-mile-long strip – known as the Mother Lode – north from Yosemite along the western slopes of the Sierra Nevada mountains. Almost every community here prides itself on preserving its 19th-century buildings that, together with ubiquitous gold-mining museums, evoke a potent sense of rough and ready gold-rush days. The down side is that every town seems uncannily like the last.

California's Far North, separated from the North Coast by the Klamath Mountains and reached by Interstate 5 from the Gold Country, provides greater variety, not with its towns, which are forgettable, but with its ravishing scenery: alpine forests, canyons and sparkling rivers, wondrous lava formations at the Lava Beds National Monument, and bubbling mud pits, hot springs, and hot gases issuing furiously from the ground at Lassen Volcanic National Park.

High hopes: panning for gold

A 'walk-through' giant sequoia at Calaveras Big Trees State Park, carved before conservation awareness banned such practices

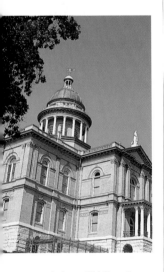

Auburn Old Town's 19th-century elegance

▶ Amador City   210B2

Officially California's smallest city, Amador City is as pretty as a picture and stretches for just one block along State Road 49, holding a handful of cafés, bed-and-breakfast inns, and art and antiques shops.

▶ Angels Camp   210C1

Mines at Angels Camp (named for the two Angel brothers who opened a shop here in 1848) yielded $19 million worth of gold between 1886 and 1910, but – bizarrely – it is frogs and not precious metal that have brought the town lasting fame. Every May since 1928, the **Jumping Frogs Jamboree▶** – in which frogs compete over three measured hops for a $1,000 prize (going to the winning owner, not the champion frog) – has brought tens of thousands of spectators to Angels Camp, and accounts for the frog motifs that appear on many of the town's buildings.

The frog fixation is actually an expression of the town's literary claim to fame. Legend has it that writer Mark Twain was relaxing in the bar of the **Hotel Angels▶** (1287 Main Street) during the 1860s, when he heard the miners' tale about jumping frogs that inspired his first published story. Another writer, Bret Harte, also has links with the town; for more on both scribes, see panel (left).

Besides frogs, Angels Camp can muster only a few souvenir shops to fill travellers' spare minutes.

▶▶ Auburn   210B2

Thirty miles from Sacramento on Interstate 80, Auburn is fast becoming the state capital's favourite suburban community. Down the hill from the nondescript modern town, however, Auburn's cheerful **Old Town▶▶** has many restored mid-19th-century buildings – including an 1892 fire house, the state's oldest continuously used post office, a domed neoclassical courthouse, and a tiny Chinatown district – battling for tourists' attention with restaurants and antiques stores (and some rummageable junk shops).

The highly commendable **Gold Country Museum▶▶** (1273 High Street) charts Auburn's past with a collection of gold-mining implements and explanatory displays, backed up with Native American items and intriguing pieces from early Auburn's Chinese community.

Next door to the main museum, the **Bernhard Museum▶** is a complex of late 1800s buildings intended to replicate Victorian life: you will find a period-furnished home, a working blacksmith's yard, and a former winery now housing an art gallery.

▶▶ Calaveras Big Trees State Park   210C1

Much less famous nowadays than their counterparts in the Sierra Nevada's national parks, the giant sequoia trees at what became Calaveras Big Trees State Park were the first of their kind to be discovered – by a local settler chasing a bear in 1852 – and were first thought to be the only giant sequoias in the world. Widespread disbelief greeted press reports of their size (in terms of bulk, giant sequoias were long considered the earth's largest living organisms) and there followed a 'tree rush'

212

of tourists and naturalists to California. The **Big Trees Visitor Center** provides a thorough grounding on the trees, which lie in two sections of the park. The North Grove is looped by a mile-long foot trail; nine miles south, the less visited South Grove, which requires a bit more walking, shelters more than 1,000 sequoias in atmospheric seclusion.

▶ Chinese Camp 210C1

In 1851, one in ten of California's 250,000 miners were Chinese, and 5,000 of them lived in Chinese Camp, nine miles south of Jamestown at the junction of State Road 49 and State Road 120. Not helped by the 'foreigners' tax' (described on page 219), few Chinese made a profit from mining and many went on to provide the labour for the transcontinental railroad, before retreating to San Francisco's Chinatown following the government's anti-Chinese Exclusion Act of 1882 and widespread 'Yellow Peril' hysteria.

Nothing remains of Chinese Camp except crumbling brick and adobe buildings, and it is mainly left up to a tourist information office to keep the place's name on the map.

▶▶▶ **REGION HIGHLIGHTS**

State Capitol Building
page 221

California State Railroad Museum *page 221*

Lassen Volcanic National Park *page 224*

Marshall Gold Discovery State Historic Park
page 219

Mount Shasta *page 226*

Grass Valley *page 218*

Nevada City *page 220*

Indian Grinding Rock State Historic Park
pages 218–19

Railtown 1897 State Historic Park *page 214*

Drive

State Road 49: Jamestown to Placerville

See map on page 210.

Begin in Jamestown, at the Railtown 1897 State Historic Park.
Jamestown's **Railtown 1897 State Historic Park**► ► preserves the engines, carriages, and equipment of the Sierra Railway Company, founded in 1897.

From Jamestown, drive three miles east on State Road 49 to reach Sonora.
One of the wealthiest gold-rush towns, **Sonora**► ► continues to thrive, thanks in part to the railway and also to the well-preserved historical buildings in the old section of the town that make it a much sought-after address.

Panning for gold in Columbia State Historic Park

Continue for four miles on State Road 49 to Columbia State Historic Park.
The outstanding **Columbia State Historic Park**► ► creates an intriguing impression of life in a gold-rush town (see page 215).

Continue for 19 miles on State Road 49 to Angels Camp.
Curiously, **Angels Camp**► is the only gold-rush town better known for its frogs than its preserved buildings: writer Mark Twain penned his first published story about them, and nowadays a Jumping Frogs Jamboree is held each May (see page 212).

Continue for 11 miles on State Road 49 to San Andreas.
In **San Andreas**►, legendary outlaw Black Bart (see panel on page 223) was tried and sentenced in 1883 at the County Courthouse, an immaculately restored building that is now the **Calaveras County Historical Museum and Archives**►.

Continue for 16 miles on State Road 49 to Jackson.
The seat of tiny Amador County, Jackson is home to the **Amador County Museum**►, which offers a lively examination of gold-mining techniques with working scale models.

Continue for 14 miles on State Road 49, passing Amador City (described on page 212), on the way to Plymouth.
The route passes through Drytown, named for the condition of the local creek, not sarcastically for the 27 saloons that stood here in gold rush times. A side road from Plymouth leads to Fiddletown, settled by fiddle-playing Missourians in the 19th century.

Continue for 20 miles on State Road 49 to Placerville.
In **Placerville**►, once known as Hangtown, the well lit but chilly innards of the **Gold Bug Mine**► can be toured, and the **El Dorado County Museum**► ► stores a hoard of miners' tools and machinery.

▶▶▶ Columbia State Historic Park *210C1*

In 1854, bustling Columbia was beaten by two votes by Sacramento in the race to become California's state capital. Consequently, as soon as its mines closed so too did the town, leaving the 12 square blocks that now form **Columbia State Historic Park**. Its 50 wooden buildings preserved in the park include Columbia's saloon, hotel, schoolhouse, and even its dentist's office, all staffed by guides in period dress.

▶ Coulterville *210C1*

Coulterville should be on your itinerary because of the engrossing accounts of mining-era life in the **North Mariposa County History Center▶**, inside the community's former Wells Fargo office. Take a walk, too, along Main Street to view the thick-walled adobe buildings of the 1850s, such as the Jeffrey Hotel and the Magnolia Saloon, and the Sun Sun Wo Co Store, a survivor of Coulterville's Chinatown district.

▶ Downieville *210B3*

Flaunting its dubious distinction of being the only mining community to hang a woman, Downieville not only preserves many of its 1850s structures but also keeps a shine on the town gallows. Once a Chinese store and opium den, the **Sierra County Museum▶** on Main Street has photographs and knick-knacks.

▶ Folsom *210B2*

More than a quarter of Folsom's 23,000 residents are unhappily enduring what Johnny Cash immortalised in song as Folsom Prison Blues. Such is the fame of the town's prison that it has its own museum, devoted to crime and its perpetrators. A more orthodox historical collection fills the **Folsom Museum▶**. Nearby Lake Folsom has water skiing, swimming, and sailing.

A stagecoach is part of the scenery in Columbia State Historic Park

CHINESE 'WARS'
The Chinese endured more racism than any other ethnic group during the gold-mining days, and there was much disappintment in the non-Chinese community when a 'Tong Wars' battle, which raged in Chinese Camp for several hours in 1856, left only four dead.

GALLOWS HUMOR
The group of public-spirited Downieville citizens who got together in the late 1980s to finance the restoration of their community's most historic landmark – its gallows – rejoiced in the title, The Friends of the Gallows.

The image of the lone prospector standing beside a river patiently sifting through a panful of slush in the hope of finding yellow flakes is somewhat removed from truth. In reality rivers were diverted and dredged, entire hillsides were blown to smithereens, and immense machines kept whole towns awake at night as they hammered quartz to powder. The same technology that made California rich also inflicted scars across its Sierra foothill landscapes that – a century after the damage was done – are only just starting to heal. Many museums in the area showcase the history of gold-mining technology.

A gory reminder of the summary justice practised in the early days of the Gold Country, seen here at Jamestown helping attract attention to a business offering gold prospecting tours

Placer mining Panning was the simplest form of 'placer mining' (the term stemming from the idea of the gold being 'in place' in rivers and streams), the 'placer' scooping up a panload of gravel from the riverbed and carefully removing the lighter material to leave (hopefully) the heavier gold remaining at the bottom. Most of the gold found this way was actually tiny flakes of gold dust nicknamed 'color.'

A more sophisticated form of placer mining came later with the use of the 'rocker,' a long box into which one placer shovelled riverbed detritus while a second miner shook the contraption, hoping to capture gold in the cleats at the bottom as the dirt fell through.

A further refinement was the 'long tom,' a wooden trough about 12 feet long that needed three placers: one shovelling, one mixing and the third directing a jet of water into the trough. The contents drained out through a 'ripple box,' which caught any passing gold.

Later, productivity was increased with complex sluice systems, but by the 1850s it was widely accepted that most of the rivers had yielded all the gold they were going to and attention turned to the gold-bearing Sierra rock.

Hydraulic mining During the early 1850s, surface rock was removed from whole hillsides with high-pressure jets of water using adapted fire-fighting equipment and nozzles weighing a ton to expose the seams of gold.

Highly productive (although many tons of rock had to be removed to yield a few ounces of gold) but also highly pollutive, this so-called hydraulic mining wreaked havoc on the natural landscape, destroying wildlife habitats and clogging rivers with so much mud and gravel that the state's farmland came under threat. Because of such damage, 'hydraulicking', as it was known, was banned in 1884.

Quartz (or hard-rock) mining Around the time hydraulic mining commenced, it was discovered that gold was embedded in quartz veins, or lodes (hence the term 'Mother Lode', applied to the whole Gold Country but misleadingly implying that there was a single large lode), which occurred throughout the Gold Country.

Dynamite, invented in 1860, was used to blast into the hillsides and the first tunnel mines were constructed, often stretching for many miles underground.

Miners descended into the depths and attacked the quartz lodes with pickaxes and shovels, the quartz chunks they hacked out being carried to the surface on mule-drawn wagons. Mules were also used to turn the *arrastra*, a cumbersome machine of Mexican origin resembling a large pestle and mortar, which slowly ground the quartz.

Pulverising the quartz was greatly speeded up by stamp mills, enormous machines weighing several tons (and now the prize exhibits of many Gold Country museums); hammering day and night, the stamp mills often could be heard in surrounding towns. Gold was extracted from the pulverised quartz through a chemical process, and then, in molten form, it was poured into molds to make ingots.

Dredge mining From the 1890s, dredging machines began gouging up the riverbeds where the earlier placer miners had worked, depositing the resultant material in huge sluicing machines. The tons of waste that this process created were unceremoniously dumped in any available space, often burying vegetation and changing the course of many rivers. Subject to strict controls, limited dredge mining continues today.

GOLD PANNING TODAY
Some people believe the 'Mother Lode' has plenty of gold left to yield, and dredge mining and gold panning both have plenty of serious adherents, even today. The pans handed out to tourists at a few spots around the Gold Country, however, are unlikely to produce anything other than minuscule amounts of gold.

217

Small amounts of gold can still be found by panning California's rivers

The wealth produced by gold mining left its mark in the elegant buildings of Grass Valley

LOLA MONTEZ
Having danced her way across the United States, thrilling audiences with her saucy 'spider dance', Irish-born Lola Montez settled in Grass Valley. Flamboyant and glamorous, Lola's was a bemusing presence to miners but not to Lotta Crabtree, a local six-year-old later to become the highest-earning entertainer in the United States, to whom Lola passed on her dancing skills. Leaving Grass Valley after her husband shot her pet bear, Lola underwent a religious conversion and spent the next few years delivering theosophical lectures in Australia and Europe, before dying penniless in New York in 1861, aged 42.

▶▶ **Grass Valley**   *210B2*

The biggest and most lucrative mine in California made Grass Valley one of the state's richest communities by the late 1800s. The buildings, a shaft and many of the machines of the state's most technologically innovative mine – which ceased operations only in 1956 – can be seen at the **Empire Mine State Historic Park▶▶**, spread across both sides of State Road 174 a mile east of the town. The mine produced almost 6 million ounces of gold during its lifetime, in 367 miles of underground tunnels and workings that sometimes reached 11,000 feet beneath the surface.

After the mine closed, Grass Valley kept itself in style through farming and the lumber trade and by exploiting the tourist appeal of its many balconied 19th-century buildings – and the restaurants serving 'English-style' food, a throwback to the days when many Cornish miners settled here.

A less likely settler was Lola Montez, a vivacious dancer and a former lover of the King of Bavaria (see panel). A replica of her home (at 248 Mill Street) houses the tourist office and many mementos of her life.

Elsewhere, the **Grass Valley Museum▶** (corner of Church and Chapel streets) fills an 1865 schoolhouse with historical displays that include reconstructed period rooms and a 10,000-volume collection of antiquarian books, and the **North Star Mining Museum▶** (intersection of State Road 20 and State Road 49) has detailed exhibitions on mining technology.

▶▶ **Indian Grinding Rock State Historic Park**   *210C2*

Many generations of Miwok grinding nuts to make flour have left over 1,000 identical *chaw'se*, or mortar cups, indenting a large limestone outcrop at Indian Grinding Rock State Historic Park, between Amador City and Volcano; several hundred petroglyphs also mark the rock. More recent additions to the park are a re-created

Miwok Village and a Museum Cultural Center, which describes the use of the *chaw'se* and profiles the 10 tribes native to the area.

▶ Malakoff Diggins State Historic Park   *210B3*

Sixteen miles from Nevada City, a massive gash on the side of a mountain caused by hydraulic mining has become a serene expanse of meadows and canyons populated by deer, coyotes and squirrels. A few restored buildings recall the mining settlement here, but it is the extraordinary regenerative abilities of nature that impress most throughout the 3,000-acre park.

▶ Mariposa   *210C1*

Most who pass through Mariposa are less interested in the Gold Country than Yosemite National Park, which lies just 30 miles east. If you are one of them, stop off at least long enough to explore the **Mariposa County History Center▶▶** (corner of Twelfth and Jessie streets), a rewarding collection revealing plenty about life during the gold-rush times and featuring a miner's cabin and a lady's boudoir among a group of reconstructed period interiors.

Outside, the lawlessness of the old days is suggested much less by the grand **Mariposa County Courthouse▶** (5808 Bullion Street) – finished in 1854 and the state's longest-serving place of justice – than by the nearby Old Mariposa Jail, a grim affair in use until 1960.

Two miles south of Mariposa, the **California State Mining and Mineral Museum▶▶** holds ample proof that this region yielded the Gold Country's most spectacular finds, with diamonds and gold nuggets among 200,000 precious pieces.

▶▶▶ Marshall Gold Discovery State Historic Park   *210C2*

California changed forever on January 24, 1848, when James Marshall, building a sawmill for landowner John Sutter, chanced upon flakes of gold beside the American River in the settlement of Coloma, commemorated as the Marshall Gold Discovery State Historic Park.

Within a year, 10,000 people were busy with pickaxes and shovels in the vicinity, although they quickly departed as richer veins were discovered elsewhere, leaving Coloma to decline and a disillusioned Marshall to die in 1879 in his cabin, which still stands here.

Among many restored buildings, the park also has a working model of Sutter's Mill and a museum tracing the colossal effect Marshall's find had on the state.

▶ Murphys   *210C1*

Named after the two Irish brothers who founded it in 1848, Murphys barely extends beyond its tree-lined Main Street, where the **Murphys Hotel▶▶** has stood since 1856, hosting luminaries such as writer Bret Harte and future US president Ulysses S Grant. The clutter of curiosities filling the **Oldtimer's Museum▶** attests to the mining community's dislike of throwing things away.

North of Murphys off Sheep Ranch Road, a guided tour of **Mercer's Caverns▶▶** leads to bizarre limestone formations discovered by chance in 1885.

THE FOREIGNERS' TAX
Passed by the state legislature in 1850, the Foreign Miners' License Tax imposed a monthly $20 levy on all miners who were not U.S. citizens. Initially it was directed at Mexicans, who had staged an uprising against U.S. vigilantes enforcing racist mining codes in Sonora. In practice it came to be only Chinese miners who were subject to the tax: $15 went to the state and $5 to the local sheriff.

Raised sidewalks, wooden balconies and imitation gas lamps are features typical of well-preserved Gold Country communities

The traffic may be modern but many of the buildings in this Nevada City street date from the town's 19th-century prosperity

CORNISH CALIFORNIANS
The Cornish pasty, meat and potatoes wrapped in pastry, is a dish commonly found in Grass Valley and Nevada City, and is a legacy of the Cornish immigrants who brought advanced mining techniques to the Californian gold field from the 1870s. Most had learned their trade in the tin mines of Cornwall, England, and some arrived in California via the lead mines of Wisconsin and Illinois. Many subsequently left California for the silver mines of Nevada.

►► **Nevada City**   *210B2*

Like neighbouring Grass Valley, Nevada City benefited from mining to a much greater degree than most Gold Country communities, and is still comfortably well off, with much from its past lining its narrow streets.

Serving travellers since 1850, the antique-scattered bar and dining rooms of the **National Hotel** (211 Broad Street) do much to evoke the past have been renovated recently. More evidence of the town's formative days is provided by the **Nevada County Historical Society Museum** (also known as the Firehouse Museum), inside the tall, narrow 1861 fire station at 214 Main Street. The museum also features displays of local Native American crafts and outlines the sad tale of the Donner Party (see page 200).

Still more historical exhibits are to be found at the **Miners' Foundry and Cultural Center**►► (325 Spring Street), a one-time metalworks turned into a theatre and music venue. Adjacent is the **Nevada City Winery**, dating from 1870 but reopened in 1980.

Only two buildings in the old town are not Victorian: the art-deco Courthouse (on Church Street) and the 1937 City Hall (317 Broad Street).

►► **lumas-Eureka State Park**   *210B2*

Enclosed by rough granite peaks and hillsides streaked green by fir and sugar pine trees, pretty Plumas-Eureka State Park sits above 70 miles of tunnels that belonged to the Sierra Buttes Mining Company. The park office and a well-planned **mining museum** fill the miners' former bunkhouse.

► **Rough And Ready**   *210B2*

In an act of drunken bravura and in protest at a miners' tax, Rough And Ready seceded from the United States in 1850 (returning two months later), the only town ever to do so. Today, there is no incentive to pause on your way to the **Bridgeport Covered Bridge,** built in 1862 and spanning 233 feet across the Yuba River – the longest such bridge in the country, in use until 1971.

Today, Sacramento may seem an odd choice for state capital, but in 1854 it was the gateway to the gold mines, and men, machinery and money were streaming through it. As California's first fortunes were being made, it was here that the Big Four rose to prominence, and established the power base from which they shaped the state's future.

Buildings Eclipsing everything around it, the **State Capitol Building**▶▶▶ (east end of Capitol Mall), completed in 1874, is not only an impressive example of the neoclassical style that defined US public building for decades; it is also, at a cost of $2.5 million, a lasting testament to the incredible wealth of gold-rush California. Inside, you can see several restored offices on free guided tours (or on your own), and the state legislature can be witnessed in action.

Sacramento's earliest building, the largely adobe **Sutter's Fort**▶▶ (2701 L Street), was erected in 1839 by German-born John Sutter as a commercial base for his considerable landholdings. Several reconstructed workshops stand in the fort's grounds, as does the **California State Indian Museum**▶, making a valiant attempt to chronicle California's 104 native peoples with a fine collection of handicrafts and ceremonial objects.

Beside the Sacramento River, the wooden sidewalks of the **Old Town**▶▶ link six blocks of restored 19th-century buildings, the genuine history – revealed by several excellent small museums – sitting slightly awkwardly alongside gift shops and cafés.

Museums The Old Town also boasts the **California State Railroad Museum**▶▶▶ (111 I Street), a dazzling collection of old locomotives and imaginative displays clarifying the crucial role of railways in California's development, and the **Sacramento Discovery Museum**▶▶ (101 I Street), which plots the growth of the town and its surroundings. Just outside the Old Town, the

Crocker Art Museum▶▶ (216 O Street) has striking tiled floors and curving staircases and is said to be the West's first art museum.

Continue west along I Street for the Old Town.

❏ The 'Big Four' – Charles Crocker, Mark Hopkins, Collis P Huntington and Leland Stanford – were Sacramento businessmen who, in the late 1850s, financed the plans of a railway engineer, Theodore Judah, for a transcontinental railway linking California with the rest of the United States. The success of the venture resulted in the Big Four's Southern Pacific Railroad Company enjoying a monopoly of communication links, making them the biggest political power brokers in state history. ❏

221

The Sacramento River

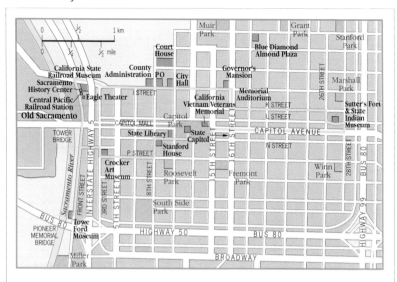

Walk

Sacramento

From the State Capital, described on page 221, walk east along Capitol Avenue, turning left along 28th Street for Sutter's Fort.
Sutter's Fort, the town's earliest building, is described on page 221.

Walk along K Street, turning right into 16th Street for the Governor's Mansion.
At 1526 H Street, the 1877 **Governor's Mansion** is now a museum of Victoriana.

Continue west along 1 Street for the Old Town.
The **Old Town** with restored buildings and museums, is described on page 221.

Walk through the Old Town for the Towe Ford Museum.
At 2200 Front Street, the **Towe Ford Museum** displays gleaming Ford vehicles from 1903 on.

Walk east along O Street for the Crocker Art Museum.

❑ Born in Germany but living in Switzerland when he went bankrupt, John Sutter arrived in (then Mexican) California in 1839, taking advantage of internecine squabbles to acquire 48,000 acres around the confluence of the Sacramento and American rivers. When gold was discovered on his land in 1848, Sutter's workers became gold prospectors overnight, leaving their boss's possessions to rot. By 1852 Sutter was again bankrupt, and he died impoverished in 1880. ❑

For information on the elegant **Crocker Art Museum**, 216 O Street, see page 221.

Walk east along P Street, turning left along Eighth Street for the Stanford House.

On the corner of N Street, the **Stanford House** (under continuing restoration) was a home of railway magnate Leland Stanford, one of the Big Four (see page 221), from 1871.

Walk east along N Street to return to the State Capitol.

▶ Sierra City   210C3

Evocatively perched in the Sierra foothills beneath towering granite peaks, Sierra City's **Sierra Historical Park** does a great job of re-creating the homes and illustrating the lifestyles of mining folk. It also does justice to the memory Ohio-born inventor Lester Allen Pelton, who arrived in California in 1850 hoping to strike gold. Pelton failed in this quest, but did change the face of Californian mining by devising the Pelton Wheel, which enabled the mines' enormous stamp mills to be powered by small jets of water.

In common with many Gold Country towns, Sonora has grown from 19th-century origins, its early buildings still forming a historic centre, into a leafy and pleasant town where contemporary homes dot tree-lined hillsides

223

▶▶ Sonora   210C1

The Mexican miners who founded Sonora were driven away by North American settlers before the town became one of the richest gold-rush towns, and later, thanks to the railway, the commercial hub of the entire region. Even now, Sonora is a coveted address, its tranquillity bringing many new residents from the cities.

The old section of Sonora is extremely well preserved, and many of the town's 19th-century leading citizens lived in mansions still clustered together along Washington Street. Here, too, is the red-and-white **St James Episcopal Church▶▶**, dating from 1859.

A leaflet detailing the historic homes can be picked up in what used to be the County Jail (188 W Bradford Avenue), now doubling as a tourist office, and the **Tuoulomne County Museum▶**, whose local history exhibits and Old West paintings fill the former cells.

▶ Volcano   210C2

A meandering back road (off State Road 88) gives access to Volcano, which takes its name from the crater-like landscape in which it sits, which once had a population of 5,000 and a reputation for riotous nightlife. Only a couple of hundred people live here now, and the chief reminder of the halcyon times is the splendid 1864 **St George Hotel▶**.

BLACK BART
Wearing a mask and wielding a shotgun, Black Bart (an alias of one Charles Bolton) relieved 28 Wells Fargo stagecoaches of their gold between 1875 and 1883, often leaving his victims with a self-penned poem. Finally traced by, and captured through a dropped handkerchief, Bart was tried in San Andreas and served five years in San Quentin prison. Following his release he vanished from the public eye – rumoured by some to be receiving a Wells Fargo pension on the understanding that he never robbed from them again.

A sign warns visitors of the dangers of venturing off the trail leading to Bumpass Hell in Lassen Volcanic National Park. Like the county in which it partly sits, the park was named after Peter Lassen, a Danish-born blacksmith and frontiersman who arrived in the area in 1839

224

▶▶▶ Lassen Volcanic National Park   *210B4*

A seven-year period of intermittent eruptions culminated in 1915 when Lassen Peak, California's only active volcano and the southernmost of the Cascade mountain range, threw a cloud of dust seven miles high, tossed out five-ton boulders, and smothered the surrounding countryside in a 20-foot-deep mud flow.

Lassen Peak, the world's largest 'plug' volcano and one unlikely to erupt again for many decades, sits in Lassen National Park, 50 miles east of Redding, the tallest but by no means the only volcanic peak in a geologically very busy region. It occupies a caldera – or crater – left behind by the collapsing dome of a vast prehistoric volcano.

Along State Road 89, which steers a 30-mile course through the park, the major points of interest are indicated by numbered markers corresponding to explanatory descriptions in a leaflet distributed at the park entrance.

A mile-long trail from the road reaches the park's largest hydrothermal area, **Bumpass Hell▶▶▶**, a steaming cauldron of fumeroles – pressured gases hissing to the surface through gaps in the lava rock – hot springs and bubbling pits of mud. It is hard to believe that such violent scenes are only mild manifestations of the earth's energies.

The same phenomenon on a less imposing scale is repeated at several points throughout the park, but once your nostrils have had their fill of the sulphur gas – and its pervasive rotten-egg smell – you should pay attention to the park's meadows, resplendent with wildflowers in midsummer and sometimes with grazing deer, and pause by a few of the numerous lakes, often hauntingly still and reflecting nearby peaks in their calm surfaces.

Nature's tranquil qualities are also apparent at the **Devastated Area▶▶**, where stands of young trees are beginning to reclaim a landscape rased of all vegetation by the mud flows and gases unleashed by the 1915 eruption.

Hiking trails through the park, and to the summit of Lassen Peak, are described on page 226.

▶▶ Lava Beds National Monument   *210B5*

Few visitors make the effort to reach Lava Beds National Monument, tucked away in the state's north-east corner, but the reward for those who do is an eerie, often foggy plateau ridden with volcanic craters, cinder cones and lava tubes formed over 1,000 years ago by cooling magma flows.

Many of the hundreds of lava tubes lie a few feet beneath the ground as cylindrical caves, which can be explored with flashlights borrowed from the visitor centre beside State Road 139, at the monument's southern entrance.

Near the visitor centre, exhibits inside the illuminated **Mushpot Cave▶▶** aid understanding of the area's geological curiosities, and several unlit caves lie within easy reach on the three-mile **Cave Loop▶**. If you find the darkness daunting, opt for the guided tours that are conducted daily in summer.

THE MODOC WAR
Resisting forcible resettlement, a group of Modocs returned to their ancestral lands (what is now the Lava Beds National Monument) in November 1872, turning the area's volcanic formations into a natural line of defence against the troops sent to remove them. The five-month Modoc War that ensued became the only Native American war fought in California. It needed a two-day mortar attack to finally shift the Modoc, following which their chief, Kentipoos (known to Caucasians as Captain Jack), along with three other Modoc, were tried by a military court and executed.

The single road through the monument's desolate terrain passes many more caves, whose isolation deters all but the most adept explorers (who must get permits from the visitor centre), before reaching the area known as Captain Jack's Stronghold. This was named after a Modoc chief who held out here with 52 of his people against 1,000 US soldiers, using the natural landscape as a shield (see panel on page 224).

(see panel on page 224).

▶ Redding   210A4

Given the alluring natural wonders all around it and the scores of fast-food joints and motels within its boundaries, it is not surprising that most people use Redding, the Far North's largest town, only for eating and sleeping.

The **Carter House Natural Science Museum▶** (48 Quartz Hill Road), provides a moderately successful introduction to the Far North's flora and fauna, and the **Museum of Art and History▶** (56 Quartz Hill Road) places temporary local art exhibitions alongside permanent regional historical items, including a large collection of Native American basketry. Both museums are located in Caldwell Park, which sits on the north bank of the Sacramento River (a good picnic spot in fine weather).

WEATHER CHECK
Lassen National Park's extremely volatile weather is a more pressing concern than the likelihood of volcanic eruptions. Temperatures range from cool to very cold, with July and August being the only months dependably free of snow. Whenever you plan to come, check conditions before setting out by phoning the park headquarters on 916/595–4444.

Compressed gases burst through crevices in the lava rock at Bumpass Hell

225

It's almost impossible to drive through the Far North without feeling the urge to explore the landscape more closely. In Lassen National Park, and to a lesser extent in the Whiskeytown-Shasta-Trinity National Recreation Area, many miles of hiking trails await – and none require great strength, although some may be snow-covered even in summer.

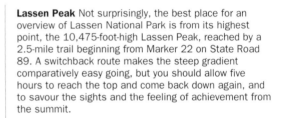

CLIMBING MOUNT SHASTA
Mount Shasta can be reached only on very steep trails beginning at Ski Bowl and Horse Camp. You will need to set out at dawn to be sure of returning from the majestic (and mysterious, being a setting for many strange occult tales) mountain before nightfall.

226

Lassen Peak Not surprisingly, the best place for an overview of Lassen National Park is from its highest point, the 10,475-foot-high Lassen Peak, reached by a 2.5-mile trail beginning from Marker 22 on State Road 89. A switchback route makes the steep gradient comparatively easy going, but you should allow five hours to reach the top and come back down again, and to savour the sights and the feeling of achievement from the summit.

Other hikes Lassen Peak is a prime objective for many hikers, however, so if you want equally spectacular views and fewer people to share them with, try **Brokeoff Mountain**, the second-tallest peak in the national park, reached along a trail from Marker 2 on State Road 89.

Entering the eastern section of the park on State Road 44 (which, unlike State Road 89, does not cross the park) gives access to the backcountry, where you can hike for several days at a stretch – though the area may well be snowbound even in the summer.

The best hikes The pick of the shorter hikes in this region is the **Cinder Cone Nature Trail**, starting from Butte Lake, a potentially ankle-twisting trek through loose rock, but passing the aptly named Fantastic Lava Beds and Painted Dunes – multicoloured lava flows dating from the 1850s.

Much of the **Whiskeytown-Shasta-Trinity National Recreation Area** (see page 227) is geared towards boating rather than walking. The best bets for modest exertion here are the Hirz Bay and Samwell Cave trails, close to Lake Shasta and designed to illustrate local nature and history. Perpetually snow-capped Mount Shasta, 30 miles north of Lake Shasta, is on many hikers' Far North itineraries, but the 14,162-foot-high peak is not to be underestimated, as it is prone to avalanches, rock falls, and constantly changing weather.

STRANGE SHASTA
Many of the strange tales surrounding Mount Shasta – regarded as a sacred place since pre-European times – focus on the mountain's supposed role as a gateway to Lemuria, an ancient but highly advanced subterranean civilisation. The first written account on this theme appeared in the 1880s, and there has been no shortage of alleged sightings of secret tunnels, gold-domed temples and mysterious entities on its slopes ever since.

For the adventurous hiker For longer and more isolated hikes, make for the Clair Engle (also known as Trinity) Lake area, and the **Salmon-Trinity Alps Primitive Area**, with 400 hikable miles of trails through forests, meadows and canyons, beside waterfalls and beneath glaciated peaks. Be aware that local weather is unpredictable and service stations are scarce (for information, tel: 916/623–2121).

▶ Shasta   210A4

Shasta flourished during the late 1800s because of the lucrative gold mines that surrounded it. Remains and detailed reconstructions of Shasta's buildings form the **Shasta State Historical Park▶**, on State Road 299, six miles west of Redding.

▶▶ Whiskeytown-Shasta-Trinity NRA   210A4

Covering nearly 250,000 acres, the Whiskeytown-Shasta-Trinity National Recreation Area divides into three sections, each one adjacent to a dam-formed lake. Sailing, windsurfing and water- and jet-skiing (supply permitting, most equipment can be rented on arrival) make the lakes, and Whiskeytown especially, intensely busy each summer. Lake Shasta Dam, reached with State Road 155 off Interstate 5, is the area's most spectacular man-made sight and the second-biggest dam in the United States: It diverts three rivers to irrigate California's Central Valley farmlands. A film describing the dam's construction is shown at the visitor centre, while crossing the lake on Interstate 5 takes you over the **Pit River Bridge▶**, the world's biggest double-decked bridge, carrying a railway line as well as the highway.

Turn a visit to Lake Shasta into a day-trip by continuing to the **Lake Shasta Caverns▶**; guided cavern tours by boat start from O'Brien, on the eastern side of the lake, and feature stalactite and stalagmite formations.

Close to Clair Engle Lake, on the western fringes of the recreation area, **Weaverville▶▶** has many 19th-century buildings as reminders of its gold-prospecting days. During the 1850s, half of Weaverville's population was Chinese, some of whom contributed to the building of the **Joss House**, a Taoist temple decorated with tapestries and ornaments set around a 300-year-old altar. Now the centrepiece of **Joss House State Historic Park▶▶**, the temple has guided tours every half hour.

A LAKE WITH TWO NAMES
Part of the Whiskeytown-Shasta-Trinity National Recreation Area, the title of Trinity Lake – fed by the Trinity River – was officially changed to Clair Engle Lake to commemorate the state senator who oversaw its damming. Trinity still appears on many maps, however, and is also still in use locally, not least by the resentful residents who formerly owned the land now at the bottom of the reservoir that the dam created.

Mount Shasta, 14,162 feet high and usually snow-capped all year, was first climbed in 1854

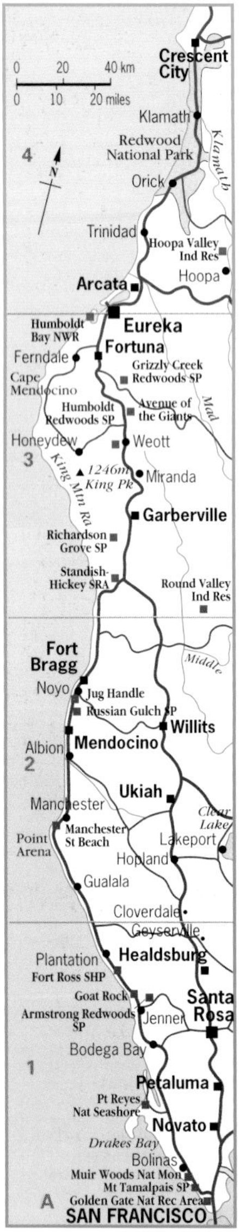

0 20 40 km
0 10 20 miles
Crescent City
Klamath
Redwood National Park
Klamath
N
4
Orick
Trinidad
Hoopa Valley Ind Res
Hoopa
Arcata
Humboldt Bay NWR
Eureka
Fortuna
Ferndale
Grizzly Creek Redwoods SP
Cape Mendocino
Humboldt Redwoods SP
Avenue of the Giants
Mad
Honeydew
Weott
3
King Mtn Ra
1246m King Pk
Miranda
Garberville
Richardson Grove SP
Standish-Hickey SRA
Round Valley Ind Res
Fort Bragg
Middle
Noyo
Jug Handle
Russian Gulch SP
Willits
Albion
Mendocino
2
Ukiah
Manchester
Clear Lake
Manchester St Beach
Point Arena
Lakeport
Hopland
Gualala
Cloverdale
Geyserville
Plantation
Healdsburg
Fort Ross SHP
Goat Rock
Santa Rosa
Armstrong Redwoods SP
Jenner
Bodega Bay
1
Petaluma
Pt Reyes Nat Seashore
Novato
Drakes Bay
Bolinas
Muir Woods Nat Mon
Mt Tamalpais SP
A
Golden Gate Nat Rec Area
SAN FRANCISCO

A WORLD AWAY Far from the affluent cities, crowded sands and persistent sunshine of southern California, the state's North Coast – between San Francisco and the Oregon border – is heavily forested and almost continually damp, populated by a bizarre mix of lumber workers, marijuana farmers, back-to-nature artists and radical ecologists.

Despite its size – accounting for almost a third of the state's Pacific seaboard – the North Coast has always been one of California's most sparsely inhabited and least accessible corners; even today, there are only a couple of viable routes through it. The coast-hugging Highway 1 is the most scenic option but covers just half the region before swinging inland to join Highway 101, which links the inland settlements and the northernmost coastal towns before continuing into Oregon and deep into the Pacific Northwest.

CLIMATE The North Coast's summer temperatures can be searing, but fogs regularly block out the heat and, in winter, the area is one of the wettest in the United States. Clearly, this is no place to acquire a tan (and typically, the region's best beaches are slivers of sand enclosed by jagged headlands at the end of winding foot trails), yet it is just this climate that allows the North Coast's most prized feature to flourish: the gigantic coastal redwoods, the tallest trees in the world, found only here.

There are strands of redwoods within easy striking distance of San Francisco at the Muir Woods National Monument, part of the Golden Gate National Recreation Area, and at Point Reyes National Seashore. But travel further north to Humboldt State Park or the Redwood National Park and you will find these incredible trees – their slender trunks often rising more than 300 feet.

Even without the redwoods, the North Coast would be exceptionally strong on natural spectacle. At almost every turn throughout 200 miles of coastline there is a fresh vista to excite – wave-sculpted rock arches, gale-tormented bluffs, schools of basking seals and (at the right time of year) migrating whales. The scenery attracts many weekending San Franciscans, as do the region's small, romantic inns and quality restaurants.

Gull Rock, on the Pacific Coast

TOWN LIFE Small and far apart, the towns of the North Coast generally provide a sedate accompaniment to the wild scenery around them. Most sprang up during the mid-19th century, when their sheltered bays made perfect landing points for men and machinery destined for the Gold Country, and later grew into busy lumber ports as timber became the region's economic backbone.

Several communities – notably Fort Bragg, halfway along the North Coast – are still dominated by the logging industry, despite the fact that depressingly large sections of the North Coast's forests have been reduced to stumps and pressure from the environmental lobby has stimulated a rethinking of tree-felling methods. This is part of a reassessment of priorities as the region's other staple trades, fishing and farming, face decline.

ALTERNATIVE INDUSTRY From the early 1970s, some landowners in the slumbering agricultural hamlets sought an alternative source of income by cultivating marijuana. This illegal enterprise grew into a highly productive business, particularly in the region around Garberville, nicknamed 'the Emerald Triangle.' In the mid-1980s, however, the government initiated a clampdown intended to end large-scale cultivation. Despite several high profile raids, however, it is thought that the illegal crop is still a major contributor to many local incomes, whether directly through growing or indirectly through the supply of equipment.

These days tourism is seen as the financial future of the North Coast, something that causes commercial interests and conservationists to lock horns with increasing regularity. The battle between the rival factions is clearest at Mendocino, a lovely artistic town with many restored mid-1800s buildings that is struggling to maintain its charm as gift shops and bed-and-breakfast inns proliferate.

Elsewhere, larger communities such as Arcata and Eureka pack their centres with preserved Victorian homes, and make good bases from which to discover the best of the North Coast's natural pleasures. The quirkiest historical sight is the remnant of a 19th-century Russian fur-trapping settlement at Fort Ross.

One more North Coast curiosity is the notorious San Andreas fault, the line of geological instability that has been responsible for many of California's biggest earthquakes, which scars the landscape with its presence before moving away beneath the ocean.

A North Coast small town: Mendocino

▶ **Arcata** *228A4*

These days a hotbed of student politics and ecological activism, Arcata was founded as a mining supply base and gained notoriety in 1860 by booting soon-to-be-famous writer Bret Harte out of town for publicising a massacre of Native Americans.

Numerous Victorian homes and a lovely central plaza bring character to Arcata, and the small town is kept bubbling by the students of the North Coast's only university.

All the sights worth seeing are natural ones: the **Historic Logging Trail**▶ traces the impact of the lumber industry on a section of Arcata Community Forest; landfill sites around **Arcata Bay**▶▶ have been turned into a wildlife preserve and bird sanctuary; and azaleas, rhododendrons and a host of wildflowers blooming at various times throughout the year ensure that some colour is always beautifying the 30-acre **Azalea State Reserve**▶.

▶ **Bodega Bay** *228A1*

An encouraging first glimpse of the North Coast if you are arriving from the Wine Country, and a good base for exploring the Sonoma Coast State Beach (see page 241), Bodega Bay's tall cliffs and sandy beaches look out over the vessels of a declining fishing fleet, whose plaid-shirted workforce is not overly enamoured of the gift shops, bed and breakfasts and boutiques that are spreading through their village.

If Bodega Bay's immense population of gulls, egrets, pelicans and herons gets on your nerves, it will come as no comfort at all to learn that it was here (and at the nearby inland town of Bodega) that Alfred Hitchcock shot his 1963 film *The Birds*.

▶ **Bolinas** *228A1*

Just south of Point Reyes National Seashore, Bolinas is so well liked by its residents that they are known to tear down road signs directing traffic to it. As it

Oysters being barbecued in a region where the harvest of the sea has traditionally provided a livelihood as well as sustenance

happens, Bolinas may be a nice place to live but it is entirely uninteresting to visit.

Much more deserving of attention in the area are the birds swooping for fishy snacks at **Bolinas Lagoon**, and the many and various marine creatures inhabiting the tidal pools of **Duxbury Reef**.

▶▶ Eureka   228A3

A glut of Victorian residential architecture has made industrialised Eureka, easily the largest town on the North Coast, into an impressive showcase of turn-of-the-century California living. There is no more eloquent example of the style than the **Carson Mansion**▶▶▶ (143 M Street), complete with painted window frames, turrets and towers, built in 1885 by a builder who did not know when to stop.

Using timber to a different end, the **Romano Gabriel Sculpture Garden**▶▶ (325 Second Street) is an intensely colourful collection of people, plants and symbols carved from disused packing cases with a chain saw. It is either epic folk art or simply a mess – either way, you will kick yourself if you miss it.

The Carson Mansion, one of over a hundred preserved Victorian homes in Eureka, was built mostly of redwood for wealthy lumber mogal William Carson and is now an exclusive men-only club

Old Town The downbeat bars and flophouses that were once a feature of Eureka's dockside area have been transformed into trendy galleries, boutiques and eateries. These occupy newly painted restored buildings collectively titled the **Old Town**▶ – all a bit contrived and pricey, but nonetheless the area makes for an enjoyable stroll.

Nearby, the **Clarke Memorial Museum**▶ (240 E Street) keeps the dust off myriad exhibits from Eureka's pioneer times, and maintains a ravishing stash of basketry from the Northwest's Native American tribes.

By contrast, Eureka's 1853 Fort Humboldt was built to launch attacks on Native Americans. At **Fort Humboldt State Historic Park**▶▶ (3431 Fort Avenue) only the redwood hospital of the fort's 14 buildings remains upright, and its exhibits – not surprisingly – dwell on logging rather than on genocide.

▶▶ Ferndale   228A3

Almost every one of the thousand or so residents of Ferndale, 20 miles south of Eureka, has a well-looked-after Victorian pile to call home. The few antiques and period furnishings not in daily use are stored inside the **Ferndale Museum**▶ (515 Shaw Avenue), a collection that sets the seal on this wondrous time-locked community.

▶ Fort Bragg   228A2

You will not find a fort in Fort Bragg, but you will find lumber mills and freight yards that diminish the scenic setting of this hard-working coastal town. The **Guest House Museum**▶ (on Main Street) unfurls an uncritical account of the timber industry, but you are better off opting for a stroll along the two miles of trails weaving through the 17-acre **Mendocino Botanical Gardens**▶▶ (18220 N Highway 1), where craggy, wave-lashed headlands vie with blooming wildflowers for your attention.

BOAT TOURS
The cold and choppy waters off the North Coast generally do little to encourage boat tours. An exception is Eureka's sheltered Humboldt Bay, enjoyably cruised on a narrated 75-minute sailing aboard a 1910 ferry, departing from the C Street harbour (for details, tel: 707/445–1910). Also in Eureka, the Image Tour includes a boat trip as part of a five-hour guided town tour (details from the Chamber of Commerce, tel: 800/356–6381).

Found only along a slender section of the coast between Big Sur, on the northern half of California's Central Coast, and central Oregon, the tall and comparatively slender coast redwoods (Sequoia sempervirens) should not be confused with the slightly shorter and much stockier giant sequoias (Sequoia gigantea) that live on the western slopes of the Sierra Nevada mountains.

THE SKUNK TRAIN
Between Fort Bragg and Willits, the Skunk Train – which earned its name from the aromatic qualities of its diesel engine – makes a scenic 40-mile trip, criss-crossing the Noyo River and riding on trestles high above redwood groves. Tourists have replaced timber as the main cargo, although the train still makes unscheduled stops to deliver mail and supplies to the tiny settlements on its route. Operating twice daily in summer, and daily in winter, the Skunk Train should not be missed.

232

The tallest trees in the world As a species, the redwoods have been around for 60 million years. When dinosaurs roamed the earth, the trees covered large - sections of the North American and European continents. As global weather patterns changed, the redwoods retreated to the United States' West Coast, where the heavy rainfall and regular fogs are much to their liking.

Often growing as high as a football field is long, the coast redwoods are the world's tallest trees – the tallest among them reaching 368 feet – although their life span of up to 2,600 years is less than that of the giant sequoias of the Sierra Nevada, which can live up to 3,400 years. Because of logging, however, many of the trees you will see along the North Coast are second-growth redwoods and comparative youngsters.

Like the giant sequoias, the coast redwoods absorb rainwater through shallow root systems. Such roots render them unstable in high winds, however, and as a consequence they grow in areas sheltered from ocean breezes and cluster together in tight groves.

With heat-resistant barks, both types of sequoia are able to take advantage of forest fires, dropping their winged seeds to the freshly cleared forest floor, where sunlight is able to reach the sprouting sequoias.

As well as by seeds, sequoias can regenerate in a strange cloning-type process, which enables new trees to grow from fallen branches, stumps or roots, each one bearing the genetic imprint of its progenitor.

The Skunk Train, now mainly tourist transport

The 'harvesting' of the redwoods The dark and damp redwood groves were seldom penetrated by Native Americans, who traditionally regarded such places the domain of spirits. The redwoods' isolation changed when US settlers arrived. The first sawmills appeared in the region during the 1830s, but it was the gold rush that turned lumberjacks into lumber barons overnight.

Mining and a fast-expanding population brought a huge demand for timber, the raw material for tunnels, dams, sluices, fences, and flumes, and for the buildings of the new gold-rush towns. The redwoods' fire-resistant properties made their timber a valued commodity, and as early as 1870 the best of the state's redwood trees had been felled.

With no thoughts of reforestation, commercial logging continued apace for the next 40 years using the highly destructive clear-cutting method. This involved an entire hillside or waterside section of forest being sawed down, leaving a desolate stump-strewn landscape where any remaining groves were exposed to erosion and where local wildlife was devastated.

Saving the trees As the lumber industry made fortunes and kept a large contingent of Californians in work – especially along the North Coast – voices of dissent

233

Timber became big business when settlers arrived

struggled to be heard. In 1918, the Save-the-Redwoods League was founded and teamed up with the Sierra Club to promote awareness of the dangers faced by California's forests. During the 1930s, the Civilian Conservation Corps increased forest protection against fires, diseases and pests, and helped pave the way for 18 forests (including Klamath National Forest on the North Coast) to be given National Forest status. This placed them under the control of the US Forestry Commission, which regulated logging activity at least to the extent of providing financial and technical assistance to maximise the forest's commercial potential.

It is only recently that the arguments of environmental-ists (some of whom became derisively known as 'tree huggers') that continued clear-cutting will eventually destroy the logging business as well as the forests, has struck home with local commercial interests. Sustained-yield timber harvesting – cutting down no more than the amount grown each year – has now become more accepted as the sensible way ahead.

WHO PROTECTS WHAT?
The various categories of natural areas and historic sites in California can be confusing. National Forests, National Parks, and National Monuments are all federally run from Washington, DC (forests by the Forestry Service, which is part of the Department of Agriculture; parks and monuments by the Department of the Interior). State Parks, State Recreational Areas, State Historical Parks, and the sole State Historical Monument (San Simeon) are administered by California's State Department of Parks and Recreation, based in Sacramento. But many anomalies exist; for instance, within the Redwood National Park are at least three state parks.

The North Coast

MEAT-EATERS' DELIGHT
Particularly in the region's northern reaches, restaurants are likely to offer delectable morsels such as elk steaks, roasted bear, wild boar and even antelope sausages. Vegetarians who eat fish might console themselves with salmon jerky, a traditional Native American creation that involves drying and smoking the fish.

▶▶ Fort Ross   228A1

Founded in 1812, Fort Ross was a social centre for a colony of Russians, who arrived to grow wheat to supply their compatriots in Alaska and to hunt sea otters for their pelts.

Most of the buildings were destroyed after the Russians' departure in 1841, but many, including the exceptional Orthodox Chapel, have been carefully reconstructed and authentically furnished at Fort Ross State Historic Park, beside Highway 1, 20 miles north of Bodega Bay.

▶ Garberville   228A3

When devoted marijuana smokers began forsaking San Francisco for the country, many arrived in Garberville and began cultivating their own patches of the illicit weed.

Discovering a booming market for home-grown hemp, Garberville's pioneers became major dealers, buying up large pockets of land and installing elaborate security systems to guard their crops.

These days, marijuana money contributes much less than it did to the economy of the tiny town, which gets most of its visitors during July, when top musical names from Jamaica perform at the Reggae on the River music festival.

▶▶ Golden Gate National
Recreation Area   228A1

The Golden Gate National Recreation Area (GGNRA) spreads from San Francisco across the Golden Gate Bridge to the southernmost few miles of the North Coast, rubbing shoulders with Stinson Beach (see page 242) and the Point Reyes National Seashore (see page 241).

A network of foot trails penetrates the GGNRA's Marin Headlands, offering exceptional views of San Francisco and the Golden Gate Bridge while traversing an immense acreage of pristine, scrub-covered hillsides to the tops of granite cliffs, buffeted far below by angry ocean waves.

Make for Point Bonita and the half-mile trail that negotiates a tunnel – gouged from the rock by hand in 1877 – and a spine-tingling rope bridge on the way to **Point Bonita Lighthouse▶**, in itself less spectacular than the views all around it despite being among the West Coast's earliest beacons; or Rodeo Beach, an impossibly slender strip of sand between the ocean and a wildlife-rich lagoon.

Above Rodeo Beach, the **California Marine Mammal Center▶** provides treatment for injured seals and sea lions, and informs the public of coastal environmental issues with hands-on exhibits.

▶ Green Gulch Farm and Zen Center   228A1

From Muir Beach (see page 240), a path climbs to the Green Gulch Farm and Zen Center, founded in the early 1970s to further knowledge of Buddhism and meditation techniques. The centre's organic farm supplies several of the city's top-ranking restaurants. Get tuned in at the free public meditation session (tel: 415/383–3134).

▶ **Gualala**   *228A2*

Claimed by some to have been named after a Spanish rendition of the Norse myth of Valhalla but actually a derivation of a Pomo word, Gualala is a sleepy former lumber town with little to admire beyond the 1903 **Gualala Hotel** at its centre, and a handful of galleries that highlight the work of Mendocino area artists, who are further celebrated by the Arts in the Redwoods festival held here each August.

Just south, **Gualala Regional Park** encompasses redwoods and beaches (some of California's few remaining abalone divers do their work here), and has a foot trail to **Del Mar Landing**, a secluded coastal reserve with only the seals basking on the offshore rocks providing company for adventuring humans.

The distinctive onion domes of the Russian-style St Orres Dining Room rise behind a field of Californian poppies on Highway 1 near Gualala

236

AN ECOLOGICAL STAIRCASE
The five-mile Ecological Staircase Trail at Jug Handle State Park, five miles south of Fort Bragg, makes a geologically fascinating trek across five rock terraces formed by the action of plate tectonics and exposed by wave action. Although only 100 feet separate the terraces, each is 100,000 years older or younger than its neighbour, and covered by entirely different vegetation. A final surprise comes at the top, with the stunted and twisted cypress and pine trees of the Mendocino Pygmy Forest.

BIG FOOT
Drive inland towards the Hoopa Valley and you will be met at Willow Creek by a (supposedly) life-size statue of Big Foot, the large and hairy ape-like creature which is believed by many to exist in North America's least accessible back-country areas. Reports of Big Foot activity have come from almost every state (and the beast has long been known to Native Americans as 'Sasquatch', but the majority have originated in this section of California. It was here, too, that the term 'Big Foot' was born in 1958, after a plaster cast was made of unexplained 16-inch-long footprints.

▶ **Hoopa Valley**   228A4

Covering 93,000 acres, the Hoopa Valley Reservation is the largest of its kind in California, but like all reservations it cannot be anything other than a depressing reminder of the wrongs inflicted by white settlers on the country's indigenous peoples. The **Hoopa Tribal Museum**▶ displays the handicrafts of the Hupa and Yurok tribes, but many people make the 60-mile drive from the coast simply to attend the Friday and Saturday night bingo sessions; legally, high-stakes bingo can be played only on reservations. Based inland, the Hupa traditionally exchanged home-grown food and animal skins for the seafood and canoes of the pre-dominantly coastal-based Yurok.

▶▶ **Humboldt Redwoods State Park**   228A3

Illuminated by beams of sunlight breaking through towering foliage, the 33-mile-long **Avenue of the Giants** winds through a section of the vast Humboldt Redwoods State Park, a 20-million-year-old forest harbouring some of the world's tallest trees. Several roadside stops and short walking trails provide a chance to become an insignificant speck at the foot of these 300-foot-high green giants.

In spring, the park's Eel River, whose course the avenue follows, becomes a torrent that brings out the region's daredevil white-water rafters and kayakers. Slowing in summer to an eminently swimmable emerald-coloured stream, the river also has sandy banks well suited to leisurely picnics.

Hiking trails and long-abandoned lumber roads thread deeper into the park, ascending from the redwood-cloaked lowlands to hillsides covered by strands of fir, where rustic cabins and rough campsites provide for overnight stays.

The Avenue of the Giants, winding for 33 miles through Humboldt Redwoods State Park

Drive

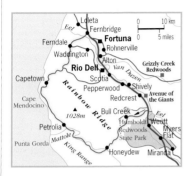

The Lost Coast

From the Rockefeller Forest section of Humboldt Redwoods State Park (described on page 236), drive west along Bull Creek Flats Road to join Mattole Road, after 12 miles reaching Honeydew.
The tiny crossroads community of **Honeydew▶** – where the centre of activity for the single-figure population is the General Store-cum-gas station – is one of the rainiest spots in the United States, with 200 inches falling annually.

From Honeydew, continue on Mattole Road, reaching Petrolia after eight miles.
At the foot of a thickly vegetated valley, eucalyptus-enshrouded

Petrolia▶ was, in the 1860s, the site of one of California's earliest commercial oil wells; the economic boom that the strike promised was soon thwarted by the remoteness of the region.

From Petrolia, take the bumpy Lighthouse Road to the Punta Gorda headland.
At the **Punta Gorda headland▶**, a jeep track leads to a disused lighthouse.

Return to Mattole Road and continue north, after six miles passing Cape Mendocino.
Bordered by black-sand beaches, **Cape Mendocino▶** is the most western point of the contiguous United States. It is believed to have been named by some 16th-century Spanish seafarers in honour of a Spanish viceroy.

Pass Cape Mendocino and continue on Mattole Road, after 16 miles reaching Ferndale.
An immaculately preserved Victorian village first settled by Swedish dairy farmers, charming **Ferndale's▶** 1,000 inhabitants make the town by far the largest settlement on the Lost Coast; see page 231 for a description.

From Ferndale, continue on Mattole Road for four miles, rejoining Highway 101 10 miles south of Eureka.

▶ The Lost Coast 228A3

Black bears and bald eagles are more common than people within the desolate, deserted landscapes of the Lost Coast, a 30-mile portion of the North Coast south of Eureka, whose dense forests, coastal bluffs and pocket-size beaches are shielded by the sharp inclines of the Kings Mountain Range.

The scenic Lost Coast can be sampled lightly by taking Briceland Thorne Road, off Highway 101 near Redway. This route leads to **Shelter Cove▶▶**, a tiny coast-hugging community adjacent to a beach at the foot of impressive granite headlands, first passing the elk-roamed **Sinkyone Wilderness State Park▶**, named after the Sinkyone tribe, who inhabited the Lost Coast from 6000 BC. At that time food, both from the sea and from the forest, was available in plentiful supplies and the Lost Coast region was North America's most densely populated place.

NATIVE AMERICAN RESERVATIONS
One of three Native American reservations in California, the Hoopa Valley Reservation has just 2,000 Hoopa people living on its 93,000 acres. Statewide, an estimated 35,000 of the state's 250,000 native population live on reservations.

In a city of predominantly wooden buildings, Mendocino's volunteer firefighters are an important part of the community

CHARLES F RICHTER
When Californians declare that they sleep through a mere 2.3, barely notice a 3.6, but know exactly what to do if an 8.9 hits, they are, of course, quoting Richter scale measurements of earthquake magnitudes. Few of them know, however, that the man who devised the Richter scale in 1935, Charles F Richter, was a 35-year-old seismology professor at the California Institute of Technology in Pasadena.

▶ Manchester State Beach   228A2

Stretching for several miles beside Highway 1 south of Mendocino Headlands State Park, Manchester State Beach is a must-see for beachcombers and hikers and for hardy campers who do not mind spending a night being buffeted by winds or waking up beside a beach cloaked in fog.

▶▶▶ Mendocino   228A2

Mendocino is set on a coastal bluff and has a plethora of well-preserved 19th-century buildings dating from its settlement by New England loggers.

Because of Mendocino's well-deserved reputation as the North Coast's prettiest town, its population of 1,000 permanent residents is frequently outnumbered by tourists, who fill the numerous bed-and-breakfasts and wander ceaselessly in and out of the many gift shops.

Crowds aside, Mendocino is very likable and very easily explored. In decline as a lumber centre, Mendocino's unspoiled beauty proved irresistible to a group of San Francisco artists in the 1950s and 1960s, who began renovating and preserving the old buildings and whose influence lingers on, most notably in numerous galleries and in the arts appreciation programmes of the **Mendocino Art Center▶** (45200 Little Lake Road).

The **Kelley House Museum▶▶**, inside an 1861 residence (45007 Albion Street), has written and photographic background information on most of the town's early buildings. Among these, the 1868 Gothic-style Mendocino Presbyterian Church (44831 Main Street) is still in use, and Mendocino's oldest residence, the 1854 **Ford House▶** (Main Street), functions as a visitor centre for **Mendocino Headlands State Park▶▶**, where three miles of footpaths weave around the wind-lashed bluff on which the town sits.

The biggest and most destructive earthquake ever to strike California, the 1906 San Francisco earthquake was caused by the 600-mile-long San Andreas fault, the longest of hundreds of geological fault lines that pass through the state, and one that runs for many miles along the North Coast.

The big shake In fact, the 1906 quake was more powerful along the North Coast than in San Francisco, though the region's moderate level of development meant that damage was limited to displaced cattle fences and slightly skewed roads. Such damage has long since been rectified, but provided you know where to look – and what to look for – the fault line is easy to recognise.

At Point Reyes, which was jolted almost 16 feet north in the few seconds of the 1906 quake, the National Seashores' Earthquake Trail follows a section of the fault, and markers indicate some of its effects.

Where the fault lies From Point Reyes, the fault follows the line of Tamales Bay and continues to Bodega Bay, where it passes between Bodega Head and the mainland. Although it is mostly concealed by sand dunes, the fault's presence here is marked by tell-tale deposits of mixed and crushed rock. The fault continues under the ocean beyond Bodega Head and returns to land just south of Fort Ross, which lost several of its early Russian buildings in the 1906 quake. Follow the Fort Ross Road inland for a few miles looking for furrows on the hillsides, further evidence of the 1906 quake.

As it travels just inland from the coast, the fault cuts a straight valley through the hills, causing many streams to change their course. This fact explains why the Gualala River flows parallel to the coast for several miles, instead of draining directly into the ocean.

Close to Point Arena, the fault again dips under the ocean. Until recently, experts believed the sharp breaks in the headlands further north around the Lost Coast were proof of the fault staying close to the shore. A more recent hypothesis, however, suggests that it is only a branch of the San Andreas fault that lies along this part of the coast and that the main line runs some miles offshore, veering west under the Pacific.

239

A sample of the earthquake damage suffered in San Francisco

From the summit of Mount Tamalpais is a dramatic panorama encompassing San Francisco, the Golden Gate and the East Bay

▶ Mill Valley 74A5

Full of rural charm despite being a San Francisco commuter base, Mill Valley sits on the eastern slopes of Mount Tamalpais. Attracting many of the big city's well-off but liberal souls, the town sports a surprising number of coffee bars, and even stages its own film festival – with the emphasis on independent productions – every autumn.

▶▶▶ Mount Tamalpais State Park 228A1

A switchback road leads almost to the top of Mount Tamalpais, but you will feel you have earned the scintillating views – of San Francisco and far inland to the Sierra Nevada mountains – only if you have attained the summit after a day's hike from the redwood-filled canyons of Mount Tamalpais State Park or tackled the network of five roads around the slopes by mountain bike. Weather permitting, concerts and performing arts are staged at the park's **Mountain Theater▶**, where more than 3,000 people can enjoy an outdoor show against a stunning natural backdrop.

▶▶ Muir Woods National Monument 228A1

When San Franciscans feel they are living in a concrete jungle, they head 17 miles north-west to the Muir Woods National Monument (also visited by numerous bus tours from San Francisco), where six miles of trails lead through a dark, cool grove of redwoods. These are not the biggest examples of the North Coast's redwood trees, but at over 250 feet high they are unlikely to disappoint; if they do, push on to the slender semi-circular cove holding **Muir Beach▶**, and mingle with the anglers and bird-watchers.

▶ Point Arena Lighthouse 228A2

Interrupt the lengthy drive between Bodega Bay and Fort Bragg with a tour of the 1908 **Point Arena Lighthouse** and its museum, which details the many ships that have come to grief off this wild and rugged coastline.

WILLIAM KENT'S DONATION
It is hard to belive today, but both Mount Tamalpais and the redwood grove that became the Muir Wood National Monument were once in private hands. The land formed part of the family holdings inherited by William Kent, a conservation-mined Congressman who settled in Main County in 1907. His donation asked for the latter to be named after naturalist John Muir, who did much to encourage the preservation of wild California.

►► Point Reyes National Seashore   *228A1*

Formed by, and still subject to, seismic activity, the 100-mile coastline of the Point Reyes National Seashore encompasses granite headlands, beaches, dunes and marshes, and reaches inland to hills topped by pine-fringed ridges. The area's geological background is outlined at the **Visitor Center**, beside Highway 1, and the adjacent easily walked **Earthquake Trail►►**.

Longer trails aim to please bird-watchers and beach-combers, and another leads to **Kule Loklo►**, a re-created Miwok village. If ocean breezes deter walking, drive to the 1870s **Point Reyes Lighthouse►** on the seashore's western extremity.

► Richardson Grove State Park   *228A3*

A few miles south of Garberville, Richardson Grove State Park has three lush redwood groves and numerous backcountry hikes. But when the summer temperatures send warm air into the otherwise cool groves, the park becomes one of the North Coast's most popular and crowded camping areas.

Close by, the dot-on-the-map settlement of Piercy seeks to lure campers, and any passing traffic on Highway 1, with the optimistically titled World Famous Tree House, a room built 50 feet up a redwood tree, and Confusion Hill, a collection of visual conceits.

►► Sonoma Coast State Beach   *228A1*

Between Bodega Bay and the Russian River hamlet of Jenner, the Sonoma Coast State Beach spans 13 miles of secluded beaches slotted between craggy headlands, many of which have formed sea stacks and arches.

Trails lead to the beaches from Highway 1, and there are connecting paths linking the whole Sonoma coast. Splendid scenery is common to all, yet each beach has its own admirers: fishermen favour **Portuguese Beach►**; **Shell Beach►** delights beachcombers, delivering a rich harvest with each receding tide; and the picnic tables at **Rock Point►►** provide settings for picture-perfect meals.

241

Dark sands, and wind- and wave-lashed rocks, are typical of the Sonoma Coast State Beach

CALIFORNIA GRAY WHALES
Many places along the North Coast make excellent points to observe the migrating California gray whales, which pass by on their 6,000-mile journey between the Arctic sea off Alaska, where they feed, and the warmer waters off Baja California, where the females give birth. The whales are thought to use coastal landscapes to navigate, and can be sighted at any time from December to July, though the largest numbers are usually visible in March.

Old machinery forms part of the historical potpourri at the Mendocino County Museum

▶ **Stinson Beach**   74A5

Unchallenged as the North Coast's finest and busiest strand, the broad and inviting Stinson Beach sits at the foot of Mount Tamalpais within easy reach of San Francisco. Its 3-mile-long crescent-shaped sands stretch north to the Bolinas Lagoon (see pages 230–1).

Because Stinson is spared the strong currents that affect much of the North Coast, swimming is popular here, although many don diver's wet suits before braving the cool waters. If swimming or sitting in the sun does not suit you, try one of the hikes from the beach to Mount Tamalpais State Park or the Muir Woods National Monument.

Three miles north, the wooded canyons of the **Audubon Canyon Ranch**▶▶ are cherished by birdwatchers, especially from March to July, when egrets and blue herons make their nests in the redwood branches and visiting hours to this wildlife research centre are extended. Hiking trails here offer amateur ornithologists close-up views of egrets, blue herons and many other species.

▶ **Willits**   228A2

Taking the Skunk Train from Fort Bragg (see panel on page 232), you will find yourself 40 miles inland at Willits, a likable small country community that conserves its energy for regional rodeos. Other than serving wholesome traditional fare in its diners, it offers only the Native American basketry and pioneer-period artefacts of the **Mendocino County Museum**▶ (400 E Commercial Street) for out-of-towners to pass the time before their journey back.

Provided you are not sick of the sight of the North Coast's redwood trees by the time you reach it, the Redwood National Park, filling 100,000 acres of California's north-west corner and encompassing four state parks, offers an unrivalled chance to delve among the tall trees and their related flora and fauna, and to strike out across 40 miles of California's utterly untrammelled shoreline.

Far from the crowds: Smith River, Jedediah Smith State Park

Take a hike Dozens of short foot trails lead off Highway 101 (which passes through the park), and longer hiking routes connect the four state parks that form the key sections of the national park.

The southern entrance is close to Orick, where the **Redwood Visitor Center** provides geographical orientation and a wealth of ecological information. Close by, the aptly named **Tall Trees Grove**▶▶ contains three of the world's tallest trees, including the 368-foot Howard Libby Redwood. Its statistics impress most; though, from the ground, the tree looks no more enormous than its neighbours.

The park's inland sections Farther on, **Prairie Creek State Park**▶ spans a large tract of grassland between the redwoods and the ocean, with numerous trails leading to tidal pools and coves. The park's inland sections are kept lush and fertile by heavy winter rainfall, and its landscapes are at their best at Fern Canyon, a moss-covered floor enclosed by 60-foot-high fern walls. The park also boasts a sizable elk herd; you will see some of them grazing in meadows beside Highway 101, and more can be spotted on the coastal trails.

243

❑ Jedediah Smith State Park, and the Smith River which runs through it, are named after Jedediah Strong Smith, a New York-born fur trapper who became a California frontier legend in 1826, after making the first nonnative crossing of the Sierra Nevada mountains. ❑

Summer fogs are frequent in the northerly reaches of the national park, especially at **Del Norte State Park**▶▶, where the redwood groves reach almost to the shore. Once the fog lifts, seek out the area's main attractions: tide pools, coves and isolated beaches.

Further inland and less affected by fog, **Jedediah Smith State Park**▶▶ is the least-visited section of the national park yet also one of the most enjoyable. Take the meandering Howland Hill Road, a one-time stage-coach route, and stop at Stout Grove to admire the immense girth of the so-called Stout Tree. Salmon fishermen and canoeists are brought to this park by the Smith River, which has many placid sections ideal for swimming and for taking in the rural tranquillity from sandy banks.

The Wine Country

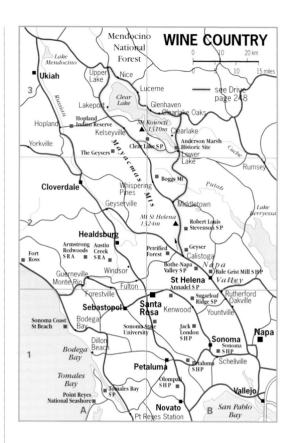

CALISTOGA'S WINERIES
Though better known for its spas, Calistoga also has several notable wineries. Occupying a French-style castle, Château Montelena (1429 Tubbs Lane; tel: 707/942–5105) produces an acclaimed Chardonnay and overlooks Lake Jade, where formal Chinese gardens are laid out on the banks of the lake. The champagne-making Schramsberg Vineyards (Schramsberg Road; tel: 707/942–4558) were immortalised in 1880 by Robert Louis Stevenson's book *The Silverado Squatters*.

PLEASURES OF THE PALATE You will find wineries all over California, but only in the Wine Country – beginning 48 miles north of San Francisco and encompassing three separate valleys – is the grape the main attraction of an entire region.

Hot summers, moist winters, fertile volcanic soil – courtesy of the long-extinct Mount St Helena – and heaps of publicity bring hordes of tourists to the Wine Country, whose wineries range from high-tech modern plants to century-old family-run operations in stone buildings. Most of these run tours and tastings and have become adept at turning beginners into connoisseurs of California's finest within an hour.

STATE GRAPE Spanish missionaries produced California's earliest wine, but a take-charge Hungarian named Agoston Haraszthy was the first to bring choice European vine cuttings to the state. Their yield of familiar Mediterranean grapes brought a rush of European vintners to settle the region from the 1880s.

Decades of patient refining were rewarded in the early 1970s when California wines were acknowledged as being among the world's best. Everyone from the Coco-Cola Company to Moët & Chandon began sinking money into the Wine Country, and the region underwent an unexpected tourist boom.

Among the 200 wineries in the Napa Valley, on the Wine Country's eastern edge, are the nation's biggest and most prestigious wine producers. Three million visitors annually beat a path through the compact valley, their cars jamming the main route, State Road 29, between the sprawling town of Napa (whose name derives from the Native American word for 'abundance') and the historic spa resort of Calistoga, every summer weekend.

SOFTER OPTIONS An alternative to Napa Valley is the less congested Sonoma Valley, immediately west, where apple orchards partner the vines on softly sloping hillsides, and meandering country lanes pass some of the Wine Country's most reputable and longest-established small wineries, while linking amiable rural towns such as history-laden Sonoma, site of the most northerly and last-completed of California's Spanish missions.

On the coastal side of the Wine Country, the Russian River Valley also has its share of smaller wineries. Here, though, the Russian River's sandy banks and thick redwood groves provide appeal beyond wine consuming, and Guerneville, one of the largest communities, fully justifies its reputation as a lively resort town.

Château Souverain in Geyserville is one of the many wineries in this area offering tastings

The entrance to Château Souverain, scene of wining and dining and open-air summer concerts

Calistoga see page 247.

► Geyserville   224A2

Two towers aping traditional hop kilns on a small hill just outside Geyserville belong to **Château Souverain► ►** (400 Souverain Road; tel: 707/433–3141), whose fame dominates the village. Besides arriving to sample its Chardonnay and Cabaret Sauvignon, most Californians come to Souverain for its widely acclaimed restaurant.

By contrast, the **J Pedroncelli Winery►** (1220 Canyon Road; tel: 707/857–3531) has been producing a good cross-section of low-priced red and white wines since 1904.

► Guerneville   224A2

Carefully preserving its rustic charms, turning canoeing and kayaking on the Russian River into growth industries, and keeping its bars and discos jumping into the small hours, Guerneville (pronounced 'GURN-ville') is the Wine Country's liveliest resort town and has become the weekend place-to-be for a large gay contingent from San Francisco.

On the edge of town, foot trails penetrate the dark, damp groves of the **Armstrong Redwoods State Reserve►**, and continue into the bright open meadows of the **Austin Creek State Reserve►**.

Korbel Champagne Cellars► ► (13250 River Road; tel: 707/887–2294) has produced the bubbly – as well as some excellent brandy – since 1862.

► ► Healdsburg   224A2

Filled with Victorian homes and prettified by a century-old tree-lined plaza, Healdsburg, at the northern end of the Russian River Valley, also has a dozen wineries.

You can also read about wine at the **Sonoma County Wine Library►** (corner of Center and Piper streets), stocked with more then 3,000 wine-related volumes, or bone up on it in the **Healdsburg Museum►** (221 Matheson Street). Visit Healdsburg on a summer Sunday and you might well find music in the air – the town stages an excellent series of free concerts in the plaza's park.

THE BOHEMIAN CLUB
Founded in 1872 as a social club for San Francisco newspapermen, and including socialist writers such as Jack London and Ambrose Bierce among its early members, the Bohemian Club is now best known for its Bohemian Week, which takes place annually in July. Scores of high-flying (and exclusively male) bankers, industrialists, congressmen, foreign diplomats and even ex-US presidents arrive at the club's summer retreat, Bohemian Grove, a Russian River Valley redwood grove near Monte Rio, for seven days of nefarious activities behind high-security fences.

Bottled and sold throughout the state, sparkling spring water from Calistoga furthers the fame of a Napa Valley town already noted for its mineral-rich spas, which have been earning the respect of dedicated sybarites since the first health resort was founded here in 1859 by millionaire Mormon Sam Brannan.

Take the waters The cheapest way to find out what all the fuss is about is by taking a dip in the mineral pools at Calistoga Springs Hot Spa (1006 Washington Avenue) or Golden Haven Spa (1713 Lake Street).

A more thorough spa session typically costs $30–$50 (an extra $20–$30 with a massage) and includes a volcanic-mud bath, a soak in a mineral-water whirlpool, a smothering in sweat-inducing blankets, and finally a massage to induce a nirvana-like state of well-being. Purveyors of this relaxing therapy include Nance's Hot Springs (1614 Lincoln Avenue) and Indian Springs (1712 Lincoln Avenue), built around Sam Brannan's resort.

Sam Brannan The founder of Calistoga, Sam Brannan arrived in San Francisco from New York with a boatload of fellow Mormons in 1846. Seeking farmland and religious tolerance, they were dismayed to find that California had joined the United States just prior to their landing. The 26-year-old Brannan published San Francisco's first newspaper and quickly became one of the fledgling state's wealthiest, most flamboyant figures. His investment in Calistoga did not pay off, however, and he spent his final years drunk and destitute in Escondido, near San Diego, dying in 1889.

Calistoga's more adventurous spas are devising weird – and nearly always wonderful – treatments using herbs, eucalyptus steam and Japanese-style enzyme baths; one such is the International Spa (1300 Washington Street), soothing souls with the aid of New Age music and environmental art.

❏ Five miles west of Calistoga, the Petrified Forest (4100 Petrified Forest Road) is the result of a redwood grove being uprooted and turned to stone by volcanic mud and ash that was spewed out by Mount St Helena. ❏

247

Old Faithful Geyser Another way to enjoy the legacy of the area's volcanic activity is simply by looking at it. A mile north of Calistoga, the Old Faithful Geyser (1299 Tubbs Lane), heated by an underground river, sends a high-pressure jet of boiling water 60 feet skyward every 30 or 50 minutes (depending upon seismic activity in the region).

The Old Faithful Geyser, producing natural energy near Calistoga

Calistoga–Clear Lake Loop

See map on page 244.

Drive 10 miles north from Calistoga on State Road 29 for Robert Louis Stevenson State Park.
On the site of Silverado, a disused mining camp, author Robert Louis Stevenson and his wife honeymooned during 1880 in what is now **Robert Louis Stevenson State Park▶▶**, whose 3,000 undeveloped acres include a trail to the summit of Mount St Helena.

Continue seven miles north on State Road 29 for Middletown.
Middletown marks the halfway point of the former Calistoga–Lakeport stagecoach route, which State Road 29 follows. Immediately east of the town, on Butts Canyon Road, the **Guenoc Winery▶** was once owned by English actress Lillie Langtry.

Continue for 15 miles on State Road 29 to the Anderson Marsh Historic Site, just north of Lower Lake.
At the **Anderson Marsh Historic Site▶**, 10,000-year-old sites of Native American habitation have been discovered; another section of the 1,000-acre site is a wildlife refuge,

Clear Lake State Park

protecting bald eagles among many other species.

From Lower Lake, continue on State Road 29 to Clear Lake State Park.
Set on land still bearing evidence of Native American occupation, **Clear Lake State Park▶** is popular with anglers who hunt catfish and perch in the park's volcanic, rather than 'clear', lake.

Continue on State Road 29 for 10 miles to Lakeport.
Besides the usual exhibits, **Lakeport's County Historical Museum▶** holds a glittering cache of locally grown diamonds.

Continue for nine miles on State Road 29, turning east on to State Road 20 at Upper Lake and driving for 21 miles to State Road 53.
Quiet lakeside villages punctuate the drive east from Upper Lake.

From the junction with State Road 53, drive nine miles south on State Road 29 to Lower Lake, continuing for 32 miles to return to Calistoga.

❏ Robert Louis Stevenson spent part of his honeymoon in a miners' cabin on the slopes of Mount St Helena. He was so impressed that he used it as the model for Spyglass Hill in *Treasure Island.* ❏

▶ Oakville
244B1

Among the Wine Country's best tours are the free and highly instructive offerings at Oakville's **Robert Mondavi Winery▶▶** (7801 St Helena Highway; tel: 707/963–9611), which has you winding through the establishment's underground passages; a tasting is included.

Along the road, a geodesic dome covers the workings of the reputable De Moor Cellars (7481 St Helena Highway; tel: 707/944–2565), as well as the winery's visitor centre.

▶▶ Petaluma
224B1

Long famed for its poultry and dairy farms, Petaluma stages a riotous Butter and Eggs Day parade each April. The colourful procession winds through the centre of this riverside town, where carefully maintained 19th- and early 20th-century architecture creates a picture-postcard image of small-town America. In fact, it should be no surprise that Petaluma's streets have served as backdrops for successful nostalgia movies such as *American Graffiti* and *Peggy Sue Got Married*.

The name Petaluma is thought to derive from a Miwok (the indigenous peoples of the region) word meaning 'flat bank', probably a reference to a local hill. A great deal about the town's origins and the commercial importance of the Petaluma River on which it sits can be discovered by taking a visit to the **Historical Library and Museum▶** (20 Fourth Street), which is housed within the imposing 1906 Carnegie Library Building. Find the time, too, to stroll the riverside footpaths that add greatly to this tiny community's appeal.

Early days There is evidence of still earlier times on a hillside across Highway 101, where the **Petaluma Adobe State Historic Park▶▶** holds the well-restored 1836 two-storey adobe building that was at the centre of one of Mexican California's largest land holdings, a vast rancho with which General Mariano Vallejo – the founder of Sonoma – established himself among the province's rich and powerful.

▶ Rutherford
244B1

Several of the Napa Valley's major wine producers lie close to the hamlet of Rutherford and offer novice-friendly tours. The **Rutherford Hill Winery** (200 Rutherford Hill Road; tel: 707/963–7194) is a winery that welcomes beginners and the uninitiated and that, like most of its rivals, ages its wine in caves, though these particular underground tunnels are said to be the biggest such system in the world.

Chateau tasting Wine enthusiasts who happen to be claustrophobic might prefer to visit the ivy-covered stone chateau, complete with stained-glass windows, housing **Niebaum-Coppola** (1919 St Helena Highway; tel: 707/963–9099), where tastings are complemented by a wine museum and exhibits on film-making – your clue that the the property's co-owner is film director Francis Ford Coppola.

CALIFORNIA'S CHEESE
A popular accompaniment to wine drinking, dry and nutty Monterey Jack, California's native cheese, was first produced in 1892 on dairy farms close to Monterey under the control of an unpopular Scottish migrant called David Jacks. Since then, the Sonoma Valley has become a significant cheese-producing area, with the Sonoma Cheese Factory (2 West Spain Street, in Sonoma) and the Creamery Store (711 Western Avenue, in Petaluma) both giving tours of the manufacturing process – and dispensing bite-size free samples.

249

Verdant its valleys may be, but only teetotallers visit the Wine Country for its scenery. For everyone else, a trip through the region begins and ends with a glass in the hand and, given the large number of winery tours and wine tastings offered, it is a glass that you'll know a lot more about by the time you reach the end of a trip than you did at the beginning.

AGOSTON HARASZTHY
Remembered as a pioneering vinter, father of California wine, and founder of Buena Vista Winery in Sonoma, Hungarain aristocrat Haraszthy arrived in California in 1849. A sheriff in San Diego County before moving to the Sonoma Valley, Haraszthy was an impulsive adventurer who later moved to Nicaragua to start a sugar plantation; he disappeared in the jungle, presumed drowned in 1869.

250

A round of drinks
Larger wineries have daily tours and tastings for which reservations are sometimes necessary, while smaller wineries may open only for a few hours a week. Always phone ahead.

Tour one of the major producers first, for a look at the wine-making process and for a broad introduction to the state's wines. Later, move on to the more specialised small wineries, whose products reveal their subtleties only to the initiated.

Grape stuff California's wine types are known by their grape. The main whites include Chardonnay, Chenin Blanc, Gewurztraminer, Riesling, and Sauvignon (or Fumé) Blanc; the main reds are Cabernet Sauvignon, Merlot, Pinot Noir, and Zinfandel.

The extremely versatile Zinfandel also appears as White Zinfandel, actually a 'blush' wine, which is pink rather than red because the grapes' skins are removed during the fermentation process.

Sparkling wine (it is bad form to use the term Champagne to refer to a product that does not come from France) is also found in the Wine Country, and some of the more interesting sparkling-wine producers use the traditional Méthode Champenoise, with fermentation carried out in the bottle rather than in casks.

On the train Known locally as the 'swine train' for the noise it makes rumbling through the valley, and set up in an attempt to ease traffic congestion, the Napa Valley Wine Train (tel: 800/427–4124 or 707/253–2111) pulls restored Pullman cars on a three-tour trip between Napa and St Helena, serving pricey gourmet food accompanied by selections from the valley's wineries. The basic round-trip fare does not include meals, but the train, environmental considerations aside, is hard to beat if you have only half a day to see the Wine Country.

Wine-tasting tips It is a good idea to visit no more than three wineries on any single day. Every wine that you sample affects the taste buds, and red wines tend to coat the tongue, so after you've tasted a few, it becomes harder and harder to appreciate a wine's subtleties of flavour.

Also stick to either the whites or the reds at any given tasting. Or at least begin with the whites, move

on to the reds and rosés, follow with the dessert wines and, finally, try the sparkling wines.

Young wines Do not feel cheated if your host produces a recent wine to sample. Because the climate varies little from year to year, vintages count for far less in California than they do in Europe, though certain wines are noted as being exceptionally good in certain years (not least the 1973 Cabernet Sauvignon, which won a prestigious European tasting in 1976 and helped put California's wines on the world map). The final verdict on a wine's qualities is for you alone to determine, although there are well-established stages in forming judgements.

Step-by-step tasting First look closely at the wine to judge its colour. All wines should be free of clouding; whites should have a yellow to golden shading; rosés should be pink, possibly with an orange hue; reds should have a purple hint and may vary in tone from a light crimson to a rich ruby.

Second, swirl the wine to release its fragrance, or 'nose' – something that results from a combination of the 'aroma', supplied by the grape, and the 'bouquet', which comes from the winemaking process.

Third, sip the wine and roll it around your tongue to determine texture and balance. Flavours are a complex field, and range from a Chardonnay's dry fruitiness to a Zinfandel's zippy spiciness.

At tastings, never feel embarrassed about seeming ignorant. California's vintners are eager for their products to become more widely appreciated, and they respond much better to the genuine interest of a beginner than the witless comments of a wine snob.

Typically, wineries in the Napa Valley charge $2–3 for a tasting and a glass, which you may keep; elsewhere tastings are often free.

THE MYSTERIOUS ZINFANDEL

While most Californian grapes are clearly of European origin, the roots of Zinfandel are shrouded in mystery. A Black Zinfandel wine appeared on the US's east coast in 1838, and Zinfandel grapes were first grown in California 20 years later, but where the grapes actually come from is uncertain. The son of Agoston Haraszthy, the state's earliest vintner, falsely claimed that his father was the first to import them (but did not say where from), and more recently experts have variously cited southern Italy, Slovenia, and even California itself, as the true home of Zinfandel.

251

Wine tasting at Oakville's Robert Mondavi Winery, which has one of the region's best introductory tours

The stained-glass windows of Santa Rosa's Church of One Tree, holding the Ripley Memorial Museum

BALLOON TOURS
When you tire of looking at it through the bottom of a wine glass, you can view the Wine Country from above, wafting across the valleys in a balloon. Prices start at around $125 for an hour, and many flights touch down in a scenic spot for a champagne picnic. Numerous widely advertised companies run flights, among them Bonaventure Balloon Company (tel: 800/243–6743); Napa Valley Balloons (tel: 800/253–2224); and Sonoma Thunder (tel: 800/759–5638).

▶▶ St Helena   244B2

Ten miles south of Calistoga, St Helena sits fortuitously at the heart of the Napa Valley, cashing in on its location with its upmarket restaurants and craft shops.

One person who passed through St Helena was impoverished writer Robert Louis Stevenson who, having married Fanny Osbourne in 1880, honeymooned north of the town in what is now **Robert Louis Stevenson State Park▶▶**. Occupying a special wing of the St Helena Public Library (1490 Library Lane), the **Silverado Museum▶▶** celebrates the Stevenson connection with manuscripts and memorabilia.

▶ Santa Rosa   244B1

Levelled by the 1906 earthquake, Santa Rosa has made a dramatic comeback. It is now the fastest-growing Wine Country community.

The restored 1920s buildings of Railroad Square and the pre-earthquake railroad terminal in Railroad Park show off their community's roots, but Santa Rosa does a better job at commemorating two former inhabitants.

The Church of One Tree (492 Sonoma Avenue) – not the base of a tree-centred religion but built entirely from a redwood felled in 1875 – contains the **Ripley Memorial Museum▶▶**, devoted to local man Robert Ripley, whose cartoon strips – recounting strange and exotic phenomena – were hugely popular beginning in the 1920s.

Self-taught horticulturalist Luther Burbank arrived in Santa Rosa in 1875 armed with 10 Burbank potatoes, early examples of what was to be a lifetime's devotion to developing vegetable, fruit and plant hybrids. The **Luther Burbank Home and Memorial Gardens▶** (415 Steele Lane) preserves Burbank's Greek Revival-style house and the gardens where his creations evolved.

▶ Sebastopol   244A1

Americans know Sebastopol for its reddish-yellow Gravenstein apples, grown here and celebrated by April's Apple Blossom Festival. Otherwise, the area is notable for its dry wines, particularly Pinot Noir, best sampled at the **Dehlinger Winery** (6300 Guerneville Road; tel: 707/823–2378).

In addition to a winery at every turn, the Sonoma and Napa valleys boast a formidable group of state parks. Combining historic and scenic interest, the parks also provide a head-clearing pick-me-up for anyone who has overdone the wine tasting.

Inspirational country A prolific writer, and the first millionaire author in the United States, Jack London eulogised the Sonoma Valley in his 1913 book *Valley of the Moon*. At the time he had already put into practice the return-to-nature way of living that its pages advocated, turning a large tract of grassy hillside beneath Sonoma Mountain into an experimental farm, and building the 26-room Wolf House for himself and his wife.

His ranch is now **Jack London State Historic Park▶▶▶**, in the bucolic hamlet of Glen Ellen, just west of Sonoma. Only the ruins of the fire-destroyed Wolf House remain, but the park's House of Happy Walls Museum is well stocked with mementos of London's far from peaceful life (see panel on this page).

At the northern end of the Sonoma Valley Hiking and horseback-riding trails criss-cross the 5,000-acre **Annadel State Park▶**, rising from meadows and marshes into steep-sided canyons. Even more rugged terrain fills **Sugarloaf Ridge State Park▶**, 14 miles east of Santa Rosa, where wine-induced lethargy will quickly be forgotten after a brisk hike over chaparral-covered ridges on the way to the summit of Bald Mountain.

Just north of St Helena in the Napa Valley, a ramble through the **Bale Grist Mill State Historic Park▶** (3801 St Helena Highway) leads to a restored 19th-century water mill, built for an English ships' surgeon who became a prominent Napa Valley landowner after his vessel ran aground at Monterey in 1837.

Immediately south Greater hiking opportunities are presented by **Bothe-Napa Valley State Park▶**, whose trails pass through strands of coastal redwoods. One leads to the remains of the valley's earliest church and to a pioneer-era graveyard, where several members of the ill-fated Donner party (see page 200) lie buried.

JACK LONDON
The illegitimate son of an itinerant Irish astrologist, Jack London led an eventful life that began in San Francisco in 1876. Largely self-educated, he earned a living variously in Oakland's waterfront canneries, as a harbour policeman, as a sailor, and as a gold prospector before becoming (much to his surprise) a financially secure author, having turned his experiences into a vast body of realist fiction. His *Valley of the Moon*, published in 1913, bestowed a lasting nickname on the Sonoma Valley (resulting from a mis-translation of a Native American word), where London lived until his death – probably by suicide – in 1916.

HITCHCOCK'S RETREAT
Much of the Bothe-Napa State Valley Park occupies the 1,000 acres of creekside land bought by Doctor Charles Hitchcock as a weekend retreat in 1872. An arm doctor posted to San Francisco in 1851, Hitchcock was the father of Lille Hitchcock (married name Coit), whose flouting of convention made her the talk of San Francisco society and whose obsession with fires led to the construction of the city's Coit Tower (see page 39).

The Wine Country

FESTIVALS

Guerneville stages the Russian River Jazz Festival and the Russian River Rodeo every September and, in March, the bizarre Slug Festival; Healdsburg's Harvest Hoedown marks September; Petaluma hosts the World Wristwrestling Championships in October; and Sonoma holds Living History Days during May and October.

A stately palm tree stands before Sonoma's City Hall, inside which is a tourist office

▶▶ **Sonoma**   *244B1*

With a history far more illustrious than its contemporary importance, Sonoma has many restored adobe buildings that provide an evocative window on the turbulent decades that saw California switch from Spanish to Mexican and finally to US rule. A host of bed-and-breakfasts make the small town a good base for exploring the Wine Country, though Sonoma itself is easily covered by a half-day walk.

Surrounded by historic hotels, Sonoma's eight-acre **plaza** was constructed in 1835 and is the largest in California. In the centre is **Sonoma City Hall▶**, dating from 1906 and presenting a symbol of early US authority in the town. The **Bear Flag Monument▶**, on the plaza's north-east corner, commemorates the 1846 hoisting of the Bear Flag, denoting an independent California Republic. Across Spain Street, on the corner with First Street East, is the much-restored **Mission San Francisco de Solano▶**. Founded in 1823, this was the last and most northerly of California's Spanish missions. It also saw service as a saloon, a warehouse, and a barn; a small museum tells its story.

At 285 First Street West, the **Depot Museum▶**, across Depot Park from First Street East, mounts changing temporary exhibitions on local heritage themes. The main buildings of **Sonoma State Historical Park▶▶** are across First Street West: several important structures form this far-flung park, among them two former homes of General Mariano Vallejo – wealthy rancho owner and the founder and first mayor of Sonoma – and the Sonoma Barracks, whose storming by the US cavalry in 1846 was part of the Bear Flag Revolt – briefly turning California into an independent republic.

Enjoying a bucolic setting on the outskirts of Sonoma, the **Buena Vista Winery▶▶** (18000 Old Winery Road;

tel: 707/938–1266), founded by Agoston Haraszthy (see panel, page 250) in 1857, is the oldest commercial winery in the state.

Although it only opened in 1986, Yountville's Domain Chandon shows off some historic wine-making equipment

▶ Ukiah   244A3

Native American culture keeps a decidedly low profile throughout the Wine Country, a fact that makes the **Grace Hudson Museum and Sun House▶▶** (431 Main Street) all the more welcome. It houses lyrical studies of the Pomo by painter Grace Carpenter Hudson and her husband's extensive ethnographical collections, one of the main sources of information on Pomo culture. The layout of the museum is based on the geometry used in Pomo crafts. Remarkably, this outstanding collection crops up in what is a run-of-the-mill lumber town, with only tastings and tours at the **Parducci Wine Cellars** (501 Parducci Road; tel: 707/462–WINE) providing other diversion.

▶ Yountville   244B1

A rural counterpart to sprawling Napa, 14 miles south, pleasant Yountville became a stop on the wine tourists' circuit in 1986 following the opening of **Domain Chandon▶▶** (W California Drive; tel: 707/944–8844) by the top-bracket champagne and brandy producer, Moët & Chandon. Tours describing the sparkling-wine-making process are free, but you have to pay if you would like to sample a glass.

If you like to shop, visit Domain Chandon only after a tour of **Yountville 1870▶**, where upscale boutiques, art galleries, and antiques outlets fill an imaginatively restored 19th-century railroad station; the area could seriously lighten the wallet of any less-than-clear-headed browser.

THE SILVERADO TRAIL
Used during the 1800s to carry cinnabar from mines at Mount St Helena to the river docks in Napa, the Silverado Trail crosses the east side of the Napa Valley and makes for a quieter passage than the busy State Road 29, which it parallels.

Complementing the peaceful mood, several tourable and rarely crowded small wineries line the trail.

Arranging a trip
Flights and packages
Competition between tour operators specialising in US holidays and transatlantic airlines is fierce and you are well advised to shop around for the best deal.

Package holidays, involving any combination of flights, accommodation and car hire, and widely advertised in travel agents' brochures, can save legwork once you have arrived, but will not necessarily be the best or the cheapest travel option.

If you are booking a flight independently, take advantage of the reduced fares regularly offered during quiet periods (autumn and spring) by the major airlines – American, British Airways, United, TWA and Virgin – which fly non-stop between London and California (the least costly flights from Europe to the US are via London) or use a discount ticket agent. Being under 26 or a student will bring further reductions.

Three US airlines – **Continental**, **Delta** and **Northwest** – have services from London to California via other US cities, which allows for greater choice as to where you land in California – many small towns are well served by domestic flights.

The majority of scheduled non-stop international flights land at Los Angeles; fewer touch down at San Francisco. Some charter airlines fly direct to San Diego or Oakland (for San Francisco) from London and regional UK airports.

Arriving in California
Visas, Immigration and Customs
Citizens of the UK, most European countries and New Zealand need a full passport to visit the US, but do not need a visa for a stay of 90 days or less (provided they have a return ticket). It is necessary, however, to fill out the visa-waiver form issued on the plane.

Citizens of Australia do need visas. Passengers will also be given customs and immigration forms to complete. These will present no difficulties if you are visiting the US on holiday; if you are planning to live and/or work in the US you will need proof that you can do this legally.

If travelling with a major airline, it is likely that an immigration check (a computer check of passengers' names against those of known miscreants) will be carried out when you check in. A sticker will then be attached to your passport to speed your passage through immigration control when you land. On arrival, your passport will be stamped and part of the immigration form will be fixed in your passport; this is only removed when you leave.

Duty-free allowances include a quart (just under a litre) of alcoholic spirits or wine and 200 cigarettes or 50 cigars. Among items not allowed into the US are meat, fruit and plants.

Banks
California banks usually open Monday to Thursday 10–5, Friday 10–5.30. Major branches may also be open longer hours and on Saturday 10–1 until 1 or 2.

Beaches
With almost 1,000 miles of coastline, California is well supplied with beaches. They are endlessly fascinating: you can walk on them, lie and sunbathe on them, watch seabirds and hunt for shells, dig clams or spot seals and sea otters at play. From December through to March you can watch the migrations of the gray whales.

What you can't always do is swim. From San Francisco northwards, the water is simply too cold for any but extremely hardy souls. Some beaches, even along the southern half of the coast, are too dangerous for swimming because of the undertow.

Park rangers patrol beaches and enforce regulations, such as those on pets (dogs must be on a leash at all times), alcohol, dune buggies and fires.

Access to beaches in California is generally excellent. The state park system includes many fine beaches, and oceanside communities have their own public beaches.

In addition, through the work of the California Coastal Commission, many stretches of private property that would otherwise seal off the beach from outsiders have public-access

Travel Facts

Travel Facts

paths and trails. Again, the best advice is to look for signs and obey them.

Bed-and-breakfast

California's most atmospheric lodgings, bed-and-breakfasts, are often restored Victorian homes with a small number of guest rooms, with private or shared bathrooms, decorated with antiques. Here, guests are encouraged to mingle, and breakfast itself is normally a hearty affair served around a large table. Prices per room range from $45 to $200, depending on location and facilities.

The **California Office of Tourism** (see Maps and Tourist Information) publish the free *Bed and Breakfast Inn Directory*, and reservations can be made through an agency such as Bed and Breakfast International, PO Box 282910, San Francisco, CA 94706 (tel: 800/272–4500).

Camping

Most of California's 264 state parks have well-equipped campsites costing $10–$15. Places can be reserved up to eight weeks in advance through **DESTINET** (tel: 800/444–7275). Larger state parks may also have very basic hikers' campsites ($2–$6) in the backcountry.

For information on camping in national parks, such as Yosemite, whose facilities range from large campsites with all amenities to rough plots in the wild, contact the National Park Service, PO Box 37127, Washington, DC 20013-7127 (tel: 202/208-4989).

In addition, there are many privately run camping-grounds throughout the state. One of the larger operators is the **California Travel Parks Association**, Box 5648, Auburn, CA 95604 (tel: 916/885–1624).

Car hire

Car hire companies – all the major international names and smaller local firms with links to European operators – have desks at the airports (and offices throughout the state). Here, you can collect a pre-booked car or hire on the spot. Driving is

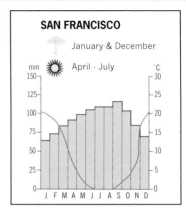

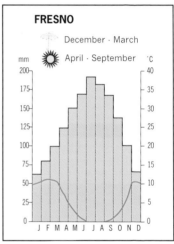

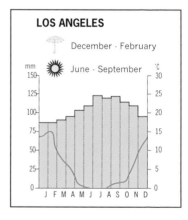

legal with a valid licence of most European countries or with an International Driving Licence.

Prices between car rental companies vary little but it is usually cheaper to arrange car hire before arrival in the US. Do not neglect to read the small print, particularly if you are intending to leave California from a different city from where you arrived (some companies do not allow for this and you might incur extra charges). Be aware that full third party insurance (sometimes called Supplementary Liability Insurance) is not included in most standard rental agreements. Without booking ahead, anyone under 25 and/or without a credit card may have problems hiring a car.

Here are toll-free numbers for some of the car-hire firms agencies in California:

American International Rent a Car (AI), tel: 800/633–1331
Avis, tel: 800/331–1212
Budget Car and Truck Rental, tel: 800/527–0700
Dollar Rent a Car, tel: 800/421–6868
Hertz, tel: 800/654–3131; (in Canada 800/263-0600)
National Car Rental, tel: 800/328–4567
Thrifty Car Rental, tel: 800/367–2277

Children
Rarely in California are children regarded disdainfully. Hotels and motels usually provide a crib or extra bed in the parents' room for under 12s at no extra charge, and restaurant staff are likely to appear with games, the children's menu, and – if required – a high chair. If you are hiring a car, ask for a car seat when you make your booking.

The state has much that will amuse children: Disneyland is just the most famous of a number of theme parks; many museums provide hands-on exhibits; and the state's parks and forests can make an excellent introduction to the natural world.

Climate and clothing
The common perception of California as a sun-drenched paradise applies only to the southern half of the state, and even here there are variations:

San Francisco's finest – the 'Smokey Bears'

humidity-free San Diego ranges from mild to warm; Los Angeles can be hot and sticky in summer, warm but potentially wet during winter; inland, the baking deserts are off-limits to humans throughout the summer and are merely hot during the rest of the year.

In the north, San Francisco's temperatures are mild, but persistent fog can mean a cool start to even the sunniest day; further north along the coast, expect more fog and colder, damper conditions; inland, the Gold Country can be scorching in summer while the higher elevations of the Sierra Nevada region are welcomingly mild – in winter, snow covers the mountains and their immediate surroundings.

If you are travelling widely around the state you should pack with varying climates in mind. California dress is almost always casual, but bare feet and swimsuits are not acceptable in public buildings, and the most elegant restaurants require formal attire. The national and state parks, and much of the undeveloped coastline, are best seen by walking, so bring suitable footwear.

Crime
Theft of money and valuables from your room is easy to avoid simply by handing them over to the hotel

California crabs

and allow a companion to travel free provided you have a doctor's certificate. Car-hire companies are able to arrange vehicles equipped with hand controls provided they receive advance notice; all public parking lots have spaces that are specially marked for people with disabilities.

Many US-based organisations specialise in providing information for the traveller with disabilities. One of the largest is the **Society for the Advancement of Travel for the Handicapped**, 347 5th Avenue, Suite 610, New York, NY1001 (tel: 212/447–7284).

staff to put in a safe. Being robbed in the street is statistically very unlikely but does happen, usually to people who have been careless enough to make things easy for the robber – by carrying easily snatched handbags or having wallets sticking out of their back pockets.

Lost travellers' cheques are quite easy to replace (read the instructions when you buy the cheques), but replacing a stolen passport is much harder and begins with a visit or phone call to your country's nearest consular office (those in San Francisco and Los Angeles are given in the regional gazetteer).

Straying into dangerous areas of cities is another potential hazard. San Francisco is fairly safe (but not completely), San Diego slightly less so, and Los Angeles much less so; get local advice and follow it.

Travellers with disabilities
California leads the United States in providing facilities for travellers with disabilities. All public buildings have to be wheelchair accessible, and wheelchair users will find public transport equipped with 'kneeling' buses, and (in San Francisco) lifts to the underground BART system. Trains and airlines are obliged to provide services for people with disabilities if requested, and **Amtrak** (the US train service) has earned a reputation for doing this well. Though less comfortable than trains, Greyhound buses are more frequent

Driving
With petrol typically costing from $1.20 to $1.50 a gallon and public transport (see page 262) far from comprehensive, you will save money and time by touring California by car.

California's roads fall into several categories depending on who pays for their upkeep. The Interstates and US Highways are part of the federally run road network; State Highways and State Roads tend to be smaller than Interstates and US Highways, and are financed by the state government; much less frequently you will be travelling on County Roads – most typically winding lanes through isolated rural areas. Petrol stations are easy to find in all but the most secluded or inhospitable regions.

Eating
One of the greatest pleasures of the Golden State is eating, which can be done extremely well, and if your budget demands, extremely cheaply. Your biggest problem could simply be succumbing to temptation and over-indulging, although the potential for gluttony is balanced by a well-established trend towards healthy eating. Even major fast-food outlets offer low-fat alternatives to burgers and french fries.

To sample what people generally consider California Cuisine, you can venture into any of the haute temples of gastronomy in Los Angeles or San

Francisco, or experiment with myriad bistros that line neighbourhood streets. California cooking is light, fresh and extremely creative (sometimes unappetisingly so). It affords shredded Thai chicken on pizza and goat cheese and sun-dried cherries in salad. Don't be afraid to stretch your palate. You might be surprised to find how delicious some concoctions can be.

Perhaps ethnic food offers the best value for money. Both Los Angeles and San Francisco feature large and varied ethnic communities, which have enriched the city's respective restaurant scenes with a full range of eateries – everything from upmarket Japanese sushi palaces to down-and-dirty Mexican bogedas. An ethnic restaurant filled with people of that ethnicity is a good sign that the cooking is authentic and very good.

California is also one of the great wine regions of the world, and it would be a shame to experience the food without sampling the best of the barrels. California wines are mostly categorised by varietal, labelled by the grape name rather than the region or producer. The Chardonnays are typically big and oaky while the Cabernet Sauvignon are bold and tannic. They offer a perfect accompaniment to the vibrant cooking of the area.

The relaxed atmosphere of even the most formal restaurants makes dining in California even more enjoyable. A Hawaiian shirt is usually all you need to don to eat in Los Angeles, while a cable-knit sweater will generally suffice in cooler San Francisco.

Traditional Coffee shops and diners are abundant and don't stay in business long if they don't deliver good food at good prices. Most offer gigantic breakfasts for around $6, washed down by as much coffee as you like for the price of a single cup. For lunch, they serve sandwiches (actually a whole hot meal) and salads (actually a whole cold meal) for $6–$9. Some coffee shops and diners close after lunch, but some provide substantial dinners for $10–$15.

At the top end of the scale are the gourmet restaurants, whose chefs are the leading practitioners of California cuisine: an ever-inventive manipulation of local produce to create attractive and nutritionally balanced meals – worth a $30–$80 splurge at least once during your stay.

Electricity
The US electrical supply is 110–115 volts (60 cycles) and appliances use two-prong plugs. European appliances are designed for 220 volts (50 cycles) and can only be used with an adaptor. These can be bought before leaving (though first make sure the adaptor is suitable for the US) or in the US.

Festivals and events
From county fairs to frog racing, thousands of festivals and special events take place in California each year. Somewhere, at some time, in California there's bound to be an event celebrating everything you can think of and some more besides. The pick of the bunch is in the regional gazetteer. For a (very long) full list, contact the **California Office of Tourism** (see Maps and Tourist Information).

Gay and lesbian travellers
California in general and San Francisco in particular are welcoming places for gay and lesbian travellers. Gay and lesbian bars, clubs, accommodation and information centres are well established in the major cities, and gays and lesbians are unlikely to encounter open public hostility.

Health and insurance
It is essential, though not compulsory, to have insurance when you travel anywhere in the US. Besides the obvious benefits of compensation for stolen articles and disrupted travel, being insured will guard against an astronomical bill if you are unfortunate enough to need medical treatment.

If you need to see a doctor, find one by looking under 'physicians' in the phone book; hospitals have emergency rooms, but if you are dealing with a serious injury call 911.

Holidays

Banks and all public offices will be closed on all the following holidays, but shops may be open on some of these days: New Year's Day (1 January), Martin Luther King's Birthday (third Monday in January), Lincoln's Birthday (12 February), Washingtons's Birthday (3rd Monday in February), Memorial Day (4th Monday in May), Independence Day (4 July), Labor Day (1st Monday in September), Columbus Day (12 October), Veteran's Day (11 November), Thanksgiving Day (4th Thursday in November), Christmas Day (25 December).

In addition, Good Friday is a half-day holiday and Easter Monday is a full day holiday. The actual date may vary if the holiday falls on a weekend.

262

Hotels and motels

The major American mid-range hotel chains (usually $70–$90 a night), such as Holiday Inn, Best Western, Travelodge and Vagabond, are heavily represented in California, offering double beds, colour TVs, private bathrooms and phones in their clean, comfortable rooms.

Such hotels are rarely the best value, however. Many smaller hotels and motels – including budget-priced chains such as Hampton Inn, Days Inn and Comfort Inns ($40–$70) – often offer the same things as the pricier hotels, minus room service and an on-premises restaurant.

Thousands of small, owner-run motels are likely to have even lower prices ($35–$70), especially during quiet periods when the rooms would otherwise be unoccupied. Although you should always check the room before booking in, bargain-priced motels nearly always offer perfectly acceptable accommodation and include in-room phones, private bathrooms and TV.

Three people sharing can often add an extra bed to a double room for an additional fee of $10–$15 above the regular rate.

Besides the standard sales tax (see page 265), some areas impose a 'bed tax' of 5–15 per cent on the standard room charge.

CONVERSION CHARTS

FROM	TO	MULTIPLY BY
Inches	Centimetres	2.54
Centimetres	Inches	0.3937
Feet	Metres	0.3048
Metres	Feet	3.2810
Yards	Metres	0.9144
Metres	Yards	1.0940
Miles	Kilometres	1.6090
Kilometres	Miles	0.6214
Acres	Hectares	0.4047
Hectares	Acres	2.4710
Gallons	Liters	4.5460
Litres	Gallons	0.2200
Ounces	Grams	28.35
Grams	Ounces	0.0353
Pounds	Grams	453.6
Grams	Pounds	0.0022
Pounds	Kilograms	0.4536
Kilograms	Pounds	2.205
UK Tons	Tonnes	1.0160
Tonnes	UK Tons	0.9842

MEN'S SUITS

UK	36	38	40	42	44	46	48
Rest of Europe	46	48	50	52	54	56	58
US	36	38	40	42	44	46	48

DRESS SIZES

UK	8	10	12	14	16	18
France	36	38	40	42	44	46
Italy	38	40	42	44	46	48
Rest of Europe	34	36	38	40	42	44
US	6	8	10	12	14	16

MEN'S SHIRTS

UK	14	14.5	15	15.5	16	16.5	17
Rest of Europe	36	37	38	39/40	41	42	43
US	14	14.5	15	15.5	16	16.5	17

MEN'S SHOES

UK	7	7.5	8.5	9.5	10.5	11
Rest of Europe	41	42	43	44	45	46
US	8	8.5	9.5	10.5	11.5	12

WOMEN'S SHOES

UK	4.5	5	5.5	6	6.5	7
Rest of Europe	38	38	39	39	40	41
US	6	6.5	7	7.5	8	8.5

Language

When California joined the Union in 1850, Spanish was spoken as a mother tongue by two-thirds of the state's population. It was only with the influx of English speakers from the east during the gold rush that the language lost its predominance.

Now, after 100 years, Spanish is once again widely spoken in California. Spanish speakers are concentrated in the most densely populated third of the state: over a quarter of the population of Los Angeles, America's second-largest city, are Hispanic Americans. Many face discrimination and prejudice. Controversy has raged about education provision in Spanish schools and the rights of Spanish speakers. Despite opposition from civil

rights groups, Californians voted in a state-wide referendum to make English their official language. A Spanish speaker can easily understand Mexican Spanish. The main difficulty is in vocabulary: Mexican Spanish has

agua fresca	cold water
arroz	rice
cafe	coffee
cerveza	beer
el guacamole	avocado purée
el jitomate	tomato
el licuado de agua	fruit juice with water
el licuado de leche	fruit juice with milk
el mojo de ajo	fried with garlic in butter
el refresco	soft drink
empanizado	fried in breadcrumbs
la botana	appetiser
la carne de res	beef
la cena	dinner
la cochinita pibil	spicy pork Yucatan-style
la comida	lunch
la comida corrida	set menu
la crepa	crepe
la cuenta	the bill
la papa	potato
la torta	roll with meat, lettuce, avocado, cream
las puntas de filete	thin slices of beef (sometimes in a sandwich)
las enchiladas suizas	tortilla filled with chicken, covered with cooked cheese and cream
las carnitas	small pieces of grilled pork
las crepas con cajeta	crepes with sweet sauce
las papas fritas	french fries
los tamales	dumplings
los totopos tacos	dips
pan	bread
pescado	fish
pollo	chicken
vegetariano	vegetarian
verduras	vegetables

Mission Beach Broadwalk

a standard form of payment for major expenses such as car hire and accommodation, and are also an indication that you are a credit-worthy person.

The US currency you will be handling most frequently are the identical looking notes: $20, $10, $5 and $1; and the variously sized coins: 25¢ (a 'quarter'), 10¢ (a 'dime'), 5¢ (a 'nickel') and 1¢ (a 'penny').

Nightlife

To discover the best of the nightlife look for the free local newspapers distributed in bookshops, bars, restaurants or just piled up on street corners. Each community has at least one and they are dependable (and opinionated) sources of information.

Post offices

All towns have post offices and most open Monday to Friday 8.30–5, Saturday 8–12 noon.

Public transport

It is possible to see most of California without a car, but it's difficult: public transport is decidedly thin outside cities and non-existent in many country and coastal areas.

There is a limited train service connecting San Francisco, Los Angeles and San Diego. A more common form of long-distance travel is Greyhound bus; for some this is the classic way to travel, but can be comparatively expensive.

Costs over very long journeys might be reduced with an Ameripass ticket, which offers unlimited Greyhound travel over a fixed period – from four to 30 days. Bear in mind that buses often fall hours behind schedule and that the routes miss much of the state's finest scenery.

With the exception of San Francisco, which has a good public transport network, getting around cities without a car is also problematic though again not impossible, provided you study the local schedules carefully.

When using city buses, take care not to miss your stop and unwittingly stray into dangerous areas (this is especially important after dark); the driver will be ready to give advice.

been much enriched by words from Nahuatl, the language of the Aztecs.

On page 263 is a basic vocabulary to help you in Hispanic restaurants.

Various Asian languages are also spoken in pockets around the state.

Maps and tourist information

Almost every community has a Visitors' Bureau or Chamber of Commerce equipped to provide free maps, leaflets and information. The offices are usually signposted and their addresses are always in the phone book. Most keep regular business hours; those in major cities are often open on weekends, too.

Information on and reliable maps of the whole state are provided by the **California Office of Tourism**, which is based at 801 K Street, Suite 1600, Sacramento, CA 95814 (tel: 916/ 322–2881). Detailed topographical maps of California national parks are available from the United States Geographical Survey (US65), Box 25286, Denver Federal Center, Denver, CO 80225 (tel: 303/202–4700).

Money and currency exchange

Before arriving in the US, convert your spending money to US dollar travellers' cheques, accepted as cash in shops, hotels, restaurants and so on. Foreign currency can be changed in some banks and at a small number of exchange bureaux, but rates and commissions are never good. Credit cards should be carried, too; these are

Sales tax
The state sales tax is 7.25 per cent plus local taxes.

Shops
Shops in California span everything from gigantic city shopping malls to country stores beside rural crossroads. Opening hours vary and are usually Monday to Saturday 9–5.30.

Sports
While California's spectator sports enjoy a high profile and regularly fill TV screens, more popular are participant sports, which range from surfing to scuba diving to skiing and white-river rafting. Details are given in the appropriate section of the regional gazetteer.

Taxis
In cities, taxis can be hailed in the street though it is more common to phone for one; many companies are listed (under 'taxicabs') in the Yellow Pages. Hotel and motel lobby staff will usually call a taxi for you.

Telephones
Found on the street, in hotel lobbies, bus stations, bars, restaurants and, indeed, in most public buildings, California's public telephones almost always work and, by European standards, are cheap. Local calls cost only cents (the phone has slots for quarters, dimes and nickels, which should be inserted before dialling), although calls further afield can be very costly.

To phone out of the US dial 011 and then your country code: Australia 61: Eire 353: New Zealand 64: UK 44.

Emergency calls (dial 911) and calls to the operartor (dial 0) or the international operator (dial 01) are free.

Time
California uses Pacific Standard Time, three hours behind the US's East Coast, eight hours behind the UK and nine hours behind the rest of Europe. Australia is between 16 and 18 hours later than California; New Zealand is 20 hours later.

Tipping
After using restaurants, bars or taxis, leave a tip of 15–20 per cent of the bill. If a hotel porter carries your luggage, tip 80¢–$1.50 per bag.

Wine and beer
International recognition draws many visitors to sample the produce of California's Wine Country; the state's native beers are also worth investigating. San Francisco's Anchor Steam Beer has gained worldwide acclaim, and there are many micro-breweries creating good brews that blow away the weak and relatively tasteless mass-market beers.

Youth hostels, YMCAs and YWCAs
Youth hostels and a small number of comparable YMCAs and YWCAs are scattered throughout California and, at $12–$15 a night, offer by far the least costly form of accommodation.

Most hostels have small, shared rooms (usually with six to eight beds) and a few single and double rooms (around $25) and simple cooking facilities. A three-night limit operates when the hostel is fully booked, as is very likely during the summer.

Views of California

SAN FRANCISCO

Accommodation
Expensive

Campton Place, 340 Stockton Street (tel: 415/781–5555 or 800/235–4300). Housed in a small brownstone building, this hotel offers discreet service and surroundings, and is filled with antiques. The rooms are understated and elegant.

Fairmont Hotel & Tower, 950 Mason Street (tel: 415/772–5000). An elite hotel in Nob Hill and a survivor of the 1906 earthquake; the marble-pillared lobby is just the beginning of the grand opulence that awaits.

Hotel Griffon, 155 Stewart Street (tel: 415/495–2100). Classy accommodation on the Embarcadero waterfront; hotel guests get free use of the adjoining fitness centre.

Huntington, 1075 California Street (tel: 415/474–5400 or 800/227–4683). Comfortable accommodation with excellent service and individually decorated rooms.

Inn at the Opera, 333 Fulton Street (tel: 415/863–8400 or 800/325–2708). Opera and ballet stars, classical musicians and top-billed thespians are likely to be among the fellow guests with whom you may be sharing the breakfast buffet at this extremely cosy and tastefully decorated hotel.

Mandarin Oriental, 222 Sansome Street (tel: 415/885–0999 or 800/622–0404). Experience some of the best views of the city from the rooms on the upper floor. Guests enjoy health club privileges, dining and gracious service.

Mark Hopkins Inter-Continental, 1 Nob Hill (tel: 415/392–3434). This old Nob Hill favourite still retains its individuality and charm.

The Miyako, 1625 Post Street (tel: 415/922–3200). A discreet and luxurious retreat in Japantown that is a harmonious blend of Japanese and Western ideas.

Ritz-Carlton San Francisco, 600 Stockton Street (tel: 415/296–7465). A neoclassical landmark filled with antiques, paintings and chandeliers. Extensive amenities such as a health club, pool, excellent dining and excellent service.

San Francisco Marriott, 55 Fourth Street (tel: 415/896–1600). While the facade has inspired great debate, the interior is extremely comfortable.

Tuscan Inn, 425 North Point (tel: 800/648–4626 or 415/561–1100). The pick of the hotels in touristy Fisherman's Wharf. Warmly furnished rooms, personable staff and a complimentary wine hour.

The Westin St Francis, 335 Powell Street (tel: 415/397–7000). Over 90 years old, this hotel offers old-world luxury and elegance. Services include dining, a beauty salon, shopping and a health club.

Moderate

Abigail, 246 McAllister Street (tel: 415/861–9728). Delightfully old-fashioned and stuffed with mementos from earlier days, when it catered to visiting theatre companies; comfortable and renovated.

Alamo Square Inn, 719 Scott Street (tel: 415/922–2055). Bed and breakfast in an atmospheric rambling Victorian building with fabulous views; in a fast-improving area between Haight-Ashbury and Pacific Heights.

The Alexander Inn, 415 O'Farrel Street (tel: 800/843–8709). Compact and stylishly furnished; a good choice in a central area.

Cartwright Hotel, 524 Sutter Street (tel: 415/421–2865). Small rooms but comfortable and very competitively priced this close to Union Square. Complimentary afternoon tea served in the book-lined study.

Economy Inn, 1 Richardson Avenue (tel: 415/922–0810). Run-of-the-mill motel near Fisherman's Wharf, and reasonably priced.

Edward II Suites & Pub, 3155 Scott Street (tel: 800/GREAT-IN or 415/922–3000). Four-poster beds and whirlpool baths in Pacific Heights; price includes a glass of sherry in the adjoining bar.

Hotel Diva, 440 Geary Street (tel: 415/885–0200 or 800/553–1900). Italian design and a VCR in every room.

Hotel Essex, 684 Ellis Street (tel: 415/474–4664 or 800/453–7739). Pleasant, well placed and good value.

Hotel Union Square, 114 Powell Street (tel: 415/397–3000 or 800/553–1900). Well-known 1930s hotel, stylishly revamped; extras include complimentary croissants and herbal teas.

Kensington Park, 450 Post Street (tel: 415/788–6400). An impressively presented boutique hotel; breakfast is included and complimentary afternoon sherry is served to the sound of the resident pianist.

The King George, 334 Mason Street (tel: 415/781– 5050 or 800/288–6005). Pleasant if unspectacular rooms in the heart of Downtown; serves 'English-style' afternoon tea to piano music.

Laurel Motor Inn, 444 Presidio Avenue (tel: 800/552–8735). Unspectacular but good value and slightly removed from the strongly touristed areas.

Maxwell Hotel, 386 Geary Street (tel: 415/986–2000). Unexceptional but friendly; useful Downtown location.

The Pickwick, 85 Fifth Street (tel: 415/421–7500). Up-and-coming hotel in increasingly fashionable SoMa district; good value despite steadily rising prices.

The Red Victorian, 1665 Haight Street (tel: 415/864–1978). A 1904 structure with soothing décor, a meditation room, in-house masseurs, and healthy breakfasts – a true San Francisco experience.

Stanyan Park, 750 Stanyan Street (tel: 415/751–1000). Elegantly renovated and facing Golden Gate Park; rates include breakfast.

Hotels & Restaurants

Victorian Inn on the Park, 301 Lyon Street (tel: 415/ 931–1830 or 800/435–1967). Twelve antique-decorated rooms, some with original fireplaces, in a lovely 1897 house. Rates include fruit, croissants and freshly brewed coffee for breakfast.

Washington Square Inn, 1660 Stockton Street (tel: 415/981–4220 or 800/388–0220). Antiques-laden bed-and-breakfast in a prime North Beach setting; rates include afternoon tea and evening wine and cheese.

Budget

Adelaide Inn, 5 Isadora Duncan Court (tel: 415/441–2261). Small, pleasant rooms with shared bathrooms and a friendly atmosphere in a quiet cul-de-sac off Taylor Street.

Brady Acres, 649 Jones Street (tel: 415/929–8033). Pleasant rooms equipped with coffee-makers and microwaves.

Central YMCA, 220 Golden Gate Avenue (tel: 415/885–0460). Plain single and double rooms in an uninteresting neighbourhood; a solid budget option.

European Guest House, 761 Minna Street (tel: 415/861–6634). Cosy and low-cost option with an easy-going, youth-oriented mood and a mix of dormitory beds and double rooms.

Grant Plaza, 465 Grant Avenue (tel: 415/434–3883 or 800/472–6899). Tremendous value in the centre of Chinatown, with small but thoughtfully decorated rooms and a stained-glass dome on the top floor.

Hostelling International San Francisco-Fort Mason, Building 240, Fort Mason (tel: 415/771–7277). Massive youth hostel. Three night limit in summer, five nights in winter.

Hotel David, 480 Geary Street (tel: 415/771–1600). An all-you-can-eat breakfast and a discounted dinner from the ground-floor deli are both included in the room rate and make the small but clean rooms temptingly good value for the budget-minded visitor.

Hotel Sheehan, 620 Sutter Street (tel: 415/775–6500 or 800/848–1529). A converted YMCA with large but not pricey rooms; the Olympic-sized swimming pool and a gymnasium are free for guests.

International Guest House, 2976 23rd Street (tel: 415/641–1411). Aimed at backpacking students, with dormitory bunk beds and a few private rooms.

Marina Motel, 2576 Lombard Street (tel: 415/ 921–9406). On a busy street in the largely residential Marina District, offering choice of regular and kitchen-equipped rooms.

Mary Elizabeth Inn, 1040 Bush Street (tel: 415/673–6768). Friendly and low-key women-only accommodation since 1914.

San Remo Hotel, 2237 Mason Street (tel: 415/ 776–8688). Comfortable if spartan rooms with shared bathrooms; good value in a good location.

Sutter Larkin Hotel, 1048 Larkin Street (tel: 415/474–6820). The bare necessities at a very low price in a convenient Downtown spot.

24 Henry, 24 Henry Street (tel: 415/864 5686). Five-room guesthouse on a tree-lined Castro side street; a friendly and affordable base for gay men.

Restaurants
Expensive

Aqua, 252 California Street (tel: 415/956–9662). Painstakingly prepared and artfully presented seafood that draws a style-conscious crowd. One of the city's top restaurants.

Boulevard, 1 Mission Street (tel: 415/543–6084). Nancy Oaks cooks for adoring fans at this SoMa hot spot, where the food typifies California cooking: inventive, healthy, and delicious.

Café Majestic, Majestic Hotel, 1500 Sutter Street (tel: 415/776–6400). California cuisine in an ultra-elegant, classically furnished dining room.

The Dining Room, The Ritz-Carlton San Francisco, 600 Stockton Street (tel: 415/296–7465). Elegant French fare by former Le Cirque chef Sylvian Portay served in an exquisite - setting, complete with antiques and stunning flower arrangements. The service is extremely accommodating, and there is also an excellent wine cellar.

Farallon, 40 Post Street (tel: 415/956-6969). Picture the Little Mermaid meets Jacques Cousteau. The setting is fantasmagorical, the seafood imaginative and delicious.

Fleur de Lys, 777 Sutter Street (tel: 415/673-7779). Hubert Keller's inspired French cooking competes only with the richly appointed dining room, draped in hundreds of yards of rich, batiked fabric.

Greens, Building A, Fort Mason (tel: 415/771–6222). Rarified state-of-the-art gourmet vegetarian cuisine, using ingredients grown on a Zen Buddhist farm across the bay in Marin County.

La Folie, 2316 Polk Street (tel: 415/776–5577). Outstanding French food served in a refreshingly unstuffy setting; options include a five-course dinner designed to reveal the chef's talents.

Jardinière, 300 Grove Street (tel: 415/861–5555). The elegant contemporary décor is comfortable and inviting. Sit back in plush velvet surroundings, listen to soft piano music, and enjoy chef Traci Des Jardins' sophisticated French-inspired cooking with a California flair.

Masa's, 648 Bush Street (tel: 415/ 989–7154). The inventively prepared and presented French menu is set off by the understated surroundings. The staff is knowledgeable and attentive and the wine selection is admirable. One of the city's best places to eat.

Postrio, 545 Post Street (tel: 415/776–7825). The Asian- and Mediterranean-inspired California menu is overseen by superstar chef

The North Beach area, San Francisco

Wolfgang Puck at this popular, attractive spot. Enjoy specialties such as Chinese duck, and excellent desserts. They also serve a great breakfast.

Rubicon, 558 Sacramento Street (tel: 415/434–4100). An elegant outpost of New York restaurateur Drew Nieporent's empire (Nobu, Montrachet); the menu has inventive Mediterranean fare.

Silks, Mandarin Oriental Hotel, 222 Sansome Street (tel: 415/986–2020). Inventive 'architectural' cuisine with an emphasis on strong flavours and beautiful presentation.

Moderate

Angkor Wat, 4217 Geary Boulevard (tel: 415/221–7889). Elegant eatery with seating on floor cushions and top-notch Cambodian cuisine.

Basta Pasta, 1268 Grant Avenue (tel: 415/434–2248). Late-night North Beach restaurant with fine pastas and succulent wood-fired pizzas, and large windows well suited to people-watching.

Bix, 56 Gold Street (tel: 415/433–6300). Everything about this lounge-cum-restaurant is cool: the hidden entrance, the jazz music, the dim lighting, the copious martinis and the delicious food.

Blue Light Café, 1979 Union Street (tel: 415/922–5510). South-western cuisine, spicy and predominantly meat-based; few vegetarian options.

The Buena Vista, 2765 Hyde Street (tel: 415/474–5044). One of the few places in the Fisherman's Wharf area that are good value; a good selection of basic breakfasts and lunches, but more famous for its Irish coffee.

Café Rocco, 1131 Folsom Street (tel: 415/554–0522). Northern Italian fare and a lovely patio. Breakfast and lunch daily; dinner Thursday to Saturday.

Calzone's, 430 Columbus Avenue (tel: 415/397–3600). Wood-fired pizzas with inventive, exotic toppings.

Capp's Corner, 1600 Powell Street (tel: 415/989–2589. Delicious pasta lunches and huge 5-course set dinners. Owned by a former boxing champion.

Cha Cha Cha, 1805 Haight Street (tel: 415/386–5758). A small and lively spot that pulls a diverse crowd for its (predominantly) Cuban lunches and dinners at reasonable prices.

The Élite Café, 2049 Filmore Street (tel: 415/346–8668). Good Cajun and Creole fare.

Fog City Diner, 1300 Battery Street (tel: 415/982–2000). A faux 1950s diner, complete with neon lights and stainless-steel fittings. The California cuisine is creative – and affordable.

Fringale, 570 Fourth Street (tel: 415/543-0573). Contemporary French bistro with a congenial atmosphere and satisfying cuisine.

Gold Spike, 527 Columbus Avenue (tel: 415/421–4591). A North Beach institution that serves six-course Italian dinners.

John's Grill, 63 Ellis Street (tel: 415/986–0069). Exceptionally good steak, seafood and pasta for lunch and dinner. Mentioned in Dashiell Hammett's *The Maltese Falcon.*

Judy's Homestyle Café, 2268 Chestnut Street (tel: 415/922–4588). Hunger-busting omelets and sandwiches and a trendy Marina District crowd.

Lulu, 816 Folsom Street (tel: 415/495–5775). Delicious, fresh food (with an emphasis on grilling) is served is family-sized portions at this trendy casual restaurant in the SoMa neighbourhood.

Max's Diner, 311 Third Street (tel: 415/546–6297). Ample platefuls of traditional American fare – meatloaf, turkey sandwiches, burgers, milkshakes and much more – dished up in a 1950s-style diner.

North Beach Pizza, 1512 Stockton Street (tel: 415/392–1700). Famous all over town for expertly made pizzas, with a long list of toppings. Always busy.

Pastis, 1015 Battery Street (tel: 415/391–2555). A great French bistro with satisfying food and friendly service. A sister to Fringale (570 4th Street), but less expensive and easier to get a table.

Perry's, 1944 Union Street (tel: 415/922–9022). Famed Pacific Heights rendezvous serving large portions of traditional American food.

Rose Pistola, 32 Colombus Avenue (tel: 415/399-0499). Friendly setting for hearty, contemporary food, bold flavours and large portions.

The Slanted Door, 584 Valencia Street (tel: 415/861-8032). Exciting, modern Vietnamese food served in a chic, casual setting.

The Stinking Rose, 325 Columbus Avenue (tel: 415/781–7673). Every dish, and many of the drinks, make liberal use of garlic at this predominantly Italian spot.

Yank Sing, 427 Battery Street (tel: 415/781–1111). Not cheap but among the best dim sum restaurants in the city; always busy.

Budget

Café Caravan, 1312 Chestnut Street (tel: 415/441–1168). Locals' diner with fast and friendly service. Good value.

Café Flore, 2298 Market Street (tel: 415/621-8579). Salads and other light fare are the way to go at this people-watching paradise in the heart of the city's Castro districts.

Caffè Trieste, 601 Vallejo Street (tel: 415/392–6739). A long-established Italian coffee-house legendary for its espresso and its live opera on Saturday afternoons.

Dottie's True Blue Café, 522 Jones Street (tel: 415/885–2767). Healthy diner food heavy on fresh fruit and cereals in a Downtown location.

Eagle Café, Pier 39, Fisherman's Wharf (tel: 415/433–3689). The building, which dates from the 1920s, was shifted by crane to its current position in 1978. The café serves wholesome coffee shop staples to a mix of wharf workers and tourists.

Eats, 50 Clement Street (tel: 415/752–2938). Mammoth portions of fast, cheap and very succulent food at breakfast and lunch.

El Toro Taqueria, 597 Valencia Street (tel: 415/431–3351). Popular fill-up stop for tasty, down-to-earth Mexican food.

Flying Saucer, 1000 Guerrero Street (tel: 415/641–9955). As zany as the Mission neighbourhood in which it is located; a fun-filled place with a congenial atmosphere and creative food.

Hamburger Mary's Organic Grill, 1582 Folsom Street (tel: 415/626–1985). Great burgers, loud music, and an eye-catching clientele.

House of Nanking, 919 Kearny Street (tel: 415/421–1429). Always packed for inexpensive, excellent northern Chinese fare.

La Cumbre Taqueria, 515 Valencia Street (tel: 415/863–8205). Cafeteria-style outlet for delicious low-cost Mexican favourites.

St Francis Candy Store, 2801 24th Street (tel: 415/826–4200). Wonderful, long-established provider of sandwiches and famous, frothy milkshakes.

San Francisco Bar-B-Cue, 1328 Eighteenth Street (tel: 415/431–8956). Spicy meat dishes Thai-style.

Tad's, 120 Powell Street (tel: 415/982–1718). Good spot for cheap breakfast and lunch; also serves burgers, soups and sourdough bread.

Thai Stick, 698 Post Street (tel: 415/928–7730). Enjoyable, good-quality Thai restaunt. It's easy to order more than you can eat and still spend less than you expect.

Ton Kiang, 3148 Geary Boulevard (tel: 415/752–4440), 5821 Geary Boulevard (tel: 415/387–8273). An amazing array of dim sum (with over nine types of shrimp dumplings) served in a contemporary setting.

Village Pizzeria, 3348 Steiner Street (tel: 415/931–2470). A budget-priced eatery in an expensive area; pizza sold whole and by the slice.

THE BAY AREA

Accommodation
Expensive

Claremont Resort Hotel and Tennis Club, Ashby and Domingo avenues, Oakland (tel: 510/843–3000 or 800/327–7500). Refurbished 1916 mansion on landscaped grounds in the Oakland hills; saunas, swimming pools and whirlpools.

Moderate

The Hensley House, 456 N Third Street, San Jose (tel: 408/298–3537). Tiny but luxurious 1884 house offering bed-and-breakfast.

Hotel Durant, 2600 Durant Avenue, Berkeley 9 (tel: 510/845–8981 or 800/238–7268). Ageing but comfortable, and within an easy walk of Berkeley campus.

Budget

Hotel De Anza, 233 W Santa Clara Street, San Jose (tel: 408/286–1000 or 800/843–3700). This hotel was built in 1930 and has been thoughtfully restored to its original splendour. The staff is efficient and the rooms are well equipped.

Motel 6, 2560 Fontaine Road, San Jose (tel: 408/270–3131). Part of the nationwide budget chain of plain but functional motels.
Sanborn Park Hostel, 15808 Sanborn Road, Saratoga (tel: 408/741–0166). A lovely rustic youth hostel, formerly a hunting lodge.

Restaurants
Expensive
Chez Panisse, 1517 Shattuck Avenue, Berkeley (tel: 510/548–5525). The birthplace of California cuisine is as innovative and popular as ever.
The Lark Creek Inn, 234 Magnolia Avenue, Larkspur (tel: 415/927-7766). Contemporary American cuisine by award-winning chef Bradley Ogden is served in an idyllic setting. Ravioli with shredded ham hocks among the many signature dishes.
Viognier, 222 E Fourth Avenue, San Mateo (tel: 650/685-3727). Award-winning chef Gary Danko now cooks in this casual but sophisticated restaurant situated in what many believe to be the best gourmet store in the country.

Moderate
Chez Panisse Café, 1517 Shattuck Avenue, Berkeley (tel: 415/548–5409). This offshoot is a chance to sample delectable California cuisine at a far more affordable price than the main restaurant downstairs.
Frankie, Johnny, and Luigi's Too, 939 El Camino Real, Palo Alto (tel: 650/967–5384). Earns the favour of locals, including many Stanford students, for its delectable pizzas.
The Good Earth, 185 University Avenue, Palo Alto (tel: 650/321–9449). Only healthy, natural ingredients are used to whip up

omelets, salads and sandwiches; also has a counter for muffins to take away.
Palermo Ristorante Italiano, 394 S Second Street, San Jose (tel: 408/297–0607). Popular spot for pasta and pizzas; convivial.

Budget
The Blue Nile, 2525 Telegraph Avenue, Berkeley (tel: 510/540–6777). Absurdly cheap East African food, ideal for vegetarians and anyone looking for a culinary bargain.

CENTRAL COAST NORTH

Accommodation
Expensive
Highlands Inn, on Highway 1 four miles south of Carmel (tel: 415/624–3801 or 800/682–4811). Where Madonna honey-mooned: every room has an ocean view.
Inn at Depot Hill 250 Monterey Avenue, Santa Cruz (tel: 408/462–3376 or 800/572–2632). Housed in a 1901 railroad depot building, this inn overlooking the water is a sophisticated and unusual choice. The railroad theme extends to the restaurant, which is designed like an old-fashioned dining car.

271

Moderate
Carmel Village Inn, Ocean Avenue and Junipero Street (tel: 408/624–3864). Good value for pricey Carmel, with comfortable rooms and nice grounds.
Darling House, 314 W Cliff Drive, Santa Cruz (tel: 408/458–1958). Delightful 1910 clifftop home offering cosy bed-and-breakfast accommodation.

Seals guard the pier at Monterey

The Monterey Hotel, 406 Alvarado Street, Monterey (tel: 800/727–0960). Elegant, historic, and in the heart of town.

Budget

Motel 6, 2124 Freemont Street, Monterey (tel: 408/646–8585). By just a few dollars, the cheapest in town; early booking essential but plenty of alternatives along this motel-lined street.

Motel 6, 1010 Fairview Avenue, Salinas (tel: 408/758–2122). The least expensive of two of this bland but dependable motel chain in Salinas.

Super 8, 321 Riverside Avenue, Santa Cruz (tel: 408/464–5100). One of the best of the many plain and simple motels located close to the beach and the Boardwalk.

Restaurants
Expensive

Matsuhisa, 129 N La Cienega Boulevard, Beverly Hills (tel: 310/659-9639). Before there was the show-stopper Nobu in New York City, there was this tiny Matsuhisa in Los Angeles, where Hollywood celebrities come to enjoy extraordinary Japanese food in a dated 1980s setting.

Michael's, 1147 Third Street, Santa Monica (tel: 310/451-0843). Michael McCarty virtually invented California cooking at his favourite haunt of Los Angeles' glamour scene.

Pacific's Edge, at the Highlands Inn on Highway 1 four miles south of Carmel (tel: 408/622–5445). Scintillating ocean views and fabulous food from a menu that varies according to what is in season.

Patina, 5955 Melrose Avenue (tel: 213/467-1108). Inspired modern-French cooking issues forth from Joachim Splichal's kitchen. Sparse, elegant dining room and casual but efficient service.

Moderate

Dolphin Restaurant, Municipal Wharf, Santa Cruz (tel: 408/426–5830). Several restaurants line the wharf but none is better than this one, located right at the end and open all day, serving a winning mix of seafood and general dishes.

India Joze, 1001 Center Street, Santa Cruz (tel: 408/427–3554). Inspiring mix of Indian and Indonesian fare given the California treatment.

Pinot Bistro, 12969 Ventura Boulevard, Studio City (tel: 818/990-0500). An off-shoot of Joachim Splichal's Patina, this less-expensive bistro features satisfying fare such as crispy whitefish with roasted garlic sauce.

Rappa's, Fisherman's Wharf, Monterey (tel: 408/372–7562). Fresh seafood and a lively, congenial atmosphere.

Budget

Kathy's Restaurant, 700 Cass Street, Monterey (tel: 408/647–9540). Open for breakfast and lunch; best for chunky omelets and sandwiches. Patio tables.

Rosita's Armory Café, 231 Salinas Street, Salinas (tel: 408/424–7039). Mexican eatery popular for its low-cost lunches and dinners.

Tuck Box, Delores and Seventh streets, Carmel (tel: 408/624–6365). Shepherds pie, Welsh rarebit and scones are some of the dishes in this shoebox-sized restaurant.

Zachary's, 819 Pacific Avenue, Santa Cruz (tel: 408/427–0646). American breakfasts and lunches served with delicious homemade breads.

CENTRAL COAST SOUTH

Accommodation
Expensive

El Encanto Hotel, 1900 Lausen Road, Santa Barbara (tel: 805/687–5000 or 800/346–7039). Ordinary rooms inside the 1927 Spanish-style main building, but more appealing are the small cottages dotting the expansive grounds.

Four Seasons Biltmore, 1260 Channel Drive, Santa Barbara (tel: 805/969–2261). There are breathtaking views of the ocean or the mountains in most of the rooms at this stunning resort-style hotel. Enjoy many outdoor sports, a restaurant, and a full programme of children's activities.

Simpson House, 121 E Arrellaga Street, Santa Barbara (tel: 805/963–7067 or 800/676–1280). Built in 1874, this estate has been restored to one of the area's top hotels. The rooms are furnished with antiques and fresh flower arrangements.

Moderate

Adobe Inn, 1473 Monterey Street, San Luis Obispo (tel: 805/549–0321). Once a run-of-the-mill motel, it has been expertly converted into a stylish bed-and-breakfast.

Casa Del Mar, 18 Bath Street, Santa Barbara (tel: 800/433–3097). Lovely Mediterranean-style small hotel, with 20 rooms around a courtyard and pool.

Inn on the Beach, 1175 Seaward Drive, Ventura (tel: 805/652–2000). All rooms have beach-facing balconies; complimentary breakfast, wine and cheese.

Keystone Inn, 540 Main Street, Morro Bay (tel: 805/772–7503). The pick of the town's mid-range motels.

Budget

Californian Hotel, 35 State Street, Santa Barbara (tel: 805/966–7153). One of Santa Barbara's few budget-priced hotels.

Peach Tree Inn, 2001 Monterey Street, San Luis Obispo (tel: 805/543–3170 or 800/227–6396). Quiet and reasonably priced on this motel-lined street.

Restaurants
Expensive

The Palace Café, 8 E Cota Street, Santa Barbara (tel: 805/966–3133). A mixture of Cajun and Caribbean cuisine; open evenings only.

Moderate

Andria's Haborside Restaurant, 336 W Cabrillo Boulevard, Santa Barbara (tel: 805/966–3000). Locals and tourists alike come here for the substantial breakfasts and the equally filling lunches and dinners.

Paradise Café, 702 Anacapa Street, Santa Barbara (tel: 805/962–4416). Plain but good American cooking in a simple setting.

Rose's Landing Restaurant, 725 Embarcadero, Morro Bay (tel: 805/772–4441). Deservedly popular seafood restaurant with a view over the bay and the massive Morro Rock.

Budget

Dorn's Original Breakers Café, 801 Market Street, Morro Bay (tel: 805/772–4415). Unsurpassed for inventive breakfasts, and also good for lunch and dinner.

Joe's Café, 536 State Street, Santa Barbara (tel: 805/966–4638). There is always an eager crowd for the large helpings of meat and fish dishes.

Kyoto/China Brown, 685 Higuera Street, San Luis Obispo (tel: 805/546–9700). Chinese and Japanese food from a help-yourself buffet.

Woody's Beach Club and Cantina, 229 W Montecito Street, Santa Barbara (tel: 805/963–9326). Barbecued ribs and chicken to bring joy to every carnivore's heart; the menu also includes sizable burgers and spicy chili dishes.

LOS ANGELES

Accommodation
Expensive

The Argyle, 8358 Sunset Boulevard, Los Angeles (tel: 213/654–7100). Gargoyles overlook the entrance to this redone art-deco masterpiece. The rooms are individually furnished, many with luxury touches.

Beverly Hills Hotel, 9641 Sunset Boulevard (tel: 310/276–2251). One movie-world legend that everyone has heard of, complete with pink awnings and bungalows. The service may not be great unless the staff have heard of you.

Chateau Marmont Hotel, 8221 Sunset Boulevrd, 90046 (tel: 213/656-10110 or 800/242-8328). Well known for its literary connections (Gore Vidal and Dominick Dunne are just two famous residents); cottages and bungalows as well as suites and rooms.

Four Seasons, 330 S Doheny Drive, Los Angeles (tel: 310/273–2222). This high-rise in downtown Los Angeles is known for attracting rich and famous Hollywood types. The pool and open-air health club are particularly attractive.

Hotel Bel-Air, 701 Stone Canyon Road, Los Angeles (tel: 310/472–1211). A beautiful resort-style property situated on 10 acres of garden landscape. The rooms are light and airy. The restaurant and poolside service are exceptional, and the staff is extremely accommodating.

Hotel Oceania, 849 Ocean Avenue, Santa Monica (tel: 800/777–0758). Evokes a Caribbean mood with pastel-coloured rooms grouped around a pool, across the road from the ocean.

Hyatt Regency Los Angeles, 711 S. Hope Street, 90017 (Tel: 213/683-1234). Good for business functions. Wood decorations and good views of the city from every room.

Loews Santa Monica Beach Hotel, 1700 Ocean Avenue (tel: 310/458–6700). An architectural showpiece beside the ocean and Santa Monica Pier.

New Otani Garden Hotel, 120 S Los Angeles Street, Downtown (tel: 213/629–1200 or 800/421–8795). In Little Tokyo, Downtown; try the Japanese-style rooms for maximum value.

The Peninsula, Beverley Hills, 9882 Little Santa Monica Boulevard, Beverley Hills (tel: 310/551–2888 or 800/462–7899). One of the top hotels in Los Angeles, every detail is exquisite, including the full service spa, rooftop pool, huge bathrooms, plush lounge and the excellent restaurant, Belvedere.

Shutters on the Beach, 1 Pico Boulevard (tel: 310/458–0030 or 800/334–9000). Santa Monica's latest luxury hotel, with every facility imaginable and fabulous ocean views from every room.

Wyndham Checkers Hotel Los Angeles, 535 S Grand Avenue, Los Angeles (tel: 213/624–0000). The rooms are particularly comfortable at this historic Los Angeles building. Also featured is a restaurant and health club.

Moderate

Bay Blue Inn, 1670 Ocean Avenue, Santa Monica (tel: 310/393–2363). Small and cosy bed-and-breakfast inn just a few strides from the beach.

Crescent Hotel, 403 N Crescent Drive, Beverly Hills, (tel: 800/451–1566). Comfortable if unelaborate rooms at a good price.

Del Capri Hotel, 10587 Wilshire Boulevard (tel: 310/474–3511). Homey and good value in expensive Westwood; most rooms have kitchenettes.

Figueroa Hotel, 939 S Figueroa Street, Downtown (tel: 800/421–9092). Relaxed hotel with an appealing Spanish look.

Highland Gardens Hotel, 7047 Franklin Avenue (tel: 213/850–0536). Good facilities on a residential Hollywood street.

Holiday Inn, 1755 N Highland Avenue (tel: 213/ 462–7181). Unexciting but dependable mid-range chain hotel within walking distance of many of Hollywood's sights.

Hollywood Metropolitan, 5825 Sunset Boulevard (tel: 800/962–5800). Nicely furnished high-rise making a comfortable base for Hollywood touring.

273

Hotels & Restaurants

Hollywood Roosevelt, 700 Hollywood Boulevard (tel: 213/466–7000). Steeped in Hollywood tradition but the rooms are less impressive than the lobby; adequate but ordinary.

Huntley Hotel, 1111 Second Street, Santa Monica (tel: 800/556–4012). High-rise near the beach; aim for a room that has a view of the ocean.

La Reve Hotel, 8822 Cynthia Street, West Hollywood (tel: 800/835–7997). A pleasant location for attractively furnished and well-equipped suites.

Le Parc, 733 West Knoll Drive, West Hollywood (tel: 310/855–8888). Quiet, low-key elegance on a residential street and a pleasing, fashionable neighbourhood.

The Mansion Inn, 327 Washington Boulevard (tel: 800/828–0688). An inviting bed-and-breakfast within walking distance of Marina Del Rey and Venice Beach.

Shangri-la Hotel, 1301 Ocean Avenue, Santa Monica (tel: 310/394–2791 or 800/345–7829). Unmistakable art-deco delight that has been carefully restored to its original 1930s style; all rooms overlook Santa Monica Bay.

Wilshire Royale, 2619 Wilshire Boulevard (tel: 800/421–8072). A 1920s art-deco hotel greatly renovated and within easy reach of Downtown. The mini suites are ideal for several people sharing.

Budget

Banana Bungalow AAIH, 2775 Cahuenga Boulevard (tel: 800/4–HOSTEL). Wonderful backpackers' hostel nestled in the Hollywood Hills; free transportation to airport and beaches.

Bevonshire Lodge Motel, 7575 Beverly Boulevard (tel: 213/936–6154). Extremely well-priced and well-located small motel.

Cadillac Hotel, 401 Ocean Front Walk (tel: 310/399– 8876). Low-cost shared or private rooms beside Venice Beach.

Carlyle Inn, 119 S Robertson Boulevard, 90035 (tel: 310/275-4445 or 800/322-7595). A small hotel in a safe neighborhood close to Beverly Hills. Complimentary buffet breakfasts.

Crest Motel, 7701 Beverly Boulevard (tel: 213/931–8100). Clean, tidy and quiet, and surprisingly low-priced for its West Hollywood/ Beverly Hills location.

Econo Lodge Hollywood, 777 N Vine Street (tel: 800/446–3916). Not the safest area by night but ideally placed for daytime sightseeing in Hollywood.

Hollywood Downtowner Motel, 5601 Hollywood Boulevard (tel: 213/464–7191). Austere, but perfectly placed for exploring Hollywood.

Los Angeles International Hostel, 3601 S Gaffrey Street, Building 613, San Pedro (tel: 310/831–8109). Removed from the centre of LA life but handy to South Bay and airport.

Motel de Ville, 1123 W Seventh Street, Downtown (tel: 213/624–8474). Garish décor but adequate, no-frills rooms.

274

Orchid Motel, 819 Flower Street (tel: 213/624–5855). Attractive budget option Downtown.

Park Plaza Hotel, 607 Park View Street (tel: 213/384-5281). Small, plain rooms in an art-deco megalith overlooking MacArthur Park; unsafe area by night.

Royal Host Motel, 901 W Olympic Boulevard (tel: 213/626–6255). Located Downtown and including refrigerators and minibars in the very well-priced rooms; student discount.

Santa Monica International Hostel, 1436 Second Street, Santa Monica (tel: 310/393–9913). Large, modern hostel in a safe and enjoyable area.

Winona Motel, 5131 Hollywood Boulevard (tel: 213/663–1243). Small and well-appointed hotel right in the heart of Hollywood.

Restaurants
Expensive

The Belvedere, The Peninsula, Beverly Hills, 9882 Little Santa Monica Boulevard (tel: 310/788–2306). This quintessential California restaurant is one of the most popular in the area. The décor is exuberant yet formal, and the service is excellent.

Chasen's, 246 N Canon Drive, Beverly Hills (tel: 310/858–1200). This LA stalwart retains much of its original star-studded ambiance. The kitchen does an admirable job of presenting classic American fare.

Chinois on Main, 2709 Main Street, Santa Monica (tel: 310/392–9025). The flagship of celebrity chef Wolfgang Puck serves astronomically priced but gastronomically perfect California cuisine with Far Eastern touches.

Citrus, 6703 Melrose Avenue, West Hollywood (tel: 213/857–0034). For food and design, the most creative restaurant in LA.

Coco Pazzo, 8440 Sunset Boulevard, West Hollywood (tel: 213/848–6000). Located in the casually elegant surroundings of the incredibly hip Mondrian hotel, this is a current favourite in the city. It is more than just a scene, however, for the northern Italian food is always excellently prepared.

Dining Room, 9500 Wilshire Boulevard, Beverly Hills (tel: 310/275-5200). California cuisines served in an elegant setting.

Fenix, The Argyle Hotel, 8358 Sunset Boulevard, Los Angeles (tel: 213/848–6677). Impressive art-deco style with exquisite views of the city from the outdoor terrace. The French-influenced California cuisine completes the experience.

L'Orangerie, 903 N La Cienega Boulevard, Hollywood (tel: 310/652–9770). Elegant French food, an extensive wine cellar, and decorated in grand style. It is extremely expensive but, according to most, well worth it.

Jiraffe, 502 Santa Monica Boulevard, Santa Monica (tel: 310/917–6671). This casually chic California bistro has a menu based on seasonal items purchased at a nearby farmer's market.

Spago, 8795 Sunset Boulevard, West Hollywood (tel: 310/652–4025). With exotic pizzas and mouth-watering pasta dishes, Spago has been setting LA's culinary standards for years – reserve weeks ahead.
Spago of Beverly Hills, 176 N Canon Drive, Beverly Hills (tel: 310/358–0800). Rub elbows with who's who of Los Angeles at the latest addition to Wolfgang Puck's legendary chain. The California cuisine is as good as ever.
Valentino, 3115 Pico Boulevard, Santa Monica (tel: 310/829–4313). World-class Italian food and a long and diverse list of exceptional daily specials.

Moderate
Aunt Kizzy's Back Porch, 4325 Glencoe Avenue, Marina Del Rey (tel: 310/ 578–1005). Big portions of southern favourites prepared with a distinct California style.
Book Soup Bistro, 8800 Sunset Boulevard (tel: 310/657–1072). Stylish American dishes and a literary atmosphere; the legendary Book Soup bookstore is next door.
Caffe Luna, 7463 Melrose Avenue, West Hollywood (tel: 213/665–8647). Regional Italian fare consumed by a trendy, fashionable crowd.
Campanile, 624 S La Brea Avenue, West Hollywood (tel: 213/938–1447). Tasty northern Italian fare and a predominantly young and arty clientele.
Coast Café, 1700 Ocean Avenue, Santa Monica (tel: 310/458–6700). In the fashionable Loews hotel; excellent for people-watching.
Country Life Vegetarian Buffet, 888 S Figueroa Street (tel: 213/489–4118). Exactly what its name suggests: a bountiful array of fare entirely free of animal or dairy products.
Dar Maghreb, 7651 Sunset Boulevard, Hollywood (tel: 213/876–7651). Morocco re-created Hollywood-style complete with belly dancers. The food is reasonable and comes in large amounts.
El Cholo, 1121 S Western Avenue, Wilshire District (tel: 213/734–2773). Good Mexican food in a restaurant once patronised by Hollywood's biggest names.
Hollywood Athletic Club, 6525 Sunset Boulevard, Hollywood (tel: 213/962–6600). A 1920s Hollywood landmark restored to the style of the halcyon years, but the menu is uninspired.
House of Blues, 8439 Sunset Boulevard, West Hollywood (tel: 213/650–0476). Specialising in well-prepared southern dishes at reasonable prices, this is an extremely popular spot. The atmosphere is lively, especially at their gospel brunch.
Jackson's Farm, 439 N Beverly Drive, Beverly Hills (tel: 310/273-5578). Home-style cooking in a restaurant designed to look like a farmhouse.
Kachina Grill, 330 S Hope Street, Downtown (tel: 213/625–0956). Sizzling south-western specialties plus classy pasta and seafood.

Mon Kee, 679 N Spring Street, Chinatown (tel: 213/628–6717). Justifiably busy Chinese eatery specialising in seafood.
Orleans, 11705 National Boulevard, near Beverly Hills (tel: 310/479–4187). Cajun and Creole dishes served in a relaxed atmosphere.
Pacific Dining Car, 1310 W Sixth Street, Wilshire District (tel: 231/483–6000). Succulent ribs and steaks in a room fitted out as a luxury railway dining car; open 24 hours. The breakfasts are also worth sampling at any hour.
Water Grill, 544 S Grand Avenue, Downtown (tel: 213/891–0900). Delicious seafood stylishly served in a light, spacious and modern art-filled dining room.

Budget
Barney's Beanery, 8447 Santa Monica Boulevard, West Hollywood (tel: 213/ 654–2287). Burgers, chili and imported beers in poolhall-cum-eatery-cum-bar.
Canter's, 419 Fairfax Avenue, West Hollywood (tel: 213/651–2030). New York-style deli serving generous portions for decades.
Clifton's Brookdale Cafeteria, 648 S Broadway, Downtown (tel: 213/627–1673). Help yourself from the array of steaming trays, then pay at the cash register.
Dive!, 10350 Santa Monica Boulevard (tel: 310/788-3483). Steven Spielberg's theme restaurant is popular with children. Fish swimming behind screens and simulated submarine dives. Food is mainly submarine sandwiches.
Ed Debevic's, 134 N La Cienega Boulevard (tel: 310/659–1952). One of the first retro-diners, complete with 1950s-style décor and garishly dressed staff. Massive burgers.
The Gumbo Pot, at Farmer's Market, 6333 W Third Street (tel: 213/933–0358). Tempting Cajun and Creole food in an eat-and-run setting.
Hot Wings On Melrose, 7011 Melrose Avenue (tel: 213/930–1233). Chicken wings, sandwiches and other snacks at the lowest prices to be found on this trendy shopping and eating strip.
The Kings Head, 116 Santa Monica Boulevard (tel: 310/ 451–1402). Pseudo-English pub serving top-notch fish-and-chips alongside imported British beers.
The Pantry, 877 S Figueroa Street, Downtown (tel: 213/972–9279). Famous but unprepossessing coffee shop; the best value in Downtown – and always open.
Philippe's the Original, 1001 N Alameda Street, Downtown (tel: 213/ 628–3781). Serving wholesome American food since 1908 at shared wooden bench tables.
Pinks Famous Chili Dogs, 711 N La Brea Avenue, Hollywood (tel: 213/931–4223). Burgers, hot dogs and chili dishes, served from a giant hot-dog shaped stand in what is inexplicably an LA fast-food legend.
Yorkshire Grill, 610 W Sixth Street (tel: 213/ 629–3020). Long-serving and highly rated deli, ideal for low-cost breakfast or lunch.

275

AROUND LOS ANGELES

Accommodation
Expensive

The Disneyland Hotel, 1150 W Cerritos Avenue, Anaheim (tel: 714/778–6600). The official Disneyland hotel, every bit as theme-oriented as the famous park itself and with almost as much innocent amusement.

Inn on Mt Ada, 598 Wrigley Road, Santa Catalina Island (tel: 310/510–2030). The former Wrigley family home is now a luxurious bed-and-breakfast inn, complete with grand piano and crystal chandeliers in a splendid hilltop setting.

The Ritz-Carlton Huntington Hotel, 1401 S Oak Knoll Avenue, Pasadena (tel: 626/568–3900). A 1907 Pasadena landmark restored to its original grandeur and elegance.

Moderate

Doubletree Hotel, 191 N Los Robles Avenue, Pasadena (tel: 626/792–2727 or 800/222–TREE). Chic and stylish, and ideally placed for seeing Pasadena.

Howard Johnson's Hotel at Disneyland, 1380 S Harbor Boulevard, Anaheim (tel: 714/776–6120 or 800/442–4228). With its plush landscaped grounds, an almost unrecognisable link in the nationwide mid-priced chain; within easy walking distance of Disneyland.

Malibu Beach Inn, 22878 Pacific Coast Highway (tel: 310/456–6445). Highly conducive to a relaxing stay, each room has an ocean-view balcony.

Seacliff Inn, 1661 S Coast Highway, Laguna Beach (tel: 714/494–9717). Unpretentious motel with the best rates in this otherwise very costly town.

Vista Del Mar, 417 Crescent Avenue, Santa Catalina Island (tel: 310/510–1452). Pleasing bed-and-breakfast inn with glorious views over Avalon; the smaller rooms are tremendous value.

Zane Grey Pueblo Hotel, 199 Chimes Tower Road, Santa Catalina Island (tel: 310/510–0966). Former home of the western writer and the island's most atmospheric hotel.

Budget

Candy Cane Inn, 1747 S Harbor Boulevard, Anaheim (tel: 800/345–7057). Pleasantly furnished rooms, a complimentary muffin and coffee breakfast, and free transportation to Disneyland.

Colonial Inn Youth Hostel, 421 Eighth Street, Huntington Beach (tel: 714/536–3315). Well placed for the busy local beach and easily reached by bus from LA's airport.

Comfort Inn, 2452 E Colorado Boulevard, Pasadena (tel: 818/405–0811). A cut above the many chain motels that line this thoroughfare just west of central Pasadena.

Econo Lodge, 1570 S Harbor Boulevard, Anaheim (tel: 800/854–0199). Chain motels are plentiful in the area; this is consistently one of the best for price and service.

Fullerton Hacienda Hostel, 1700 N Harbor Boulevard (tel: 714/738–3721). Tiny hostel just five miles from Disneyland – book early.

Restaurants
Expensive

Café Del Rey, 4451 Admiralty Way, Marina del Rey (tel: 310/823-6395). The inventive French/Japanese cooking of Katsuo Nagasawa offers such delectable dishes as spicy black pepper-crusted hamachi and pan-fried sea tower with lemon caper olive oil.

The Cannery, 3010 Lafayette Avenue, Newport Beach (tel: 714/675–5777). The ramshackle exterior conceals one of Newport Beach's longest-running and most popular seafood eateries.

Fresco, 514 S Brand Boulevard, Glendale (tel: 818/247–5541). Draws fussy eaters from all over LA to its world-class Italian menu.

Tommy Tang's, 24 W Colorado Boulevard (tel: 818/792–9700). Thai cuisine exquisitely prepared and presented with panache.

Moderate

Armstrong's Seafood Restaurant, 306 Crescent Avenue, Santa Catalina Island (tel: 310/510–0113). Freshly caught swordfish and mahi-mahi among the mesquite-grilled delights.

Gladstone's 4 Fish, 17300 Pacific Coast Highway, Malibu (tel: 310/573–0212). Fine, fresh sea fare with ocean views and, at dinner, memorable sunsets.

Inn of the Seventh Ray, 128 Old Topanga Canyon Road, Topanga Canyon (tel: 310/455–1311). California flower power lives on in this long-running and rightly popular health-food restaurant.

Parkway Grill, 510 S Arroyo Parkway, Pasadena (tel: 626/795–1001). Scintillating fresh salads and a mouth-watering selection of pizzas and pastas, plus quality fish and meat dishes and a well-stocked California wine cellar.

Route 66, 425 S Fair Oaks Avenue, Pasadena (tel: 626/793–8462). Classy California cuisine served amid art celebrating the American automobile and one of the nation's best-loved highways.

White House, 340 S Coast Highway, Laguna Beach (tel: 714/494–8088). Impressively diverse and uniformly good menu. You can shake a leg on the dance floor after dinner.

Budget

The Busy Bee, 306 Crescent Avenue, Santa Catalina Island (tel: 310/510–1983). Simple but filling breakfasts and lunches at patio tables.

Country Harvest, 1630 Katella Avenue, Anaheim (tel: 714/539–2234). Huge buffet certain to satiate the most ravenous of appetites.

Green Street Restaurant, 146 S Shoppers Lane, Pasadena (tel: 818/577– 7170). Inventive and nourishing burgers, sandwiches and salads, and other American staples.

Mrs Knott's Chicken Restaurant, 8039 Beach Boulevard, Buena Boulevard (tel: 714/220–5200). The chicken dinners that begat the Knotts Berry Farm theme park, plus tempting fruit pies.

Ruby's, Balboa Pier, Newport Beach (tel: 714/431–RUBY). Art-deco diner at the end of the pier with great location and superb milkshakes. Other food is just average.

SAN DIEGO

Accommodation
Expensive
Catamaran Resort Hotel, 3999 Mission Boulevard (tel: 800/288–0770). Alongside Mission Bay and an ideal base for water-sports fans.

Hotel Del Coronado, 1500 Orange Avenue (tel: 800/HOTEL–DELL). A wooden architectural marvel, steeped in history.

US Grant Hotel, 326 Broadway (tel: 619/238–1818 or 800/221–3802). Pampering presidents and celebrities for many years. Full of character.

Moderate
Glorietta Bay Inn, 1630 Glorietta Boulevard, Coronado (tel: 800/283–9383). One-time home of sugar mogul J D Spreckels, now expanded into a mixture of regular rooms and expansive suites; complimentary breakfast.

Hotel St James, 830 Sixth Avenue (tel: 619/234–0155). Classy but not large rooms in an appealingly restored building.

Hotel San Diego, 339 W Broadway (tel: 800/824–1244). High-class lodgings in a renovated Downtown landmark.

La Jolla Cove Motel, 1155 Coast Boulevard (tel: 619/459–2621). No frills but a fine base for discovering La Jolla.

La Pensione Hotel, 1654 Columbia Street (tel: 619/232–3400). Clean and quiet with a European flavour.

Loma Lodge, 3202 Rosecrans Street (tel: 619/222–0511). One of the better values on the Point Loma peninsula.

Ramada Hotel Old Town, 2435 Jefferson Street (tel: 800/355–2544). Classy accommodation adjacent to the Old Town.

Budget
HI-Elliot Hostel, 3790 Udall Street (tel: 619/223–4778). Friendly hostel with small, shared rooms; perfectly sited for the local beach but some miles from the city centre.

Inn at the YMCA, 500 W Broadway (tel: 619/232–1133). Big and rather soulless but with simple rooms for men and women at bargain rates.

Jim's San Diego, 1425 C Street (tel: 619/235–0234). Hostel aimed at backpackers, with complimentary breakfast and a weekly barbecue.

Killager Lodge, 660 G Street (tel: 619/238–4100). Remarkably low rates for such welcoming rooms.

The Maryland Hotel, 630 F Street (tel: 619/239–9243). Basic but clean and central.

Pickwick Hotel, 132 W Broadway (tel: 619/234–9200). Drab but cheap on Downtown San Diego's main street.

YWCA, 1012 C Street (tel: 619/239–0355). Exclusively for women; dormitory beds or small, private rooms. In a slightly seedy section of Downtown.

Restaurants
Expensive
George's at the Cove, 1250 Prospect Street (tel: 619/454–4244). Justly acclaimed for its creative seafood dishes and divine pastas.

Grant Grill, US Grant Hotel, 326 Broadway (tel: 619/239–6806). Long favoured by the city's power brokers; meats and seafood, but best known for its mock turtle soup and meal-in-themselves salads.

Marius, 2000 Second Street, Coronado (tel: 619/435–3000). Just about the best formal French dining in town, with a somewhat stuffy but accommodating atmosphere.

Moderate
Anthony's Star of the Sea Room, 1360 Harbor Drive (tel: 619/232–7408). Extensive range of succulent seafood served overlooking the harbour.

La Gran Tapa, 611 B Street (tel: 619/234–8272). Mesmerising tapas; excellent paella nightly.

Old Town Mexican Café y Cantina, 2489 San Diego Avenue (tel: 619/297–4330). Always packed, but worth the wait for the best Mexican food in Old Town.

Sfuzzi, 340 Fifth Avenue (tel: 619/231–2323). Cosy Italian eatery serving fresh pastas and tasty wood-fired pizzas.

The Spot, 105 Prospect Street, La Jolla (tel: 619/459–0800). Fine affordable food, including steaks, seafood, and pizzas.

Budget
Broken Yolk, 1851 Garnet Street (tel: 619/270–0045). Immense range of omelets at next-to-nothing prices.

Dick's Last Resort, 345 Fifth Avenue (tel: 619/231–9100). Lively atmosphere and generous portions of American favourites.

El Indio, 3695 India Street (tel: 619/299–0333). Good-quality Mexican fare in a fast-food setting.

Grand Central Café, 500 W Broadway (tel: 619/234– CAFE). Wholesome American fare and many daily specials are on offer at this spacious café inside the YMCA building.

Ingrid's Cantina, 818 Fifth Avenue (tel: 619/233–6945). Chunky breakfast omelets, and tasty chili dishes and burgers served into the wee hours.

La Jolla Brewing Company, 7536 Fay Avenue (tel: 619/456–2739). House-brewed beers are the main attraction; delicious soups, salads and burgers help the ale go down.

277

Old Columbia Brewery & Grill, 1157 Columbia Street (tel: 619/234–2739). Meat and seafood dishes in large portions; the beer is brewed on the premises.
Village Kitchen, 2497 San Diego Avenue (tel: 619/294–4180). A cheap and cheerful Old Town spot for Mexican and American fare.

THE DESERTS

Accommodation
Expensive
Givenchy Hotel & Spa, 4200 E. Palm Canyon Drive, Palm Springs (tel: 800/276–5000). Spare no expense and pamper yourself senseless in this top-class facility offering luxury villas and spa treatments.
Hyatt Regency Suites Palm Springs, 285 N Palm Canyon Drive, Palm Springs (tel: 760/322– 9000). All of the rooms are suites, many with private balconies, at this modern, well-appointed hotel. Main attractions are golf, a pool and whirlpool, and nightly entertainment.
Marriot's Desert Springs Resort and Spa, 74855 Country Club Drive, Palm Desert (tel: 760/341–2211 or 800/331–3112). The impressive lobby, complete with a waterfall, is the first glimpse of this enormous resort complete with its own lake, beach, 5 swimming pools, golf, tennis and a spa.
The Ritz-Carlton, Rancho Mirage, 68–900 Frank Sinatra Drive, Rancho Mirage (tel: 760/321–8282). An exceptional resort with views of the desert and mountains. Activities include golf, tennis, and personal training. A truly luxurious experience.

Moderate
Budget Host Inn, 1277 S Palm Canyon Drive, Palm Springs (tel: 800/283–4678). Very attractive rates for simple but clean and comfortable rooms.
Casa Cody Country Inn, 175 S Cahuilla Road, Palm Springs (tel: 760/320–9346 or 800/231–2639). Choice of tastefully decorated rooms and suites.
Furnace Creek Ranch, Death Valley (tel: 760/786–2345). Fairly charmless but a prime base for touring Death Valley.
Hampton Inn, 1590 University Avenue, Riverside (tel: 909/683–6000). Part of a nationwide chain noted for its good value.

Budget
Motel 6, 660 S Palm Canyon Drive, Palm Springs (tel: 760/327–4200). The larger of two Motel 6s in town and the one most likely to have space.

Restaurants
Expensive
Cuistot, 73111 El Paseo, Palm Desert (tel: 760/340–1000). California cuisine that pleases the desert communities' wealthiest residents.
Le Vallauris, 385 W Tahquitz Canyon Way, Palm Springs (tel: 760/325–5059). Top-notch, French–California cuisine.

Moderate
Flower Drum, 424 S Indian Canyon Drive, Palm Springs (tel: 760/323–3020). Classy cuisine from five regions of China served alongside an indoor waterfall.
La Casuelas Terraza, 222 S Palm Canyon Drive, Palm Springs (tel: 760/325–2794). Consume well-prepared Mexican food on the micromist-cooled patio.

Budget
Churchill's English Fish & Chips, 665 S Palm Canyon Drive, Palm Springs (tel: 760/325–3716). Enormous servings of what its name suggests.
Elmer's Pancake and Steakhouse, 1030 E Palm Canyon Drive, Palm Springs (tel: 760/327–8419). Pancakes and waffles galore at prices to incite gluttony.
Louise's Pantry, 124 S Palm Canyon Drive, Palm Springs (tel: 760/325–5124). Simple coffee-shop favourites in a shed-sized diner.
Nate's Delicatessen, 100 S Indian Avenue, Palm Springs (tel: 760/325–3506). A deli seemingly transplanted from New York, offering unlikely desert fare such as chicken soup and corned beef sandwiches.

SIERRA NEVADA

Accommodation
Expensive
Ahwahnee Lodge, Yosemite Valley (tel: 209/252–4848). A 1927 creation in local stone and concrete fitting perfectly into beautiful natural surroundings.

Moderate
Inn By The Lake, 3300 Lake Tahoe Boulevard, South Lake Tahoe (tel: 800/877– 1466). Relaxing, well-equipped, and a few strides from Lake Tahoe.
Montecito Sequoia Lodge, 8000 General's Highway (tel: 209/565–3388). Comfortable rooms in rustic surroundings within easy driving distance of Kings Canyon and Sequoia national parks; breakfast included.
Snow Goose Inn, 57 Forest Trail, Mammoth Lakes (tel: 800/874–7368). Welcoming bed-and-breakfast.
Wawona Hotel, Mariposa, Yosemite National Park (tel: 209/252–4848). Charming Victorian hotel nicely distanced from the park's busiest sections.

Budget
Creekside Inn, 725 N Main Street, Bishop (tel: 619/ 872–3044). Bright, spacious and temptingly priced.
Motel 6, 2375 Lake Tahoe Boulevard, Lake Tahoe (tel: 916/542–1400). The cheapest for miles; reserve ahead.
Winnedumah Hotel, 211 N Edwards Street Independence (tel: 619/ 878–2040). Lovely, historic inn; very comfortable.

Restaurants
Expensive
Ahwahnee Dining Room, Yosemite Valley (tel: 209/372–1489). Formal dining in a grand setting.

Moderate
Giant Forest Lodge Dining Room, Sequoia National Park (tel: 209/561–3314). Indulgent dinners to finish off a day in the forest.
Whiskey Creek, Highway 203 and Minaret Road, Mammoth Lakes (tel: 619/934–2555). Mainly popular for its steaks and ribs, but also doing imaginative things with seafood and sauces.
Wolfdale's, 640 N Lake Boulevard, Tahoe City (tel: 916/583–5700). Ideal venue for scrumptious vegetarian meals.

Budget
Jack's Waffle Shop, 437 N Main Street, Bishop (tel: 619/872–7971). Solid nourishment 24 hours a day.
Rosie's Café, 571 N Lake Boulevard, Tahoe City (tel: 916/583–8504). Sandwiches, soups and burgers with a smile.
Village Cafeteria, Giant Forest Village, Sequoia National Park (tel: 209/ 561–3314). Unpretentious, filling fare for tree lovers and dedicated hikers.
Yosemite Trails Inn, Highway 395, Lee Vining (tel: 619/647–6369). Great food in big portions; breakfast, lunch and dinner all served.

GOLD COUNTRY

Accommodation
Expensive
Delta King Hotel, 1000 Front Street, Sacramento (tel: 916/444–5464). Rooms on a 1927 riverboat moored next to Old Town.

Moderate
Abigail's, 2120 G Street, Sacramento (tel: 916/441–5007). Homey bed-and-breakfast in a 1912 Colonial Revival home.
Amber House, 1315 22nd Street, Sacramento (tel: 916/444–8085). Fourteen individually furnished rooms and a hearty breakfast served each morning.
National Hotel, 211 Broad Street, Nevada City (tel: 916/265–4551). Believably claims to be the oldest hotel in the west, operating since 1856.
Ryan House, 153 S Shepherd Street, Sonora (tel: 209/533–3445). Competitively priced bed-and-breakfast in a mid-19th-century miner's home.

Budget
Coach & Four Motel, 628 S Auburn Street, Grass Valley (tel: 916/273–8009). A light breakfast is included in the competitive room rates.
National Hotel, 77 Main Street, Jamestown (tel: 209/984–3902). Simple, inexpensive rooms in one of this town's oldest lodgings; tremendous atmosphere.

Restaurants
Expensive
Biba, 2801 Capitol Avenue, Sacramento (tel: 916/455– 2422). Upmarket Italian dining, drawing stylish, well-heeled crowd.

Moderate
City Hotel Dining Room, Main Street, Columbia (tel: 209/532–1479). French cuisine in a gold-rush era setting.
Murphys Hotel Restaurant, Main Street, Murphys (tel: 209/728–3444). Exotic dishes such as calves' liver and frogs' legs alongside the more usual American fare.

Budget
Greta's Café, 1831 Capitol Avenue, Sacramento (tel: 916/442–7382). Soups, sandwiches and substantial salads.
Marshall's, 203 Mill Street, Grass Valley (tel: 916/272– 2844). The town's tastiest examples of the local delicacy: Cornish pasties.
Rubicon Brewing Company, 2004 Capitol Avenue, Sacramento (tel: 916/448–7032). Home-brewed beer and wholesome meals.
Wilma's Café, 275 S Washington Street, Sonora (tel: 209/532–9957). Earthy, coffee-shop staples served from 6am till late.

NORTH COAST

Accommodation
Expensive
Eureka Inn, 518 7th Street, Eureka (tel: 707/442– 6441). Tudor-style mansion with elegant, spacious rooms and attentive staff.

279

Moderate
Carson House Inn, 1209 4th Street, Eureka (tel: 707/443–1601 or 800/772–1622). Bland but comfortable motel.
Grey Whale Inn, 615 N Main Street, Fort Bragg (tel: 707/964–0640). This four-storey redwood mansion served as the local hospital until 1971 and is now an impressive place to stay.
The Lady Anne Inn, 902 14th Street, Arcata (tel: 707/822–2797). Gracious Victorian mansion offering bed-and-breakfast accommodation.
MacCallum House, 45020 Albion Street, Mendocino (tel: 707/937–0289). Homely and comfortable bed-and-breakfast in an 1882 house with some of the original fittings.
Mendocino Hotel, 45080 Main Street, Mendocino (tel: 800/548–0513). Extremely cosy, antiques-filled hotel dating from 1878; the lounge fireplace is ideal for relaxing on those chilly North Coast evenings.

Budget
Downtowner Motel, 424 Eight Street, Eureka (tel: 707/443–5061). The pick of the town's preponderance of simple, low-cost accommodation.

Eureka Streets

Fairwinds Motel, 1674 G Street, Arcata (tel: 707/ 822–4824). A bargain in this surprisingly expensive town.
Surf Motel, 1220 S Main Street, Fort Bragg (tel: 707/964–5361). Simple, clean and very affordable.

Restaurants
Expensive
Café Beaujolais, 961 Ukiah Street, Mendocino (tel: 707/937–5614). Also serves moderately priced breakfasts and lunches, but it is the more expensive dinners that demonstrate creative flair.
St Orres, on Highway 1 near Gualala (tel: 707/ 884–3303). Spot the onion domes of this distinctive Russian-style building overlooking the ocean, and feast on a fixed-price gourmet meal.

Moderate
Lost Coast Brewery, 617 Fourth Street, Eureka (tel: 707/445–4480). Fantastic soups, stews and sandwiches to accompany the beer brewed on the premises.

Budget
Egghead Omelettes of Oz, 356 N Main Street, Fort Bragg (tel: 707/964–5005). Cosy, relaxed diner delivering plenty of what its name suggests – and much more.
Mendocino Market and Café, 45051 Ukiah Street, Mendocino (tel: 707/937–FISH). Excellent clam chowder to go. Locals come for the enterprising mix of Thai and American cooking.
Stanton's, 1111 5th Street, Eureka (tel: 707/442–8141). Pleasant coffee shop.

WINE COUNTRY

Accommodation
Expensive
Auberge du Soleil, 180 Rutherford Hill Road, Rutherford (tel: 707/963–1211 or 800/348–5406). This relaxed inn, situated in an olive grove, overlooks the hills of Napa Valley and has a European air. The service is top-notch and the restaurant, bearing the same name, is one of the best in the area.
Kenwood, 10400 Sonoma Highway, Kenwood (tel: 707/833–1293 or 800/353–6966). Located in the heart of the Sonoma valley, this Italianate villa with views of the surrounding vineyards is an excellent retreat. All of the rooms have fireplaces and there is a full service spa on the premises.
Meadowood, 900 Meadowood Lane, St Helena (tel: 707/963–3646 or 800/458–8080). This secluded resort has excellent croquet, tennis and golf facilities. Guests are housed in bungalows and many rooms have fireplaces and patios.
Sonoma Mission Inn and Spa, 18140 Sonoma Highway, Sonoma (tel: 800/862–4945). Luxury rooms, gourmet dining and a fully equipped health spa set within rolling acres.

Moderate
Brannan Cottage, 109 Wapoo Avenue, Calistoga (tel: 707/942–4200). Highly rated bed-and-breakfast in 1860 cottage built by Sam Brannan, the famous California pioneer who founded the health resort here in 1859.

The Gables, 4257 Petaluma Hill Road, Santa Rosa (tel: 707/585–7777). An atmospheric Victorian home serving a substantial home-cooked breakfast with your stay.
Victorian Garden Inn, 316 E Napa Street, Sonoma (tel: 707/996–5339). A 19th-century farmhouse converted to a bed-and-breakfast inn, enclosed in colourful gardens.

Budget

Calistoga Inn, 1250 Lincoln Avenue, Calistoga (tel: 707/942–4101). A positive bargain deal by Wine Country standards, with cosy rooms and a complimentary breakfast.
Motel 6, 2760 Cleveland Avenue, Santa Rosa (tel: 707/546–1500). A Wine Country rarity of uninspiring, yet genuinely cheap, accommodation.
Swiss Hotel, 18 W Spain Street, Sonoma (tel: 707/938–2884). Tiny, atmospheric adobe building in a convenient central location.

Restaurants
Expensive

Auberge du Soleil, 180 Rutherford Hill Road, Rutherford (tel: 707/ 963–1211). Delectably prepared and presented nouvelle French and California cuisine in a rural location.
Domaine Chandon, 1 California Drive, Yountville (tel: 707/944–2892). Set in a grand dining room overlooking the adjacent vineyard, this restaurant serves creative California/French cuisine from a menu that changes daily.
The French Laundry, 6640 Washington Avenue, Yountville (tel: 707/944–2380). This unassuming restaurant is considered one of the best in the country. The food is contemporary French, perfectly executed, and delicious, served by extremely knowledgeable and attentive staff.

Terra, 1345 Railroad Avenue, St Helena (tel: 707/963–8931). A casually elegant setting in a renovated foundry, and a menu serving California, French and northern Italian fare. Try specials such as broiled *sake*-marinated sea bass, and the excellent desserts.
Tra Vigne, 1050 Charter Oak Street, St Helena (tel: 707/963-4444). Large, fun, contemporary restaurant that feels like an Italian trattoria crossed with a French bistro. The satisfying menu is informed by the regional cooking of Italy.

Moderate

Calistoga Inn and Brewery, 1250 Lincoln Avenue (tel: 707/942–4101). Varied range of classy meat and seafood dishes; outdoor eating in summer.
Mustards Grill, 7399 Highway 29, Yountville (tel: 707/944–2424). Delicious grilled morsels in a California cuisine style.

Budget

Boskos, 1364 Lincoln Avenue, Calistoga (tel: 707/ 942–9088). The freshly made pasta is followed up by some very tempting desserts.
Dempsey's Ale House, 50 E Washington Street, Petaluma (tel: 707/765– 9694). Sociable spot overlooking the Petaluma River; good food and great beers.
Sonoma Cheese Factory, 2 W Spain Street, Sonoma (tel: 707/996–1931). More than 100 homemade cheeses, perfect for including in your picnic basket.

Buena Vista Winery, Sonoma, is the oldest winery in the state

Index

Index

Index

Index/Acknowledgements

Picture credits

The Automobile Association would like to thank the following photographers, libraries and associations for their assistance in the preparation of this book. **CALIFORNIA DEPT OF PARKS AND RECREATION** 97 Monterey area beach, 200 pools across the meadows; **J PAUL GETTY TRUST** 154; **IMAGE BANK** front cover, woman inline skating; **IMAGES COLOUR LIBRARY LTD** 19a zodiacs; **MARINE WORLD** 87 elephants, dolphin; **MARY EVANS** 22 Native Americans and Jesuit missionaries, 23 Mission San Diego, 26 prospector, 28 earthquake, 29 cartoon; **PICTOR UNIPHOTO** front cover, surfer; **POPPERFOTO** 16 Charles Manson, 30 gentlemen of Paramount, 32-3 police and demonstrator; **REX FEATURES** 132 Beach Boys, 133 The Doors; **ROYAL GEOGRAPHIC SOCIETY** 20 map; **SPECTRUM COLOUR LIBRARY** 75 fireworks, 97 fruit, 102 oil platforms, 128-9 Hollywood sign, 137 University of California, 202-3 Sierra Mountain lake, 207 Kaweah River, Mount Whitney Trail, 239 earthquake damage, 243 Smith River; **TONY STONE IMAGES** front cover, Merced River; **WALT DISNEY CO**. 160 Sleeping Beauty's Castle; **ZEFA PICTURE LIBRARY (UK) LTD** 136 LA Westwood village, 144 Hard Rock Cafe, 145 Sunset Boulevard, 148 LA airport, 149 Yellow cabs, 162 Catalina Island, 164 LA freeways and skyline, 175 Mission Bay, 201 Sequoia tree, 228 Gull Rock, 257 LA harbour.
The remaining pictures are held in the association's own photo library **(AA PHOTO LIBRARY)** and were taken by **ROBERT HOLMES** with the exception of the following pages which were taken by **HAROLD HARRIS** 15, 35, 78, 80, 245; **KEN PATERSON** 8, 13b, 14b; **BARRIE SMITH** 38, 39, 51, 52, 53, 60, 62, 63, 68, 70, 72, 73, 88, 125, 259, 265, 266, 267, 268, 269; **JAMES TIMS** 19b, 19c cybercafe; **PHIL WOOD** 4, 5, 6-7.

Contributors

Revision editors: Donna Dailey, Grapevine Publishing Services Ltd   **Original editor**: Diana Payne
Revision verifier: Mick Sinclair